The Word and Its Witness

The Word and Its Witness

The Spiritualization of American Realism

GREGORY S. JACKSON

THE UNIVERSITY OF CHICAGO PRESS   CHICAGO AND LONDON

GREGORY S. JACKSON is assistant professor of English and American studies at Rutgers University.

The University of Chicago Press, Chicago 60637
The University of Chicago Press, Ltd., London
© 2009 by The University of Chicago
All rights reserved. Published 2009
Printed in the United States of America
17 16 15 14 13 12 11 10 09   1 2 3 4 5

ISBN-13: 978-0-226-39003-1 (cloth)
ISBN-13: 978-0-226-39004-8 (paper)
ISBN-10: 0-226-39003-9 (cloth)
ISBN-10: 0-226-39004-7 (paper)

Library of Congress Cataloging-in-Publication Data
Jackson, Gregory S.
    The Word and its witness : the spiritualization of American realism / Gregory S. Jackson.
        p. cm.
    Includes bibliographical references and index.
    ISBN-13: 978-0-226-39003-1 (cloth : alk. paper)
    ISBN-13: 978-0-226-39004-8 (pbk. : alk. paper)
    ISBN-10: 0-226-39003-9 (cloth : alk. paper)
    ISBN-10: 0-226-39004-7 (pbk. : alk. paper)
    1. American literature—History and criticism. 2. Realism in literature. 3. Religious literature—History and criticism. 4. Religion and culture—History. 5. Popular culture—Religious aspects. 6. Social gospel in literature. 7. Religion in literature. I. Title.
    PS169.R43J33 2008
    810.9—dc22

                                                              2008024434

FOR MY PARENTS, PHIL AND NINA JACKSON,
AND MY STUDENTS

Contents

Illustrations

Acknowledgments

In a work that is about the education of individuals, communities, and coteries, it is both fitting and a pleasure to remember so many—students, teachers, friends, and family—who have had a part in mine and, thus, in the production of this book. I wish first to acknowledge Rutgers University, whose generous support has made this work possible and whose colonial origins and Revolutionary setting on the Raritan ford inspire the religious historian in me. To my mind, my colleagues' intellectual generosity and collegiality set the professional standard. The stream of conferences, colloquia, speaker series, and institutes that they convene puts our department at the center of university life. Myra Jehlen, Chris Iannini, Ann Fabian, Brad Evans, Meredith McGill, Richard Miller, Dianne Sadoff, John Kucich, and Michael McKeon, in particular, have offered guidance, perceptive criticism, and friendship.

My research benefited from an American Council of Learned Societies fellowship in 2005, and over the last five years, this book has largely taken shape at the Huntington Library, whose extensive archives and renowned gardens are conducive to reflection and conversation, and whose interdisciplinary fellowship remind me that scholarship is, at its best, collaborative. Special thanks to the archive staff for their assistance and friendship over the long haul: Mona Shulman, Susie Krasnoo, Kate Henningsen, Meredith Berbée, Juan Gomez, Anne Mar, Bert Rinderle, Laura Stalker, Jennifer Watts, and Catherine Wehrey. A number of institutions and colleagues have provided occasions to speak about my work as it unfolded. Donald Pease and Robyn Wiegman invited me as a plenary speaker to the "Futures of American Studies" symposium at Dartmouth; Chris Looby welcomed me to the UCLA "Americanist Reading Colloquium," whose participants energetically tested my crit-

ical convictions; and the English departments at the University of Red-
lands and Connecticut College provided me with spirited interlocutors.
Edgar Dryden twice invited me to present my research at the *Arizona
Quarterly* symposium, and I am grateful for his thoughtful remarks and
those of colleagues there. Roy Ritchie invited me to share work with the
Huntington's "Society of Fellows," a community of donors whose generosity and keen intellectual interests in culture and history are embodied by J. D. and Nancy Hornberger. For provocative critiques of my work
in American Studies Association and Modern Language Association
panels over the years, I am appreciative of colleagues from a range of
disciplines, particularly John Corrigan, Cecilia Tichi, Tobias Gregory,
Erika Doss, R. Marie Griffith, Jeanne Halgren Kilde, and Miles Orvell,
who were respondents to talks drawn from materials taken from chapters 2 and 3. I am also grateful for conversations with Bill Brown, Daniel
Walker Howe, Lars Larson, Caroline Levander, Leerom Medevoi, Dana
Nelson, Michael Warner, Charlie Bertsch, William Gleason, Andrew
Sargent, Eric Slaughter, Erin Smith, and Priscilla Wald.

For the last five years, I have benefited from intensive workshops with
my colleagues in the Southern California Americanist Group (SCAG);
their collective wisdom, encouragement, and friendship have provided
real sustenance. I would like to express my deep appreciation for Paul
Gilmore, Mark Goble, Mark McGurl, Eric Hayot, Sianne Ngai, Sha-
ron Oster, Elisa Tamarkin, and Stuart Burrows. I am grateful to *Representations* and *PMLA* for permission to reprint portions of chapters 3
and 4 and to their readers, Sam Otter and David Leverenz, and to those
who remained anonymous for their perceptive insights. Russ Castronovo
and the readers for the University of Chicago Press—more than any—
offered extensive, engaged, and generous critiques, focusing the book at
the crucial moment. My editor Doug Mitchell and his team—Timothy
McGovern, my copy editors, Vivian Kirklin and Carol Saller, and Robert Hunt—have shepherded this book through press with precision, cre-
ativity, and commitment to an ongoing conversation that has improved it
at every stage. To that end, my former student Matthew Evans has been a
dedicated and exacting research assistant and friend.

Over the years, I have been fortunate to have a scattered coterie of
colleagues whose expertise, arguments, and affection have challenged
me and my work. Jennifer Bryan and Susan Aiken have read the book
more than a few times, braving the manuscript in its earliest stages and,
over time, helping to plot the arc of its transformation. Jen's expertise

in medieval Catholicism and lay devotion fostered my commitment to a trans-Reformation perspective, and her commitment to ideas and women's religious history has been an inspiration since our school days. Susan, who first hired us, was a model chair and mentor, a close reader, and an exquisite stylist. Paul Gilmore and Sarah Rivett read numerous drafts, helping me to think through the implications of my homiletic theory and reframe and broaden my arguments. My colleague Eric Hayot has been a great friend and intellectual sounding board; he recognized early and often what it was I was trying to say, and his rare gift for concretizing ideas sharpened my thinking and this book. Chris Carroll has been a sage counselor and friend, and, for years, has reminded me of the simple joy of storytelling, demonstrating often what he would teach. Angela Mullis's religious expertise and personal partisanship have been deeply felt in my work and life.

From our days in the London House in Mecklenburg Square, Arthur Combs has been a fellow adventurer in the realm of academe, politics, ideas, and disputation. My work owes much to his devil's advocacy and unswerving support. Chapters 3 and 4 silently register my debt to the historian Clark Davis; I wish he were with us to see the book's completion. Tony Eilert took me on a tour of Charles Sheldon's Topeka, Kansas, and his knowledge of evangelical history has given me insight into late-nineteenth-century devotional life in the rural Midwest. Sam and Roberta Jackson and Tammy Eilert, on numerous occasions, have mercifully interrupted my scholarly itinerancy and insularity with great affection. Jonathan Auerbach, Renée Bergland, Kathleen Donegan, Jennifer Fleissner, Karen Keely, Jason Kelly, Tobias Gregory, John Herron, V. A. Kolve, Cheryl Koos, Maurice Lee, Roxanne Mountford, Bran Noonan, Nick Petzak, Anne Sheehan, Ivy Schweitzer, Debora Shuger, Brian Wagner, Tom Augst, and Neil Van Leeuwen read parts, each cheering progress at important junctures. Nancy Bentley's friendship and intellectual generosity have left their mark as well. Her rare capacity to interweave culture, history, and texts to reveal profound insights has, for me, been an influential mode of critical analysis. Likewise, readings of Barbara Packer's and Joyce Appleby's works—the surprising revelations of thought, depths of knowledge, and eloquence of expression—have been genuine sources of learning and aspiration.

For debts longest overdue: I had the great fortune to work with Eric Sundquist and Martha Banta on a different project. They guided me through the critical methodologies and archives of American literary, cultural, and religious history. Over the years, Eric has been the model of personal and intellectual generosity, integrity, and devoted friendship. Martha has been a great friend and skilled professional advisor. In another time, small communities of faculty and students fostered my early literary interests: Matthew Titolo and Chris Hamilton, more than any, set the pace of my research and career. William L. Andrews, Margaret Doody, Ron Dreiling, Richard Hardin, Nathan Hatch, Karen Rowe, and Valerie Smith all contributed to my work by contributing to my education. With nostalgic reverie, I recall Moreland Hall and my deep affection for four great scholar-teachers there: Bob Jones, Robert Schwartz, Michael Oriard, and Kerry Ahearn. To Peter Bierma, Grant Armbruster, Tim John, Brian Monihan, Scott Duyck, Mark Jackson, and Tami Volz, my comrades there who gave me direction and, occasionally, misdirection, my admiration. With fond obligation, I recall Barbara Baumgartner, Myrtle Caswell, Mildred Mitchell, Harold Williamson, Jim Hirsch, Bonnie Putnam, and Nelson Jones, whose passions for reading and knowledge were contagious.

John Carmichael and Steve Childers have patiently sat through so many readings that I have lost count, and, with the rest of my cohort at the Pasadena Shire—Michael and Priscilla Bransby, Anthony Nittle, Dino Parenti, Mandy Siegel, Jason Wurtz, Meghan Connealy, Michael and Wendy Churukian and my nephew Brett Jackson—have for years made up for my lapses, excused my deficiencies, and reminded me of the true measure of friends who are also family. Finally, I come to my parents, Phil and Nina, my brothers and sisters, nieces and nephews, my godchildren—the Monihans—and Mavy Terry-Stoddard, who have tolerated my absences and repaid my neglect with love and affection. My thoughts often run back to the Oregon ranch communities in the Calapooia Valley, where solitude early awoke me to the pleasure of reading, and where over the generations time has altered life so little.

Spiritual Realism and the Work of Homiletic Narrative

"When for the time ye ought to be teachers, ye have need that one teach you again which be the first principles of the oracles of God; and are become such as have need of milk, and not of strong meat. For every one that useth milk is unskillful in the word of righteousness: for he is a babe." Because they were babes, they needed to be taught again the first principles. . . . They need to be converted anew, to lay the foundation of faith and repentance anew. —Jonathan Edwards, "Subjects of the First Work of Grace May Need a New Conversion"

In explicating the book of Hebrews (5:12–13),[1] Jonathan Edwards foregrounds a theory of Protestant education that would stress appropriate material for new converts, gradually training them in increasingly difficult doctrine that they might steadily grow from "babes" to seasoned teachers. He outlines a trajectory of participatory learning in which the young and inexperienced can at each stage of development engage the process of conversion and spiritual growth toward what he and many of his followers believed was America's special millennial dispensation. This model of escalating engagement is at the root of homiletic practices today, as exemplified in what might be seen as the newest realm of religious pedagogy, video games. Set in the near future, in the time following the Rapture when those already saved ascend into heaven, and before Christ's return and thousand-year reign, the 2006 *Left Behind: Eternal Forces* video game invites players to "conduct physical & spiritual warfare, using the power of prayer to strengthen . . . troops in com-

bat and wield modern military weaponry."² As foot soldiers in a paramilitary group known as the Tribulation Force, whose mission is to remake
the nation as a Christian theocracy ready for Christ's return, players receive high-tech weapons and engage the infidel in the streets with prayer,
worship, and, if necessary, deadly force.³ The game's official Web site
stresses its narratological and mimetic import, inviting users to "enjoy
a robust single player experience . . . in story mode."⁴ As they "command forces through intense battles across a breathtaking, authentic depiction of New York City"—what *Newsweek* magazine characterizes as
an "eerily authentic reproduction" of Manhattan—each character is provided with a life story and sets of missions predicated on an escalating
structure.⁵

In encouraging its players to imagine themselves as soldiers for
Christ, to visualize the landscape of their self-transformation, and to
take on as intimately as possible the responsibility of their actions inside
an imaginary representational space, *Left Behind: Eternal Forces* stands
as a powerful contemporary instance of what I call "the spiritualization
of American realism." Based on the phenomenally successful fourteen-
novel Left Behind series, which has sold tens of millions of copies in the
United States, the game suggests the continuing interaction between visual technologies and printed texts at work throughout this study.⁶ Set in
the premillennial landscape of the Apocalypse envisioned in the book of
Revelations, the Left Behind novels celebrate an intrepid band of Christians left behind after the Rapture who battle the gathering forces of
the Antichrist, embodied in the charismatic Romanian politician Nicolae Carpathia (acclaimed in the fictional plot by *People* magazine as the
"Sexiest Man Alive").⁷ The video game, which shares the novels' homiletic drive, targets both the series' youngest readers and those of the
spin-off forty-novel series Left Behind: The Kids. In a significant rever-
sal of the historical trajectory of Protestant literacy, it also targets large
numbers of the young who are unlikely to read religious narratives in any
form—though they may, on encountering the imaginary forces of global
evil in the game-world established by the Left Behind series, find themselves encouraging Satan's minions to do some reading of their own by
handing them equally imaginary copies of the Bible. At no point do the
forces of good encourage conversion by asking the forces of evil to play
the *Eternal Forces* video game, and thus, the game references the centrality of reading to Protestant pedagogies to bolster its own claims for

converting the nonbeliever or strengthening those in need of the "milk," rather than "strong meat," of spiritual truth.[8]

From the perspective organized by this study, the game marks the culmination of a representational history that will take us, in the following chapters, from the vividly visual sermons and homiletic theory of Jonathan Edwards—whose religious philosophy had for more than a century after his death served the cross-purposes of a range of Protestant theology, from the orthodox and rational to the evangelical and emotional—through subsequent homiletic enactments of redemption: eighteenth- and nineteenth-century sermons and devotional exercises by such influential preachers as John Wesley, Charles Grandison Finney, Zilpha Elaw, and Henry Ward Beecher, who invoked visual imagery to engage congregants in a kind of virtual experience; the postbellum emergence of what I call the "homiletic novel," which used fictional narrative to motivate real conversions;[9] the parallel development of the Social Gospel movement; and the Social Gospel Movement's late nineteenth- and early-twentieth-century offshoots, including the vision-oriented homiletic pedagogy of urban reformer Jacob Riis, who deployed the emergent technology of photographic projection to stimulate audience intervention in the suffering of the "undeserving poor."[10] As such, this study attempts to meet the visual historian Barbara Stafford's challenge that the late-twentieth-century transformation from "lens culture" to "digital culture"—from Riis's photo-tableaux to such modern homiletic technologies as the *Eternal Forces* video game—could be better understood if we attempted to situate it historically.[11] That is to say, that to understand this video game, the forms of media and religious culture it represents, and their power and attraction for a broad section of American evangelicals, we must reconstruct the historical origins of homiletic literature. Through this history, the new media form of the video game not only becomes comprehensible within contemporary religious culture, but also integrally linked to a broader history of homiletic practices.

The *Eternal Forces* video game highlights how evangelicals have long understood participatory pedagogies as key to developing volitional agency.[12] Running through a vast constellation of films, novels, artwork, Psalters, primers, catechisms, homiletic pamphlets, and other forms of representation that make up the history of American religious life, these pedagogies encapsulate the major themes of this study: the post-Reformation shift in epistemology that emphasized personal experience

for salvific transformation and spiritual growth; the emergence of hermeneutic and narrative modes that fostered new forms of readerly identification designed to engender that experience; and the gradual shift in
Protestantism from a conceptual realism initiated by narrative and sermon heuristics to an external, materially based, simulated reality epitomized by various interactive and performative pedagogies and emerging
visual technologies.

The Word and Its Witness provides what we might think of as a narrative progress of Protestant education in order to elucidate how cultural
and social conditions shaped the devotional purposes and practices of
homiletic works, and how, in turn, these pedagogical instruments further
shaped the lives and cultures to which they responded. By "homiletic
works" I mean a broad spectrum of parabiblical materials that sprang up
despite the commitment of American Protestants, Calvinists in particular, to the principle of *sola scriptura* or "scripture alone." Through such
materials, various Protestant movements and leaders sought to train the
faithful in particular interpretive and reading practices, and in so doing,
to orient diverse groups across a vast landscape, not with the precision of
a sextant's bearing but more broadly in a cardinal direction that distinguished them generally from their European counterparts.[13] In demonstrating how this homiletic tradition came to articulate an increasingly
wide range of related but shifting developments and genres, the termi-
nology I use will expand to define both complementary and contradictory cultural and religious interests and literary forms.

The Word and Its Witness thus revises a particular understanding of
the history of American Protestantism by showing how elite religious
discourse was shadowed—sometimes even overshadowed—by a wealth
of popular narrative material organized around sermons, novels, and
other homiletic spaces. It traces the fascinating story of how "formal"
doctrine and theology coming out of synods and seminaries, churches
and conclaves, and the private studies of ministers were transformed by
remarkable men and women on the ground, whose lives' work was to sow
the seeds of revival pietism and, in due season, reap harvests of souls,
swelling the ranks of salvation's army in a new and rapidly changing
America. The historical development of popular Protestant narrative—
a pilgrim's progress in which successive experiments in narrative form
and medium were thought to lead believers ever closer to spiritual
salvation—shows how American Protestants struggled to integrate the
experience of America and American modernity into a narrative of spir-

itual salvation and communal destiny. The materials I sample demonstrate a continuing engagement with such problems as individuals' religious responsibility to American geography and the gift of the New World; the development of new markets for devotional narrative; the arrival on the religious scene of diverse regional, racial, national, or cultural idioms; and the public awareness of new forms of knowledge, like psychology, sociology, and biology, that offered competing explanations for human behavior and community development. They show how the interventionist energies of evangelical exhorters and their proselytes were, through homiletic frames, converted into a national ethic of social intervention that became the hallmark of such humanitarian endeavors as abolition, the Social Gospel, and Progressive Era urban reform.

In following the history of American religious representation through these successive crucibles, this book ultimately argues that their cumulative work produced a uniquely American form of literary representation that developed through the narrative strategies and theological innovations as they were adapted to the particularity of New World experience. Designed to draw readers and auditors into the frame of homiletic allegory, this representational system bound an intensely optic imagination with specific Protestant strategies for engaging visual, oral, and literary texts. A particular way of seeing and narrating social reality that I call an "aesthetics of immediacy" emerged as a project of self-education aimed at allowing all good Americans to live simultaneously in the United States and in Christ, simultaneously in history and outside time. In Harold Bell Wright's best-selling novel *That Printer of Udell's* (1902), for example, the narrator describes the effects of such an aesthetics of immediacy, as a young minister brings his sermon vividly to life:

He recalled to their minds the Saviour of men, as He walked and talked in Galilee. He pictured the Christ feeding the hungry and healing the sick. He made them hear again the voice that spake as never man spake before, giving forth that wonderful sermon on the mount, and pronouncing His blessing on the poor and merciful. Again the audience stood with the Master when He wept at the grave of Lazarus, and with Him sat at the last supper, when He introduced the simple memorial of His death and love. Then walking with Him across the brook Kedron, they entered the shadows of the Olive trees and heard the Saviour pray while His disciples slept. . . . And then they stood with the Jewish mob, clamoring for His blood. . . . Then under the spell of Cameron's speech, they looked into the empty tomb and felt their hearts throb in ecstasy, as the full meaning of that silent vault burst upon them. Looking up they saw their risen Lord seated at the right hand of the Father, glorified with the glory that was His in the beginning.[14]

In taking up the particular strategies by which ministers and spiritual stewards engaged audiences in the reality of worldly sin and suffering, helping them to structure their daily lives and social commitments, *The Word and Its Witness* proposes a history of the rise of American realism as integral to secular literary realism, demonstrating surprising epistemological continuity across seemingly disparate domains of late-nineteenth-century knowledge formation. Realism thus emerges in this study as a culminating practice in a long history of discursive techniques designed to access knowledge through an aesthetic negotiation between form and lived experience. American homiletic realism mediates between the spiritual and the empirical in ways that mirror secular realism's movement between the typological and the specific. Spiritual and secular forms thus share a genealogy that produced the formal and thematic conventions that we have come to associate with eighteenth- and nineteenth-century pictorial and discursive realism broadly and with the postbellum emergence of literary realism.[15]

Homiletic Realism and the Forms of Fiction

In the introduction to his influential 1982 collection *American Realism: New Essays,* Eric J. Sundquist offers what is still a fair assessment of the realist movement. He notes that this aesthetic embodied a "complexity of response" that "no specific ideological or theoretical program" can adequately explain.[16] As Amy Kaplan observes, however, critics have repeatedly attempted to reduce realism to just such a program. In the early twentieth century, progressives like V. L. Parrington celebrated "critical realism" as the apogee of the American progressive tradition that began in the eighteenth century. They viewed literary realism as a tough look at the unexamined optimism generated by industrialized modernity. In the 1930s Marxists such as Granville Hicks and Bernard Smith similarly praised American realism's gritty depiction of the dark underbelly of capitalism, while modernist-aestheticists like F. O. Matthiessen located literary realism in a democratic genealogy that received its political and aesthetic impetus from Walt Whitman. The institutionalization of the New Criticism, with its emphasis on lyric poetry, both initiated and, for more than a generation of criticism, finalized American realism's decline from the literary pantheon. Finally, poststructuralist critics such as Michael Fried reread literary realism, in Kaplan's words, and found the power of realist narratives "in their ability to deconstruct their own claims to referentiality," positing a kind of metarealism.[17] As Phillip Barrish has recently argued, what links these critical reinterpretations of American literary realism is a contest of one-upmanship in which characters, authors, and twentieth-century critics (who, according to Barrish, participate in the same contest since they reject what they perceive as less real in favor of something more so) all claim the rhetorical status of "realer than thou."[18]

Rather than seeking to achieve a critical synthesis, I want to flesh out one dimension of that period's complexity and, as a consequence, its influence on literary modes of representation. In so doing, I aim to extend the generic parameters of American literary realism by accounting for how homiletic literature's discursive strategies were constitutive in its formation. To understand the intersection of Protestant narrative with literary realism in the late nineteenth century requires attending to their similar roots in the intersections between modern empirical epistemology and American spiritual pedagogies. The focus on realism as an epistemological mode, as both a register of the real and a catalyst for the convert's self-transformation, provides my subtitle, *The Spiritualization of American Realism*. This phrase does not mark a point of origination but a revitalization, beginning in the late seventeenth century, of a pre-Reformation mode of reading—an increasingly lay-oriented religious hermeneutic that imaginatively transformed moral hypotheticals and doctrinal abstractions into vivid encounters with spiritual reality. By marking the emergence of homiletic realism's aesthetics as a crucial trigger for spiritual conversion and moral and social reformation, this subtitle also announces an alternative vision of postbellum literary realism that moves beyond recent criticism's concern with generic distinctions, psychological motivations, the mimetic capacity of language, or epistemic orientations produced within sociological and demographic registers.[19] Tracing the epistemic origins and development of homiletic realism, this study adds to this critical discussion a heretofore unexamined account of the Protestant hermeneutic operative within canonical American realism. I break with the deeper epistemological pretext that realist criticism to date presumes from the outset in order to reconfigure the onto-

logical categories that underpin received assumptions of both the realist
movement and its secular, philosophical orientation—namely, the dialectical relationship between realism and idealism.[20] This conventional critical binary has tended to reify other corresponding oppositions such as
realism and romance, reason and imagination, or literary realism and
sentimentalism—idealism's debased, popular generic form.[21]

Barrish's description of a contest over what is more real exposes a
struggle for a material authenticity that homiletic authors eschewed at
the outset. For eighteenth- and nineteenth-century evangelical readers,
like their counterparts today, the clear division between the real and
the imaginative was a symptom of an increasingly divergent epistemological investment—one, broadly speaking, characterized by the disparate tracks taken by secularism on the one hand, and by the fusion of
nineteenth-century popular Christianity and spiritualism on the other.[22]
By blurring the distinction between the real and the figural, between
worldly fact and sermonic hypotheticals, homiletic narrative confirmed
for countless readers that such designations simply perpetuated a false
ontology. In relation to the eternal verities, after all, all forms of worldly
truth or empirical reference—human wisdom by any measure—were but
representations, symbolic registers that simply verified that *the Real* resided not in the material world at all but in a universal design beyond human perception.[23] As the Christian author of *Ideal Suggestion through
Mental Photography* put it in 1893, asserting an epistemological alternative to strict empiricism, "Our divine heritage . . . gives us the power to
invoke and uprear a mental structure either symmetrical or deformed. If
we *will* we can turn our backs upon the lower and sensuous plane, and
lift ourselves into the realm of the spiritual and Real, and there 'gain a
residence.'"[24]

Homiletic realism posited a radical, modern *imitatio Christi* as a
transformative structure of identification with the oppressed. In so doing, it sought to weaken the link between the agent's capacity to represent social oppression and his or her moral complicity in it. Because, following John Calvin, Anglo-American Protestantism subscribed to the
Augustinian theology of human depravity—the seventeenth-century
foundation of Protestant antihumanism—homiletic realism rejected empiricism as the sole evidentiary mode for determining authentic social
knowledge. For practitioners of homiletic realism—from the eighteenth-
century revival sermon to the *Eternal Forces* video game—the temporal world could never be more real than the veracity of our perceptions

of it; that is, more real than the limits of the instrument by which it was known. Homiletic realism assumes the fallibility of an epistemology degraded by humanity's culpability in original sin. In essence, original sin trumps any possibility for representing the social world because its consequence is a reality solely composed of fallen reason and perception.[25] In the Messianic tradition, original sin's a priori status requires a more radical orientation to the material world, to the human suffering that inhabits it, and to our understanding of the perceived ends of human volition and social intervention.

In this fundamentally Augustinian moral order—a reformulation of Plato's metaphysics—fact and fiction are two sides of the coin of representation; both offer insight only as they directly mediate an invisible, spiritual reality. Even when, for the religious, perception is uncommonly acute, embodied in literary or artistic genius, the natural world that one scrutinizes for either social facts or providential signs is itself an unreliable filter, the dark glass through which humanity obliquely peers. Late-nineteenth-century homiletic authors were thus less vulnerable to the representational conundrum that ensnared secular realists, who, as Sundquist observes, proved unable to negotiate the complexity of a postindustrial modernist society—what Stephanie Foote characterizes as the "radically unbalanced cultural landscape"—and to synthesize its excesses into a coherent, stable vision of the "real."[26] Witnessing intensified urban industrialization, immigration, class struggles, and the codification of vast economic divisions, the decades between the Civil War and World War I marked a time of turbulent social change. Yet cultural differences and social fragmentation were not universal. The fin de siècle was also a time when the vast majority of Americans characterized themselves as active Christians. For many of these individuals, worldly reality shadowed a greater reality, a universal absolute to which morality, knowledge, and truth were moored. Oddly, not unlike recent critical suspicions of language's capacity to represent a stable, unified meaning—yet toward different ends—homiletic authors understood the real as perpetually emptying out into yet another instance or category of the real that claimed a more authentic status. Then as now, homiletic readers found the distinctions between reality and representation serviceable only insofar as they gestured toward universal truths outside the temporal, outside the deceptive authenticity of empiricism and materiality.[27]

Ministers digested the slippage between empirical fact and the eternal real into a stern scriptural warning, exhorting the faithful not to lay up

treasures on earth, where moth and rust doth corrupt (Matthew 6:19)—
an admonition all the more credible for its "red-letter authority," its at-
tribution to Christ.[28] Homiletic realism instilled a weaker sense of the
differences that distinguished the real and the hypothetical; it generated
tolerance for the ambiguities that it itself affirmed between the autoptic reality of the material and the immutable facts of the invisible world.
Mistaking this rejection of empirical reference as an end in itself for the
inability to constitute mimesis, critics of literary realism have tended to
dismiss the homiletic novel as romance or, worse, sentimentalism.[29] But
in the context of homiletic literature, the relationship between realism
and idealism might be more usefully configured not between the particular and the universal, or, as in its debased sense, between reality and
romance (fantasy or the "ideal"), but rather between divergent ontolo-
gies of the real, what we can discretely delineate as material *and* spiritual reality.[30]

How might this reformulation alter our understanding in a specific instance? Recent criticism tends to view nineteenth-century realism as an
urban style focused less on mimetic representation than on a close-up
perspective (primarily the narrator's) that, though experimental, remains
deeply committed to the empiricism and the immediacy of personal experience. Critics have further defined literary realism against the pervasive conventions of sentimentalism.[31] In his study of Stephen Crane, for
instance, Alan Trachtenberg qualifies the realism of Crane's urban tales
by contrasting them with Jacob Riis's sentimental strategies, which, in
his view, were largely "devices to preserve distance—devices of picturesque perspective or sentimental plot that protected the reader from the
danger of a true exchange of point of view with the 'other half.'"[32] Such
devices, I argue, appear to produce distance only from a modern perspective, according to an increasingly secular and skeptical epistemology. Because it overlooks a religious tradition grounded not solely in a
sense-based psychology but in an idealist epistemology that still credited the faculties of intuition, empathy, instinct, extrasensory perception,
and revelation, Trachtenberg's representative criticism is a historical ret-
rojection of a modern epistemological and ontological hegemony onto
a past in which the struggle between idealism and "realism" still evenly
galvanized ideological partisanship over the nature of reality in religion,
psychology, philosophy, and science.[33]

Taking for granted metaphysical capacities (what Jonathan Edwards
referred to as "divine and supernatural light" and the later Christian

pragmatist Josiah Royce, citing Edwards, called "apperception" and "insight"), Protestant ministers from Edwards to Charles Sheldon defied the limits of perception as understood within Cartesian dualism and the Lockean legacy of scientific empiricism, and hence defied the existentialism toward which the "sociological" works of Crane, Jack London, Theodore Dreiser, and Frank Norris tended. The importance that nineteenth-century ministers placed on human volition and the individual's moral agency contested naturalism's focus on "pessimistic determinism"—what Donald Pizer artfully softens in his assessment of Dreiser not as "an exercise in determinism," but as "a subtle dramatization" of how a "distinctive temperament" interacts with a specific environment.[34] This emphasis on volition and moral agency also contested literary realism's assumption that reality exists apart from experience—at least a single's individual's experience—such that the authenticity and accuracy of an individual's perception must be evaluated in relation to a body of perceiving individuals (narrator, author, or reader), or measured against an implied omniscience. By contrast, anchored in spiritual self-evaluation and an eighteenth-century emphasis on individual volition that emerged with contractualism's consensual imperative and the concomitant decline of predestinarianism, religious adherents of homiletics assumed personal experience, illuminated by spiritual insight, to be the measure of reality.

Thus, while secular literary realism anatomized the experience of *reality* (what homiletic novelist Henry Wood ridiculed as "pen-photography," Charles Dudley Warner described as the "realism" that wallows in "the disagreeable, the vicious, the unwholesome," Henry James disparaged as "dingy realism," and Ambrose Bierce scoffed was "nature as it is seen by toads"[35]), homiletic realism focused on the reality of *experience*. Following Augustine's figure of this life as a dry run for the next, homiletic authors understood that experience was managed, at least in part, by the individual's volitional agency and commitment to the temporal as an allegory of the eternal. The difference here had a great deal to do—or so opponents of naturalism and realism believed—with the moral purposes of art. In "The Novel and Its Future" (1874), George Parsons Lathrop, a sympathetic critic of religious themes of moral elevation and associate editor of *Atlantic Monthly,* scolded the emerging school of realists for failing "to grasp the difference between realism and that which is merely literalism," for conflating reality with tawdry social detail, lamenting its "mere transcription of facts" that "look[s] into the roots of things" without an appreciation for "the value of calm, unchanging heights, upon which to build securely and live happily."[36] Lathrop's figuration of moral and spiritual foundations epitomizes one side of the "coded diction" that Pizer identifies in his introduction to *Documents of American Realism and Naturalism* as marking the criticism of both the early purveyors and the opponents of literary realism.[37]

What these divergent worldviews have in common at least as late as the turn of the century is their belief in a cosmic design, whether deterministic—governed by the laws of a Newtonian physics either indifferent or hostile to human plight—or providential. Even among many intellectuals, aesthetics and ethics often had their moorings in the cosmic design outside the material domain. In his 1888 article "The Art of Fiction," for instance, Henry James—an agnostic and thus a mediating figure in a modernity divided between religious and secular perspectives— shares the assumption that art and morality are coanchored in the larger universal structure: the "essence of moral energy," he writes, "is to survey the whole field and create the 'perfect work,'" draw a "picture" that "partake[s] of the substance of beauty and truth."[38] Similarly, writing at this same time in defense of idealism, particularly its intimations of immortality suggested in the mutability of the material, the Christian pragmatist Josiah Royce reminded the anti-Kantian purveyors of the "new realism" that the very act of discerning between the ideal and the real, right and wrong, fact and fiction—realism and romance—assumed the existence of a universal standard by which such distinctions were calibrated. Such echoes of a premodernist, prematerialist ontology reveal turn-of-the-century belief systems to be more in flux, even in the secular and professional domain, than the fixed categories that twentieth-century critics have often heretofore assumed.

Thus to focus, as some recent criticism does, on realism's failure as a mimetic project or as social critique is to become mired in an analysis of the material—in a never-ending adjudication of what is *more* or *less* real—that, unlike homiletic purposes, makes the material and its representation the end of analysis rather than its beginning.[39] How might a nuanced sense of the interplay between the real and the ideal, latent yet still perceptible, change our views about conventional constructions of literary realism or further complicate the insights of critics like Kaplan, who seek not to expose the failure of realism's "claims to represent U.S. society," but rather "to ask *what* realistic novels do accomplish and *how* they work as a cultural practice"?[40] That is, how might a more complete account of the contending status of nineteenth-century ontology and epistemology render traditional teleologies newly visible? More to my purpose, what might it tell us about homiletic literature's response to urban blight and human suffering, or about the agency and social intervention such literature advocated? Seen from this perspective, the "realism" of nineteenth-century homiletic works and their offshoots—from Louisa May Alcott's *Little Women* and Sheldon's didactic novels, to Riis's haunting virtual-tour narratives, to the *Eternal Forces* video game—requires that we reassess the values that underlie conventional definitions of realism: the disdain for religious faith and teleological worldviews, cynicism toward Progressive Era belief in social intervention, and a "scientific" or evolutionary determinism that naturalizes social constructivism as ontological certainty.[41] At the very least, we need to reassess our assumptions about what realist authors, secular or religious, imagined themselves to be doing and to what purpose.[42]

At the risk of making what June Howard and others have dismissed as naive claims about the mimetic capacity of literary conventions or other linguistic practices to reflect reality, *The Word and Its Witness* takes seriously the possibility that words, images, and heuristics might simulate reality for religious auditors and readers for whom imitation and authenticity amounted to the same thing: registers of a realness lodged not in the temporal but in the eternal.[43] Realism, as Roman Jakobson famously contends, works metonymically, utilizing "synecdochic details" to capture the reality of particular characters and then moving both "from the plot to the atmosphere and from the characters to the setting in space and time."[44] The realist novelist thus tends to work by selecting representative cases to reveal a social truth, to describe particulars in order to reveal the truth about the whole. Homiletic exercises, on the other hand, do not posit absolutes in or about the social world. Instead, they work more through metaphor, through the recognition of the similarity between two different realms altogether. That is, they engage the material through experiential templates in an effort to illuminate the spiritual conditions of the real that reside beyond the empirical. In this sense, both the realist and homiletic novel bespeak not a struggle to be "realer than thou," but merely to be real *enough*. Despite the difference in referential mode, the homiletic novel's emphasis on acting as Jesus would in this world—the thrust of the modern *imitatio Christi*—shades into the realist novel's tendency to read the social as the product of individual ethical choices, and the realist novel's attempt to capture a social totality, a world beyond the intellectual scope or experience of individual characters, bleeds into the homiletic gesture to a world elsewhere. Homiletic realism, Thomas P. Hughes wrote of "new developments" in religious literature in 1904, "throw[s] around our material life the grandeur of something better, and . . . lift[s] us from that which is temporal and selfish to that goodness, beauty, and truth which seem to belong to another and better world than this."[45] By returning the homiletic tradition to its prominent place in late nineteenth-century American literary culture, this study argues that the aesthetic innovations of literary realism emerged not only from a cosmopolitan embrace of scientific empiricism but also from this homegrown, indeed parochial, heuristic tradition of Protestant homiletics.

Babes in Christ

Though only a few of the primers, manuals of piety, psalm books, sermons, novels, and lectures I study here invoke the millennialist Christian "end times" as forcefully as the *Left Behind* video game, they share with it the desire to use forms of visual and narrative identification to induce Christians to rehearse as realistically as possible the kinds of moral decisions deemed crucial to their long-term fate as sinners in the hands of a temperamental and exacting God. The quasi-pedagogical motives of such representations owe their impetus, then as now, to a particularly Anglo-American sense of the relationship between religious experience and the child, which drew extensively on various colonial adaptations of the seventeenth-century British philosopher John Locke and, later in the eighteenth century, a host of Lockean theologians, Anglo-American essayists, and colonial cottager philosophers and empiricists.[46] Before discussing how empiricism altered colonial Calvinist pedagogy, it will be useful to examine further how the changing concept of children's spiritual aptitude altered homiletic theory, a subject that conjoins the putative audience for a twenty-first-century video game with the new forms of human being theorized by a host of empirically focused epistemologies that cropped up in the wake of Locke's enormously influential *Essay concerning Human Understanding* in 1689.

To uncover the way in which homiletic literature shaped the nineteenth-century conception of human volition—individuals' capacities to alter themselves and their environment, most vitally in the decades before and after the American Civil War—this book begins with this focus on children. At its base, Protestant interest in epistemology, education, conversion morphology, and moral surveillance was deeply informed by a concern for children—beliefs about their spiritual condition, assumptions about their moral and mental aptitudes, and perceptions about the role of education in preparing them to meet spiritual challenges in a world hostile to God's own. Those concerns produced thousands of sermons in the centuries before the American Civil War that were addressed to children, their parents, and their teachers. Similarly, worries over children's spiritual welfare—constellated around discussions of psychology; the child's perceived volitional capacity to make, review, and revise moral choices; and perceptions about how best to instill moral discipline—were at the heart of eighteenth-century revival manuals and became, in the next century, the focus of a large number of homiletic manuals aimed at children's salvation.[47]

In colonial times, ministers created catechisms and compiled primers to assist new converts in their semi-autonomous quests for spiritual enlightenment. In ear-scorching sermons, preachers warned their parishioners of the dangers of death without redemption. Over time, however, as the hellfire sermons of the eighteenth century continued to thunder at parishioners without producing the soul-wrenching effect that led to conversion, and as views of human psychology changed, ministers experimented with new narrative forms. Using a kind of aversion therapy, they expanded interactive sermon and catechistic exercises to produce narratives that took young listeners on imaginative tours of hell where the damned howled in pain, on tours of brothels where they encountered residents in intensifying stages of disease and suffering, and on tours of taverns where wide-eyed readers gaped at the spectacle of the young sinking into lives of escalating crime and depravity.

Through other discursive strategies that would lead toward such twenty-first-century pedagogies as the *Eternal Forces* game, the "Jesus Camp," and the hell house (in which the young tour exhibits depicting the eternal consequences of particular sins), religious educators created scores of allegorical guidebooks to lead spiritual novices in transforming their own lives according to familiar typological patterns.[48] By the early antebellum period, as the novel finally began to supersede the sermon in the United States, ministers and religious educators like Mason Locke Weems (the peripatetic "parson") began novelizing homiletic pedagogy, creating new modes of discursive realism that showcased sumptuously graphic and visually detailed narratives intended to exercise the

volition of the young while feeding their appetites for newly popular
literary forms.[49] Like Weems before them, Jacob Abbott, John Belton
O'Neall, George Lippard, Susan Warner, and countless other popular
authors whose sermons and tracts were published under the auspices of
such emerging institutions as the American Bible Society, the American Tract Society, and, especially, the American Sunday School Union,
paired morality and spirituality with emerging sentiments of republican virtue, welding the religious and the political together in imaginative modes of literary realism that asked young readers to identify with
and emulate a cast of characters whose heroic feats merged biblical and
national hagiography.[50] Combined with colonial and national millennialism, these works informally mounted an American Testament that both
complemented and competed with the New Testament in its transfigura-
tion of biblical history, typology, and prophecy into a unique and sacred
national eschatology.[51]

Increasingly visual forms of representation and technology, what David S. Reynolds has identified as the "new religious style," added to this
spiritualization of American realism, helping to shift the reading epistemologies for audiences of all ages from imaginatively conceptualized
sermon homilies to externally visible homiletic pedagogies in which narrative combined with a range of viewing technologies, including stereopticon slide shows and photographic exposés published as "lay sermons"
in scores of Christian and secular magazines after 1880.[52] As we will see
in the following chapters, human volition and agency increasingly became the focus of social intervention after the Civil War, and as the vividly graphic sermons of the past began to lose the novelty of realism, religious reformers incorporated these visual and theatrical technologies
into the novel's homiletic strategies. Seeking to simulate lived experience
for religious audiences already trained in transforming visually oriented
rhetoric into their spiritual reality, these reformers created vivid forms of
realism, blending a narrative tradition steeped in an imaginatively interactive readerly hermeneutic with the empirical immediacy and the seemingly self-referential veracity of visual media.[53] Only by assisting novices in developing a fund of experience—albeit simulated, an instance of
what I will be calling "inoculation theology"—could they hope either to
inoculate would-be reformers against the fear of moral and physical contagion or to render the young resistant to the surprises of sin in an effort
to prepare a salvific army fit for battle on multiple fronts.

These materials sprang from and reflected particular beliefs about children that were notably in flux during much of the eighteenth and nineteenth centuries. While early Protestants held firmly to the belief that all humanity was born into sin—bearing what Jonathan Edwards's Boston colleague William Cooper referred to as the "hereditary stain"— children were regarded as particularly vulnerable to further corruption.[54] The least experienced in the ways of the world, with little awareness of their fallen nature, children were thought to have weak moral defenses. Yet as childhood increasingly came to be perceived as a time when children should be protected from the responsibilities (moral and physical) of adulthood, many eighteenth-century ministers worried that too much protection could weaken individual wills and that cloistered generations would come of age unprepared to cope with the spiritual peril surrounding them.[55] The Calvinist view of humanity's innate depravity was encountering growing challenges from new pedagogical theories. Protestant ministers increasingly embraced John Locke's sensual psychology, engaging to varying degrees the scores of emerging theologies supporting and refuting the empirical basis of modern epistemology that steadily suffused colonial Enlightenment culture.[56] While Edwards's intersectarian generation of colonial Calvinists could not quite come to terms with the infant as tabula rasa, a blank slate with no fixed ideas either good or evil, it gradually took the sense-based epistemology for granted: the most authentic form of knowledge came from personal experience.

This epistemology generated problems, particularly where children were concerned. For if the young were tabulae rasae, lacking an innate moral sense, how could they safely accrue what Locke called a "settled standard," a fund of experience against which to measure the accuracy of new sensations, so that they could properly exercise their volition through the appropriate moral understanding?[57] By the mid-eighteenth century, experience had come to occupy so important a place in Anglo-American Protestant theories of moral development and spiritual maturation that it led to an arsenal of training exercises and homiletic instruments meant to provide the inexperienced with controlled exposure to sin. Puritan divines in Edwards's generation shaped homiletic pedagogy as a defense against a perceived decline in moral vigilance and the worldly encroachment it presaged. Seeking to shape children's conception of the material world, Edwards's and his cohort's sermons increasingly came to rely on homiletic realism's aesthetics of immediacy: visual language, the personalization of religious narrative and doctrine, and the evocation of intense emotions, especially fear—all of which, as with the *Eternal Forces* video game, worked to create an intensely identificatory structure.

Although he had no neurological research to confirm his supposition, Edwards believed that the need for immediacy and participatory identification were marks of an unformed or unregenerated mind. A more rational (though still fallen) creature might be swayed by divine reason, biblical logic, highly intertextual rhetoric, and self-evident moral truths channeled through Ramistic and Aristotelian systems of logic, but children, the inexperienced, and those Edwards identified as "persons of mean capacities"—and Isaac Watts, referring to "children" and "servants," called "the more ignorant parts of mankind,"—needed something else entirely if their attention were to be diverted from sin and directed toward salvation.[58] Only by simulating the terrible consequences of sin and suffering through new forms of literary and dramatic realism could ministers and spiritual leaders help new converts anticipate the moral snares around them or learn to recognize evil cloaked within the seductive guise of beauty.[59] In their attempts to simulate experience through homiletic lessons, guardians of the faith assumed that to be forewarned is to be forearmed. They wrote voluminously on child development and forms of reading appropriate to the perceptions of spiritual truths, and they authored texts for children, parents, converts, and religious advisors in an effort to guide new "professors" along their spiritual journeys toward salvation.[60]

The nineteenth century saw further changes to the meaning of childhood, and particular Protestant communities adopted to varying degrees the new attitudes circulating in Western society more generally. Many evangelical Protestants came to believe that children were born naturally good and, in a popular form of romanticism corresponding with Rousseau's child psychology, uncorrupted by society. Coleridgean Platonism—taken up by a number of American idealists—reinfused the Cambridge Platonism borne to the New World with the Puritan migration of Congregationalists, Presbyterians, and Baptists in the seventeenth and eighteenth centuries, and Christian idealism enjoyed new vogue as children, and often those racially deemed "primitives," were perceived to enjoy privileged access to the divine.[61] Their unfocused gaze, distractibility, untroubled slumber, prelinguistic bursts of laughter, and unfettered joy all signified lingering memories of heaven, if not latent angelic affinities. Influenced by Scottish common sense philosophy, religious and secular educators alike in the 1820s and 1830s developed pedagogies around the assumption that children were more malleable and more attuned to the spiritual and to their own better feelings than adults.[62]

Horace Bushnell, the great nineteenth-century Congregationalist minister, helped frame and concretize this new ethos for generations to come with his immensely influential work *Views of Christian Nurture* (1847).[63] Equally important in popularizing this view was Jacob Abbott's enormously popular "Rollo" series (*Rollo at Work, Rollo at Play, Rollo's Experiments*). This theological shift accompanied changes both in institutional attitudes toward children—including a spate of laws governing children's capacity to form legal or political consent, and their criminal culpability—and attitudes about child rearing in the home. These changing attitudes toward children appear in a number of the texts examined in this study.

Devising educational theories, homiletic programs, and catechisms compatible with early modern epistemology thus meant addressing children's emotional, mental, and moral needs, while neither overshooting nor underestimating their spiritual aptitude.[64] In the seventeenth and eighteenth centuries (as we will see in chapters 1 and 2), catechisms, primers, conversion manuals, and sermons trained the young in typological and providential interpretations of contemporary events, while spiritual autobiographies, the martyr sections of primers, and other forms of narrative hagiography taught them how to narrate their own lives within and around these events. Later, more sophisticated homiletic strategies absorbed the task of self-discovery, helping the young to link experience with knowledge. Over time, both religious epistemology and the perception of a child's moral aptitude and responsive capacity changed, at times occasioning and at times occasioned by profound doctrinal shifts. These shifts altered homiletic forms—initially none more than the sermon— sometimes through innovations, in other periods and places through reversion to more conventional forms. While the narrative forms that American Protestants used to spread and instill their pedagogical beliefs changed often, some popular forms—in particular, the nineteenth-century homiletic novel—flourished, even after the pedagogical beliefs they advocated ceased to resonate widely outside religious readerships. Broadly speaking, *The Word and Its Witness* is the story of these changes and the homiletic strategies they advanced, and of how each altered or, in more dramatic ways, transformed American culture beyond spiritual life.

However significant these developments in Protestant homiletic approaches to children may be, this study is not primarily about children or childhood—at least not in the physical or material sense. While it prominently features the battle for the spiritual salvation of children, it does so in order to show how Protestantism has often used children as figures for the pressing concerns of adults. Since the Reformation—more specifically, after the emergence of empirically focused pedagogies in the eighteenth century—Protestants have perceived children's spiritual capacity as the litmus test for religious instruction of all types. To foster the moral musculature of all, ministers created a range of heuristic and devotional exercises applicable to the moral development and religious autonomy of individuals with a variety of spiritual needs, arming the faithful against the onslaught of an evil for whom the young and new converts were merely the first and easiest objects of attack. Although beliefs and practices diverged among the Protestant branches and denominations, and changed often and even radically from the seventeenth to the twentieth century, the spiritual welfare of the child continued to set the bar for religious education. It was a fail-safe position. Individuals inoculated against evil as children carried their immunity into adulthood. And if a spiritual guide worked for children, it could work for anyone, for of course all new Christians, regardless of age, were considered "babes in Christ" (I Corinthians 3:1), reflecting the Pauline trope of rebirth and regeneration in Christ's death.

In conversion, Paul wrote, the soul went through a terrible travail as the "new man" emerged from the shell of the old or "natural" man, who as Adam's heir had been born into death. This "old man" was crucified on the cross with Christ and resurrected from Christ's death in sin into a new flesh and a new life (Romans 6:1–28). Well before the Reformation, devotional literature had figured the spiritually unadvanced—novice monks, women, and especially the laity—as children in need of particular kinds of nourishment: bland portions of scriptural meat, easily digested and unquestionably wholesome. "Simple creatures," one popular author wrote around 1410, "as childryn haven nede to be fedde with milke of lighte doctrine, and not with sadde [serious] mete of grete clargye and of hye contemplacion."[65] Chaucer's Prioress, reflecting the language of the Little Office of the Virgin and the Mass of the Holy Innocents, describes herself as a babe sucking at the breast: "a child of twelf month oold, or lesse / That kan unnethes [hardly] any word expresse."[66] Medieval English morality plays like the widely popular *The Castle of*

Perseverance and *Mundus et Infans* opened with the figure of Mankind as a baby.[67] Devotional texts described the Christian's daily trials and temptations as "the chastising of God's children" (the title of one particularly popular guide).[68]

The familiar theme of spiritual infancy and childhood gained new power and meaning after the Reformation, thanks in part to the Protestant emphasis on conversion and spiritual rebirth as absolutely necessary for every soul that was to be saved, and to a concomitant doctrinal shift from infant baptism to late-preadolescent baptism (initially the doctrine of Anabaptists), with an emphasis on the convert's requisite capacity to form consent.[69] The idea of spiritual education took on added significance in a culture of new readers, where every person was expected to be able to interpret the Bible for him or herself. In contrast to their view of Catholicism's in-loco-parentis model of mediation between the spiritual supplicant as child and the cleric as father, Protestants envisioned the rebirth of converts as the beginning of a process of spiritual maturation. Through careful regulation, converts would grow from spiritual toddlers spoon-fed with small, partially digested doctrinal portions, to adults able to digest complex doctrine and to discriminate between what was healthy and what might be unsalutary, noxious, or even lethal.

Of course, Protestants had very different ideas about what counted as sustenance for fragile digestions. For example, in his hard-hitting primer and catechism *Spiritual Milk for Babes: Drawn out of the Breasts of Both Testaments* (c. 1646), the famed minister John Cotton, the first-generation New England immigrant and dynastical head of the Mather clan, offered a diet of fear, rebuke, and retribution, warning of hell's misery and the fiendish pleasure of its terrible minions.[70] While the text was a pillar of Protestant education among many sects in the eighteenth and nineteenth centuries and was edited by a host of interdenominational ministers and laity, many nineteenth-century middle-class educators, particularly those from an emerging genteel evangelical tradition, found it and works like it deeply objectionable, capable of impairing developing minds and withering sensitive spirits.[71]

Long before the advent of modern psychology, Puritans believed that problems encountered in adulthood could be traced to childhood origins. In the sermon quoted in the epigraph to this introduction, for example, Jonathan Edwards tells his adult audience that their faulty educations and ineffective conversions have stunted, warped, or arrested their spiritual development. He explains that many of them have been given an adult's diet with a child's digestion, and that they are wandering far from the true path, though they presume themselves converted. In a fruit-of-the-poison-tree analogy that reflects a broader pattern of what we might think of as a kind of Calvinist eugenics, Edwards warns that bad husbandry produces inferior fruit, and inferior fruit produces bad seeds. He thus encourages his audience to regress to the condition of babes in order to undergo their early training again. By returning to the "first principles" and undergoing "repentance anew," he suggests, they can correct the missteps in their religious understanding and lay the "foundation of faith" required for proper spiritual development. The materials this study explores, ranging from early catechisms, sermons, and spiritual autobiographies to homiletic novels and the "virtual-tour" narratives of late-nineteenth-century Social Gospel reformers, were grounded in just such beliefs about the maturational processes of physical and spiritual children alike. This book will thus be concerned with how these maturational processes were represented in various kinds of Protestant pedagogy in the eighteenth and nineteenth centuries, and with how ministers' understanding of such processes shaped the creation of homiletic exercises and imaginative spiritual works.

Homiletic Patterns

While popular homiletic literature in America was designed in part to address the spiritual development of the inexperienced, it was also a response to fears about the growing diversity, diffusion, and fragmentation of American Protestant communities. One side of the story this book unfolds concerns the masterplots that Protestants used to organize their various spiritual journeys. From the first settlements, ministers worried about the potential for spiritual atomism in an expansive wilderness without institutional or cultural infrastructures.[72] Here, religious values and views could spread virtually unimpeded, a potential increasingly realized in later years as immigrants poured into the colonies and branched out into the wilderness beyond the immediate control of their charismatic ministers. Church leaders—initially intra- and later interdenominationally—believed that the unifying forms of homiletic practices could slow the centrifugal forces of Protestant sectarianism while preserving pilgrims' independence.[73] Homiletic materials thus aimed to assist individuals in their personal devotions, guiding them during the times between direct contact with spiritual leaders, whether a week or more extended periods, in the cases of those who could not attend regular church meetings. Such texts also helped popularize public piety; in the overheated decades of the 1730s and 1740s, for instance, ministers ushered a number of sixteenth- and seventeenth-century manuals of piety and conversion through the presses in an attempt to regulate the enthusiasm generated in the wake of the colonial revivals that came to be known as the First Great Awakening.[74]

Ministers struggled to create narrative forms and homiletic exercises to provide the least experienced, the least educated, with patterns and practices that would sharpen their moral sense in the absence of spiritual counselors and firsthand experience, since the perceived survival rates against encounters with moral temptation were indeed low. What emerges from the vast body of American homiletic materials—sermons, religious journals, hymnals, newspapers, homiletic booklets, tracts, pamphlets, and even novels—is a series of remarkably unified narrative patterns. The literary and schematic forms they inhabit (traditionally referred to as heuristics, but which we might more usefully think of as homiletic templates) play a significant role in how Protestants understood and used masterplots to shape their own pilgrimages. Even as these templates shed one literary form and assumed another to meet the demands of shifting print markets and to accommodate new or alternative pedagogical views, they still contained traces of familiar masterplots and templates whose heuristic function, regardless of denominational affiliation, assisted Christians in monitoring and regulating their lives in accordance with biblical and typological patterns of redemption, spiritual progress, and salvation.

Another side of the story concerns the larger impact of these templates and the reading practices that made them relevant to a wide range of individuals on literary forms and political culture. In American literary criticism, the exclusion of religious narrative from genre studies, particularly in modes of formalism between 1900 and the midcentury apogee of New Criticism, did much to distort our current understanding of American literary history, particularly since in the eighteenth and nineteenth centuries the most widely read narratives were religious.[75] These texts ranged from Thomas à Kempis's *The Christian Pattern* (in Latin, *De Imitatione Christi*), the King James Bible, John Bunyan's *The Pilgrim's Progress,* literally tens of thousands of sermons, Jonathan Edwards's *The Life of David Brainerd,* T. S. Arthur's *Ten Days in a Barroom,* and countless "sermon stories" and spiritual narratives, to nineteenth-century homiletic novels such as the largest bestseller, Charles Sheldon's *In His Steps,* which coined the slogan, "What would Jesus do?" Only by excluding these narrative traditions from the canon—presumably because none of them, according to generations of literary formalists, measured up aesthetically, but also because of academia's increasing secularism—could New Criticism, for instance, create an enduring model of reading that rejected the "affective fallacy."[76] As I suggested earlier, recent criticism could only construe late-nineteenth-century realism as a secular development by overlooking homiletic narrative strategies that sought to concretize the abstract consequences of eternity in vivid encounters in the material world.

Homiletic readerships were not the secular, class-based coteries that, in Richard Brodhead's terms, produced "different cultures of letters."[77] While it is true that homiletic authors wrote religious material that addressed and summoned together "some particular social grouping" or produced distinctive "modes of social reality" (to invoke Brodhead's formulation), it is wrong to assume that any religious grouping was determined entirely by one social or cultural element, be it commercial interests, gender, wealth or poverty, ethnic background, or even denominational affiliation. Certainly, American homiletic readers were primarily Protestant and, after the American Revolution, increasingly evangelical, but they were also composed of conflicting sectarian interests, running the gamut from the liberal progressivism of the reformist Social Gospel to the conservative pietism of the individual-oriented, ante- and postbellum holiness movement, a branch of which would emerge in the early twentieth century as Pentecostalism and, still later, as charismatic fundamentalism. That is not to say a given work did not receive localized or culturally or ethnically charged readings. Various denominations mounted complex hermeneutic registers around specific texts, often radically altering conventional biblical commentaries.[78] The Mormon followers of Joseph Smith, for instance, reconfigured their belief around a radical reading of John 10:16 ("other sheep I have not of this fold"), reinterpreting what traditional commentaries glossed over as Christ's allusion to Gentiles as an allusion, instead, to the peoples of the precontact New World, the descendants of the legendary lost tribe of Israel. Smith's revelation announced that the Bible, corrupted in the first centuries of the church, was in need of restoration—including a history of

Christ's first-century visit to the New World—through the Book of Mormon and Doctrine of the Covenants, a latter-day dispensation of the holy scriptures.

While these masterplots endured so long as the historical circumstances from which they emerged prevailed, they also generated an infinite number of localized variations, such as the dramatic distinctions between Northern and Southern theology, or the development of a distinctly African American sermonic style.[79] Even among specific, demographically diverse spiritual coteries and communities, exact hermeneutic variations of a given masterplot were rarely stable from one group to the next, even when those populations shared similar racial, national, ideological, or doctrinal roots or circumstances. While master narratives and interpretive practices might carry the stabilizing approval of churches, congregations, conclaves, synods, or other loosely defined ecumenical bodies, they were primarily engaged by individuals in spiritual life outside institutional frameworks, in the day-to-day existence of the faithful. The personalization of scripture embedded in the Protestant tradition of *sola scriptura* trumped both local and regional sociopolitical conventions, even as changes in content tended to leave the masterplot frame intact. In the final analysis, American religion, like politics, is a local affair.

The ability to read oneself into newly interpreted typologies was vital to the cultivation and maintenance of personal faith particularly in times of affliction, for it provided a teleology that answered—even as it made newly relevant—the question, "Why me?"[80] Not only could the scriptures simultaneously sustain multiple and conflicting interpretations, but so also could many homiletic texts, explaining the cultural viability in different times and different places of, for instance, such works as Thomas à Kempis's *De Imitatione Christi,* Bunyan's *Pilgrim's Progress,* Edwards's *Life of David Brainerd,* and, as we shall see, even Alcott's *Little Women.* As a function of highly specialized hermeneutic cultures, interpreting against the grain of dominant religious narrative traditions was widespread. In spite of a fairly constant Protestant hermeneutic tradition, the imperative to read and interpret the scriptures for oneself and to experience faith in a deeply personal way made geographic and historical localization the most significant determinant in the shaping of American spiritual identity and daily religious practices.[81]

One of the mysteries of American Protestantism after the Revolution is how evangelicals could both assert denominational differences, often quite contentiously, and still assume a true church of all believers that transcended sectarianism. In the eighteenth century, Jonathan Edwards, John Wesley, and George Whitefield shared fellowship—in person or in correspondence—despite the sustained animosity their followers exhibited toward each other and each other's leaders. The American Civil War records many instances of Southern and Northern soldiers worshipping together on hiatuses between battles despite not just denominational differences in once-unified communions (e.g., Southern versus Northern Methodists and Baptists), but the deep political differences that drove the nation to war. Much as the Stone-Campbell "Christians" attempted to build a unified Protestantism in the antebellum era, the postbellum period witnessed greater attempts by national religious leaders to build inter- and nonsectarian alliances. Coming toward the tail end of a long line of ministers promoting ecumenical cooperation through such organizations as the Christian Alliance, Washington Gladden and Edward Everett Hale promoted a Christian commonwealth, writing novels about towns whose denominationally diverse churches integrated their congregations or shared resources, including church buildings, hymnals and Bibles, and community centers.[82] Similar to the Christian socialist impulses of Gladden and Hale, the more popular Dwight L. Moody and other, later evangelists like Billy Sunday downplayed denominational and doctrinal differences in their sermons to increasingly nondenominational or interfaith audiences. Yet for all these commonalities, differences persisted. This study seeks to disentangle some of the primary formative elements of this paradox.

Visualizing the Word

Visual paradigms and their relation to print culture are particularly important in understanding the impact of Protestant homiletics on religious and secular Americans' differing understandings of the epistemological and aesthetic categories of "the real" and realism. The title of my study, *The Word and Its Witness,* is meant to invoke some of the complexity of this subject. The phrase accounts for the way in which words themselves have, in particular Protestant traditions, been perceived as something vividly incarnated and materially transformative: a literalization of the "word made flesh" (John 1:1–14). The term *witness* recapitulates

its manifold meanings within a conventional Protestant idiom, signifying the intersection between the visual (watching and seeing), the jurid-
ical (testifying or giving an account of, as in "bearing false witness"),
and the spiritual (as in evangelicals "witnessing" in order to convert).
The *its* in the phrase "word and its witness" moves ambiguously between
subjective and objective genitive—not as the *jouissance* of linguistic
play but as a slippage historically relevant in the language of evangelical revivalism. For me this ambiguity points usefully toward two different modes in which the book operates. First, it is concerned with the degree to which the sacred word finds itself witnessed *by* others: the way in
which the word is spoken of, discussed, expounded on, interpreted, registered, seen, and otherwise asserted as a feature of the real. Second, it
is concerned with the degree to which the sacred word witnesses *to* others: how it appears to others as a direct mediator of their lives and their
experience, as a sui generis feature of the real that gives voice and testifies to features of the real that without its enchanted or spiritual intervention would remain shrouded in silence. It is according to this second
concern that *The Word and Its Witness* seeks to expand American realism beyond its conceptual frame. In contrast to literary realism even
broadly conceived, this version of the real is constituted through representational practices that require transcendent mediation.

It is in this context that this study participates not only in a rethinking
of literary realism but also in visual rhetoric's attempt to develop a language for describing the intersection between print and visual cultures,
taking seriously David Morgan's warning against sidelining the visual in
studies of Protestantism.[83] Such attention to the visual might seem surprising because we are accustomed to thinking of Protestant faith practices as less focused on the visual, on icons and pageantry, than are the
rich emblematic and devotional-ritual traditions of either the Roman
Catholic or the Greek Orthodox Church.[84] Even in relation to Luther-
anism and Anglicanism—the other major branches of Protestantism—
the visual and performative devotions of non-Anglican Calvinists, at
least in conventional terms, pale by comparison.[85] Popular history has
often labored under the notion that Protestants were dyed-in-the-wool
iconoclasts: image breakers. According to our popular metanarrative, it
was from the Calvinists' Spartan attitude toward leisure, creature comfort, and spiritual and social accessorizing, and from their theology,
which did not flinch at infant damnation and morally justified worldly
suffering, that our nation derived its masculine ethos, spiritual forti-

tude, and exceptionalism.[86] Homiletic materials remain largely unexamined because the evidence they provide, as Charles E. Hambrick-
Stowe has demonstrated, goes against deeply ingrained certainties about
seventeenth-century iconoclasm, about the rejection of liturgical forms
and pictorial representation; it runs counter to received notions of a distinctive national personality predicated on Max Weber's Protestant-
work-ethic thesis, in which colonial productivity and American ingenu-
ity were the payoffs for intense psychological sublimation, the denial of
art and beauty, and the repression of pleasure—most certainly, the pleasure of the text.[87]

Since V. L. Parrington in the 1920s, scholarship has broadly gestured
back to the raid on sacred icons, spiritual *visibilia* (the term C. S. Lewis
favored), and architectural homiletics in the fraught decade of the 1640s,
when a minority faction controlled the Long Parliament. Leagued with
Oliver Cromwell's army, an austere ministry simply continued the iconoclasm of the sixteenth-century English Reformation under the boy king
Edward VI (1547–53), at a time when a new class of scripturally zealous divines and an increasingly autonomous laity swept through village
parishes vandalizing sacred images, engravings of saints, nave reliefs of
biblical stories, carved roof bosses, wooden communion rails, and apse
and altar crucifixes and crèches.[88] The illustrator of John Foxe's famed
Acts and Monuments (1570; better known by its descriptive title "Foxe's
Book of Martyrs") summed up the invigorated Reformation following
Henry VIII's death in a bold allegorical representation. The frontispiece
is divided into three scenes. The lower-left corner depicts the young Edward presiding over the court's orderly transition between monarchs.
The lower-right panel reveals a congregation gathered in a simple meeting house observing the two scripturally authorized sacraments, baptism and the Eucharist or—in the anti-Catholic idiom favored by Anglo-
American Calvinists—communion. In bold contrast, the upper panel depicts the Reformation expulsion of "Papistes" from England, representing the church stripped of Catholic icons and other sacred objects, super-
stitious "trinkets" loaded aboard "the ship of Romish Church" by monks
fleeing the realm. A banner flying above the Protestant king's court pro-
claims, "The Temple well purged."

Because Foxe's martyrology was continuously published and widely
circulated among Presbyterians, Congregationalists, Quakers, and Baptists in the colonies, and its woodblock prints and narratives excerpted
in countless colonial catechisms and primers as part of emblematic ex-

ercises, this visual anecdote aptly illustrates Protestants' vexed relationship with the use of images in worship and devotion. The lower panels of
crown and church form a diptych that emblematizes the twin pillars of
the state and civic life, the institutions that at once sanction and contain
the violent iconoclasm of the upper panel. The contradiction embodied
in the frontispiece bespeaks the Protestant ambivalence toward the visual, veering between the extremes of what the Long Parliament's Ordi-
nance of 17 May 1642 called "monuments of idolatry and superstition"
and appropriate emblematic illumination. In one of the most revered
books published after the Counter-Reformation of Catholic Queen
Mary, iconography celebrates iconoclasm. Clearly, Protestants discerned
a difference between appropriate and inappropriate devotional representations, parsed between word and image.

While the ceremonial austerity of Calvinism has been overstated—
exacerbated by the scholarly centrality of New England Congregationalism at the expense of broader comparative analyses of other
seventeenth- and eighteenth-century "Puritan" sects, such as the Baptists, Presbyterians, Anglicans, and Methodists—this book looks at an
aspect of the visual often occluded by the focus on Christian images and
rituals, particularly in a field dominated in this context by the focus on
Catholicism. Much has been made of the Puritan "plain style" as the first
American aesthetic. Deemed another mode of religious iconoclasm, the
plain style advocated simplicity, clarity, and lack of such ornamentation
as rhetorical flourishes and figures, allegory, metaphor, metonymy, and
the like. Because I will later address language in greater detail, suffice
it to say here that by the eighteenth century, in response to the epistemological challenges posed by the ascendancy of sensational psychology,
Protestant pedagogy reinstituted increasingly visually oriented language
into sermons. One need only think of the catalog of sensuous, but largely
visual, images Edwards uses to describe damnation in "Sinners in the
Hands of an Angry God." The need to crystallize metaphysical abstractions such as hell, heaven, eternity, or even the unspeakable suffering of
damnation drove ministers to employ vivid visual incarnations: to embody language. The word had to witness God's omnipotence, wrath, and
retribution through the production of sensation, the epistemological register of personal experience, largely emptied out in the plain style. The
crisis about language's ability to convey experience (the extended subject of chapter 1) fostered other forms of graphic discursion.

In no period has the act of seeing been a neutral register. Scholar-

ship in visual cultural studies and visual rhetoric has formulated a set of
new theoretical praxes at emergent disciplinary intersections that make
it possible for us to talk about vision and seeing in a broader context
than that in which it has typically been construed: the perceiving subject in relation to the object world.[89] As historians of visual culture and
art history remind us, seeing, unlike vision, is not a universal experience, but a physical activity culturally constructed by deeply ingrained
modes of cultural interpretation, social expectation, perception and conception, and spiritual habits of imagination. How individuals conceive
of their environment—inflected for economic status, for religious, class,
political, and national affiliation, and for various forms of identity—
influences how they perceive their reality, whether nationally or region-
ally conceived, or conceived among particular groups defined culturally,
ideologically, doctrinally, or demographically. Thus, exploring how different communities "see" differently can broaden our understanding of
specialized readerships and the social reality they construed, not only
by *what* they read, but by *how* they read it.[90] For even against the range
of interpretive and readerly practices suggested by critics as diverse as
Michael Denning, David D. Hall, Janice A. Radway, and Jane Tompkins, many scholars tend to assume that all nineteenth- and twentieth-
century readers approached the written word with the same critical,
aesthetic, or didactic orientation—with an implicit rather than explicit
reading epistemology—regardless of their religious or secular commitments, professions, class, or cultural background.[91]

Significantly, in its focus on the visual and visual rhetoric, this book
situates the authority of Protestant epistemology and hermeneutic practices not in a secular or empirical reality measured solely by the senses,
but in a spiritual reality beyond the ken of empirical fact. These practices vividly materialized metaphysical and spiritual abstractions as if
they existed in the object world, taking paradigmatic shape. They were
viewed not simply as phenomenological evidence, but within inenarrable
structures of communal envisioning and feeling: in shared perceptions
of heaven and hell, death's ineluctable grasp or Judgment's inexorable
penalty, and the prescripted, unifying responses such perceptions evoke.
While religious art historian Margaret Miles, representing a common
bias, suggests that only "an Eastern Orthodox or Roman Catholic Christian relates to an icon," this study demonstrates the ancient embedded
visual traditions of Protestant hermeneutics and homiletic practices.[92]

A study of visual cultures thus offers fresh approaches to our understanding of Protestant interiority, the relation between spiritual and material "reality," the connections between external seeing and the inward gaze, and the fusion of language and images, vision and envisioning, sight and insight, perceiving and conceiving. The chapters to follow examine the role of epistemology in simultaneously shaping contested realities, considering, for instance, how mental concepts—spiritual paradigms or larger belief systems through which the religious interpret or understand the world—perceptually organize reality in advance of perception itself. I examine how the interplay between vision and envisioning instrumentalized individuals' identification with exemplary figures and fictional characters, thus heightening their capacity to personalize allegorical plots and typological narratives. This process, I suggest, became the modern *imitatio Christi,* a tradition popularized with the cessation of colonial aristocracies of the elect and the doctrine of predestination.

American Homiletic Realism

Broadly speaking, then, homiletic practitioners brought to their heuristic pedagogy specific strategies for engaging visual, oral, and literary texts: a particular way of seeing and narrating social and spiritual reality that I am calling as an "aesthetics of immediacy." Before moving to more specific analyses of how this aesthetic intersected with social movements, secular reading practices, and narrative genres, let me briefly lay out three of its key components. First, homiletic texts employed allegorical frames to create social environments immediately present to readers or auditors in which individuals imagined possibilities for personal transformation. Readers of homiletic narrative understood religious stories of exemplary figures—biblical personages, the subjects of spiritual autobiographies, the characters in religious novels, or characterological roles in video games—to be not merely tales particular to a time and place, but also representative stories of universal experiences, religious metanarratives, and biblical typologies, with realities and consequences both in historical and eschatological time—the temporal simultaneity that produces an aesthetics of immediacy. Homiletic allegories transformed individuals into communities of action that were expected to engage with religious material as experiential templates or moral scripts for their own lives.

Second, homiletic texts denied readers the role of passive onlooker,

presenting instead a virtual reality that demanded their narrative participation and volition in moral choices. These texts required the reader
to identify with the subjects of the texts, to engage in a dialogue not only
about his or her decisions and choices but also about their implications
for personal experience and social obligation. The lay sermons of late-
nineteenth-century religious reformers on urban poverty and destitution,
for example—anticipating the visual realism of such modern pedagogies
as the *Eternal Forces* video game—employed photographic realism not
simply to illustrate social reality at face value, but to construct religious
tableaux for audiences that still believed in representation as what, following the Edwardsian homiletic epistemology discussed in chapter 1, I
will call "second sight," an unmediated access to the inexpungible reality of the divine.

Third, the aesthetics of immediacy cultivates a kind of double vision
that allows audiences to perceive themselves as forever in a transhistorical present, or eschatological time, bearing the cross *with* their suffering
Savior.[93] Homiletic narrative drew on readers' sentimental perceptions
to invoke a spiritual world, affording those who engaged the narratives a
glimpse of their part in God's design. Particularly in the aftermath of the
Second Great Awakening—composed of scores of local revivals across
the country roughly between 1800 and 1835—identification with personal tragedy became central to the homiletic strategy for reinvigorating
Pauline scripture in Protestant life. Suffering became the primary mechanism for such identification, the epistemological bridge, Charles Sheldon wrote in *In His Steps* (1896), between subject and object made "concrete," "actual," and "personal" in the visceral experience of another's
pain.[94] It also, however, underscored the contrast between the individual's insignificant historical location and the universal and eternal significance of Christ's sacrifice on the cross. Homiletic novels by authors like
Sheldon, Alcott, Harold Bell Wright, and others illustrate the injunction
that the faithful become Christlike by becoming a "living sacrifice" for
the social world—the homiletic catechism of muscular Christianity.

This double vision fostered a weak sense of anachronism, demanding that disciples recognize, if not achieve, an Archimedean perspective
outside their historical localization—to see both history and its causality as shadow shows in a cave whose debasement of eternal realities required an epistemological reorientation and a renewed faith in humanity
to correct. Following the Neoplatonic routes of much medieval patristic
theology, this second sight bifurcated perspective, reminding the faithful

that they were *in* but not *of* the world—following Paul, not to "conform" their lives but to "transform" them (Romans 12:2).[95] In a revivification of the interactive strategies of medieval morality and cycle plays, spiritual stewards encouraged their charges to imagine themselves as participants in sacred events—Christ's birth, crucifixion, and resurrection—in the familiar setting of their own historical moment. Like the ancient Greeks' explanation of tragedy as protagonists having missed their appointed hour at the crossroads of two kinds of time—the juncture of destiny, or "God's time" (*kairos*), and historic time (*kronos*)—such a worldview imagined the possibility for the faithful to stand at the intersection of the temporal and eternal, simultaneously inside and outside time. Much as medieval art patrons had their likenesses inserted into commissioned works of sacred events, the faithful understood how the diachronic path of their lives passed through the sacred scenes of Christ's life, and thus imagined how their Savior's blood could flow from the cross not only forward through history but also back in time, extending salvation to the godly in Old Testament history.[96]

This attenuated sense of anachronism further instrumentalized Christian allegory and typology as a heuristic frame for conceptualizing a number of otherwise abstract dialectical relationships: temporal and eternal, body and soul, material and spiritual, type and archetype, and reality and representation. Revitalized by seventeenth-century Calvinists, second sight became an important supplement for the religious as the eighteenth-century Enlightenment plunged traditional metaphysics (the soul as arbiter between the material and spiritual worlds) into an evidentiary crisis. The earliest Protestant homiletic frames reveal the tie between double vision and spiritual growth, the theory for which Protestants from an array of denominations turned to Jonathan Edwards, as we will see in the next chapter. Infused with the aesthetics of immediacy, homiletic narratives immersed audiences into the contemporary world's moral, and later social, concerns, declaring that earthly challenges of their world corresponded with those of the spiritual realm. Colonial ministers encouraged the faithful to draw on their spiritual vision to anticipate, through divergent post-Lockean models of sensual psychology, the preternatural dangers that lay in wait to ensnare the young, the inexperienced, and the unaware.

A century and a half later, in a brief change that reflected a shift in spiritual conversion's salvific emphasis from individual to collective redemption, postbellum homiletics demanded that the religiously committed draw on their second sight to address human need through personal intervention in the social world. Much as colonial Baptist, Methodist, Presbyterian, and Congregational children saw the violent afterlife their charismatic ministers summoned, Social Gospel adherents saw the salvific path through virtual representation: experience that—as Jonathan Edwards, Ralph Waldo Emerson, and John Dewey similarly defined it—transformed knowledge into action. The tableaux of urban despair, for instance, that postbellum religious reformers dramatized in stereopticon-slide shows were the shadows cast by the union of allegory and new visual technologies, to which only the sympathetic identification of middle-class Christians could lend substance. Earlier homiletic authors had pressed their audiences to identify with exemplary figures like David Brainerd and Zilpha Elaw, or typological heroes like John Bunyan's "everyman" protagonist and Alcott's fictional "pilgrims." Later they sought to recreate not the universal sacrifice of Christ as a remote deity, but the particular suffering of Jesus, "the son of man" (John 8:28), whose crucifixion was the "personalized" price paid for the particular sins of each individual, regardless of his or her station in life. The Social Gospel transformed this absorption with Jesus's suffering into an identification with those deemed most Christlike: the impoverished itinerant, the immigrant laborer in tenement sweatshops, the widow and orphan, and the "undeserving poor."

As it traces the history of these identifications and interventions, this study shows how the anxieties and doubts raised by the devastation of the Civil War, technological advances, and the emergence of forensic sciences and secularism reformulated not only religious values but also new forms of expression. It is to these new forms that the latter half of this study particularly turns. Multimedia aesthetics of Protestant evangelicalism nurtured socioreligious awakenings by pairing both traditional and new oral and visual literary forms; homiletic novels and the sermon-novel hybrids I call "virtual-tour narratives" created religious fervor by asking readers to imagine themselves *as* Jesus Christ rather than simply as the imperfect impress of his divine mold. These narrative forms generated new modes of religious experience and new concepts of community, inspiring social and political reform in sites ranging from the New World wilderness, the domestic sphere, small communities in the late-nineteenth-century Midwest, and the urban ghetto.

Thus the intellectual tradition of American Protestant theology was transformed into popular practice, not as the fugitive and cloistered virtue inhabiting the seminary or divinity school, but on the ground, in what tens of thousands of ordinary men, women, and children likened, in Miltonic terms, to "the race where the immortal garland is to be run for, not without dust and heat." Homiletic practices helped channel the reformist energies of evangelical exhorters and their proselytes into a national ethic of social intervention that became the hallmark of such humanitarian endeavors as abolition, temperance, poverty relief, civil rights, "woman suffrage," the Social Gospel, and Progressive Era reform. But they also helped to structure reading practices receptive to forms of visual and discursive realism, culminating in nineteenth-century American literary realism. An understanding of homiletic literature—of how narrative forms helped to structure Americans' sense of their social and spiritual realities—is essential to a fuller understanding of both the forms of realist fiction and the "realities" those narrative forms encouraged religious reformers to perceive and reshape.

CHAPTER ONE

Hell's Plot: The Hermeneutic of Fear

If men be thoroughly scared, they will dread doing what wounds their consciences; *fear of Hell* will make men *afraid of sin.* —Solomon Stoddard, *A Guide to Christ*

Some people talk of it as an unreasonable thing to think to fright persons to heaven; but I think it is a reasonable thing to endeavor to fright persons away from Hell, that stand upon the brink of it, and are just ready to fall into it, and are senseless of their danger: 'tis a reasonable thing to fright a person out of a house on fire. —Jonathan Edwards, "The Distinguishing Marks of a Work of the Spirit of God"

The hell and destruction that Satan can bestow upon those who choose not to serve Jesus Christ. Literally, Hell House depicts choices that have the end result of ushering people into hell. —Keenan Roberts, senior pastor at Destiny Church of the Assemblies of God and creator of "The Hell House Kit"

The emergence of the hell house phenomenon among groups of evangelical fundamentalists in the 1980s has garnered public interest both inside and outside evangelical circles.[1] Credited as the brainchild of Jerry Falwell, the hell house has become increasingly popular in the last fifteen years, with growing numbers of churches and youth groups participating nationally.[2] Architecturally similar to the traditional haunted house, the hell house is meant as an antidote to the popularity of Halloween festivities with their celebration of the occult and, in the view of many evangelical fundamentalists, their dangerous demystification of the demonic. Not surprisingly, secular educators regard hell houses with

considerable dismay, deeming them potentially injurious to young audiences. The houses have also stirred controversy among the various evangelical denominations and even among their individual congregations.

Inside the hell house, a docent in demonic guise—wearing a black
gown and a skull mask, and carrying a trident—guides visitors through
seven or eight chambers, each exhibiting a graphic, disturbing vignette
of what many conservative evangelicals consider the most threatening
forms of immorality that entice the young today. Each room reveals a
different sin, with special focus not only on the act itself, but also on its
consequences both in the temporal world and in eternity. The putative
wages of sin encompass a wide array of pain, violence, lunacy, and despair. While the "sins" vary depending on the region and the denominational or doctrinal affiliation of each hell house, the popular "Hell
House Kit"—advertised as a "Satan-be-cryin,' keep-ya-from-fryin,' no
holds barred, cutting-edge evangelism tool" and sold internationally
from Denver, Colorado, to churches, youth ministries, and affiliated
organizations—offers from seven to ten standard moral themes: abortion, homosexuality, fornication, drinking and driving, drugs, suicide,
and Columbine-style mass murder. Each sin is graphically performed,
with particular attention to the verisimilitude of pain and emotional suffering it engenders and to the appearance of bodily decay commensurate with the sinning soul's supposed deterioration. The abortion chamber, for example—usually the first room of the tour—reveals a teenage
girl lying on an operating table, legs elevated and parted by stirrups, as
actors garbed in medical gowns perform the abortion with visceral realism, using strips of raw animal flesh to simulate the dismembered fetus.
The patient's cries alternate between resignation and protest, pain, and
despair.[3] The narrator tells the audience that the girl conceived as a result of being raped at a rave, having taken the drug "ecstasy" that lowered her inhibitions and impaired her moral faculties. The vignette of a
gay teenager, disfigured with open sores and skin lesions and lying in a
hospital ward, often occupies another of the house's rooms. Here the demon guide announces that the weeping boy is dying of AIDS, the consequence of sexual deviance.[4]

As a modern morality play, the hell house exposes visitors to the cycles of shame, remorse, guilt, despair, and agony that ensue from immoral
acts of the flesh—but also from such "gateway" sins as lying, cheating, alcohol and drug use, "making out," masturbation, pornography, and petty
theft. Through an enervation of the conscience, such lesser sins appear

to escalate into greater sins and their irrevocable consequences: the habituation of depravity, agonizing death, and eternal suffering. The effect
of the hell house's realism relies on the audiences' capacity to see the
narrative development implicit in such cycles of escalating sin and punishment, which, in turn, depends on the visual and aural realism the production generates. A 270-page instruction manual for producing the hell
house is included with the kit, along with a blueprint and script for each
chamber; a guide for auditioning and casting; a soundtrack of screams,
gun reports, and rave music; the moral lessons advocated; and instructions for witnessing to shaken visitors seeking redemption at tour's end.[5]

The emergence of the hell house raises numerous questions. Why
have some fundamentalist groups turned to such sensational narratives to instruct the young? Why enact sin with a realism so graphic it
induces vomiting, fainting, hysteria, and depression? What concerns induce ministers to risk such violent reactions? This chapter explores how
such rhetorical and performative practices are particularly Protestant,
particularly American. Why has Calvinism historically viewed fear as a
vital tool for moral armament against the perceived powers of evil? This
chapter answers such questions through an exploration of how the narrative development of hell altered the course of generations of Americans'
religious pilgrimages, and how it shaped their perceptions of family and
community, both in life and after death. The hell house phenomenon requires an understanding of a tradition of Protestant epistemology—of
how we know what we know and the limits of spiritual knowledge.

Narrative representations of hell hold a prominent place in Protestant narrative history. The hell house is but one example of a larger homiletic repertoire that sought to instill fear in the living in order to alter
their fates after death. Henry Ward Beecher's "The Strange Woman's
House," for instance, anticipates the hell house. In this sermon, the centerpiece of his 1843 *Lectures to Young Men,* Beecher leads his audience
through a hellish house in which each room represents the progressive
escalation of sin, leading listeners "in imagination" from one "ward" to
the next.[6] Beecher speaks with the immediacy of direct address in order
to help audiences imagine themselves within the narrative frame.[7] By invoking frightening images of the sick and dying—sinners already in the
throes of hellish torment—he creates an allegory in which audiences play
a role, demonstrating that in the moral structure of Protestant vigilance,
surveillance, and regulation, they who witness also participate. Viewers'
visceral responses to the descriptions of "bloated inmates" and "blood-

drenched walls" are themselves participatory acts. As audiences recoil
from the vividly evoked consequences of sin, their external response signifies moral opprobrium; at the same time, the saturation of lurid detail works to anathematize the sin internally, instilling an aversion aimed
at long-term inoculation. Like hell houses, Beecher's sermon serves the
homiletic tradition's interactive purpose: providing the young with the
experience of sin and its horrifying consequences without actually imperiling their souls by inadvertently triggering sin's cascade effect into a
vicious life.

Even Beecher's sermon, however, is a late innovation in a homiletic
tradition that sought to replace experience with the similitude *of* experience, offering a moral safeguard against actual sin. Many readers, extrapolating backward from Jonathan Edwards's infamous Enfield sermon, "Sinners in the Hands of an Angry God," have erroneously placed
the apogee of the fear-inducing hellfire sermon within the seventeenth-
century Puritan tradition. While fear of damnation has played a significant role in Protestant conversion morphologies since the Reformation,
and while the seventeenth-century sermon did emphasize hell as a place
of perpetual suffering, it was not until very late in the century that ministers routinely began asking listeners to imagine themselves in hell. Only
then did the spiritual motivation of Anglo-American Calvinists begin to
approximate the volition that induced medieval Christians to renounce
the flesh and labor for the coming of the Kingdom. Broadly speaking,
the nineteenth-century hellfire sermon was conceived of as a powerful
tool in the arsenal of what I call the emerging inoculation theology propounded by such early eighteenth-century ministers as William Cooper, Edwards, Thomas Foxcroft, George Whitefield, and Joseph Sewall.[8]
This chapter examines the changes leading to that eighteenth-century
development and its progression through narrative forms.

The seventeenth-century sermons of Thomas Shepard, Richard and
Increase Mather, John Davenport, Roger Williams, John Eliot, John
Norton and John Cotton, James Fitch, James Noyes, and Samuel Stone,
among others, tended to focus on sin as a condition of innate depravity rather than hell as a site of eternal damnation. In lieu of vivid descriptions of hell, sin engendered an emphasis on biblical exegesis and
on carefully delineated arguments for God's free grace, the doctrine of
election, the soul's passive reception of grace, infant baptism, and covenant theology. Harry S. Stout notes that especially in seventeenth-
century Boston among a "more liberal clergy," ministers tended to push

themes of "God's love, patience, and mercy to ailing sinners," those most in need of a stern warning.[9] While works like Lewis Bayly's *Practise of Pietie* (1612) chastened Richard Eccles, a parishioner in Thomas Shepard's Cambridge congregation, with "torments of hell which affected [his] heart," these sermons sought to inculcate hermeneutic practice, using scriptural study to teach those in a culture newly advocating vernacular literacy and an unmediated relationship with God how to translate the Bible into a living creed applicable to their lives.[10] Eighteenth-century ministers, by contrast, focused more on the evocative emotionalism produced by dramas of suffering, hellish hypotheticals of parishioners' future state. Even when seventeenth-century jeremiads thundered over parishioners' heads, threatening God's wrath in cataracts of fire, cajoling the wicked to repent, they could not match the psychosomatic intensity with which eighteenth-century ministers played on congregants' fear of eternal isolation, of suffering loved ones left behind; nor could their pulpit pounding match the visceral power of personalized exercises that asked congregants to imagine cavities in their flesh filled with worms and toads.

By envisioning the consequences of sin in allegorical vignettes that parishioners were encouraged to personalize, eighteenth-century ministers placed an almost unbearable strain on their audiences. One woman "about 30 years of age" recalled how George Whitefield, for instance, had cried out at the end of a sermon, "Ye wonder what makes these people cry so: but if the Lord would be pleased to open your Eyes, as he has done theirs, ye would see your hearts all crawling with Toads of Corruptions, and surrounded with Legions of Devils." The image "did not affect me much at the time," she reports, "yet when I came home I took on a Strong apprehension that it was so, and imagined that I felt them within me crawling up my Throat . . . , and turned away my eyes that I might not see them coming out of my mouth."[11]

What accounted for this psychological turn aimed at penetrating individuals' mental and emotional defenses, evoking nightmares and "mental anguish" capable of wrecking congregants' health or "dethroning" their reason, as Elizabeth Cady Stanton claimed of her own childhood experience in the famed "Burnt-over" district of upstate New York?[12] In *Cleansing Our Way in Youth* (1719), Thomas Foxcroft reasoned with his young parishioners: "If you are not fond of Heaven; it may be you are afraid of Hell. Hope of happiness, and fear of misery are the powerful springs of action, and the great engines to move rational creatures; and

no passion of human nature has a more constraining and governing influence, than fear. If therefore this bright prospect of eternity has not al-
lured you, I will now shift the scene, change hands, and turn the gloomy
side to affright you."[13] Foxcroft's assertion explains why sermons emphasized the unspeakable suffering awaiting sinners at their death, yet it
says frustratingly little about the reasons for the shift toward personalizing hell, what the theological historian Ava Chamberlain calls the "theology of cruelty."[14]

The pedagogical tradition of inculcating experience through fear
emerged in relation to several interlocking cultural and intellectual factors. The stability of colonial development reduced external threats of
violence, dissipating the experiential connections between the miseries
of this life and those of the next. By the eighteenth century the material
and spiritual worlds no longer manifested such clear semiotic connections. At the same time, the erosion of the doctrine of election; the slow,
subtle return of volition to mainstream colonial Calvinist theology; and
the rise of evangelicalism and Arminianism—the heretical creed associated with Jacobus Arminus (1560–1609) that held out the hope of salvific
grace for all who sought redemption and conversion—elicited new strategies for teaching congregants how to exercise their wills toward appropriate moral choices.[15] No longer would fear exclusively, or even primarily, motivate the obsessive, lifelong examination of the self to determine
one's status in relation to the elect. The eighteenth century unfolded a
religious epistemology that made fear an essential mechanism of religious conversion and the sword for motivating sinners to make conscious
choices about how they lived each day. Most significantly, an eighteenth-
century shift in religious epistemology made fear an essential mechanism of religious conversion. Concurrent with this transformation, scientific empiricism increasingly posed challenges to Calvinist thought
by making experience the regnant ingredient in moral and spiritual development. While Jonathan Edwards's theology can be understood as a
lifelong attempt to achieve a rapprochement between these contending
epistemologies, William James perhaps best explained the difficulty of
all Christians after the ascendancy of empiricism and materialism in *Varieties of Religious Experience:*[16] "How can religion, which believes in
two worlds and an invisible order, be estimated by the adaptation of its
fruits to this world's order alone? It is its *truth,* not its utility . . . upon
which our verdict ought to depend. If religion is true, its fruits are good

fruits, even though in this world they should prove uniformly ill adapted and full of naught but pathos."[17] Edwards's response to Locke—as one instance of how the dialectic between colonial religion and rational empiricism affected Protestantism—would frame the foundation of evangelical pedagogy for succeeding centuries.[18]

Throughout this chapter I focus particularly on the problems posed by the spiritual status of children, for even if they were not perfectly Lockean tabulae rasae, their relative lack of experience provided a test case for free will in a universe where inexperience exacted a steep spiritual price. Pedagogies developed for children—not unlike the modern hell house or *Eternal Forces* video game—would become the core of Protestant hermeneutic tradition and American homiletic practices, many of which will be explored in subsequent chapters. It will be useful to begin by returning briefly to the seventeenth century, to those early Puritan traditions inherited by Edwards's generation and the evangelical congregations that followed them.

Hell on Earth: The Seventeenth Century

The Protestant Reformation rejected key Roman Catholic institutions and doctrines intended to ameliorate believers' spiritual anxiety about death and the consequences of the afterlife. This is not to say that medieval Catholicism did not have its own culture of fear surrounding death and hell, a culture that became increasingly intense after the first great waves of plague in 1348.[19] I will return later to the tombs; the dances of death; the grinning, toad-infested *memento mori;* the broad hell-mouths; the *ars moriendi;* and other medieval elaborations of the terrifying kingdoms of death and hell. What I want to emphasize here is not the medieval cult of death but the ameliorative tradition of purgatory, the rejection of which would haunt Protestants—particularly Calvinists—for centuries after the Reformation.

Though not formalized until the Church Council of 1274, the doctrine of purgatory emerged in the eleventh century, affirming an intermediate zone between heaven and hell where the dead could expiate their sins and where the mitigative prayers and rituals of the living—requiem masses, indulgences, pilgrimages—could shrink the term of punishment for suffering souls. Such rituals sped the "grateful dead" on their way to

life everlasting. No longer did death without spiritual preparation con-
demn the deceased to an eternity of torment. All but the worst reprobates could take comfort in the knowledge that although their purgation
might be terrible—Hamlet's father refuses even to discuss the tortures
he endures—they could eventually achieve salvation, either through their
own expiative suffering or through the agency of family, friends, and prearranged priestly rituals. This comforting doctrine was popular enough
to survive Henry VIII's initial seizure of church lands and powers; not
until 1547 did the Church of England finally dissolve chantries and fra-
ternities, including the one founded by Henry's throne-usurping father,
Henry VII, for his own purgation. Although Protestants viewed purga-
torial rituals—personified by Chaucer's entrepreneurial Pardoner—as
among the most pernicious of papal corruptions, the liturgy lingered a
decade more, succumbing only in Elizabeth's reign to Nonconformists'
and Separatists' assaults against its scriptural authority.

In the absence of purgatory, and without the comforting intercessions
of extreme unction, the viaticum, and pardons, Protestant death assumed a finality that intensified the grief of friends and family who could
no longer be sure of the deceased's spiritual fate, much less ameliorate
it. It also heightened individuals' anxiety for their own welfare, for in the
absence of clerical intercession, they alone could discern their spiritual
condition, could know whether their contrition was sincere or hypocrit-
ical, sufficient or insufficient, accepted or rejected by God—whether, in
short, they were among the new category of "the elect," those few chosen for salvation while the great mass of humanity toppled into the fires
of hell. Following Augustine, early Calvinists grounded their theology
on the doctrine of original sin, which imputed Adam's sin to humanity.
Belief in total depravity would continue to be a mainstay of American
Protestant culture long after belief in the doctrine of limited atonement
(election) had weakened.[20] In the words of *The New England Primer,* "In
Adam's fall, we sinned all."[21] It was a catechism as familiar to New England Congregationalists and Scottish Presbyterians as snow and ice.[22]
With the Reformation's rejection of purgatory and the role of intercessions, and with its emphasis on the doctrines of original sin and predestination, the perceived likelihood of damnation seemed all but inevitable.

But if seventeenth-century Calvinists looked within for the signs of
grace or its absence, they also saw hell and its fearful torments in the
world around them. For the first generations of colonial Calvinists, life

was quite literally hell on earth. This was not because the New World émigrés did not enjoy pleasure—a myth epitomized by H. L. Mencken's remark that Puritans were haunted by the "fear that someone, somewhere, may be happy"—but because the spiritual realm spilled over into the earthly, multiplying the cares of the world. The inhabitants of hell were believed to pass through spiritual gates left ajar, much as Milton's Satan slipped his bonds and, crawl-stroking through the ether-filled void between realms, invaded the world to wreak havoc. Seventeenth-century Protestants did not need graphic sermons to bring an imagined hell to life; they needed only to recognize the correspondences between the material and spiritual to see Satan's violent minions in the physical spaces of the New World.

If colonial Americans viewed life as hell on earth, it was partly because the English sixteenth and seventeenth centuries were filled with violence and bloodshed, with religious oppression, Protestant martyrdom, and violent Catholic purges. The 1572 massacre of Protestant Huguenots on St. Bartholomew's Day, for example, became a sacrificial icon for seventeenth-century Protestants, framing the Protestant martyrdoms perpetrated by the Catholic Queen Mary and emblematized by Guy Fawkes's 1605 Gunpowder Plot. Such events filled the Protestant imagination, confirming prophecies that foretold the Antichrist's reign. Foxe's *Book of Martyrs* provided Protestants with a hagiographical exemplar, less a guide for appropriate living than a sacrificial template for dying. For Caroline-era Puritans (Congregationalists, Presbyterians, and Baptists) such as John Bunyan, Thomas Shepard, Thomas Hooker, Ezekiel Rogers, and Nathaniel Ward, or the vast number of ministers from other Puritan sects who had been expelled from English pulpits, material persecutions as instances of Satan's earthly grasp were a foretaste of the torment to come.[23] These threats helped colonists to see this life as preparation for the next, an exercise of expiation intended to drive the ungodly to atone for their sins. It was a sentiment ministers never tired of repeating. As Solomon Stoddard, Edwards's grandfather, articulated in *A Guide to Christ,* the homiletic manual he wrote for his grandson's generation (just fresh from seminary): "Every man must have so much trouble, as to make him strive earnestly after Salvation." (53). Michael Wigglesworth's widely selling treatise *Meat out of the Eater; or, Meditations Concerning the Necessity, End, and Usefulness of Afflictions unto Gods Children: All Tending to Prepare Them, for, and Comfort Them under, the Crosse* (1670) taught generations of the faithful to embrace their personal suffering as an individual-specific guide to salvation. Convinced that the "signs of the times" revealed that the time was nigh when Satan's wrath was to be unloosed on earth, Anglo-American Calvinists attributed social unrest, violence, and natural disaster to preternatural forces. By such oppressions, they measured their worth.

While Oliver Cromwell was clearing spaces for Protestant colonization in Ireland and retaliating brutally against Catholics loyal to Charles, the New England colonists were struggling against indigenous peoples to expand their foothold in the New World. For Calvinists, the natural world was the unclaimed, unsanctified space where the powers of evil amassed against humanity. Through the Pequot battles of the 1630s and the later, increasingly brutal wars against Algonquins in the second part of the century, New England Calvinists came to view American Indians as the devil's demonic henchmen, whose sneaking treachery corresponded to Satan's alluringly rational deceptions.[24] Increase Mather warned his congregation that the Indian was a cohabitant of both earth and hell. Cotton Mather records in his New World hagiography, *Magnalia Christi Americana,* how Hannah Dustin, captured by Indians, had persevered in the face of despair to avenge the slain and overcome the forces of evil.[25] In the biblical typology of Jael and Judith, she slew her captors while they slept in the night—a feat all the more impressive (and contradictory) because night was when dark powers were allegedly most active. Fearing the brutal savagery of "blood drinking" Indians, colonists imagined hell as a field of massacre, of scalped women and children, and homes engulfed in fire.[26] References to such attacks helped cement the link between material danger and eternal pain. The unbounded chaos of the forest, with its unfamiliar, disorienting terrain and predatory wildlife, concretized the otherworldliness of hell. By linking its descriptions with the natural world—in the vein of Milton's famous catalogue of hell's "rocks, caves, lakes, fens, bogs, dens, and shades of death"—colonial ministers annexed material experience to the eschatological abstraction of the spiritual.[27]

This enchanted worldview was still largely intact in rural areas as late as the 1692 Salem witch trials. Cotton Mather defended the trials in *The Wonders of the Invisible World* (1692), focusing on the dark, midnight landscapes where neighbors, friends, and even relatives allegedly cavorted with demons, sealing their fealty to the powers of darkness through carnal acts of obeisance. Coming less than three years after Locke published *An Essay Concerning Human Understanding,* the witch trials marked an epistemology in transition, epitomized by the difference between "spectral evidence" (tormenting apparitions, whether town folk or demons disguised as such) and forensic categories of evidence emerging from Baconian empiricism. It would not be long before the Lockean epistemology, largely filtered in the American colonies through Jonathan Edwards's generation, would reshape the colonial worldview and Calvinist theology and pedagogy, "diffus[ing] fairer light through the world in numerous affairs of science and of human life," as Edwards's renowned Anglican advocate Isaac Watts stated in assessing the influence of Locke's essay in 1735.[28]

The Return of Volition

The second colonial generation witnessed the rise of an important forebear of the eighteenth-century hellfire sermons: the jeremiad, a sermon that castigated Northern colonists for their perceived decline. Emerging from the conviction that congregants had lost their way, the jeremiad promised the very real miseries of Egyptian plagues and waves of crop-devouring locusts. No literary response to religious life used the tragedies, calamities, and natural disasters of colonial life to better effect. The jeremiad cataloged all such events as providential signs of God's seething wrath, ready to pour out the plague vials of Revelations on his New World church. Ministers asserted that as stewards of their parents' legacy, the new generations had failed to keep the spiritual flame burning.[29] Nothing bespoke the breach in the covenant more than the shrinking rolls of the elect. Less than twenty years after the Massachusetts Bay Colony had been established, membership in the visible church (the membership deemed elect) began to decline precipitously throughout the colonies.[30] By the early 1650s, few felt the assurance of grace, and still fewer risked the label "hypocrite," a designation for those who misread the signs of their salvation and bore false witness to it before the church.

In crisis, the leadership settled on a controversial solution. Installed as what detractors later called the "Half-Way Covenant," the compromise permitted the children of visible saints, those in the knowledge of their election, to enjoy a partial membership predicated on the assumption that, as Increase Mather put it, "God hath seen good to cast the line

of Election so, as that it doth . . . for the most part, run through the loins
of godly parents."[31] To authorize the compromise, Mather's generation,
matriculating from Harvard in the 1660s, looked to the influential divines of the first generation: men like his father-in-law John Cotton. God
promised, Cotton had announced to Boston in 1645, to "be thy God, and
the God of thy seed after thee."[32] While not full communicants, half-way
members could participate in church governance, shoring up the theocracy's infrastructure while fattening its lean administrative pool.

   Eighteenth-century hellfire sermons would take the rhetoric of the
jeremiad and turn it toward a spiritual world that had grown increasingly separate from the material one. A new generation of ministers,
including William Cooper, Thomas Foxcroft, Thomas Prince in Boston, Jonathan Edwards in rural Massachusetts, and Gilbert Tennent in
New Jersey, emerged from Harvard and Yale in the second decade of
the eighteenth century. As roughly fourth-generation colonists, they belonged to a new age. They had not personally known Indian captivities,
nor had they experienced the feast-and-famine cycles of the early years.
They had not seen the material and symbolic deprivations of the early
generations. What had been up until the eighteenth century a provincial
place at the end of the world was becoming its own center filled by immigrants who were not predominantly Congregationalists but Baptists,
Quakers, Presbyterians, and Anabaptists (Mennonites and Amish).
While Congregationalists maintained their cultural and theological hegemony for the first few generations, the 1689 Act of Toleration forced
these increasingly disparate sects to accommodate one another. Consequently, Calvinist sermon genres turned in entirely new directions—
directions that reveal much about broader Protestant theology as it both
moved away from Calvinism and responded to developing conditions in
the New World.

   One of the most significant things the hellfire sermon reveals is that
the doctrine of election—the very foundation of Calvinist belief and
practice—was weakening its grip on Calvinist communion.[33] While it
may have remained canonical in Congregational, Baptist, and Presbyterian theology, its defenders grew fainter, its practical influence diminished. How, after all, could fear of hell motivate individuals focused on
whether they were predestined to salvation or eternal death? If aimed
at audiences who could not work toward redemption, then the sermon's
graphic depictions of hell were pointless. Narratives of hell's horrors
might motivate individuals governed by predestination, but only if mem-

bership among the elect functioned as remuneration for those whose labor in the vineyard produced the most fruit, or as a competitive prize, an
immortal garland handed to those first in the field to meet the foe. Fear
of hell might induce one to seek salvation if grace were available to all,
if redemption was a matter of volition and obliging duty. But fear of fire
and fiends could never motivate individuals to strive for what they had
little hope of acquiring—had indeed been disqualified for at the outset.
In a world coming to prize rationalism, scientific explanation, and free-
market economies, predestinarianism might offer a corrective to secular
humanism's pride of achievement, its Babels of science and engineering,
but such an arbitrary fate could not be *the* sustaining basis of the individual's penitent quest for reconciliation with God.

Nor could the doctrine of limited atonement be the basis of mass-
scale evangelical awakenings, the reaping of souls in the harvest fields on
the margins of the First Great Awakening. Because evangelicalism drew
its energy from the zeal to fill heaven's rolls with the saved, it depended
on a democratizing of salvation, on a predication of free will rather than
the soul's conventional passive reception of grace. One can measure the
threat of such changes both by Jonathan Edwards's enormously influential treatise on free will and by the debates that treatise stirred in the
Anglo-American world. As the hope of salvation increasingly became
seen as available to all, its opposite—the fear of hell—became a powerful weapon in the conversion arsenal of ministers hungry for souls.
Terror helped pierce the barrier of human complacency. The fire-and-
brimstone sermon exposed and tapped the deep wells of spiritual inse-
curity from which flowed reproach, remorse, and self-loathing—the tried
and true mechanisms of conversion.

In an age marked by crown-mandated religious tolerance, when colonists began embracing emergent natural rights doctrines, and the alluring reciprocity of obligation and consent at the heart of social contract
theory was gaining sway, the idea of a sovereign who justified arbitrary
punishment by imputing to one individual the fault of another seemed
irrational and finally intolerable.[34] Such an image of God smacked of
the arbitrary tyranny that had caused Britons to recoil from the divine-
right doctrines of Locke's infamous antagonist, Robert Filmer, and the
political theory of the secular Calvinist Thomas Hobbes, who had justified the absorption of the individual's consent into the body of the
sovereign—sweetened in his phrase the "collective will."[35] Two of the
last living second-generation ministers, Increase Mather and Solomon

Stoddard—whose annual pilgrimages to speak in Boston brought out all the eminent divines—spent their old age refuting complaints about the fairness of a God who had at the world's framing, with advance knowledge of Adam's fall, preordained all his descendants to suffer the curse of one act of sin. Yet even in his widely read conversion manual for young ministers, *A Guide to Christ,* as well as in his other well-known work on the subject, *Defects of Preachers Reproved,* Stoddard's lukewarm conviction hardly achieved the pitch required to overcome the growing din of popular grumbling that by 1700 had become pronounced in Boston and Philadelphia. Stoddard stressed the need for all to have a conversion experience, despite the obvious contradiction: God had reserved eternal life for but a few. In Stoddard's one-hundred-page manual purporting to address the principle objections to predestinarian doctrine, only a paragraph, near the end, defends the doctrine of election, and then only half-heartedly, invoking as its best defense the last axiom of the Puritan theodicy: no one "merits" salvation. "To be sure," Edward Pearse told readers in his treatise on "preparation for death," "we have all over and over deserved long since to have been covered with the shadow of the Night of Eternal Darkness."[36]

What goes unnoted in discussions of the half-way covenant is the degree to which, in suggesting a genealogy of salvation, it functioned as a preparatory phase that, taken together with an emergent strand of Arminianism, would culminate with the doctrine of universal salvation.[37] By asserting that those born of visible saints were likely selected for salvation, half-way theology expanded the franchise of those qualified for election, facilitating a shift from an inward scrutiny of one's salvific status toward a covenant of works, what Brooks Holifield terms "sacramental theology," in which material success and piety were self-evident markers of redemption.[38] Erstwhile anxieties about salvific status could now be transformed into a sharp fear that elicited specific behavior. While seventeenth-century Calvinists had disengaged pre-Reformation fear as a motivation for conforming moral conduct to the norms of piety, the half-way children of the covenant reengaged it through subtle lines of doctrinal revision.[39]

Although Arminianism did not gain an institutional foothold in the New England colonies until the mid-eighteenth century, its creed seeped into the culture much earlier. The dreaded covenant of works, combined with liberal religious views coming out of Restoration England— principally a gentler image of God and a growing trust in the power of

human reason—made its way into New World Calvinist theology.[40] Stoddard, Edwards's grandfather, had himself opened communion to the full
congregation, a serious violation of covenant theology and a gesture the
old guard castigated, apparently as much for its negation of the aristocratic distinction enjoyed by half-way descendants as for its doctrinal
heresy. Less ambivalent than Stoddard's democratizing of communion
while upholding election, ministers in his grandson's generation, including John and Charles Wesley, were beginning to promote universal salvation. For a generation hungry to rekindle the godly fires of yore and to
awaken sinners to a fresh sense of their guilt and danger, the doctrine of
election proved a serious roadblock to converting the masses outside the
half-way covenant.

Although Edwards would defend the doctrine of predestination,
many in his generation undermined election in a number of ways. Some,
like the influential Benjamin Colman, simply refused to address it. In
his wilderness ministry to the Indians, David Brainerd—who once confessed, "I could not bear that it should be wholly at God's pleasure,
to save or damn me, just as he would"[41]—sent mixed signals: "When I
came . . . to answer the question, 'But how shall I know whether God has
chosen me to everlasting life?' by pressing them (his congregants from
the Delaware tribe) to come and give their hearts to Christ, and thereby
'to make their election sure,' they . . . engaged in seeking . . . an interest
in him" (*Life* 202). Brainerd here seemingly pits God's arbitrary choice,
his "sovereignty" (*Life* 20), against the Indians capacity to secure election by giving their hearts to Christ. Urban firebrands like Foxcroft, on
the other hand, revised the theology on which election depended. "Some
indeed assert that the covenant of grace is absolute and unconditionate,"
Foxcroft argued, "but this is contrary to the universal strain, and tends
to subvert the whole design, of the inspired Scriptures" (*Cleansing Our
Way* 150). He explained how his forebears had erred in their all or nothing view of grace. By dividing grace into "general" and "particular," he
inserted a kind of works while preserving the principle of free grace. In
this gentler theology, the gift of particular grace—the traditional saving
grace that only the elect received—now depended on individuals' use of
their allotment of general grace, which all received. In a consummate example of the theological casuistry from which the half-way covenant had
itself issued half a century before, Foxcroft sought to soften the doctrine
of election, but his aim implicitly struck the covenant as well.

Foxcroft's formula silently bespoke the New Testament's "Parable of the Talents," whereby a master measures his servants' worth by the interest returned on the principle (Roman currency, with its anglicized pun on *talent*) left in their care. In proportion to the individual's application of general grace—with "Repentance towards God, and Faith towards our Lord Jesus Christ, a Faith which worketh by Love and which purifyeth the heart" (*Cleansing Our Way* 150)—they received particular grace and thus the possibility of salvation. It required no Anne Hutchinson to ferret the way "works" was entering covenant theology; like Foxcroft, many among the Baptists, Whitefieldian Methodists, Congregationalists, Anglicans, and Presbyterians were importing it under the cover of preparation, the preliminary stage in which supplicants traditionally reoriented themselves to the divine in the hope of receiving grace.[42] Across the colonies ministers were, to one degree or another, preaching a process of preparation indistinguishable from acts of will and thus, to an extent, a revised doctrine of works.[43]

Even conservators of the faith opened as many theological fissures as they closed. Struggling not to imply "works," much less use the term, Stoddard repeatedly uses its synonym, "labour," a semantic distinction difficult to sustain even in his day: "The more earnestly the man follows after God and labours to get into a converted Condition," he argues, "the more hopeful it is that God has elected him" (*Guide to Christ* 13–14). Stoddard strained at gnats to swallow camels. Half measures "to get into" a converted condition suggested volition and agency, and adverbs like "more" and "earnestly" scarcely hid the action they modified. Loose language was beginning to erode doctrinal proscriptions, a costly drain on Calvinist theology since the premise of *sola scriptura*—not to mention the authority, enforcement, and defense of doctrine—relied on strict fidelity to linguistic precision.

Colonial conditions encouraged Foxcroft's generation—if not Edwards, then his immediate followers—to reject the soul's passive reception of grace, at the expense of God's total sovereignty.[44] If experience taught anything, it was the degree to which human will altered daily life. A market-driven economy and material success were demonstrating human capabilities energized by a new and newly virtuous economic ambition, an image aptly rendered in the term *homo economicus,* which, with its connotation of an evolutionary leap, captures the perceived enormity of the cultural changes underway.[45] American colonists lived in a world increasingly regulated by the British monarchy and by British customs, commerce, and military technology. In what historians refer to as "Anglicanization," the colonies, particularly in the North, were undergoing a process of cultural homogenization.[46] Under the Navigation Acts, the British Empire began the work of commercial and political colonization. The ports of Philadelphia, New York, and Boston were becoming avenues of social change, as an emergent class of merchant upstarts unbalanced old colonial hierarchies by amassing wealth in a new age of market capitalism and speculation. The Calvinist commitment to the soul as a passive vessel preselected for salvation ran up hard against impinging beliefs about individuals' semiautonomous capacity, sufficient to stand but free to fall.[47]

Changes in the perception of Calvinists' volitional aptitude are most visible in instances in which human fate was deemed most providential, to be accepted or petitioned, but ultimately in God's hands. A century earlier, for example, contagious illness had, for devout colonists, seemed an aspect of God's will to which individuals resigned themselves, but by the eighteenth century it had become something to oppose. Increase and Cotton Mather and Jonathan Edwards aggressively championed smallpox vaccination.[48] Increase Mather did so against protests that he was trespassing on God's provenance; Edwards died thirty some years later, illustrating the vaccine's efficacy. By asserting humanity's capacity to alter the moral world—symbolized here as contagion—smallpox inoculation provided Edwards's cohort with a model for how to shape volition through homiletic pedagogy. The determination to intervene in the course of nature inevitably led even Calvinists like Edwards and the Mathers—whose commitment to humanity's passive reception of grace restricted volitional capacity—to entertain the pedagogical possibilities of a theology of inoculation. Having helped install the age's bourgeois ethic, Enlightenment humanists such as Benjamin Franklin, himself a child of Puritans, garnished it with what for Calvinists was an audacious slogan touting humanity's ability to effect change: "God helps them who help themselves"—a phrase that sums up how the aged Mather answered his critics in the smallpox imbroglio of the 1720s.

Eighteenth-Century Puritan Medievalism

As human will was gradually readmitted to the workings of salvation, there was little to keep ministers from drawing on the older cults of death, fear, and hell that had worked so well for the pre-Reformation church—the common Protestant heritage, despite its rejection of Catholic liturgy and sacramental rituals.[49] The steady decline of the doctrine of election allowed eighteenth-century ministers to retrieve fear as the medieval motivational trigger missing from the seventeenth-century Calvinist conversion morphology. Medieval techniques for instilling fear of death and hell could now drive revivalists in subsequent eras to take refuge in God. While Enlightenment science might have been undermining some tenets of American Protestantism, it was also providing the religious with new models and metaphors for protecting the inexperienced. In what Edwards's generation likened to the smallpox vaccine they promoted, fear became a powerful inoculant in the campaign to help novices develop immunity to temptation and a lifelong resistance to moral contagion.

It is worthwhile, then, to recall that sermon realism and other techniques for inculcating fear had deep roots in Christian tradition, roots that grew particularly vigorous in the centuries just before the Reformation. As Johan Huizinga memorably put it, "No other epoch has laid so much stress as the expiring Middle Ages on the thought of death. An everlasting call of *memento mori* resounds through life."[50] Tombs and headstones were embossed with skulls, skeletal figures, and bones, images that underscored the difference between the mutability of the body and the immutability of the soul by emphasizing corporeal decay. What I want to highlight are the meditational devices that personalized death and suffering. The upper deck or lid of Transey tombs—macabre meditational props meant to evoke sustained reflection on sin, death, and life's vanity—depicted the living patron's life-size effigy in ornate costume and, although reposed in death, painted in the bloom of life. The lower deck or coffin interior, however, revealed the patron's corpse painted in a horrid, liquefying state of decay, with worms slithering through yawning gaps in the flesh and toads chewing on the fingers, toes, and genitals. Similarly, double-sided portraits showcased such images as young lovers hand in hand, the perfected image of youth, grace, and vigor on one side, and a pair of grinning cadavers on the other, their flesh sloughing off in ribbons, food for worms and saw-toothed toads. Such reversible diptychs were a tempus-fugit reminder, recalling to viewers that even now, in the blush of youth, they were in the throes of death, their bodies corrupting from within.

With the introduction of the popular woodcut in the fifteenth century, these crude images became widely available.[51] Other favorites were

corpses leading men and women in the dance of death, demons tormenting the dying in a last attempt to snatch their souls, and devils cavort-
ing in gaping mouths of hell. Small wonder that one of the most popular late-medieval devotional genres was the *Ars Moriendi,* or art of
dying, a genre that encouraged its readers to practice and prepare for
their last moments lest they be caught off guard by the grinning cadaver
and his troops of acrid-smelling demons. In popular verse, death reigned
supreme. "When thy soule is faren out," admonishes a typical English
lyric, "Thy body with erthe iraked [covered], / That body that was so
ronk [haughty] and loud / Of alle men is ihated."[52] Skulls circulated
among clerics and lay merchants as tokens of what awaited all, regardless of social standing.[53] Death emerged as a theme even in early modern portraiture, as memento-mori emblems appeared alongside the likenesses of the living, a reminder of life's transitory condition.

Similarly, in the seventeenth- and eighteenth-centuries, Anglo-
American family portraiture occasionally included spouses and children
already deceased; images of former wives, sons, and daughters lying on
deathbeds frequented the paintings' backdrops, personalized markers
linking specific individuals and families to a seemingly distant and de-
personalized eschatology. The posthumous inclusion of family members
in group portraits, like the later practice of photographing dead children
in their mothers' arms—or, as Sally Promey argues, "familial clusters"
of Puritan grave stones[54]—functioned both as a reminder of the unbroken circle awaiting families at the Resurrection and a caution of the frequency of unexpected death.[55] Even the funeral sermons of the devout
were occasions not to wax optimistic but to remind the living about their
fearful state. At the funeral of Lieutenant Governor Tailer of Massachusetts in 1736, for instance, William Cooper gave a representative sermon
titled "Man Humbled by being compared to a Worm," assuring grievers
that "tho' [man] be in honour," with fortune and good name—which, he
allowed, Tailer possessed—he was still "but a worm."[56]

Colonial elaborations of fleshly putrefaction, skeleton-embossed
headstones, and fear of hell and death, then, are partly a legacy of the
later Middle Ages.[57] Yet it is important to emphasize that it was the return of some sense of volition, some sense that the emotional turmoil induced by vivid realism could have salvific effect, that reinvigorated this
tradition, turning it from a suitably grim artistic and cultural heritage
into a real force in revivalist pedagogy and the emergence of what I have
been calling inoculation theology. The vagaries of life, death's sudden

surprise, and the dangers of postponing salvific assurance inspired sermons about hell's eternal tortures. In his sermon "The Certainty and
Suddenness of Christ's Coming to Judgment" (1716), Joseph Sewall offered a standard caution: "Let such as are yet strangers and enemies to
Christ, be now perswaded by the Terrors of the Lord, and of that dreadful Day which is approaching."[58] Even the unflappable psalmist-minister
Isaac Watts was shaken to the core at the sudden death of three young
boys in the mid-seventeenth century, struck by a single bolt of lightning.
In Israel Holly's widely circulated colonial funeral sermon "Youth Liable to Sudden Death; Excited Seriously to Consider Thereof and Speedily to Prepare Thereto," Watts found a salient warning for the precar-
iousness of young life, for those least prepared for salvation yet most
prone—through accident, illness, and enfeebled moral defenses—to a
sudden end.[59] Foxcroft reiterated the era's sermonic watchword: "Be as
speedy and active as possible" in the interest of your own salvation, he
cautioned, for "the nimble sands of time will run down faster than our
work goes on, and our glass will go . . . out, before we've finish'd our
Christian race" (*Cleansing Our Way* 30).[60] Multiplying the impediments
to redemption, he warned of physical fates worse than death, such as a
paralysis that might incapacitate spiritual efforts: "Some distemper may
utterly bereave us of our capacity for this work. We are incident to many
things, that may fatally impair our rational powers, and as much disen-
able us to all religious intents and purposes as death it self" (*Cleansing Our Way* 31). He catalogs "distempers"—"apoplexy," an incapacitat-
ing "lethargy," "delirium, or stupor," "bewilder[ing] melancholia," or a
fit of "madness"—that might "suddenly seize us," rendering us "as 'twere
dead, while we lived." Recalling not merely the pain with which all living in a preanesthetic culture were familiar, he also evokes the mental
effects of chronic suffering that could unnerve the will: "May we not be
harrass't with tormenting pains and restless with agonies, that shall utterly unhinge us, and unfit us for religious duties" when the end comes?
(*Cleansing Our Way* 31).[61]

Lockean Epistemology:
Homiletic Realism as Inoculation Theology

The resurgence of Puritan medievalism helped shape the rhetoric of
eighteenth-century Protestantism. Yet we cannot understand how per-

sonalizing fear came to be such an important mechanism of conversion in homiletic pedagogies like Beecher's virtual tour of hell or the modern hell house without also considering the problems posed by materialist epistemologies, emerging not only through Cartesian philosophy in the Harvard curriculum after the Restoration but also through Baconian empiricism and the colonial popularity of Locke's *Essay Concerning Human Understanding*.[62] Combined, these different strains of thought posed a number of related problems for colonial Protestants: they severely circumscribed the spiritual dimension of human existence; they rendered human faculties as passive receptors of sensory impressions; and they made children in particular the victims of environment and circumstance, clearly created insufficient to stand against the evil influences of the invisible world. Since the Reformation, the sermon had been a register of pedagogy and epistemology, concerned with how best to educate the young about sin and with how individuals know or experience both temporal and spiritual worlds. Because its form had evolved to reflect shifting perceptions about metaphysical truths, a comparative study of its progressive transformation illustrates the impact of empirical epistemology on colonial Calvinist culture.

Just as Darwinian evolution would later profoundly threaten Protestant theology, so Locke's mechanistic psychology menaced Calvinist epistemology, wherein God spoke to the mind through the soul from the signs percolating up into the consciousness. If there were no warring faculties or disguised impulses, what produced corrupt impulses, wayward senses, and excessive appetites? If the mind lacked the soul's unconscious defense, what chance did children in particular have of surviving moral corruption long enough to build up conscious moral perimeters? Without inspiration, intuition, revelation, or innate moral values—all banished from Locke's epistemology—learning was a mechanistic process badly adapted to the spiritual survival of the inexperienced.

Leading Protestants responded diversely to the Puritan-educated Locke, who emerged from the same college curriculum that had shaped the first generation of immigrant ministers to the Bay Colony.[63] Some, like the renowned Isaac Watts—close friend of Brattle Street Church's Benjamin Colman and William Cooper, and correspondent of Edwards—embraced the Lockean model, attempting to mend it from within.[64] Anglicans and Presbyterians like Francis Hutcheson and the Scottish School posited an innate "moral sense"—the "sixth sense"—that offered a mechanized view in place of the personified soul's function as guard. This innate sense functioned as a moral compass, appropriately reorienting the senses and faculties. Anglican bishop George Berkeley, the American Samuel Johnson, and Edwards, among others, applied materialist mechanics to the spiritual world.[65] Still others, like Foxcroft, simply cobbled the new sensual psychology together with conventional Calvinist epistemology. In his enormously influential manual for the young, Foxcroft personified the several faculties in order to demonstrate the need for Christian discipline. Torn between the shackled will of his seventeenth-century Calvinist progenitors and the newly liberated volition (the trigger for his generation's development of an inoculation theology), his revision of Locke had the advantage of explaining how grace worked on the passive soul, while demonstrating the mind's agency in its defense. "The rational powers have lost their moral rectitude, simplicity and order," he laments,

> and are under deplorable metamorphosis, miserably disfigur'd and degraded. The Understanding, the Eye of the Soul, has lost its Divine Light and influence, and is benighted under a vail [sic] of thick clouds and Egyptian darkness. The Will having lost its first governing principle and true native liberty, is contracted and confined to debasing and defiling objects, fastened and fetter'd in the most ignominious servitude, is . . . strongly inclin'd to that which is Evil. The Affections and Passions have broke the restraints of Reason, and cast off the reins of the Divine Law, are impetuous, imperious, and rove without control. The Memory, is corrupt and unfaithful shutting out . . . the Good, receiving and retaining the Evil, as a Sieve lets out the Flower, but keeps the bran. The Conscience is defiled, and debaucht; . . . being blinded thro' ignorance or brib'd by corrupt Affections. (*Cleansing Our Way* 4–8)

In this remarkable passage, Foxcroft evokes the depth of humanity's natural corruption while revealing the vitality of an older conception of human identity threatened by Locke's epistemology. For Foxcroft the individual is an amalgam of personalities that the soul unifies through discipline. Popular evangelicalism would later extend this vision of the disunited self.[66]

By reducing knowledge to whatever portion of the external world the senses filtered (the smallest units of which he called "simple ideas"), Locke made experience the primary constituent of knowledge. What individuals gleaned from the world through rational reflection—the processes of building speculative knowledge ("complex ideas") from emerging patterns in the understanding—was still vitally tied to experience (*Essay* 474). The more experience that individuals accumulated, the greater the sample by which they could compare, contrast, and evaluate new sense impressions, measure new experience. In its rejection of other forms of knowledge reception—revelation, intuition, innate ideas— Locke compressed the registers of things knowable and partially knowable, which Calvinists listed under the heads "visible" and "invisible." His sensual epistemology was a serious assault on any knowledge undetectable by the senses and thus unattainable through experience.

As we have seen, early colonials invested their material world with spiritual and moral significance; their landscape was the wilderness of hell or the city on the hill, and God used their environment to temper their faith and signal their spiritual status. For them, the fallen world was the canvas on which God displayed providential signs that communicated displeasure, protection, vengeance, or redemption.[67] Even demonic attacks were interpreted providentially, for only at God's pleasure could evil intrude into the lives of the saints. By the eighteenth century, however, the growing view of nature as a neutral arena vacated of good and evil forced a revaluation of the world, and eighteenth-century pilgrims turned increasingly inward for signs of God's intentions. George Whitefield, coarchitect of Methodism with John and Charles Wesley, never undertook any new adventure without an inward sign from God, a dream or impression, no matter how incidental it might appear.[68] Ministers urged parishioners to search inwardly, scouring their souls for blemishes, seeking in the mirror of the self the marks of hidden corruption.

Yet in its rejection of an unconscious, Locke's epistemology also imposed limits on interiority. In his mechanistic chain of faculty psychology, information passed from the senses through various faculties envisioned as the meshing gears of a machine, not as a clandestine inner self requiring vigilant observation. Locke's model of subjectivity thus conflicted with older models of the self as composed of potentially disharmonious factions: body and soul, reason and sensuality, or, in the Augustinian trinity, memory, will, and understanding. Foxcroft warned his congregants about the "disfigur'd and degraded" reason, the will's "debasing and defiling objects," and the conscience ("the monitor within") "brib'd by corrupt Affections" (*Cleansing Our Way* 7). In the eighteenth century, the religious were still taught that they were their own enemies. (When we refer to people as "not knowing their own minds," for instance, we articulate their indecision in the technical language of premodern psychology.) To know thyself, as sermons admonished, was to examine, discipline, and integrate one's inner faculties in a specific way, to parse out the personality into its component parts, searching the faculties for a weak link: the overwrought imagination that distorted and misinformed the reason; the truculent will that forgot its allegiance to the soul. For Locke, there could be no soul in the conventional sense. His model of an integrated self ("Locke's punctual self," as Charles Taylor calls it) precluded the idea that a part of the self could exist separately from the mind and without its conscious knowledge—as if selfhood were composed of two separate personalities, neither fully aware of the other.[69]

Locke's denial of the unconscious also damaged the Puritan model of the world as animated with the presence of evil. Consider, for example, the soul's nocturnal vigilance. According to Christian tradition, the soul kept watch over the sleeping individual in the hours between twilight and dawn, when hearing remained functional and the forces of evil flourished.[70] But Locke ridiculed the soul's vigil over sleeping minds vulnerable, like Milton's Eve, to aural attacks, the foul whisperings of demonic messengers.[71] For him, dreams were simply decaying sense impressions unprocessed by the faculty chain, a scheme that left scant room for nighttime battles for the hearts and minds of people like the Puritan Michael Wigglesworth, whose nocturnal seducers—while leaving little more than vivid dreams, vague impressions, or soiled sheets—sought gradually to wear away his soul's defenses.[72]

For the guardians of the faith, however, such dreams were proof of an unconscious and, as Peter Brown points out, were intricately tied to Augustine's "comprehensive explanation for why allegory should have been necessary," a precept the Calvinist hermeneutic tradition inherited from Augustinian theology.[73] In Bunyan's extraordinarily influential *The Pilgrim's Progress* (1678), the narrative of Christian's (and later Christiana's) pilgrimage advances as a dream text revealed to the narrator as he sleeps. In this view, dreams were communiqués from the soul to the mind, from the subconscious to the consciousness, demonstrating moral activity even in sleep. In what seems like a deliberate dig at the seventeenth-century empiricists, the title page of the first edition of *The Pilgrim's Progress* prints the word *dream* in heavy black lettering, easily three times the size of any other word.

Ironically, Locke's punctual self outstripped even the seventeenth-century Calvinist soul in its passivity, with serious implications for the

Christian's moral plight. By envisioning the faculties as reflexes responding to whatever force acted upon them, Locke's epistemology likened the
mind to a sponge, indiscriminately absorbing its environment. This idea
initially accorded well with seventeenth-century Calvinism's sense of humanity's weak volition, but at a time when colonial Calvinists were shifting away from strict predestination, Locke also denied the will's power
to act as a moral agent in the spiritual world and individuals' power to
direct knowledge formation in advance, leaving them instead to react to
whatever the senses garnered without gleaning.[74]

This loss of the power of will disproportionately threatened the inexperienced. The child as blank slate or "empty cabinet" (*Essay* 55),
without innate ideas, was radical to Calvinism, which held that children entered the world burdened, in Cooper's words, with the "hereditary stain"—but which also supposed the soul to be the child's mature,
worldly-wise guardian. Locke, however, denied both humanity's birth in
sin and the soul's preembodied wisdom, disavowing at the outset Descartes's insistence that innate ideas came into the world with the soul and
served as the foundation for subsequent knowledge.[75] Based on Locke's
assertion in *Some Thoughts Concerning Education* (1693) that "the little, and almost insensible impressions on our tender infancies have very
important and lasting consequences," Edwards's friend Isaac Watts became so concerned about the soul as tabula rasa that he warned potential fathers not to quarrel with their pregnant wives for fear that resentment might imprint the fetal soul, forever impairing the child's moral
development.[76] Logic like this posed new problems, particularly how to
guard children from base impressions long enough for them to develop a
moral musculature. If, as Locke's psychology suggested, children's faculties were undeveloped and thus inadequate to guard anything as vulnerable as the soul, then either the fundamentals of Calvinism were false, or
the moral order—creation itself—was a cruel hoax, the moral equivalent
of the coal mine canary: the first sensible sign of spiritual danger would
reveal an urgent need to resuscitate the child, already a victim of what he
or she could not, in Locke's model, detect.

Children's Spiritual Aptitude

Calvinist attitudes toward children further complicated the implications
that an epistemological shift posed for Protestant education and the

child's spiritual development. Building on Philippe Ariès's monumental *Centuries of Childhood,* social historians like John Demos and Michael Zuckerman argued for a radical change in notions about children in the eighteenth-century colonies, suggesting that by the late seventeenth century childhood was emerging as a distinct developmental stage.[77] While this thesis has been controversial, it seems entirely apt in the colonial context of Calvinist communities. In the seventeenth century the young shared the responsibilities of adults and suffered the same deprivations; Indian attacks, famine, disease, and wilderness dangers gave children no special dispensations. "The very idea of a morphology of emotional and intellectual growth," Jay Fliegelman observes, "was an alien one."[78] Likewise, Calvinist theology regarded childhood as coterminous with adulthood, not as a protracted developmental stage in the human life cycle. If the tenets of original sin and election affirmed that children were "born blasted," as Cooper affirmed in 1714, then they lacked that ingredient crucial for the emergence of modern childhood: presumed innocence.[79] Only a presumption of children's moral neutrality, free from innate depravity at birth, could compel the social, legal, and psychological imperatives that ultimately came to police, protect, and frame the moral order of modern childhood.[80]

The idea that the souls of the young were deemed to have the same moral aptitude as adults created a contradiction for Calvinist culture. How could a child be equally guilty of original sin as an adult, yet relatively less culpable by reason of immature moral capacity? If children lacked experience crucial to their own moral interests, then how could their sins compare to those of adults, whose experience forearmed their volition? Daily life, moreover, demonstrated that some were better prepared than others to combat Satan: clearly the clergy, followed by the educated, men, and the devout, while white adults in general were better equipped than the simple, people of color, women, and children.[81] If children and adults shared equally in the hereditary burden of sin, then it followed that they also ought to possess the same moral faculty. Something had to compensate for the child's weak or (*pace* Locke) missing moral compass. These contradictions vexed colonial theologians.[82]

As an early announcement of a secular determinism that grew apace throughout the eighteenth century, Locke's theory helped advance the view of childhood as a discrete phase of life—associated not just with blankness or innocence ("without harm") but ultimately, by some, with innate goodness. These developments heightened the Calvinist conundrum of how to balance children's relative moral capacity with the doctrine of their innate depravity. For Calvinist theology, Locke's chain of cause and effect, which implied that the educated and experienced stood a stronger chance of understanding scripture and fending off temptation, rendered old contradictions newly visible. If knowledge depended on human faculties alone, as Locke held, and was best acquired without reference to custom or creed, or taken on faith, then did not the immature and those with diminished acuity stand less chance in moral contests than the educated, ministers, and what Edwards called the "middling sort"?[83] How were the inexperienced to digest biblical truths in order to nourish their souls? More urgently, how were they to apprehend theological distinctions, much less discern the seductive reasoning of false doctrine? Without an accumulated moral base with which to assess evil's subtlety, they could hardly be expected to resist it. Lacking the whole armor of God worn by Paul's experienced martial Christian, they stood naked and vulnerable before the enemy's advance. How could they preserve their spiritual lives long enough to acquire that armor? Worse, if depraved experiences formed the core of the child's moral standard, would it systematically skew his or her perception of right and wrong? Would such children limp along, gathering impressions to which their senses had become enamored, until, like a millstone about their necks, the weight of depravity dragged them under altogether? The inexperienced could hardly do battle when their faculties were, as Foxcroft claimed, already in the control of the enemy, who could ply the senses with pleasure, drug the reason with casuistry, stoke the passions, and incite the imagination, shaping credulity and ensnaring volition.[84] From a Calvinist perspective on Lockean psychology, it looked for all the world as though hell was for children.

Such contradictions made visible the enormous anachronisms existing in eighteenth-century Calvinism, troubling before and well after the intercolonial revivals of the First Great Awakening. They were not easily resolved; most were still working themselves out in the final decades of the postbellum era.[85] The credence Locke's work gave to empirical epistemology added to the troubles of a theology and culture already assailed by inconsistencies and rent by social change. While Janice Knight and others have made us aware of the myth of a singular Puritan orthodoxy, the schisms of the eighteenth century made the Puritan canopy of the émigré generation seem coherent by comparison.[86] Lockean sensual psychology, the advent of childhood, the birth of evangelicalism, the clergy's diminishing cultural hegemony, and the concurrent cultural siege against the bedrock doctrines of election and original sin were convolutions with enormous ramifications, heaped on a system already struggling under the weight of its own doctrinal conundrums. These ramifications threatened none more than the young. The burning question for an emerging generation of Protestant leaders was how to adjust the theological explanation while instilling an educational system that compensated for a child's lack of experience.

*   *   *

It was largely Jonathan Edwards in his generation of colonial ministers who pulled the fraying threads of Calvinist doctrine into a more comprehensive pattern—a "New Light Theology" incorporated by Congregationalists, Methodists, Presbyterians, Anglicans, Baptists, and a spate of emergent popular denominations.[87] From Edwards's template, the next three generations—most famously Joseph Bellamy, Samuel Emmons, Samuel Hopkins, and finally Nathaniel Taylor (the "New Divinity School" and their heirs)—would devise the last great "systems," the final theodicies of a theology already morphing into the feeling-focused forms of interdenominational evangelicalism or the rational theology of Unitarians, Episcopalians, and High Church Anglicans. I turn to Edwards for the remaining sections of this chapter, for his theology and ministerial practice facilitated the epistemological shifts that engendered and promoted the spiritualization of American realism. His work from within Locke's sensory model would also facilitate the divergent routes that discursive and visually heuristic realism would take in the nineteenth century as the secular and sacred forms and conventions of that realism emerged from the sensationalism bequeathed by a broader eighteenth-century Calvinist hermeneutic of fear. What follows, then, sets the stage for the popular homiletic forms born of Edwards's evangelical descendants, whose principles still undergird the dynamic interpretive practices and representational strategies of American Protestantism.

Edwards has come to exemplify the shift in mid-eighteenth-century Calvinist theology as his work has been simultaneously used to justify Calvinism and evangelicalism: to support election and limited atone-

ment, on the one hand, and to mobilize fear in order to catalyze conversion and expand the availability of Christ's indwelling light toward
universal salvation, on the other. In some ways Edwards seems the least
likely to justify the use of fear in salvation, because he was the least
ready of his cohort to surrender the doctrine of election or the soul's
passive reception of free grace. Yet his answer to the empirical epistemologies embodied by Locke opened the way for later Protestants, who
had abandoned the doctrines of limited atonement and predestination to
embrace volition in the redemptive process and evangelicalism. Because
Locke's epistemology articulated how external stimuli acted on the passive faculties, it was, for Edwards, commensurate with Calvinism's explanation of the soul's passive reception of grace. He agreed with Locke
that the senses were the fundamental avenues of knowledge.[88] From this
basic premise, Edwards set out to resolve how the young and uneducated acquire adequate knowledge to form a spiritual standard by which
to evaluate the moral implications of new experience. Edwards's revised
epistemology would become the foundation for American Protestant
homiletic strategies and reading practices through the nineteenth century, epitomized, as we shall see in chapter 2, in the homiletic theory of
Jacob Abbott, student of Edwards's grandson Timothy Dwight. Edwards
would provide a rationale for experiential pedagogies and hermeneutical
practices that still persist, mystifying secular audiences today.

In "A Divine and Supernatural Light," likely his most critically examined sermon and one of the most important revivalist documents of the
eighteenth century, Edwards premises his revision of Locke's psychology
on Matthew 16:17.[89] Here Christ tells Simon (soon to be Peter), who has
just professed him "to be the Son of the living God" ("Divine Light" 408),
that "flesh and blood hath not revealed it unto thee, but my Father which
is in heaven." Seizing on the double significance of "flesh and blood,"
Edwards determines that no person—no one of flesh and blood—has "revealed" Christ to Simon (409). With an eye to Locke's denial of innate
ideas and extrasensory perception, Edwards interprets the verse also to
mean that no physical human faculty, no sense bound up in flesh and
blood, could reveal Christ's identity, which God alone imparts.[90]

For Edwards, God communicates to the redeemed through divine
and supernatural light: "The saving evidence of the truth of the Gospel
is such, as is attainable by persons of mean capacities, and advantages,
as well as those that are of the greatest parts and learning. . . . Persons,

with but an ordinary degree of knowledge, are capable, without a long and subtle train of reasoning, to see the divine excellency of the things of religion: they are capable of being taught by the Spirit of God, as well as learned men" ("Divine Light" 423). It was a profound statement. Edwards had ultimately rejected the "sixth sense"—the innate moral faculty—that Francis Hutcheson had affixed to the Lockean epistemology both in an effort to loosen its materialist grip and in an effort to muscularize human volitional capacity beyond the limits of the Augustinian worldview revivified through Calvinism. As with the other senses, Hutcheson opposed strict materialism by anchoring his sixth sense as a quasi-spiritual faculty in "flesh and blood." Secondly, and more troubling to Edwards, this "sense" elevated humanity's capacities, rendering individuals too active in the reception of grace. To Edwards, this view reversed the Fall's just penalties. It was the right impulse, but the wrong way.

In contrast, Edwards posited an avenue of knowledge *through* the senses, yet beyond any single faculty's capacity to achieve alone. He argued that a supernatural light emanating from the divine illuminated human experience, opening the gradations of spiritual meaning to the godly, even to "persons of low education" and the "less learned sorts" above the vaunted "masters of reason" ("Divine Light" 423). This was not revelation cast upon the mind like a ray of light from above. Rather, Edwards extended Locke's epistemology from within the model: "Grace only assists the faculties of the soul to do that more fully," he insisted, "which they do by nature" ("Divine Light" 410). Edwards was too much a product of the Enlightenment's investment in empiricism and too faithful to the conditions of the Fall to perpetuate the mysticism that modern readers often attribute to "Divine and Supernatural Light."[91] Rather, he found Lockean epistemological limitations—the subjective and physical constraints of perception—compatible with the Fall's impaired epistemology. While divine wisdom is "above nature," he argued, the "spiritual discovery" the Holy Ghost "wrought in the soul" worked through a human medium ("Divine Light" 411–12): "In letting light into the soul," God "deals with man according to his nature, or as a rational creature; and makes use of his human faculties" ("Divine Light" 416). Edwards's corrections of Locke were not revolutionary alterations so much as innovative adjustments that accommodated Lockean theory to scriptural imperatives and the logic of Calvinist metaphysics.

Part of the problem Edwards's generation perceived in epistemological explanations similar to, or grafted from, Locke's or Descartes's was their mechanistic structures.[92] In an age newly enamored of gears, cranks, and cogs, Locke's claim that information wound its way along a chain of reception, through the conventional faculties—perception, reason, passions, imagination, understanding, and will (or volition)—foreclosed the possibility that the will could preselect what it processed.[93] Similar to Foxcroft's "runagate" faculties, Locke's mechanized chain revealed a potential for disruption between information reception and voluntary action. The distance between the external senses and the will, held apart by the sequential train of other faculties, meant that the senses operated without benefit of the will. Lacking experience to bridge the ends, the senses risked corruption by their physical connection to the body and its appetites. Foxcroft warned of precisely this danger: "The senses," intended as "informers and friends to the soul, are now arm'd in opposition against it, and hold treacherous correspondence with its enemies: They frequently make false reports, and are guilty of many fatal mistakes. They are become instruments of Sin and Satan, and by means of them, the soul is often taken in snare of the devil" (*Cleansing Our Way* 8). At the end of the faculty chain, the will was relegated to sifting whatever the senses indiscriminately garnered: stimuli either haphazard or, worse, depraved. For ministers mounting a rearguard action against rationalism, the options were appalling: either no agency or, as with the pagan worldview, agency articulated through the machinations of chance or fortune. For Edwards and other eighteenth-century Calvinists, Locke's mechanist epistemology also created the problem we just examined: the lag time between perception and action, which rendered the young especially vulnerable. Even if wills were unencumbered and all the faculties sequentially meshed, the hapless child could still fall to moral snares—"inwardly slaughtered," as Cooper put it—before the understanding awakened the will to the soul's peril. In a natural world evacuated of spiritual imperatives, the *novum organun* of Baconian empiricism, rational philosophy, and political intrigue, Locke's sensationalism might prove adequate to the task of discovery. But in a supernatural world where spiritual pitfalls abounded and moral agency called for, in Foxcroft's phrase, "quick dispatch," Locke's bureaucratic mechanization left the soul a defensive line that might work with steady accuracy but at a sluggish pace. If the danger were natural—fire, blizzards, earth-

quakes, pursuit by a bear—and reaction thus involuntary, Locke's epistemology might prove adequate. But in the metaphysical realm, where
Satan seduced hearts and minds with false logic—what Edward Pearse
warned was his "way of Flattery," "his cunning fallacious Workings"[94]—
where the senses were either the first line of defense or the first domino
to fall, where, as Foxcroft lamented, the passions broke the restraints of
reason, the affections bribed the conscience, and the will was fettered or
belated, a Lockean epistemology spelled spiritual disaster.

For Edwards, experience was key for short-circuiting Locke's faculty
train, preempting the potential disruption between the senses and will
and the cognitive delay imposed by the faculties' sequential relay. He resolved both problems by demonstrating how the Holy Spirit converts experience into knowledge at the level of the senses, not by revelation—
the deus ex machina of mysticism—but by transforming physical sight
into "spiritual sight." For Edwards, spiritual sight could instantly apprehend experience as knowledge. The "evidence, that they, that are spiritually enlightened have of the truth of things of religion," he informs
his congregation in "Divine and Supernatural Light," "is a kind of intuitive and immediate evidence" (415).[95] By "intuitive," Edwards meant the
inferred connection between an object or experience and a known pattern, a notion Locke explained in this way: "for whatever ideas we have,
wherein the mind can perceive the immediate agreement or disagreement that is between them, there the mind is capable of intuitive knowledge" (*Essay* 534). Edwards's alteration is thus his emphasis on the *immediacy* that renders knowledge as experience.

Edwards fortifies his argument with scripture. Pointing to John
14:19, Christ's assertion of his followers' privileged way of seeing, Edwards explains one of the most enigmatic verses in the New Testament—
"The world seeth me no more; but ye see me" ("Divine Light" 417; John
14:19)—by transforming a conventionally metaphoric reading into a literal concept. Only the elect, the spiritually enlightened, can comprehend
the eternal forms visible through the shadows of the material world, for
only they have the intuitive capacity to render experience as "immediate
evidence," or what I have been calling "spiritual sight."

Counter to Locke's assertion that "precepts of natural religion" transcend language and scriptural knowledge and must be "intelligible to
all mankind," Edwards insists that God reserves such perceptual acuity for the regenerate alone. "Knowledge, or sight of God and Christ,"
he explains, now conflating knowledge and experience (figured as sight),

"can't be a mere speculative knowledge," cannot be inferred through humanity's fallen senses, "because it is spoken of as a seeing or knowing, wherein they differ from the ungodly" ("Divine Light" 417). The redeemed had the intuitive capacity to render experience as "immediate evidence." Avoiding the appearance of mysticism, Edwards calls this intuitive and immediate evidence "reason," humanity's highest faculty, but a human one all the same. "'Tis by reason, that we become possessed of a notion of those doctrines that are the subject matter of this divine light," he explains. "A seeing of the truth of religion from hence, is by reason," he reiterates, while in the next breath insisting, "though it be but by one step, and the inference be immediate" ("Divine Light" 422).[96] Edwards thus posits a circuit bypass between the senses and the will, effectively yoking the will—the faculty of agency and action—with experience. Supernatural light makes the faculties not passive slates on which the senses inscribe meaning, as Locke had it, but semiactive participants. Rather than a mechanistic chain of cause and effect, inference spans the cognitive gap between the senses and the will, producing Edwards's "immediate evidence." Intuition—what William James identified as imperceptible experience, but experience all the same—does not supplant or subvert the faculty process, but catalyzes its superfunctioning.[97] With a gestalt-like flash, knowledge and experience become interchangeable; for the redeemed to perceive, to know, and to do become one and the same. Thus to experience is, in effect, to will.

Significantly, herein lay the logic of homiletic pedagogy, the possibility for accruing knowledge through *simulated*—rather than actual— experience, necessitating, in the process, a revivification of active readerly or performative engagement. As we shall see, this reconfiguration of Lockean epistemology became the core of subsequent religious impulses, fueling revivals in the template established at Cane Ridge in 1798, informing Practical Christianity's reform agendas a century later, and, a decade beyond that, reappearing in the Christian pragmatism of the young John Dewey and Josiah Royce and even in William James's defense of the pragmatism of faith.[98]

In "A Divine and Supernatural Light," Edwards was inching his way toward a solution that he would rework throughout his career—a sustained effort to incorporate Lockean epistemology into a systematic theology. He had demonstrated how the young and uneducated might acquire the same spiritual insights afforded the educated; he had shown how the Holy Spirit opened a physical avenue by which experience could

link the senses with the will. He had explained how, with a flash of immediate knowledge, the young might sense moral danger, might see the face
of death behind the mask of beauty—"might," as Henry Ward Beecher
would write in a much later echo of New Divinity pedagogy, "see the end
of vice before they see its beginning."[99] Edwards had but one thorny issue left to address.

Sensational Savagery

Invoking the term "idea" ("Divine Light" 413), he now moved from faculty psychology to Locke's two categories of knowledge formation. For
Locke, an *idea* was an image of something, a facsimile of an object or
material essence: a tree or horse, a smell or taste. The world communicated itself through the senses in the form of ideas. Later, through reflection, the rational faculties paired ideas to form more complex concepts, extrapolating to increasingly less distinct ideas. In Locke's model,
experience was a product of what the faculties did with sensation, the
sense impression ("ideas") absorbed through contact with the environment. The more experience an individual had, the more readily his or
her mind categorized information, testing the "undoubted truths" (*Essay* 474) of science and philosophy, of culture and custom. Only by filling
the understanding could the mind combine ideas to form new certainties
because "the sorting of things, is the workmanship of the Understanding, since it is the Understanding that abstracts and makes . . . general
Ideas" (*Essay* 415). Edwards agreed. The greater one's experience, the
larger one's knowledge repository, the "settled standard" (*Essay* 444),
to use Locke's phrase, by which an individual could measure truth, de-
tecting not merely spurious facts and specious arguments, but—more vital for the religious—subtle deceptions and spiritual ruses, the iniquitous
casuistry that could fatally ensnare the inexperienced.

To show how "spiritual discovery" worked by a divine dilation of the
natural faculties and not exclusively through a mystical route, and how
the regenerate and unregenerate differed, Edwards followed Locke's division of knowledge into two categories: precept and experience. He distinguished between knowledge that is "notional"—either speculative or
mediated through books and lectures—and knowledge that is "sense of
the heart" ("Divine Light" 413), experience. The notional comes "when
a person speculatively judges" or infers the truth of something through

rational reflection; the sense of the heart, conversely, comes "when there is a sense of the beauty . . . or sweetness of a thing; so that the heart is sensible of pleasure and delight in the presence of the idea of it" ("Divine Light" 413).[100] The difference between knowledge categories "is between having a rational judgment that honey is sweet, and having a sense of its sweetness" ("Divine Light" 414). "A man may have the former," Edwards explains, exchanging Locke's illustration of a pineapple to honey, "that knows not how honey tastes; but a man can't have the latter, unless he has an idea of the taste of honey in his mind. So there is a difference between believing that a person is beautiful, and having a sense of his beauty. The former may be obtained by hearsay, but the latter only by seeing the countenance. . . . Speculation only is concerned in the former; but the heart is concerned in the latter" ("Divine Light" 414).

While Edwards's sense of the heart provided the regenerate with an additional faculty—an acute emotional, or feeling, sense—it did not render the other senses obsolete, or extend the epistemic limits of the unredeemed. Yet following Locke so closely—exchanging pineapple for honey precisely because for colonists in Northampton the taste of Locke's "celebrated fruit" was itself no more than a vague idea—Edwards could not avoid connecting experience with its presumed antecedent, sense. For Locke, the truest form of knowledge came only through the senses: "He that has not . . . received into his mind, by the proper inlet, the simple Idea which any word stands for, can never come to know the signification of that word, by any other words. . . . The only way is, by applying to his senses the proper object" (*Essay* 425). Locke's view that only direct sensations could provide fundamental knowledge was the point that most threatened Calvinist education. Taken to its logical conclusion, Locke had in effect denied the possibility that without the direct experience of sin, much less hell's eternal suffering, the young could attain real knowledge of it.

Supernatural light could unveil the complexities of reason—Locke's "notional" knowledge—but it could not, as Edwards acknowledged, "create" the "sense" of anything. "Reason . . . may determine that honey is sweet to others," he wrote, "but it will never give me a perception of its sweetness" ("Divine Light" 423). Herein lay the rub. Supernatural light could not enhance something of which the individual had no experience. It was an auxiliary aid—the Spirit "operating in the minds of the Godly by uniting himself to them, and living in them, and exerting his own nature in the exercise of their faculties" ("Divine Light" 411)—but the

Spirit could only bind itself to human perception in the act of perceiving *something*. It might enliven the sensation of taste, enhance the flavor of honey, prolong and enrich its lingering sweetness, but it could not impart the nectar's sense to one who had never savored it. As Edwards knew, without experience his explanation for children's moral aptitude quickly receded into the occult—God operating through a mystic mystical conduit.[101]

The logic of Locke's epistemology thus led Edwards to a genuine dilemma, one that still informs the question posed in the initial pages of this chapter with regard to the graphic realism of the modern-day hell house: If the only way for the young to have a sensible knowledge of sin's moral destruction was by experience, should preachers not provide the experience of sin in order to save the young from it, inducing a controlled disease to establish a lasting immunity? Could they do so without injuring the soul, rendering it henceforth susceptible to uncontrolled infections?[102]

Edwards could not easily dismiss this question, even though he recognized its devastating implications. A man who lay for hours in a meadow to discover how newly hatched spiders spun looped webs to harness the wind, floating off to distant locations, knew that experience was the most authentic form of knowledge. Only one who had disposed of a spider in his study by drawing it along at the end of a thread to the fireplace could so vividly describe, in his most famous sermon, how, in the proximity of hot light and imminent death, the spider reaches out, resigned to its fate in the flames.[103] As a minister concerned with bringing the unregenerate, like the spider to which he likened them, to a sensible knowledge of their fate in the flames of hell, Edwards's mind opened to the terrible implications of Locke's theory. If, as Locke insisted, the sense of something comes solely from experience, then in its final formulation it followed that individuals could not have the sense of sin or its consequences without the experience of having sinned.

To solve this dilemma, Edwards turned again to Locke: the solution, like the problem, inhered in the representational capacity of language, in the difference between the vividly imagined idea of something and the thing itself.[104] Given the assumption that experience imprinted the soul such that acts of sin were both damaging and habituating, and given that "notional" knowledge could not supplant experience, Edwards understood that ministers must rely on the vividly figural to help parishioners connect the invisible with the visible, the immutable with the material, preparing the rational faculties "to lie open to the force of the arguments for their truth" or falsity ("Divine Light" 414).

For not all words or thoughts—not even simple nouns—necessarily summoned an idea and its attendant emotions. This point was crucial for education. In an age epitomized by the frontispiece in Francis Bacon's *Novum Organum,* depicting the ship of discovery boldly passing beneath the classical pillars that had conventionally warned "*ne plus ultra*" (go no further), "here be monsters," Locke had augured a world in which the complexity of science, global exploration, and new discoveries, or commerce's emergent systems of debt and credit, and alienated labor, could lead to a critical disconnect between knowledge and experience, the theoretical and the practical.[105] In his *Essay,* Locke had imagined the modern semiotic dilemma: how, as society became increasingly literate, book educated, urban, and vocationally specialized, words might become separated from the objects they signified, might become fainter and fainter shadows of the reality they represented.[106] He cited as a poignant instance the mixed mode that signified the complex ideas of religious difference. To comprehend "moral words," he suggested, individuals "are either beholden to the explication of others, or (which happens for the most part) are left to their own observation and industry." But where individuals lack a reservoir of ideas formed through firsthand experience by which to discern "true and precise meaning," "these moral words are, in most men's mouths, little more than bare sounds" (*Essay* 480).[107] The Lockean Anglican Isaac Watts translated that warning into his *Catechisms; or, Instructions in the Principles of the Christian Religion* (1730) as a safeguard against the child simply parroting knowledge with little or no comprehension: "Words written on the Memory without Ideas or Sense in the Mind, will never incline a Child to his Duty, nor save his Soul" (*Catechisms* 17).[108] This was the semiotic breach that Edwards sought to bridge.

For him, the consequences of Locke's proposition were far greater than mere muddled minds whose layers of knowledge peeled away to hollow cores. Misunderstandings had eternal consequences. If even simple scriptural ideas from which biblical parables and homilies drew life—shepherd and fold, wheat and chaff, lighthouse and shoal, vineyard and husbandman—might become indistinct in young minds, then complex ideas and eternal verities such as sacraments, ordinations, sanctification, or the Trinity would undoubtedly fail to register with any greater authority than what Edwards referred to as "hearsay." If the young did not "*see* the countenance" of material things through words, how were they to acquire a "conviction of the truth and reality" of anything spiritual? ("Divine Light" 414; emphasis added). If the material was itself obscured by indeterminate words disconnected in the mind from the objects they signified, how could they differentiate an object transformed by spiritual sight from the vagueness of an inarticulate idea? Locke had warned, "In our Ideas of Substances . . . We must follow Nature, suit our complex *Ideas* to the real Existences, and regulate the signification of their Names by the Things themselves, if we will have our Names to be the signs of them, and stand for them" (481–82). Following Locke's assertion that "Names must be . . . unsteady" and "various in meaning, if the *Ideas* they stand for . . . refer to Standards . . . that either cannot be known at all, or can be known but imperfectly and uncertainly," Watts warned in *Catechisms,* "If children are trained up to say words without meanings, they will get a habit of dealing in sounds instead of Ideas, and of mistaking Words for Things" (*Catechisms* 36). Like Watts, Edwards worried that the emphasis on received learning would create a generation of inexperienced Christians who would undeservedly share the fate of the biblical virgins who, with untrimmed lamps, had slept through the bridegroom's return. Although these children—unlike the virgins in the parable—might dutifully watch for their Savior, they would not know him when he finally came.

Edwards proposed an answer: if knowledge produced through spiritual sight in one individual were processed through the senses of another as what, following Locke, he calls "notional knowledge" (through, say, the medium of sermons), then it could presumably also pass experientially from ministers to their congregations. This was the crucial difference between Edwards's Lockean empiricism and the mysticism of his ancestors, which as William James observes, "must be directly experienced; it cannot be imparted or transferred to others" (*Varieties* 302).[109] But empirical experience could, through the power of representation, through vivid simulation that cathected the emotions in the service of the soul.

In an age when education was becoming formalized, beginning in the controlled environment of nurseries and leading to classrooms, chapels, or churches, and when texts, lectures, and sermons seeded youthful minds with information and knowledge, substituting precepts for experience, Edwards contrarily insisted that "our people don't so much need

to have their heads stored, as to have their hearts touched."[110] Quoting
Thomas Shepard, the great seventeenth-century Bay Colony divine and
shepherd of the fledgling Harvard University, Edwards explained that
having one's heart touched—and a sense of the heart—did not require
book learning but rather experience; it required the minister, through
words, to move the congregant's affections, an act measurable by a palpable, almost tactile sense impression marked by gooseflesh, an intensified sense of love and joy, or self-loathing and remorse.[111] Drawing on
Edwards's work on the affections to create what he called a new method
of "catechistical preaching" for his Native American congregants, David Brainerd emphasized the need to transform knowledge into experience: "This was the continued strain of my preaching; this my great concern and constant endeavor, so to enlighten the mind, as thereby duly to
affect the heart, and, as far as possible, give persons a *sense* and *feeling*
of these precious and important doctrines of grace" (*Life* 200, 266; original emphasis).

For generations of revivalists this was the key to experiential templates, to the transformation of virtual experience (interactive homiletic
narratives, the *Eternal Forces* video game, hell houses, and the like) into
firsthand knowledge.[112] Preparing inexperienced souls for the dangerous
world they inhabited required realism, whether embodied in language
or through more performative pedagogies that would allow them to see
the consequences of sin in the absence of sin itself. From Edwards's precept of a supernatural light would come, as we shall see, the imperative
to provide children with the simulation of experience, with the beginnings of wisdom, that what they reaped through visually oriented, discursive forms of mimetic representation and homiletic realism might be
expanded into soul-saving knowledge and lasting faith—the whole of
God's armor.

The Word Made Flesh: Personalizing Hell

To generate experience through homiletic strategies, Edwards and his
cohorts turned the limitations of language to their advantage in two
ways. First, they found in Locke's theory of language the possibility of
connecting the word to its object of signification through vivid images
that drew on the experience of ordinary individuals. The key was to intensify the power of analogy by strengthening the link between the real-

ism of the representation and the thing it represented. The guide for this linguistic embodiment was found in Augustine, who, as Peter Brown explains, found it abundantly in the scriptures' "figural nature": "The gulf which separated a direct awareness of God from a human consciousness dislocated, as it were 'repressed,' by the Fall, had been mercifully bridged through the Bible, by a marvelous proliferation of imagery."[113] Second, they exploited the evocative yet obscure representations produced by language as an unstable mimetic medium, spurring the auditor's imagination to transform the vague but haunting scenes of hell and eternal despair into vividly personal scenes.

As a fast track to the passions, fear provided the best catalyst for this process. Clear "ideas" (images) drawn from everyday existence— corpses, burning houses, plagues, infections—could, when supercharged with fear, be transformed through a heightened sense *and* sensation to approximate the emotional immensity of hell's superlative suffering.[114] "Sinners in the Hands of an Angry God," "The End of the Wicked Contemplated by the Righteous; or, The Torments of the Wicked in Hell, No Occasion of Grief to the Saints in Heaven," and "Sinners in Zion" are sermon examples of Edwards's linguistic theory in practice. Later revivalists did more to put that theory into use through the fervency, visual rhetoric, and personalization of their sermons, and eventually through alternative technologies of visual realism, including graphic literary realism, discursively simulated virtual tours, sermonic enactments, and the incorporation of textual illustrations and photography. Increasingly, sermons focused on empirically verifiable snippets of homiletic realism to help audiences extrapolate between lived experience and afterlife abstractions. Vivid images authenticated themselves through the sensational response they evoked. Edwards imagined, for instance, that witnessing how a spider, when thrown into the fire, glowed brighter than the flame that consumed it could heighten congregants' ability to imagine themselves or their loved ones in a place where flames "pierce all their inward parts and so entirely possesse[s] them, that their whole bodies without and within, their heart and their brain and all, are more than red with the glowing heat, and yet alive."[115] J. A. Leo Lemay's characterization of Edwards's "Sinners in the Hands of an Angry God" as "the most effective imprecatory sermon in American literature" illustrates the new vogue for the repetitive and relentless catalogs of graphic images that piled up until an oppressive weight of doom overwhelmed listeners.[116] Here was the realism that rendered visible the connections between life and afterlife, producing, in turn, the experience that spiritual sight transformed into the devastating knowledge of hell's eternal suffering.

The perceived need to personalize the abstractions of the invisible in this way caused Edwards to promote vivid images drawn from daily life. If, as signs, words could be made to summon the ideas they signified with a new clarity, then even the iconographic and allegorical depictions of eternal truths could be made sensible in the minds of the young. If all language spilling out of the pulpit could be sensational—in its original meaning of producing sense impressions—then the young, with the aid of the Spirit, might experience the mysteries of the eternal while sitting in their pews. Responding in "The Distinguishing Marks of a Work of the Spirit of God" (1741) to accusations from Old Light clergy like Charles Chauncy that a hermeneutic of fear was unnecessarily cruel, Edwards rejoined that if "there be really a hell of such dreadful, and never-ending torments," it was the preacher's duty "to take pains to make men *sensible* of it" (emphasis added)—that is, to evoke its reality in the psychosomatic response of auditors' trembling, fainting, and trance-prone bodies.[117]

Yet because no sermon could create an endless chain of vivid images and sustain the engagement of listeners or readers, sermon experience also convinced revivalists of the efficacy of exploiting the indistinct idea produced by words as a catalyst to auditors' imaginative participation. Perhaps the best way to understand this process is from outside the religious context. While we have scores of accounts describing, decrying, and celebrating the Great Awakening's hermeneutic of fear from within Anglo-American religious culture, we also have tantalizing evidence that outsiders were watching the convolutions of colonial revivalism, trying to understand the relationship between experience and language.[118] For the young Lockean philosopher Edmund Burke, for example, the religious awakenings sweeping the colonies provided the perfect instance of how, within a particular hermeneutic and culture of audition, the indistinctness of language was a powerful purveyor of experience simulated through sensation. The final book of Burke's 1757 pamphlet *A Philosophical Enquiry* might even be understood as a theory of homiletic realism because of its emphasis on the word's capacity—above all the arts—to incite the passions, to simulate experience through a mode of discursive sensationalism that authenticated that experience in the reader's body as a psychosomatic response. Burke invokes the figure of the "fanatic preacher"—likely an allusion to Edwards or his revivalist ally, the renowned George Whitefield, or both—as the quintessential exam-

ple of how the power of rhetoric bridges the gap between linguistic representation and experience, between the sensational word and the sensation of experience manifest through the senses in the "flesh" as a kind of
sensory consciousness.[119]

For Burke, religion best illustrated the mechanism that allowed certain literary practices and genres to supersede even the object world in
their capacity to evoke sensation (*Enquiry* 160). Like his colonial contemporaries, he was coming to the conclusion that if sensation could
simulate the experience *of* experience, then language that evoked indistinct ideas might be as effective in its simulation of experience as words
that evoked clear and distinct ideas. Taking a more surprising lesson
from religious revivals, Burke suggests words might even be more emotionally evocative than sensations produced by the object world itself;
that is, experience simulated through narrative might be more sensation
producing—and thus, paradoxically, seemingly empirical—than genuine experience. "There are words, and certain dispositions of words," he
writes in book V of *Philosophical Enquiry,*

> which being peculiarly devoted to passionate subjects, and always used by
> those who are under the influence of any passion; they touch and move us
> more than those which far more clearly and distinctly express the subject
> matter. We yield to sympathy, what we refuse to description. . . . Words were
> only so far to be considered, as to shew upon what principle they were capa-
> ble of being the representatives of these natural things, and by what powers
> they were able to affect us often as strongly as the things they represent, *and
> sometimes much more strongly.* (*Enquiry* 160–61; emphasis added)

If such words affect us "much more strongly" than the very ideas drawn
from "the things they represent," then would not the physical sensation
produced by a fear so razor sharp that it penetrated the heart of the listener produce a simulation of experience so real that the body would
register pain? If so, in accordance with Edwardsian theology, ministers
could through a new system of homiletic narrative produce experience
strong enough to open the minds and hearts of the young in the belief
that the Spirit could transform that vision into spiritual sight. Edwards
and Burke could have found this theory of language and an explanation
for how reading or listening might be transformed from passive to active
engagement in Augustine, who believed that spiritual truths cloaked in
the obscurity of the figural "move and kindle our affection far more than

if they were set forth in bold statements." For Augustine, clear and distinct language "wholly absorbed" the soul in "material things," bringing the mind to a grinding halt. Yet "when it is brought to material signs
of spiritual realities, and moves from them to the things they represent,
it gathers strength just by this very act of passing from one to the other,
like the flame of a torch, that burns all the more brightly as it moves," demanding increasing interaction from the reader.[120]

Ministers accepting a material, sense-based epistemology must have
been aware of a mundane but haunting truth evident more than a century later to William James. Religion does not intrinsically possess and
thus evoke a special kind of love, fear, joy, or awe. If, as James writes
in *The Varieties of Religious Experience,* "religious fear is only the ordinary fear of commerce, so to speak, the common quaking of the human breast, in so far as the notion of divine retribution may arouse it"
(*Varieties* 31), then should not divine fear—fear of eternal suffering—
arouse a level far greater than worldly fear, a level in proportion to the
lasting consequences it invoked? Eighteenth- and nineteenth-century
Calvinists, like many fundamentalists today, thought so. Then as now,
it came down to preparation—the emotionally shattering period of guilt
and contrition that at once initiated and signaled the conversion process. Through the sensation of weeping and shaking, increased respi-
ration and chills, through paralysis, perspiration, and fainting, revivalists believed with Edwards that the Spirit manifested itself in word made
"flesh" in the listener's body, the most personal and thus most authentic
register of human experience.[121]

Fear evoked by new modes of literary realism became a powerful affective mechanism for audience identification. By evoking emotions
so overwhelming that the body registered them as involuntary physiological responses, ministers hoped to reverse the conversion morphology, such that effect might drive cause in those stalled in the redemptive process. The sensation of experience might open the mind to a new
awareness, preparing it for spiritual transformation.[122] The mechanism
for Edwards's reality-producing sense was emerging in revival pedagogy
throughout the colonies. Brainerd, for instance, devised what he called
a new form of "catechistical sermon" for his ministry among Indians of
New Jersey that, as we just saw, effectively employed Edwards's theory
by endeavoring "to affect the heart, and, as far as possible, give persons
a *sense* and *feeling* of these precious and important doctrines of grace,
at least so far as means might conduce it" (*Life* 266; original emphasis).

Looking back on these innovations of homiletic realism meant to simulate experience, William James writes, "Nothing could be more natural than to connect" these senses of reality "with the muscular sense,
with the feeling that our muscles were innervating themselves for action.
Whatsoever thus innervated our activity, or 'made our flesh creep'—our
senses are what do so oftenest—might then appear real and present, even
though it were but an abstract idea" (*Varieties* 58–59). This was not the
"heart versus head" simplification often used to differentiate New Light
revivalism from its rationalist, antirevivalist Old Light counterpart, but
the interactive simulation of experience through sensationalism.

This discursively simulated experience in turn received validation
by the sensational evidence of an empirically grounded epistemology
and was thus, for Edwards, a rationalized process. That this narrative
process—for Edwards, Burke, and James—could produce a reality no
less real, as James later noted, than any other experience confirmed by
the senses explains how homiletic pedagogy transforms realism into virtual experience: "The Sentiment of reality can indeed attach itself so
strongly to our object of belief," James observed, "that our whole life
is penetrated through and through . . . by the *sense* of the existence of
the thing believed in, and yet that thing, for the purpose of definite description, can hardly be said to be present to our mind at all" (*Varieties*
53).[123] For all intents and purposes, this is how the formerly unquantifi-
able spiritual experience could now, in Edwards's articulation, achieve
equal footing—at least in the minds of revivalists—with the rational, evidentiary model of scientific empiricism.

* * *

Edwards's desire to connect the word with the object it signified—to
strip language of its decorous shell—increasingly gained advocates over
the next century, even as it precipitated a transformation of conversion
morphology. In contrast to the seventeenth-century sermon, the revival
sermon targeted the individual rather than the communal in accordance
with a radical theological shift that, with the ebb of predestination, came
to see a sudden change of heart as the trigger for the conversion process.[124] From an older morphology predicated on a gradual spiritual
transformation shaped daily through devotional exercises, revivalists increasingly promoted a mechanistic model of conversion that stressed a

single moment of awakening—a psychological rupture—initiated by a sudden, overwhelming awareness of sin and the fear of imminent destruction or, following Presbyterian and Congregational New Lights, the sinner's limited salvific window, his or her "day of grace."[125] The revival sermon worked to produce that rupture.[126] Not quite the anomaly to his canon that many scholars of Edwards would have us believe, "Sinners in the Hands of an Angry God" exemplified a growing trend that enlisted new, imaginative modes of discursive realism to work on auditors' emotions.[127] This sermon is Edwards's popular legacy, not because it typifies the horror of eighteenth-century sermon rhetoric but because it illustrates a homiletic legacy that demanded that listeners personalize the text by inserting themselves within the narrative frame, and because it revivifies the connection between word and object with such clarity that the totality of the experience it produced in its auditors wrenched them physically out of their Sabbath stupor.[128]

This process of reification was key to the eighteenth-century legacy of spiritual and sermonic realism. Its lurid narratives of eternal suffering evoked particularized responses because ministers forced parishioners to personalize them by imagining themselves in places of torment, dangling from slender threads over pools of flame or bearing for all time the "weight of God's wrath."[129] Revivalists intensified terror through the use of the second-person form of address, encouraging congregants to see their sins as personal affronts to Christ that would make hell not a general space of suffering, but one uniquely tailored to their individually debased natures. "Almighty Saviour of the world is become your enemy," Foxcroft intones, "His power is armed with vengeance, and his mercy cloathed with fury, and as a consuming fire his jealousy burns against you, and will be continually discharging hot thunderbolts upon you . . . and all the billows of his flaming wrath shall be rolling over you" (*Cleansing Our Way* 96). The pronominal second person—"frequently use the pronouns you and your," Isaac Watts counseled parents in catechizing their children—would, ministers like Watts believed, "impress children much more sensibly, and lead them sooner to practical Godliness" (*Catechisms* 53–54). Such personalized descriptions—Edwards's "Sinners," for instance repeats the words *you* and *your* over 180 times—compelled identification much as Foxcroft's personified faculties encouraged readers to personalize sin and corruption: ministers evoked not general moral flaws, but flaws particular to each listener, a unique combination of faculty defects, moral weaknesses, and hidden ambitions that the individual alone could uncover through vigilant self-scrutiny and diaristic interlocution.

Edwards, Foxcroft, and like-minded ministers developed an additional range of strategies for making hell relevant to each auditor. They depicted it not as an abstract inferno, but as a place where congregants could picture themselves in relationship to loved ones and community. While the Reformation rejected the catechistic exercises of medieval devotional culture, which, through representational likenesses of Christian patrons, personalized eschatological abstractions, their homiletic tradition reinserted such likeness via rhetoric that served the same function. With a striking verisimilitude of time, place, and experience, ministers drew on personal and communal histories, inviting their congregants to imagine the Judgment and hell with the intimacy of a familiar setting that made an otherwise remote event feel strikingly present.

This semblance of continuity between the temporal and the eternal was a key device for instilling the terror of damnation. Much like the early American family portraits that posed the dead among the living, or like nineteenth-century virtual tours that encouraged the young to identify with the damned through a *radical imitatio,* eighteenth-century sermons vivified the afterlife by encouraging parishioners to identify with their future selves through personal connections in the present. Similarly, tombstones in Puritan cemeteries often marked the link between the temporal and the eternal in the explicit expectations of the dead for the living. In the Chandler Hill Cemetery in Colrain, Massachusetts, for instance, the "consort" of Lt. John Stewart—having died in 1801—warned her husband, whom she predeceased by a decade, that he had unfinished business. Her gravestone is a monument to her personalized expectation that they will be reunited again at the Resurrection: "Remember John as you pass by / As you are now once was I / As I am now so must you be / Prepare for death and follow me." If such posthumous reminders, like the family portraits that included the deceased, signified a duty to rejoin the dead in salvation, the hellfire sermon issued the terrifying warning that such reunions might not come to pass. Freighting the future with the terror of a personal loss, ministers kept fear fresh by warning that Judgment would either repair or forever extend that loss. By playing on their congregants' separation anxieties, sermons recast eternity in the concrete immediacy of the present hour.

We can see this change in a later sermon of Increase Mather that was influenced by post-Lockean Enlightenment. Mather's "Pray for the Rising Generation," the sermon he used to introduce Solomon Stoddard's *A Guide to Christ,* provides an apt illustration of one way in which ministers used this strategy. Mather begins by personalizing his own role in the Judgment, illustrating that the spiritual authority and moral gravity accorded ministers in this life would hound congregants right into the next. "If you dy in a Christless, graceless estate," Mather warned his young congregants, "I will most certainly profess unto Jesus Christ at the day of Judgement, Lord, these are the Children, whom I spake of often unto thy Name, publickly and privately, and I told them, that if they did not make themselves a new heart, and make sure of an interest in Christ, they should become damned creatures for evermore."[130] Rather than imagining Judgment in the iconographic frame of the Book of Revelations as a massive roll call of the damned, Mather shapes it as a dramatic community event, peopled by individuals performing their daily roles: ministers, teachers, and parents grieving or celebrating, condemning or commending, depending on the state of each congregant's soul. Such scenes intensified the vague terror of hell by particularizing it, transforming sermons into interactive texts. Framed as a village gathering, Mather's version of the Judgment induced shame, remorse, and anxiety by asking each listener to experience not the anonymity of nameless faces but the gaze of familiar eyes, eyes filled with alarm, disappointment, disgust, and grief at the listener's damnation. The cries of the redeemed for the damned were not the expressions of strangers, as terrifying as that might be even in the abstract. They were the deeply interested emotions of family and friends devastated by a child's spiritual death, by "your terrible end," Mather thundered, fixing the identification with the personal pronominal possessive. Intensifying this effect, he suggested that "godly parents" might even "testifie against their children before the Son of God."[131] Such threats, which became eighteenth-century pulpit staples, exploited the deepest anxiety and trauma of colonial childhood: familial abandonment, an irrevocable separation from parents and siblings, the frequency of which would have heightened sermonic verisimilitude. In "An Earnest Exhortation to the Children of New England to Exalt the God of their Fathers," for example, Increase Mather reminds his auditors, "What a dismal thing it will be when a child shall see his father at the right hand of Christ in the day of Judgment, but him-

self at His left hand: And when his father shall joyn with Christ in passing a sentence of Eternal Death upon him, saying, Amen O Lord, thou
are Righteous in thus Judging: and when after the Judgment, children
shall see their father going with Christ to Heaven, but themselves going
away into Everlasting Punishment."[132] Children's domestic life is here superimposed on the awe-inspiring yet impersonal iconographic image of
divine authority and punishment. The abstraction of God as wrathful
father and hell as an expulsion became more real when figured as an
earthly father's rejection and abandonment of his anguished child. Envisioned through the present, the personal rendered the abstraction of the
future concrete and immediate. By forcing the young to envision their
parents as participants in their Judgment, ministers like Mather wed experience to theory, an important function of homiletic practice.

   The fear of separation could also work in reverse. Ministers sometimes reminded listeners that they could be summoned at Judgment as
witnesses in the prosecution of loved ones. These sermons asked parishioners to personalize the Rapture by envisaging their parents, siblings,
children, or friends plunging headlong into the abyss. In all these interactive sermons, hell was not the wailing din of some exotic Old Testament Sodom or Gomorrah, but the local village peopled by family and
friends, whose terrible cries comprised the soundtrack to which the
damned would listen for all time.[133]

*   *   *

By the end of the eighteenth century, fear, produced by vivid homiletic
images and the personalization of sermons, had become the mainspring
in the mechanics of conversion, bridging the epistemological gap between the abstraction of language and firsthand experience, evidenced
as sensation so overwhelming that, in Burke's words, "the mind is hurried out of itself" (*Enquiry* 57). But the vivid imagery that Burke had decried in the sermons of the First Great Awakening would have a wider
impact in the second, as Edwards's heirs—including Timothy Dwight
and Samuel Hopkins, and in the next generation, Charles Finney, Lyman
Beecher, Jacob Abbott, and Nathaniel Taylor—terrified parishioners
with personalized dramas of eternal death, instigating febrile fits that
oscillated between paralyzing remorse and hectic reform. Descriptions
of God's vengeance, not merely against blasphemers and heretics, but
against lukewarm "Sabbath-day" Christians, prostrated the proud, pierc-

ing the hearts of recalcitrant sinners and recidivists who, as Jonathan Edwards reluctantly reported, returned each Monday to their wicked habits "like the dog to his vomit."[134] Dressing sermons in what, in the context of Burke, we might call a Calvinist sublime, evangelical preachers set about frightening their backsliding congregations into moral reform.

The spiritual journals, memoirs, and autobiographies of nineteenth-century evangelical Christians offer abundant evidence of how mental anguish transformed sight into spiritual sight; how, when infused by the Spirit, the immutable truths of the invisible world were manifest in experience so immediate and personal that the reality of its impact could be measured and thus verified as psychosomatic affliction. In the remarkable *Sketch of the Life of Stephen H. Bradley* (1830), the illiterate Bradley discloses an experience familiar to almost all nineteenth-century evangelical conversion narratives: "One Sabbath I went to hear the Methodist at the Academy. He spoke of the ushering of the day of general judgment; and he set it forth in such a solemn and terrible manner, as I never heard before. The scene of that day, appeared to be taking place; and so awakened were all the powers of my mind, that like Felix, I trembled, involuntarily on the bench, where I was sitting."[135] The revivalist tradition advocated vivid language that, by closing the gap between the word and the idea it signified, sought to produce the immediacy of experience so that it registered through sense impressions literally embodied in a shudder of revulsion or the gnawing pain of regret. While the personalization of suffering was perceived to open the reason to scriptural truths, it was the sharp edge of fear that turned the "notional" into a "sense of the heart," revealing, in Edwards's idiom, the sweetness of honey or the bitterness of gall.

Exhorters like Charles Finney, Lorenzo Dow, Barton Stone, and Jacob Knapp preached sermons filled with visual images to audiences prepared for the power of visual rhetoric. John Jasper, the Baptist itinerant from Virginia, was famed for speaking in "picture language," as he created with "daguerreotype vividness" the Gospel message as it must have been heard, his imitators believed, on the day of Pentecost. With an eye to the mechanism that made the spoken or written word more productive of emotional excess than real images, Burke had suggested that it was the obscurity of images summoned by words that promoted a kind of free play in the auditor's imagination. He illustrated how, in a comparison between a painting of Satan and Milton's depiction of him in *Paradise Lost,* the literary representation is more frightening because the image it summons in the mind is darker, more indistinct, and thus more conducive of personalization. Frightening depictions of hell on canvas are circumscribed; the signs produced by the artist's imagination exist in a closed field of representation.

The folk preaching of these exhorters provides an important index of how vital religion had become in the daily lives of ordinary people. Ministers and exhorters seemed locked in a contest to outdo each other in the number of souls they slew with words. If writing fresh sermons was not enough, ministers like Daniel A. Clark revised old standbys, bringing the verbal violence to a new pitch he classified as the "modern style." "If you cry to God" from hell, he assured his audience in an 1826 revision of Edwards's "Sinners in the Hands of Angry God," "he will but tread you under his feet, and although he will know that you cannot endure the awful weight, he will tread upon you without mercy, till your blood shall gush out and stain his raiment."[136] Similarly, in electrifying images depicting the eternal anguish of hell, ministers scorched the ears of their parishioners with the hot hail of fire and brimstone. The postbellum minister Washington Gladden recalled the modern style of Jacob Knapp, Clark's contemporary. In what Gladden labeled "sensational savagery," Knapp, "one of the most popular evangelists of the central states," emblematized the new realism by projecting "terrors of the future." With "descriptions of the burning pit, with the sinners trying to crawl up its sides out of the flames, while devils, with pitchforks, stood by to fling them back," Knapp aimed to inoculate his parishioners against sin. "Fear," Gladden admitted, remembering back more than half a century, "was always haunting me in my childhood; my most horrible dreams were of that place of torment."[137]

Gladden's characterization of Knapp's use of vivid language as sensational savagery should remind us that in the homiletic tradition, words were meant to evoke violent reactions, to register as experience verifiable through physical symptoms like Stanton's dethroned reason, prostrated health, and palpable fear. In the ante- and postbellum élan of camp revival, these sermons replicated, even as they precipitated, the unfolding psychology that prepared supplicants' hearts for baptism, parsing out sorrow, remorse, and rapture in ineluctable but measured waves of emotion. An evening of self-scrutiny and reproach attended by wailing and weeping led many to shed their "old man," and, through the symbolic immersion into "the watery grave of baptism," arise at the river's bank born anew.

In a tradition that would one day beget the modern hell house, ministers like Mather and Stoddard, Finney, and Knapp summoned for congregants' spiritual landscapes, embodying spiritual truths through the deadness of the material world. By encouraging parishioners to see the world around them as no more or less real than the images brought to life in the Bible they read, ministers collapsed the gradations of representation as it allegedly moved further and further away from "reality." Even when the faithful tried to undo the effect such realism had on the mind, as the late nineteenth-century Christian psychologist Henry Wood did, they had to do so in the language of Edwards's Lockean epistemology. "Sin, disease, fear, grief, and death," Wood asserted, suggesting Edwards's simulation of experience through the linguistic production of sensation, "are not entities having independent existence. They are shadows, morbid pictures, images, dreams which have only a seeming life. They give us sensations which make them real to the sensuous mind, therefore they picture themselves on the body. Displaced by the Real, they shrink to their native nothingness."[138]

As the Edwardsian homiletic theorist Jacob Abbott taught ministers like Finney and Knapp, the homiletic lesson exposes the material world as a mere shadow of the spiritual, and in so doing devalues it as just another representation. Abbott fully grasped the import of such preaching: "If this could be done, how strong and how lasting an impression would be made upon those minds. Years, and perhaps the whole of a life itself, would not obliterate."[139] His words proved prophetic: the fact that Gladden recalled the horror, nightmares, and "hauntings" of such sermons more than half a century after the pictorial language of the sinner's eternal suffering was impressed upon his mind testifies to the extraordinary efficacy of the hellfire sermon. It testifies, as well, to Edwards's extraordinary legacy of homiletic realism.

Edwards's New Light theology expanded the individual's relationship with the divine, fulfilling the Reformation logic that, nourished through literacy, offered the faithful a personal relationship with God. At its core was a new autonomy that became a key ingredient in the emergence of evangelicalism, which, taken together with Edwards's explanation of how the godly achieve spiritual authority despite pedigree, age, or education, foreshadowed an end of ministers' cultural hegemony. From the idea that God expands the knowledge of the righteous, amplifying the receptors of perception and sharpening insight, would flow the authority of nineteenth-century religious evangelicals, countless unlicensed exhort-

ers whose tongues were unloosed by the nation's Revolutionary iconoclasm of orthodoxies, received doctrine, and traditional denominations,
to reap souls in the antebellum harvest fields. Here were the evangelical outgrowths of Edwards's Lockean revision. Shunning the authority
of presbytery and episcopacy, synod and seminary, Methodist "connexion" and kirk, the self-acclaimed preachers, rude and rustic exhorters,
and free and enslaved African American men and women would trace
out the Edwardsian epistemology to its logical conclusion on the ground
in the personalization of everyday life. They would find in the supernat-
urally lit, inner counsel of one—the self-authorized individual—a new
source of moral authority and spiritual self-reliance, the harbinger of abolitionism and universal suffrage, that was at one with the emerging republican celebration of the individual's political autonomy.[140]

CHAPTER TWO

Personalizing Progress:
Spiritual Masterplots and Templates
of Redemption

It becomes us to spend this life only as a journey towards heaven, as it becomes us to make the seeking of our highest end, and proper good, the whole work of our lives; and we should subordinate all the other concerns of life to it. —Jonathan Edwards, "The True Christian's Life a Journey towards Heaven"

Let me make the school books and catechisms which the children study, and I care not who makes the laws. —George Livermore, *The Origin, History and Character of the New England Primer*

Scrambling up the packed snowdrift ramps piled against the north-west side of the stockades surrounding Deerfield, Massachusetts, a force of some three hundred French Canadians, Abenakis, Hurons, and Kahnawake Mohawks breached the village walls, taking the town by surprise in the dead of night on February 29, 1704, while the watch slept. In what the colonists called "Queen Anne's War" (one of the first episodes in the second of the four French and Indian Wars), the raiding party destroyed the town, burning nearly half the houses, killing more than fifty residents, and taking more than one hundred captive.[1] Among these was seven-year-old Eunice Williams, daughter of the Reverend John Williams, the village minister and a member of New England's powerful Mather-Stoddard-Williams clan. Of the many personal tragedies leading up to and produced by the Deerfield attack—with plenty of atrocities to

go around—Eunice Williams's experience would come to occupy the colonial imagination as did few other stories.

The first installment of the narrative came in 1707, with the Reverend Williams's account of his daughter's capture and ordeal. In *The Redeemed Captive Returning to Zion,* he relates the compelling story of the
initial attack and little Eunice's grueling journey from Massachusetts to
Montreal and beyond. Here, too, he recounts the outcome of his meeting
with his captive daughter later in 1704, a one-hour interview arranged by
the governor of Montreal. What must strike the modern reader as odd
about this conversation is that out of all the father might have said to
comfort his child, to offer hope against despair, what he fixed on was ascertaining that she still knew her catechism.[2] Even his parting words, he
reports, were an admonition that she "not forget her catechism and the
Scriptures she learnt by heart."[3] He adds that after he and his daughter parted, several Indians who had seen her told him that she had been
"much afraid she should forget her catechism, having none to instruct
her."[4] Clearly, Williams had staked his hopes for his daughter's spiritual
preservation on the *Westminster Confession of Faith* and the *Shorter
Catechism* (also called the *Assembly's Catechism*) widely circulated separately and in *The New England Primer,* a compendium of devotional
exercises for lay readers.[5]

Those hopes would be sadly disappointed. For what made Eunice's
story so haunting to generations of New Englanders was her ultimate refusal, after more than three years among the Mohawks, to be ransomed.
In his narrative, Williams laments that she has now forgotten English,
and he requests that "all who peruse this history would join in their fervent requests to God . . . that this poor child, and so many others of our
children who . . . are now ready to perish, might be gathered from their
dispersions, and receive sanctifying grace from God!"[6] In 1713, Williams again returned to Canada, this time as a commissioner in a pris-
oner exchange. He visited his daughter in Kahnawake, a village of the
Kahnawake Mohawks outside Montreal, again attempting to liberate her
from captivity, only to have his efforts rebuffed. Eunice was not coming
home.

The story of Eunice Williams highlights key issues explored in the
last chapter: American Protestants had from the beginning perceived
the vital need for education to arm their followers against the opportu-
nistic forces of evil, and they were especially concerned about children
and the newly converted, whose lack of experience rendered them par-

ticularly vulnerable.[7] Eunice's story dramatically confirmed that vulnerability. Far from knowing their catechisms, many of the young captives Williams encountered were "unable to speak a word of English" or recall the families or colonial villages from which they had been taken. But the story also, horrifyingly to Williams's readers, revealed the inadequacy of some of the pedagogies that Calvinists were relying on to arm their children.[8]

Catechizing children had long provided the foundation of spiritual training among Anglo-American Protestants, but in the New World, first-generation ministers made the catechism the central focus of spiritual education outside Sabbath-day services. "Few pastors of mankind," Cotton Mather boasted in his *Magnalia Christi Americana,* "ever took such pains of catechizing, as have been taken by our New England divines." Looking back over seventeenth-century Protestant spiritual education, he concluded, "let any . . . read the most judicious and elaborate catechisms published . . . and say whether true divinity were ever better handled."[9] By the last third of the seventeenth century, *The New England Primer* emerged as the most widely circulated catechism in the colonies. Based on such venerated works as William Perkins's *The Foundation of Christian Religion, gathered into sixe Principles* (1590) and John Craig's *A Shorte Summe of the Whole Catechisme* (1581), the primer became the official text for guiding Protestants' private devotions.[10]

Using alphabetically cued couplets that taught children their ABCs and the rudiments of reading and religious faith, the primer reinforced the Protestant link between literacy and spiritual development.[11] Like the primer, the Westminster Assembly's *Shorter* and *Larger Westminster Catechism* helped the young meet their spiritual responsibilities, a task not necessarily entrusted solely to parents. In a tradition that would emerge in colonial towns throughout the second half of seventeenth century, for example, the selectmen of Cambridge appointed a committee in 1647 whose duty it was to visit each family and catechize the children.[12] In league with such moral regulation, homiletic texts too surveilled the young with an eye to match their voice. The primer, for instance, warned young readers that if they failed to heed its teaching, it would cry out against them at the end of time, a living-word doctrine taken up by the eighteenth- and nineteenth-century sermon. While less active in its Judgment prosecution of reprobates, later homiletic narratives promised to sharpen the regret of the damned. Daniel A. Clark, for instance, balefully warned those who heard but did not heed his sermon in 1826 that "no doubt there are many present who will think of this sermon in hell, and some perhaps in a very few days, or *months* at farthest."[13] As actively as catechisms denounced the unregenerate, they were also meant to guard and fortify the soul. Their repetition of biblical aphorisms, mnemonic rhymes, and homiletic lessons were supposed to arm children against spiritual danger and, as with little Eunice, ensure their salvation against all odds. Brandished like an enchanted sword, it would keep her safe on her lonely journey through a world populated by enemies and pagans. Except that it did not.

*　*　*

In the last chapter, we saw how starting in the late seventeenth century, American Protestants began to harness the power of sensation and emotion, creating interactive experiences of sin and punishment to inoculate the innocent against temptation. Faced with congregations increasingly removed from the experience of real-life horrors, like those Eunice confronted, eighteenth-century ministers turned materialist epistemologies to their own advantage, using the senses to tap into the will, create knowledge, and increase spiritual understanding. Through vivid language, they sought to make ideas more directly present, to transmit experiential clarity by revitalizing the sensory capacity of the spoken word in snippets of homiletic realism. Simultaneously, they drew on the obscure but emotionally evocative images invoked by what Burke called "certain dispositions" of words. While chapter 1 demonstrated an emergent epistemological unification of the material and the spiritual, the personal and the universal, this chapter traces the implementation of this philosophical and theological convergence in the pedagogies of American Protestantism. Here I turn from the power of sensation to the power of narrative, focusing not on how ministers created controlled sensory experience, but on how they taught readers to interpret their own *lived* experiences according to spiritual templates.

For well over a century in the early American colonies, spiritual pedagogy had its own urgency, for the realities of life were still messy and unpredictable, and, as the story of Eunice Williams revealed, no given form—whether catechism, primer, or sermon—was necessarily adequate. If, as many colonial ministers came to believe, the insufficiency of traditional catechisms brought children like Eunice to grief, it was, they argued, because as catalogs of doctrinal truths or interlocutory examinations, they might fill the heads of the young with spiritual aphorisms but could not prepare them to apply such wisdom to everyday life, let alone to survive a crisis in which their souls were already imperiled.[14] How could parroted responses to such questions as "What is God?" "What are God's works of providence?" and "What is the chief end of men?" assist a child the age of Eunice, whose mind had already been weakened by months of trauma, fear, and deprivation? How could abstract propositions explain her role in the tragedy or provide her with an appropriate typological template for transforming her terrible ordeal into a sustaining vision with a salvific purpose? How could the catechism transform her isolation, terror, and spiritual plight into a martyr's nourishment, in the tradition of Paul's martial Christian? By the time Isaac Watts published his parental guide to catechizing the young—*Catechisms; or, Instructions in the Principles of Christian Religion*—in 1730, Calvinist pedagogy was torn between proponents of pre-Lockean psychology who relied on the catechism as a kind of prayer charm, and a generation of Enlightenment-influenced theologians committed to reevaluating children's moral aptitude according to new psychological norms. Much of Watts's influential manual, in fact, is dedicated to an emergent understanding of age-appropriate pedagogy, including sections such as "Of teaching Children to understand what they learn by heart, and of the use of different catechisms for different Ages" (*Catechisms* 17); "The Inconveniences of teaching Children what they don't understand" (*Catechisms* 26); and "Rules for composing Catechisms for Children" (*Catechisms* 38).

Concurrent with this Lockean influence, the theological decline in the doctrine of election prompted a range of homiletic practices designed to guide Christians in directing their own journeys, increasingly invested with new volitional possibility. Devising educational theories and homiletic programs compatible with the new sense-based epistemology meant creating heuristics to translate book knowledge into the practical knowledge accrued through experiences simulated through imaginative engagement with homiletic texts. In a revivification of the *sola scriptura* imperative, geographically isolated individuals with disparate spiritual aptitudes needed tools to turn their lived realities into spiritual narratives appropriate to new settings, changing doctrine, and emergent social conditions. In the seventeenth and early eighteenth centuries, Calvinist autobiography, journals, and an array of narrative hagiographies taught the faithful how to interpret contemporary events, incorporating them into familiar typological scripts. In the mid-eighteenth century, more sophisticated and flexible homiletic strategies absorbed the task of self-discovery, helping inexperienced Christians link experience to scriptural knowledge. In the next century, religious educators turned to other literary forms with a long reach into popular culture. This chapter tells the story of these changes as they become integral to Protestant literary history.

Interested Reading: The Christian Pattern

Throughout this history, the hermeneutic applied to homiletic texts preserved the privileged position of biblical exegesis. Parabiblical narratives emerged that offered new sources of spiritual inspiration and direction, yet the approach to reading these texts remained intricately tied to typological hermeneutics, to the particular way the religious interpreted the Old and New Testaments. Even as homiletic narrative moved away from traditional sermon forms, it seldom strayed far from exegetical practices of reading scripture and applying it to daily life.

Such practices were the key to reconciling the Protestant commitment to *sola scriptura* with the increasing proliferation of extrabiblical materials in Protestant textual culture—materials that could seem dangerously close to the layers of hagiography, local tradition, Marian legend, visionary narrative, and other nonbiblical material that Protestant reformers had originally sought to strip from the faith.[15] Where Catholics had pored over the miracles of the saints or accounts of visionary voyages to purgatory, American Protestants told stories of English martyrs or of captivity among the Indians. Works like Jonathan Edwards's *The Life of David Brainerd,* crafted from Brainerd's incomplete spiritual autobiography and journals, were hailed as "second Bibles."[16] Protestants used this trope to explain and perhaps justify an unease with their extraordinarily intense identifications with religious texts other than scripture, but the trope was also a source of that intensity, since homiletic texts drew spiritual authority precisely from their adaptation of biblical exegesis.

Individuals' authority to consult the scriptures for themselves without recourse to clergy, covenant, or creed undermined the cohesion of the spiritual community, and the seventeenth century saw a host of emergent sects in England and the colonies.[17] Even in unified Calvinist communities, ministers worried about the perceived vulnerabilities of spiritual autonomy: false reasoning, misinterpretation of providential signs and scripture, and invidious heretical influences. Colonial life added to the burden of New World Protestants, who lacked Great Britain's organized Anglican ministry. What would come of parishioners left to their own devices between services, or those too remote to attend Sabbath-day services regularly? If so many heresies could sprout in a settled land like seventeenth-century England, with (as colonial ministers had reason to know) such a vigilant church, what might not crop up in the colonies, whose religious authority largely depended on local governance? In the New World's open spaces (both geographical and theological), what is surprising is not that there were vast theological differences among Protestant sects, but that there were not more.

During the first century of colonial settlement, ministers exercised vigilance, sermons chastised the wicked, Sabbath-day laws mandated church attendance, and scriptural studies provided rudimentary lessons in exegesis. By the second century, however, with colonial expansion into western frontiers, these prescriptive methods made room for homiletic strategies aimed at fostering increasingly autonomous spiritual development through self-contained programs of private reading and devotion. The sermon continued as the unrivaled pedagogical form as printing presses increased its circulation and ministers took pains to translate their oratory into texts commensurate with parishioners' skill levels, transferring greater responsibility for spiritual nurture to an increasingly literate laity. In *Lessons of Caution to Young Sinners* (1733), Thomas Foxcroft expressed the advantage print offered in its extension of ministerial authority beyond pulpit and pew: "You have now in your hands a very serious and pathetical SERMON, preach'd on a solemn & awful Occasion, which it is wish'd and hop'd may, by the Efficacy of the Spirit of Grace, prove a Means of Awakening, of Restraint, and of Conversion to many of you."[18] Yet the sermon was hardly the only literary form charged with pastoral care; indeed, even with a clearly delineated five-part structure that parsed the logic in clear, digestible units, the sermon could still leave too much to the interpretive skills of the inexperienced.[19]

Spiritual leaders believed that the atomistic forces of sectarianism could be slowed, if not halted altogether, by unifying devotional forms— homiletic practices that, while preserving independence, might orient parishioners' progress toward a common horizon. In the most basic sense, the intercolonial revivals of the First Great Awakening and after unified many colonists through a common expression of spiritual experience. Conversion narratives among all Protestant New Lights—whether "heart-change" revivalists among the Methodists, Baptists, Congregationalists, or Presbyterians—are almost indistinguishable because the redeemed learned to channel their experiences through similar literary forms.[20] By listening to international celebrities like George Whitefield or John Wesley, or by reading their serialized journals or religious newspapers and books, New Lights from among all denominations, from different towns, parishes, cities, colonies, and nations, learned a common language of conversion and living.[21] On a more complex level, homiletic narrative taught individuals separated by time and space to see their religious experience in similar terms. While eighteenth-century Calvinists did not create the full array of homiletic exercises that emerged in the nineteenth century, they understood the crucial need for vigilance over their flocks, for weekly reckonings of congregants' private devotions and home Bible studies. As we will see, Wesley's career editing and promoting such texts as *The Pilgrim's Progress, The Life of David Brainerd,* and *The Christian's Pattern* reveals the range of genres that religious authors drew on, even as it suggests the narrative diversity that would lead to new heuristic forms and to the novelization of spiritual narrative.

Unlike modern habits of readerly consumption, in which individuals read narratives for plot, propelled by temporal and developmental progressions, homiletic reading demanded a different epistemology— what David Hall, drawing on the work of Rolf Engelsing, calls *intensive,* rather than *extensive* reading practice. *Intensive* articulates a level of repeated exegesis associated with sacred texts, in which such books were incorporated into momentous life-cycle activities, such as births, baptisms, marriages, spiritual changes, and deaths. *Extensive* reading, on the other hand, denotes reading practices fostered by the print revolution, in which readers read broadly for informational content or plot, what Engelsing suggested was a more passive mode.[22] Traditional exegesis assumes that scripture offers incrementally more difficult levels of spiritual illumination, based on the multiple senses in which it could be read. In its literal or historical sense, the Bible was a record of past events; in the allegorical or typological sense, these events signified spiritual truths; in the tropological or moral sense, scripture taught readers how to act; and in the analogical or prophetic sense, it foretold history and revealed eternal things. A particularly important kind of allegorical reading for our purposes was the typological, which connected the

Old Testament to the New by reading its events as prophetic figures—or "types"—of events in the life of Christ. The later extension of this practice to include postbiblical history meant that all kinds of events, even small and personal ones, could be understood as typological analogues of other events in Christian history—again, with particular reference to the life of Christ. This foundational understanding of the Bible's complexity, its ability to refer simultaneously across communities and temporalities, to the personal and the universal at once, historically fostered exegetical practices that depended for their legitimacy on repeated reading, meditation, and internalization, often figured as a slow chewing and digesting of the biblical text.[23]

Also crucial to Protestant exegetical practice was a belief in "living-word theology." According to this doctrine, the Spirit inhabits the word of God, preserving it against corruption through oral transmission and written translation and unfolding its meaning in proportion to the supplicant's understanding, his or her reservoir of knowledge—both received and experiential. This point is vital to understanding why Protestants viewed Catholicism's clerical mediation as a serious spiritual corruption.[24] Emphasizing individuals' need to read the Bible for themselves, Protestants predicated their campaigns for vernacular translation and popular biblical literacy—like John Eliot's translation of the Bible into Native American tongues in the first two decades of colonial settlement or, a century later, Wesley's ministerial campaign to create a "a reading people"—on the assumption that the Spirit communicated through the word, not simply to an audience seeking general truths about salvation, but to individuals seeking truths particular to their specific lives.[25]

According to living-word theology, reading scripture was a participatory act of spiritual engagement: the reader must approach the text in the right frame of mind and heart, with the appropriate faith. The unconverted could read the Bible, but to no salvific effect. They might find moral edification for a better life, but they could not discern, much less apply, the Spirit-directed truths from which eternal life was perceived to spring. Based on Paul's dictum that "the letter killeth, but the spirit giveth life" (2 Corinthians 3:6), Calvinists in particular believed that biblical history and scriptural injunctions were inadequate for either spiritual enlightenment or salvation. "The word of God," Calvin insisted, is "not that knowledge which, content with empty speculation, flits in the brain, but that which will be sound and fruitful . . . if it takes root in the heart."[26] Or, as John Wesley put it in *The Christian's Pattern*, the word must flow "into the soul of the pious and attentive reader, by the blessing of God, transforming it into the likeness of his image."[27]

While Reformation theology elevated the word over the image, living-word theology had its roots in the Middle Ages, in the belief in scripture as enchanted *remedia* or charmed invocation, invested with the power to rebuke temptation, cleanse sin, or fend off demonic attack.[28] While medieval Christians believed that particular formulas like the seven petitions of the *Paternoster* (the Lord's Prayer) could deflect specific acts of sin, eighteenth-century Calvinists believed that the Spirit operated in holy writ through the active engagement of Christians' faculties.[29] As we saw in the last chapter, by incorporating spiritualism into Locke's ascendant psychology while demonstrating how the Spirit also works through the scripture to alter material reality, Edwards rationalized this erstwhile mystical view, transforming individuals' experiences—both those accrued through living and those gleaned in homiletic study—into divine knowledge. By configuring the reception of divine truth as a process wrought by the Spirit *through* the human faculties, Edwards augmented the senses' role in comprehending the invisible, supernatural world.

Many of Edwards's nineteenth-century heirs, like the most radical eighteenth-century New Light Separates—the name taken by revivalist Congregationalists—reframed their religious experience as a mystical relationship with God. Particularly after the American Revolution, Methodists, Freewill Baptists, African Methodists, Elias Smith's Christians, and the followers of Barton Stone and Alexander Campbell, groups whose earliest leaders rose out of poverty, felt "called," in Smith's words, "like the ancient prophets, and apostles, from the handles of the plow, the fishing boat, sail-making, and other useful avocations."[30] For these popular faiths, religious experience was more important than theological knowledge. They might agree with Edwards that religious authority emanated from conversion, but they remained suspicious of formal education and wary of the seminary trained.[31] The folkways they brought to revivalism included a radical biblical literalism and a belief that God communicated directly with his chosen through visions, dreams, impressions, and voices. For more traditional Edwardsian revivalists like the Presbyterian and Congregational followers of Charles G. Finney and Lyman Beecher, spiritual knowledge was an absolute that could be perceived only with the Spirit's assistance through the faculties, never solely through rational processes. Like lay exhorters such as Zilpha Elaw, Jarena Lee, and Benjamin Abbott—who at his conversion claimed "to see the Lord Christ standing by me, with arms extended wide"—Beecher and Finney professed seeing Christ and Satan in times of trial, but, unlike these popular exhorters, took pains to explain how these visions were a manifestation of the mind wrought by the Spirit.[32] Nevertheless, both of these divergent outlooks, populist and educated, affirmed, whether through mysticism or rationalism, the individual's collaboration with the Spirit. It was this collaboration—through the act of willing and through the faculties—that personalized divine knowledge, rendering it specific to each individual's needs. Nothing better illustrates how holy writ could appear both personal and universal than the prevailing belief among Protestants (a standard pulpit threat) that sacred texts—the Bible, primers, or catechisms—would cry out at the day of reckoning against each individual who read but failed to heed its redemptive message.

These, then, were some of the beliefs, practices, and reading epistemologies that readers would bring to bear on the homiletic texts assuming increasing importance in American life, as interdenominational ministers armed parishioners for their journeys through the wilderness (literal and allegorical), and church leaders sought to unify devotional practices across a range of alternative spiritual narratives. We can get a better idea of how these practices operated by looking at one of the most popular of these narratives, John Wesley's edition of Thomas à Kempis's *De Imitatione Christi*—translated, since the mid-seventeenth century, under the title *The Christian Pattern*.[33] Wesley's homiletic instruction in his preface provides insight into how eighteenth-century ministers revivified medieval homiletic practices in an effort to shepherd their following in the privacy or isolation of Protestant devotional life.

*   *   *

The original *De Imitatione Christi,* written by a fifteenth-century German canon, was part of a late-medieval reform movement called the *Devotio Moderna,* or Modern (New) Devotion. This movement initially centered on small lay communes in the Low Countries, where men and women, usually of the middle or lower classes, worked and prayed together (the communities aspired to full self-sufficiency), but where individuals took time each day for private devotional reading and self-examination, with most texts in the Middle Dutch vernacular. These periods of private study, as the historian John Van Engen explains, focused on an individual and affective identification with particular moments in Christ's life, chiefly his passion, the result or purpose of which was ideally fourfold: to "relive" with Christ his virtuous life and saving passion, to have him ever present before one's eyes, to manifest his presence to others, and to orchestrate, as it were, all of one's mental and emotional faculties around devotion to him.[34]

Although *De Imitatione Christi* was a Catholic text, the Reformation broadened its influence: its emphasis on the benefits of honest work and its commitment to the vernacular proved particularly adaptable to Protestant culture. Its program of inward identification with Christ's life, an identification strengthened by mental, emotional, and even sensory intensity and deepened by repeated reading and structured meditation, appealed to Protestant ministers.[35]

It appealed particularly to John Wesley, founder of the Methodist sect. This new evangelical "heart religion" assumed individuals' psychological isolation and promised them salvation through inner change—a focus that predisposed Methodism for extraordinary success in the New World, where an ever-expanding frontier made the pilgrimage theme a powerful trope. In 1735, he brought out the most influential of those works, his own translated edition of *De Imitatione Christi* ("corrected throughout"): what he called *The Christian's Pattern*, a subtle but significant titular alteration, its singular possessive stressing the individual. In his introduction, Wesley begins by defending the book's use as a devotional for assisting Christians in the maturation of their faith—a necessary apologia given the anti-Catholicism to which his readers were heir. "The style of the treatise is a compleat and finish'd work," he explains, "comprehending all that relates to Christian perfection, all the principles of the internal worship, with which alone we worship God in Spirit and in truth" (*Christian's Pattern* ix). In a sentence, he justifies the book's Protestant application. *The Christian's Pattern* does not, he emphasizes, simply provide spiritual instruction. Rather, the work is an invaluable tool for assisting readers in their daily practices, particularly suited for the privacy of "internal worship," when pilgrims "alone"—without ministerial guidance or the communal compass of congregational discussion and debate—worship God, inspect their souls for moral blemishes, and pursue their semiautonomous spiritual quests.

The reading practice Wesley describes runs counter to our contemporary secular notions of reading as a process of information consumption.[36] Wesley evokes a practice that recovers the religious derivation of "edification," not merely as something instructional, but rather as a practice that fosters "building up the soul, in faith, and holiness," "imparting a moral and spiritual stability and strength."[37] Like the modern gym for the body, homiletic works, guides to piety, and manuals of conversion like *The Christian's Pattern* or the equally popular Thomas Fuller's *Good Thoughts in Bad Times* (1652) gave converts exercise, developing moral musculature, building spiritual strength, and increasing the soul's endurance. They also trained readers in a hermeneutic based on the process of reading and interpreting scripture. *The Christian's Pattern,* Wesley announces, requires study and exegesis, meditation and repeated readings because, as with the allegorical tiers of scripture, it offers levels of spiritual illumination. Intended to facilitate self-paced growth, its design aims both to meet readers at the level of their spiritual development and to open new meanings with each subsequent encounter, as their interpretive abilities progress in concert with their moral maturation.

In asserting the text's likeness to scriptures, Wesley calls it a "second bible" (*Christian's Pattern* ix), thus underscoring its usefulness as a homiletic manual through the theology of the living word: "And herein it greatly resembles the Holy Scriptures that, under the plainest words, there is a divine, hidden virtue, continually flowing into the soul of the pious and attentive reader, and by the blessing of God, transforming it into his image" (*Christian's Pattern* ix). Only the pious and attentive reader can discern and receive the upwelling of "hidden virtue" through the Spirit's action. Presumably, the book's original Catholic readers could not have received this illumination, yet the continuing presence of the Spirit in the text allowed Protestant readers to find truths particular to their lives, geared specifically to their spiritual capacities at the appropriate level of their spiritual development. Reading was a collaboration with the Spirit dwelling in and through the text.[38]

Thus *The Christian's Pattern* and other homiletic texts fostered private study, offering varying levels of knowledge to a diverse readership and encouraging the faithful to extraordinary levels of readerly commitment. But as Wesley asserts of *The Christian's Pattern,* "A serious mind will never be sated with it, tho' it were read a thousand times over; for those general principles are as fruitful seeds of meditation, and the stores they contain can never be exhausted" (*Christian's Pattern* ix). That a text can be read a thousand times and never "sate" "a serious mind," nor have its "stores . . . exhausted," might seem a claim associated with the popular caricature of the "naïve reader" (though also congruent with sophisticated formalist theoretical assumptions about the inexhaustibility of texts. These practices also owe much to medieval Midrash and Christian exegesis, as scholars have noted).[39] Yet the claim is perfectly in line with homiletic practices found in medieval Catholic devotional exercises revivified in early Protestant catechisms like John Craig's (*Craig's Catechism*), in which he counsels that it would be "frutefull to you, yf ye cause this short summe *to be oft and diligently red* in your houses: for hereby ye yours selves, your children, and servants may profite *more and more* in the principall points of your Salvation."[40]

Because homiletic narrative absorbed literary forms that competed with holy writ, ministers like Wesley articulated the process by which readers could circumscribe texts' spiritual authority with divine safeguards that affirmed their subordination to the gospel. One such safeguard was the invocation prayer with which Protestant ministers began their sermons, Sunday school lessons, and Bible studies, entreating God to open the word and reveal scriptural truths.[41] In the next century, the homiletic theorist Jacob Abbott, for example, begins *The Corner Stone* (1851)—fourth in the popular "Young Christian Series," comprised of homilies, moral hypotheticals, and spiritual instruction—by reminding young readers of the need for divine assistance: "Pray then, before you proceed any farther. You will then have God's guidance and assistance as you go on. You will be preserved from error and led into the truth. Your heart being opened, the instruction which this volume may present, will enter into it, and contribute to its improvement and happiness."[42]

But homiletic interpretation required the "agency of the Holy Spirit" to do more than open meaning: it also needed to elevate perception to achieve spiritual sight. Inheriting the linguistic problem Edwards expressed in "A Divine and Supernatural Light," homilists like Abbott worried that repeated readings could actually dull, rather than enhance, the reader's perceptions. In *The Young Christian* (1832), the first book in his series, Abbott reminded educators of the necessity of vivid, picturesque language to transport the young listener into the narrative frame. "Words that have been often repeated gradually lose their power to awaken vivid ideas in the mind," he reminds them. "The clock which has struck perhaps many thousand times in your room, you at last cease to hear. . . . The oft-repeated sound falls at last powerless and unheeded on the ear" (226–27). His injunction recalls the Edwardsian homiletic legacy and Locke's warning that, through imperfect understanding or constant repetition, "moral words are, in most men's mouths, little more than bare sounds" (*Essay* 480). Paraphrasing Edwards's union of experience and Spirit in "A Divine and Supernatural Light," Abbott asserts that the "evidence which is most . . . convincing . . . and on which . . . Christians generally, and especially young Christians, chiefly rely, is the experiential—the effects of the gospel, under the agency of the Holy Spirit, in changing the character and saving from the suffering and sin" (*Young Christian* 138). He contrasts a father's "cold reading" of a Bible passage to a vivifying homiletic rendering: "Suppose that this same father could, by some magic power, show to his children the real scene which these verses describe. Suppose he could go back through the eighteen hundred years which have elapsed since these events occurred, and taking his family to some elevation . . . from which they might overlook the country of Galilee, *actually show* them *all that this chapter describes*" (*Young Christian* 226–27; emphasis added). Alluding to Edwards's Lockean revision, Abbott explains how homiletic exercises create "experiential" evidence through which the Spirit transforms the auditor's fallen senses into "spiritual sight." Such a heuristic structure of reading reiterates living-word theology by suggesting that a universal truth has to be understood through experience rather than rationalism. "Each reader," Abbott explains,

> can, if he will take his imagination, paint for himself the scenes which the Bible describes. And if he does bring his intellect and his powers of conception to the work, and read, not merely to repeat, formally and coldly, sounds already familiar, but to bring to his mind vivid and clear conceptions of all which is represented there, he will be interested. (*Young Christian* 227–28)

As with all homiletic reading, the Spirit cannot operate without readers' cooperation; they must engage the text's interpretive levels, while also imaginatively engaging its scenes, revivifying the connection between representation and the object represented. In this context, Abbott's use of *interested* reveals a meaning vital to this passage and to the larger hermeneutic it illustrates. The term had a particular spiritual inflection: "to invest (a person) with a share in or a title to . . . a spiritual privilege."[43] To read for *interest* in Abbott's sense meant not simply to be engrossed, but rather to become invested in God's plan for salvation (just as the term "values" has both moral and economic implications). Recalling Increase Mather's earlier injunction to "gain an interest in Christ," David

Brainerd's praise in 1745 for a group of Delaware Indians "almost all affected with joy in Christ Jesus, or with the utmost concern to obtain an
interest in him," or Edward Pearse's deathbed warning to the living that
"there is no repenting, no believing, no turning to God in the Grave . . .
no getting an Interest in Jesus Christ," or Edwards's terrifying taunt in
"Sinners in the Hands of an Angry God"—you "have no interest in the
Mediator"—Abbott's use of the term implies incorporation, becoming
vested in the design of salvation through a particular form of interactive
reading.[44]

While I want to suggest that Abbott's homiletic training played a
broad role in Protestant hermeneutic practice, I am not implying that
every denomination used the same homiletic materials. Whatever their
chosen materials, however, all shared this interested method of reading
that invested individuals in history. How works were understood across
time provides an index of the pervasiveness of this personalized reading
mode. Secular readers miss the embedded hermeneutic in works such
as John Bunyan's *Pilgrim's Progress,* Mary Rowlandson's captivity narrative, Zilpha Elaw's spiritual autobiography, and Louisa May Alcott's
Little Women that made them Baedekers of the soul for generations of
the faithful. How might knowledge of homiletic practices alter our understanding of the role homiletic texts played in devotional life? The re-
mainder of this chapter will trace the application of knowledge to lived
experience through homiletic frames that preoccupied American devotional culture for much of its history—and that, like the twenty-first-
century hell house or *Eternal Forces* video game, remain a vital concern
for a broad cross-section of evangelicals today.

Everyman's Spiritual Biography: *The Pilgrim's Progress*

One text stands preeminent in its influence on American religious allegory: John Bunyan's great dream-vision, *The Pilgrim's Progress,* published in 1678. To be sure, it was not the only homiletic allegory in circulation, but through the nineteenth century, it was the most significant:
repeatedly revised, digested into tract form, inserted into new narrative
frames, used as a plot device for fiction, and modernized for later generations weaned on the novel. When the Presbyterian missionary John
Bailey Adger wished to develop a self-sustaining spiritual program for
Armenian converts in Smyrna (now Izmir, Turkey) in the 1830s, for ex-

ample, he translated the New Testament, *The Westminster Shorter Catechism,* and *The Pilgrim's Progress,* confident that these works could sustain the novice Christian's pilgrimage. As we will see in chapter 4, Bunyan's allegory would even bridge secular and religious reform initiatives and Progressive Era social intervention, becoming the regnant figure for imposing structure on the disorder of urban poverty and providing reformers with a prescripted role as the advance guard in salvation's army. Because *Pilgrim's Progress* remained vital to American evangelical culture—whatever form it took—it provides a unique opportunity to track changes in homiletic practices, to examine how parabiblical texts trained Christians in imagining their lives as journeys toward piety, redemption, and salvation. In many ways, Bunyan's allegory was America's *ur* homiletic text. In its seminal relation to American homiletic narrative and Protestant pedagogy, it became the most influential heuristic for helping readers not simply to profess but to *live* their faith. It was the homiletic template's template.

The power of Bunyan's text derives from the fact that—unlike Bunyan's own spiritual autobiography, *Grace Abounding to the Chief of Sinners*—it maps the spiritual journey not of a particular man, but of an Everyman figure named Christian as he undertakes a journey from the City of Destruction to the Celestial City, from the figure of this world to the figure of salvation in the next. Christian's pilgrimage makes explicit and available the allegorical patterning already underlying seventeenth-century Protestant autobiography. In Augustinian terms, he travels from the City of Man to the City of God. Along the way, he encounters dangerous enemies, monsters within and monsters without. He must struggle against miscreant faculties, inner weaknesses embodied as personae of the undisciplined self. Yet he is also tempted by worldly thoughts and the glitter of materiality, the Vanity Fairs from which issue pride, envy, and greed. Christian's resignation to spiritual death, for example, becomes the Giant Despair who confines him in his dungeon.[45]

Worldly dangers also impede the pilgrim's journey, each more or less menacing in relation to its capacity to exploit Christian's moral weaknesses. While the arguments of Formalist and Hypocrisy are, to Christian, transparent in their casuistry, Worldly-Wiseman seduces him from his course with logic that at times appears commonsensical. But no spiritual progress, regardless of its difficulty, lacks divine assistance. In times of crisis, the figure of Evangelist appears, like Isaiah for Job, to admonish, exhort, and lead Christian aright once again. When sorely tempted, he also receives aid from virtuous friends, such as Patience, Penitence, and Hope, who timely arrest his progress when he strays from the proper path, directing him around moral snares and pulling him out of the various bogs, swamps, and sloughs that trap and destroy the faith, hope, and redemptive spirit of the wayfaring pilgrim. While not evincing the urgent concern for the less fortunate that would become a hallmark of the Social Gospel's 1880s and 90s revision of Bunyan's pilgrimage as communal intervention, Christian assumes the role of spiritual counselor, adjuring other struggling pilgrims he meets along the way to forbear, persevere, and overcome.

Along the road to true piety, Christian learns the most valuable lesson of all: that no single weapon in the arsenal of the faithful is a panacea against all sins and temptations. Though he fights and vanquishes Apollyon, the demon-monster of spiritual doubt, with the sword of faith, he learns that the sword cannot defend him from the perils that await him in the demon-haunted valley beyond. Only the weapon called All-Prayer can light the way out of that valley's darkness. Christian learns to meet and match what lies ahead through recourse to the gospel, prayer, and Christian virtues—Faith and Hope—personified as the steadfast companions of the spiritual pilgrimage. So he climbs Mount Calvary and the Hill of Difficulty, the Hill of Caution, Mount Mammon, and the Hill of Error. And so he bypasses "the Land of Vain Glory," travels through the Valley of Humiliation and the Valley of the Shadow of Death—through which all must pass en route to salvation—and crosses the River of Death, finally to stand at the gates through which the godly enter the Celestial City.

It is worth recalling the ways in which Bunyan's text draws both on a long tradition of pilgrimage literature, penitential exercise, and dream-vision allegory—all discourses with roots in the Middle Ages, some stretching back to Augustine—and on an already-vibrant tradition of Puritan life writing. Throughout the Middle Ages, pilgrimage was not only a literal practice but also the most popular metaphor for the course of human life, both individual and social. Augustine had urged Christians not to get distracted by roadside attractions en route to the city of God; for him the journey was far less important than the destination. And while poets like Chaucer might have sanctioned a bit of "wandering by the way" (the Wife of Bath notoriously makes her pilgrimage—literal and allegorical—into an occasion for finding husbands), the seriousness with which medieval audiences took the metaphor is suggested by the immense popularity of late-medieval devotional texts like Guillaume de Deguilleville's *Pilgrimage of the Soul* and *Pilgrimage of Human Life*. As Nine Miedema points out, the idea of the individual's "inner" or spiritual pilgrimage was quite common by the early sixteenth century.[46]

Such allegorical pilgrimages often operated according to the psychomachia Bunyan uses, an inner battle assuming a self composed of various, not always harmonious, faculties. For example, William Langland's great fourteenth-century dream vision *Piers Plowman* finds a character named Will wandering through the allegorical "field full of folk" in search of a Christ-figure named Piers the Plowman.[47] The dream landscape (which includes a city on a hill) is populated with allegorical figures both external (e.g., Clergy, Study) and internal (e.g., Pride, Imagination). Eventually, late-medieval morality plays like *Everyman* and *Mankind* would encourage audiences to relate such characters explicitly to their own spiritual development, to imagine characters named Good Angel and Bad Angel sitting on their shoulders in times of spiritual crisis, whispering in their ears.

These narrative developments were a response to the requirement of annual confession instituted by the Fourth Lateran Council in 1215. This mandate resulted in a great outpouring of confessional and penitential discourses in the later Middle Ages, discourses designed to teach individuals how to identify their sins and confess them properly: thoroughly, accurately, and with true contrition. Since self-examination was the prerequisite to examination by a priest, medieval parishioners needed a range of homiletic exercises to help them identify and contemplate their failings, and to mend them. In the fourteenth and fifteenth centuries, with increases in literacy and controversies over corruption in the church, private reading and self-reflection became a more important arena for this kind of self-examination, self-understanding, and spiritual improvement.[48] Here, readers were more likely to undertake spiritual pilgrimages, to receive communion imaginatively rather than literally, and to become present at the death of Christ through intense textual meditation and the operation of the "inner eye." As we have seen, Thomas á Kempis's *De Imitatione Christi* was one of the most influential works in a new vernacular literature of private spiritual progress centered around meditation on, identification with, and imitation of the life of Christ. Readers learned to imagine Christ's literal wounds and death as if they were physically present in the scene, witnessing "with their bodily eyes." This immediacy caused them to receive the spiritual wounds of compassion and contrition for their sins, paving the way for true confession. In her fifteenth-century autobiography, for example, Margery Kempe relates how a priest, annoyed by the violence of her devotions, informs her that "Jesus is dead long since," to which Margery sharply replies, "Sir, his death is as fresh to me as if he had died this same day, and so I think it ought to be to you and to all Christian people."[49] Margery's anguish over Christ's death causes her to confess her entire life to priests all over England—and eventually issues in her remarkable written history.

For the most part, however, ordinary medieval Christians—despite their habits of self-examination and the marked increase in their autobiographical discourses in the fifteenth century—were not in the habit of committing their life stories to writing.[50] But after the Reformation—after oral confession had been abolished, print culture had taken hold, and Puritans felt compelled to examine their lives to determine whether or not Providence had placed them among the elect—spiritual diaries and autobiographies, what Tom Webster, following Michel Foucault, calls "technologies of the self," became the provenance of everyday Christians and a critical genre for Protestant self-justification.[51] Instead of confessing to priests, Puritans confessed to their diaries. Instead of receiving absolution and blessing from the church, they had to puzzle out for themselves—tracking the signs of God's grace like bloodhounds—whether they might be among the chosen few who would be saved. Account inventories of vices and virtues or expressions of piety, guilt, and sinning, the colonial Calvinist diary exemplified by Brainerd's journals charted the individual's spiritual progress, providing an index by which one measured spiritual aptitude, gauged moral lethargy, and uncovered evidence of grace or reprobation.[52]

But the discursive introspection these texts promoted also allowed authors to find meaning and to shape identity in the act of narrating experience. Colonial Calvinist life writing, conversion narratives, and deathbed testimonies emerged, in part, in response to the anxieties of living in a new land.[53] In an age of terrible violence, intrigue, conspiracy, and exile, the diurnal account compiled, over time, a record that the religious perceived to contain a hidden providential pattern, discernable only in retrospect. Interpretations of the discrete events of life helped weave a larger fabric of meaning and shape a spiritual destiny, transforming the personal idiom into a universal message for community consumption, while also whetting readers' appetites for a mode of realism—the novelized life—in advance of the eighteenth-century Anglo-American novel.

As the most crafted form of life writing, autobiography especially allowed the faithful to see the divine interpenetrating daily life. Life writing allowed individuals to find meaning in otherwise inscrutable events: John Williams, for instance, interpreted his wife's death in the second day of captivity as a sign of her redemption, and read his daughter's refusal to return to her family as an illustration of the horrors that await those who remain "unransomed" at the journey's end.

The sense that providential history contained recurring patterns was fundamental to Christian belief, part of the typological hermeneutic uniting the Old and New Testaments. As they did with the Hebrew Bible, Christian writers had always sought traces and prefigurings of Christianity in pagan texts; the parallels Augustine found in the works of Plato and those Thomas Aquinas found in Aristotle, for example, led patristic authors to believe that these Greek philosophers had glimpsed the eternal behind the material, auguring the spiritual dispensations to come. Just as Dante discovered a pattern of holy wayfaring in Virgil's great epic, so Christians in later times imagined they saw in particular cultural practices discernable patterns of Christian tradition. This is one reason *The Pilgrim's Progress* has been both successfully updated for new generations and found prophetically applicable to individuals in non-Christian cultures.[54]

The medieval church had organized ritual time so as to highlight the predictable, cyclical recurrence of these patterns. Each day, the religious—and those laypeople who imitated them through the use of books of hours—followed the narratives of Christ's birth, life, and death as if these events were taking place in the present moment. As the calendar year progressed, its holy days and feast days not only commemorated the events of Christian history, but also made them new again. The great cycle plays for the feast of Corpus Christi made clear, through strategic anachronism, that the birth and death of Christ were not confined to first-century Palestine, but were always recurring: thus in the *Second Shepherds' Play,* the shepherds who are called to witness the birth of Christ are played as fifteenth-century Yorkshire husbandmen, made miserable not by Roman occupation but by the abuses of a contemporary and recognizably local social hierarchy.

Because the Reformation violently unmoored Christian patterning and historical repetition from the predictable rounds of the monastic routine and the ritual year, however, Calvinists needed to exercise greater independence to find the signs and patterns littering their tem-

poral experience, to see the outlines of the masterplot and make sense
of the grand allegories in which they felt themselves to be living. Their
strategies for doing so are visible in the spiritual autobiographies that
became prominent even in the first generation of American colonial settlement. When *The Pilgrim's Progress* appeared on American shores, it
was greeted by readers already well versed in interpreting the evidence
of providential design in the facts of daily life.

One of the best examples of early spiritual life writing is Thomas
Shepard's autobiography (1647). Vying with John Cotton and Thomas
Hooker as one of the most prolific writers of the first New England generation, Shepard was an important architect of colonial Congregationalism, with an influential role in solidifying the conversion process and
membership in the visible church (the presumed elect). His autobiography chronicles his role in the initial stages of the Puritan revolt in England, even as it models for New England posterity the spiritual pilgrimage Christians must undertake toward salvation. Absorbing personal
history into this divine eschatology, Shepard brings the incidents of his
life—from his arrival in the world, which he identifies with the Catholic Gunpowder Plot of 1605, to his journey's end as a conservator of the
"New Jerusalem" and the incipient Harvard College—into sync with the
journey pattern undertaken by countless saints before him.

Sacvan Bercovitch has observed that in the personal literature of the
Puritans, "self-examination serves not to liberate but to constrict; selfhood appears as a state to be overcome, obliterated."[55] Shepard's text is
the consummate manual on self-abnegation. Only by examining his sufferings, accidents, and tragedies can he piece together God's plan, using biblical paradigms and typological templates to "read" the universal
meaning of isolated and obscure temporal events as part of an unbroken lifelong journey. In revealing his providential path, Shepard demonstrates how the indiscernible signs of daily life unfold in patterns that
direct the course of all Christians. Shepard's readers who knew to see
themselves in emblematic terms saw in his autobiography the representative images of a proper pilgrim, which they could then appropriate as
their own. Puritan life writing could serve as a model in this way because, as David Brainerd's own autobiography—influenced by his reading of Thomas Shepard's autobiography and journals—made clear, in
that all Christians possessed the image of Christ, they all looked alike.[56]
For, Brainerd records, the righteous know their salvation by God's revealing "his own glorious perfections *in the face of Jesus Christ*" in in-

dividuals' souls (*Life* 316; original emphasis). Such Puritan hagiographies offered a frame by which readers could focus their contemplative energies in the task of visualizing the hidden Christian self, the visage of the divine discernible in the deferral of the resurrection. By framing the hagiographic subject, this genre claimed to hold a mirror up to readers that they might see themselves or their absence in the saintly reflection they beheld. Such saintly mirrors were never static or complete, but illustrated the self-in-process. Shepard's self-analysis, for instance, appears in the implied rhetorical interrogatives: Why would God allow him to encounter so many evils—religious persecution, near imprisonment, wreck at sea, the deaths of his wife and children, and Indian attacks— and to prevail, if not to bring him to an awareness of God's saving grace? When, for instance, he resolves to flee England in fall 1634, he arrives at the coast near Ipswich only to find the ship unprepared to depart. Initially confused by these signs, Shepard realizes that he has let his desire overrule God's direction. "And the Lord saw it good," he recalls in his autobiography,

> to chastise us for rushing onward too soon and hazarding ourselves in that manner; and I had many fears, and much darkness (I remember) overspread my soul, doubting of our way. . . . I learnt from that time never to go about a sad business in the dark, unless God's call within as well as without be very strong, and clear, and comfortable.[57]

Translating a seemingly disjointed historical record into the recognizable patterns of preordained destiny, Shepard's autobiography (circulating privately until 1832) provided countless generations with a model of how individuals should transform their own lives into a pilgrimage.[58] These were deemed instances of merciful affliction when God intervenes on behalf of the faithful. Such instances signify grace, within the limits of the doctrine of grace. From Jonathan Edwards on, the eschatology of the life narrative both draws on this trope of the blessed assurances of grace and transforms them into more direct evidence of the *imitatio Christi* operative within the text. Spiritual life writing would thus shift in the century after Shepard by unifying the signs of Christic imitation with the life journey of the saint. As Edwards would later urge, underscoring the Protestant *imitatio Christi* tradition, "We must be traveling towards heaven in a way of imitation of those that are in heaven, in *imitation* of the saints . . . [who] spend their time in loving, adoring, serving, and praising God and the Lamb."[59] For Christians throughout the colonies from every sect, Shepard, likely the most quoted colonial minister after Edwards, was most certainly in heaven, and, thus, a consummate model for imitation.

By beginning his life narrative with the Gunpowder Plot, Shepard makes a definitive connection between autobiography and allegory. Linking his spiritual life and political events, he shows how human history shadows divine history, how the temporal and the spiritual are two sides of the struggle Christians engage in the battle between good and evil. To show how ordinary people can be at the center of history, he details his life with precise dates, revealing the identities of those who helped or deterred his progress and thus the Kingdom's. Through these narrative strategies, Shepard merges England's and New England's history into a New World teleology of sacred renewal and special election. As such, the New World journey becomes an allegory for the spiritual one, naturalized through a typology of deliverance, exodus, and journey to a promised land. Such a masterplot constitutes one colonial template of homiletic realism as it unfolds a particular and enduring American eschatology. Bunyan's allegorical journey becomes literalized while losing none of its embeddedness within a sacred millennial history. This history simultaneously maintains a purchase on the national imagination, investing manifest destiny with a messianic aura, and on individual lives and their attendant narrative forms that comprise this lived landscape of typological fulfillment.

Shepard's correlation between colonial history and sacred design thus exemplifies the tendency of Americans to interchange national history and providential destiny, to view nationhood itself as a preordained path composed of individual pilgrimages, making the life of each Christian integral to humanity's larger errand in bringing about the Kingdom. In the interstices between life journey and religious errand, typology expands beyond its classical status as a semiotically stable interpretive link between Old and New Testaments into a series of individualized perspectives within the cycles of sacred history with Christ at the center and scriptural patterns available to be superimposed on the community and the self.[60]

Like Shepard's typological reading of his flight from England to the New World as a spiritual pilgrimage, colonial captivity narratives also figured physical movement both as allegory and reality, type and lived experience. A literary response uniquely adapted to Indian warfare, the

captivity narrative bracketed the pilgrim's journey within a specific temporal frame, functioning as a narrative inset or close-up of the larger
spiritual journey. Captivity narratives externalized the colonial fear of
demon possession, manifesting in flesh and blood the soul's struggle not
merely against the things of this world, but against "principalities" and
"powers" and "rulers of darkness of this world," and "spiritual wickedness in high places" (Ephesians 6:12). While readers imagined the captors as corporeal beings, they also depicted them as Satan's henchmen, an
index of the genre's effort to suture form and spirit, literal and symbolic
meaning. A legacy of Augustine's Platonism, such interpretations understood the material world as just another form of representation, a shadow
of divine reality, but also a space of typological unfolding in which divinity could be materialized. Edwards recapitulated that legacy in *Images
of Divine Things:* "Why should not we suppose that [God] makes the inferior in imitation of the superior . . . to have a resemblance and shadow
of them? We see that even in the material world God makes one part of
it strangely to agree with another; and why is it not reasonable to suppose he makes the whole as a shadow of the spiritual world?"[61] In this
sense, we see how allegory sits precariously alongside historical particularity, at times contributing to this representational reading and at times
taking a subordinate position in relation to the more secure typological
register. We can also see how for the religious, language was always already typological, and how in the pilgrimage masterplot, like the captivity narratives, physical survival and death, like the wilderness itself, were
perpetually slipping into the registers of allegory, bequeathing to homiletic realism a double valence—an implicit and explicit epistemology.

Captivity narratives figured the individual's separation from Christian
society as a kind of descent into hell. In so doing, they initiated a pedagogical genre that, in the nineteenth century, produced elaborate, visually evocative sermons encouraging the young to envision their own descent into sin, suffering, and moral death. This genre produced, as well,
new modes of literary realism—precursors of the hell house—in spin-off
narratives that captivated religious and secular audiences with "true accounts" of Protestant girls forced into nunneries, fugitives from Jesuit
pursuers, or tales of abduction, rape, and incest.[62] In one of the earliest captivity narratives (published in 1682), for example, Mary Rowlandson, like Bunyan's Christian, turned her days in captivity during "King
Philip's War" into twenty "removes" figured as incremental stations
along the road of the cross. Each remove marks her progress away from

godly community, incrementalizing her struggle to retain her faith. Yet if her narrative made spiritual pilgrimage an inward journey, it also reaffirmed it as an outward, physical one. By collapsing the difference between geographical and spiritual progressions, Rowlandson renders her captivity visible as a spiritual allegory, a pilgrim's progress impeded by physical snares, bodily deprivation, and spiritual peril. With the spiritual valences accorded such terms as *ransom, redeemed, journey, captivity, struggle,* and *bondage,* her physical journey into the world as hell chiasmically traces her inward journey toward salvation; geographical sites become the stations of the cross that inversely mark her inward spiritual ascension, even as the lesson her narrative inculcates transforms her into an everywoman. Rowlandson's generation thus inaugurated a New World literary form that dissolved the barrier between sacred and desacralized space, making the road to the cross pass through every colonial village, town, and forest.[63] Her narrative remained one of the best-known seventeenth-century martyr stories, providing a template for life narration well into the antebellum period, influencing such emergent, largely spiritual genres as the African American slave narrative. As late as the mid-nineteenth century, readers still identified with Rowlandson's ordeal because it continued to figure the universal Christian journey toward a deeper faith along a road encumbered by doubt, despair, and danger embodied in the hazardous environs of the nation's frontiers, literalizing for many readers Bunyan's allegorical story.

In the aftermath of Bunyan, the pilgrimage masterplot declined in England, where it had to a large extent lost its literal edge. Not so in America, where the physical movements of emigration, colonization, settlement, captivity, and finally westward migration continued to lend an imaginative vitality to the religious template Bunyan offered. The oscillation between physical and spiritual hardship, between literal and allegorical terms, is abundantly evident in colonial journals and sermons, as when, for example, Jonathan Edwards's description of what it took for the righteous to reach heaven sounds remarkably literal, evocative of a pioneer experience on the frontier: "While they were on their journey, they underwent much labor and toil. It was a wilderness that they traveled through, a difficult road; there were abundance of difficulties in the way, mountains and rough places. It was a laborious, fatiguing thing to travel the road; they were forced to aly out themselves to get along and had many wearisome days and nights."[64] Edwards's young would-be son-in-law David Brainerd sought to turn his life into a pilgrimage in the pattern of the apostles: "I long and love to be a pilgrim, and want grace to imitate the life, labors and sufferings of St. Paul among the heathen" (*Life* 101). Brainerd's Delaware Indian converts found their own itinerancy between central New Jersey and the Susquehanna wilderness similarly conducive to the pilgrimage typology. On one of several occasions, Brainerd records that an eighty-year-old Indian woman relayed to him how in a dreamlike trance she traveled a narrow wilderness path encumbered by snares, roadblocks, and bodily deprivation which she interpreted typologically as a spiritual quest.[65] As Benjamin Franklin's childhood encounter with *Pilgrim's Progress* attests, when Bunyan's allegory appeared in the colonies, it fit immediately with the way colonial Calvinists imagined their lives, making it applicable to a broad audience. It offered Calvinists a clearer, ready-made language to talk about salvific patterns, which proved particularly helpful for children who, like little Eunice Williams, might not yet be able to see how their lives resembled Thomas Shepard's, Rowlandson's, or Brainerd's. *Pilgrim's Progress* caught on and maintained popularity in colonial America because it anticipated the inadequacy of the providential type to align fully with lived experience. As an *ur* template of homiletic forms, the story of Christian's pilgrimage became a universal one awaiting the overlay of personal details.

The degree to which readers emphasized the literal dimensions of the pilgrimage template, however, depended to some extent on race and class. In the next section, we will see that African Americans and poor white men and women would read as literal the hardships offered by the template. Seventeenth-century spiritual autobiographers had played up the correlation between biblical metaphors and their lives as struggling farmers. They compared themselves to shepherds and sheep, to husbandmen who labored in the Lord's vineyards. But it was in the nineteenth century, with the rise of the industrial revolution, the increasingly visible disparity between the very wealthy and the very poor, between agrarian labor and urban industry, that spiritual autobiographers—particularly adherents of the populist New Light denominations, African Methodists, Freewill Baptists, Methodists, Stone-Campbell Christians, and interdenominational revivalists—became aware of the possibility of recasting their poverty in the virtuous mold of primitive first-century Christians. Such a narrative construction not only revalued their lives—devalued in a modernizing, secular economy increasingly driven by either immigrant labor or machines—but also accorded a new viability to biblical parables and homiletic allegories as structures for imagining and living their lives, for transforming grueling hardship and physical suffering into the biblical idiom of laborer, soldier, and servant.[66] By privileging poverty and suffering, these narratives fostered a fascination with first-century Christianity, with itinerancy and simple piety that had an immediate impact on Christian narrative. Fictional accounts of first-century Christianity such as E. L. Carey's *The Martyr* (c. 1820) and Henry Hart Milman's *The Martyr of Antioch* (1822), both of which enjoyed wide circulation in the United States, multiplied after the second decade of the nineteenth century and would later inspire Lew Wallace's *Ben-Hur: A Tale of the Christ* (1880) and Hall Caine's *The Christian* (1897). In the introduction to his drama, Carey offers a description of the earliest converts that would have resonated among the nineteenth-century rural poor, day laborers, poor farmers, and free and enslaved African American men and women: those "bred in the camp and the field, encompassed with hardships and dangers, would be little encumbered with learning or philosophy, therefore more open to conviction."[67] As we will see, postbellum novels would incorporate the homiletic pattern to teach readers the significance of the seemingly fragmented and inconsequential hardships of life, making them fit new masterplots not only, or even primarily, for the poor, but also for middle-class success. But these narratives of suffering piety would also merge the two social classes in strident calls for social activism and moral renewal.

Journeying to Jerusalem: Pilgrimages Old and New

Awaiting a sign that God intended her to enter the ministry as an itinerant evangelist, Zilpha Elaw began to doubt her calling. Recounting this crisis in her 1846 *Memoirs,* Elaw, a devout believer in providential signs, recalled her worry that she had misinterpreted the indicators of God's will. As an uneducated African American woman, following a vocation regarded as the province of educated white men, she had good reason to doubt.[68] Yet doubt also signaled weak faith, and looking back on her resistance to the Lord's plan, she describes this and other temptations as the detours that could lure Christians from their spiritual pilgrimage: "Oh! How amazingly difficult it is for the Christian, when decoyed by erratic gleams, or delusive principles, he misses his way, wanders from his proper compass point, and flounders amongst the marshy reeds of worldly principles and properties, to detect his error, espy the gospel beacon, and regain his path; thus it was with me."[69]

Elaw's vision was a product of the Second Great Awakening, that up-surge of revivalist evangelicalism that swept America in the early decades of the nineteenth century. As we have seen, the First Great Awakening had already dramatically altered the Calvinist colonial conversion morphology: for many conversion was no longer a slow, lifelong process, but a sudden heart change, which struck so violently that new converts were often left prostrate, paralyzed, writhing on the ground, or unconscious. Promoted especially by Methodists, this "new birth" (which emerged from the "New Light" conversions in the First Great Awakening) became the regnant sign of redemption and salvation.[70] Yet even as conversion morphology changed and Calvinist congregations diversified, pilgrimage remained a dominant template for organizing spiritual narrative. Invoking this trope, Elaw's description would have resonated with readers for whom works like *The Pilgrim's Progress, The Life of David Brainerd,* Rowlandson's captivity narrative, and Shepard's autobiography were still viable models of spiritual progress. While conforming the individual's religious experience to an archetypal pattern, the progress paradigm proved versatile in its capacity to organize a range of experiences, beliefs, and practices.

* * *

Literary historians like William L. Andrews and Wilson J. Moses have traced the ways in which seventeenth- and eighteenth-century captivity narratives influenced nineteenth-century fugitive slave narratives.[71] What has been underemphasized, however, is how nineteenth-century itinerant evangelicals, especially among the poor or disempowered, reoriented existing paradigms of migration, reading the hardships of their journeys within the context of the Christian-pilgrimage template. The physical challenges that lay ministers like Elaw, her black mentor-companion Jarena Lee, John Jea (the "African Preacher"), Catherine Ferguson, Absalom Jones, Daniel Alexander Paine, Harry Hosier, and Nancy Grove Cram endured as they traveled the back roads of colony and nation, witnessing to the poor, became metaphors of Christlike suffering, at once literal and spiritual.[72] Nothing better illustrates this tem-

plate's vitality than the life of the young New York–born slave, chris-
tened Isabella, who, after her enslaved parents, siblings, and children
were sold away, experienced a spiritual transformation on what she
called a "pilgrimage" to bring salvation to the impoverished.[73] As a symbolic affirmation that the road to the cross led from one makeshift pulpit to the next along the nation's byways, she changed her name to Sojourner Truth. In this context, the scores of extant nineteenth-century
pilgrimage narratives explicitly recall the autobiographical works of earlier ministers and Indian captives, in which physical movement external-
izes the individual's inward quest for salvation, illustrating again how in
the American pioneer setting, in desolate frontier communities, isolated
farms, lumber camps, and other sites of drudgery and toil, spiritual identification easily moves between the registers of the personal and the universal, the literal and allegorical.

    Spiritual autobiographies like Elaw's reveal this unbroken genealogy
between seventeenth-century spiritual narratives and their eighteenth-
and nineteenth-century offspring. Fresh chapters from George Whitefield's and John Wesley's widely circulated journals—published serially
throughout their lives as separate volumes—demonstrated the travail
that attended the lives of even the most eminent Christians. Well into the
nineteenth century, evangelicals continued to read and cite Lewis Bayly's *The Practise of Pietie* (1612), Samuel Smith's *The Great Assize* (1617),
Henry Scudder's *The Christian's Daily Walke* (1627), Arthur Dent's *The
Plaine Man's Pathway to Heaven* (1601), Foxe's *Book of Martyrs, The
New England Primer,* and the works of Benjamin Keach, just as children
continued to recite John Cotton's catechism "for soul's nourishment,"
Spiritual Milk for Babes: Drawn out of the Breasts of Both Testaments,
and the Westminster *Shorter Catechism.*[74] All these texts—read and reread, passed from one believer to another—sustained the early, tremu-
lous struggles of new converts. Scores of nineteenth-century autobiographers attest to the popularity of these works, recalling how tattered
copies, falling into the hands of struggling supplicants, lifted them from
deep despair, sustaining them in their sorest hours of spiritual need. John
Belton O'Neall, for instance, carried into old age the recollection of how
avidly, in childhood, he read *Pilgrim's Progress.*[75] In middle age, George
Livermore continued to draw strength from *The New England Primer,*
feeling "many thrilling associations . . . aroused by the mere mention of
its name!"[76] "I see again the picture and I remember the history," he recalls, his account peppered by exclamation points,

"Of John Rogers, Minister of the Gospel in London, who was burnt at Smith-
field in February 14, 1554. His wife with nine small children and one at her
breast following him to the stake." How many times, in childhood have I cried
in thinking of his sad fate and the sadder condition of the surviving martyrs,
the poor orphans![77]

Narratives recounting the hardship and suffering of individuals who endured persecution, ministered to the sick with little regard for their own
safety, or, like Brainerd's patterning his itinerant mission among the Indians on St. Paul's among the gentiles, traveled in all seasons to preach
the Gospel evoked biblical descriptions of the apostles and their disciples, capturing the imaginations of thousands of nineteenth-century
evangelicals who themselves suffered from poverty, illness, itinerancy, or
sorrow over the loss of loved ones.

Indeed, Methodist theologians promoted these works almost as a new
hagiography. Just as he had with *The Christian's Pattern,* Wesley celebrated Edwards's *Life of Brainerd* as a model of Christian perseverance: "Find preachers of David Brainerd's spirit," he advised in 1767,
"and nothing can stand before them."[78] And as he had with Bunyan's allegory, Wesley edited a version of Brainerd's *Life,* urging it as a spiritual
model: "Let every preacher read carefully over *The Life of David Brainerd,*" he exhorted. "Let us be followers of him, as he was of Christ, in absolute self-devotion, in total deadness to the world, and in fervent love to
God and man."[79] Wesley referred to Brainerd's early death, accelerated
by his refusal to halt his mission travels among the Indians—covering
three thousand miles, for instance, between March 1 and September 1,
1745—long enough to convalesce from a chronic lung infection. For Wesley, the Christlike Brainerd, whom even the laconic William James un-
characteristically referred to as "that genuine saint" (*Varieties* 175),·
made the ultimate sacrifice for humanity, his incredible odyssey of suffering serving as his personal *imitatio.* Through acts of readerly identification, Wesley's followers learned to model their lives on Brainerd's just
as he had modeled his life on Christ's. Understanding their labors within
the allegorical frame of a pilgrimage enabled readers to concretize the
abstractions of biblical injunctions to suffer for Christ, even to the death.
The young missionary Pliny Fisk (1792–1825), for example, recorded in
his diary in 1823 how, during a terrible bout of illness in Egypt, he took
comfort from Brainerd's example: "What must not Brainerd have suffered, when sick among the Indians?"[80] By comparing his suffering with

Brainerd's, he figures his life within a specifically textual genealogy. As we shall see, one of the most important elements homiletic fiction borrowed from the life-writing tradition was the theme of suffering—particularly for another.

*   *   *

Zilpha Elaw's memoirs provide an exemplary instance of how specific groups of disenfranchised readers and writers continued to enliven and extend this narrative tradition after the American Revolution. Born around 1790, she came of age in the early Republic, a time bustling with political and religious energies. She reached adulthood as the second Great Awakening—sparked by a resurgent Methodism—was sweeping the nation, from the tent revivals of Kentucky in the early nineteenth century to upstate New York twenty years later.[81] The widespread "Methodist Connexion" in the United States developed a ministry based on the injunction attributed to Christ in Matthew 16:15—the same verse Elaw's friend Jarena Lee identified in her autobiography with the pattern of her own conversion: "Go ye into all the world and preach the Gospel to every living creature."[82] These words became the rallying cry of American itinerant ministers, who traveled prearranged routes, or "circuits," to the edges of the American frontier, turning the road to every village into a pilgrim's path, both literally and metaphorically.[83] Their forays into remote communities created a growing demand for religious exhortation and spiritual communion, whetting the appetites of rural folk for spiritually emotive, charismatic speakers like Elaw and Lee. As migration to and across the American continent increased, the pilgrimage motif would gain increasing strength, emerging as one of the foundational stories underwriting a distinctively American eschatology.[84]

    This revivalist movement combined with the iconoclastic energies of the Revolutionary era to open up new avenues for women and African Americans in the forum of public worship. Taking advantage of the political populism emerging from the Revolution, evangelicals were united in their distrust of social hierarchy and jealous of the least liberty, and for two generations, this impulse led to new social freedoms to the disempowered.[85] Evangelicalism offered particular solace in a world dominated by poverty and suffering. Not surprisingly, antebellum evangelicals tended to come from the lower and disfranchised classes, both white and black. They preached extempore to illiterate audiences, leaving no

record of their sermons or work in the field. Camps of thousands dismantled in the early dawn, leaving little in their wake but trampled fields, the
embers of campfires, and the contrite hearts of local supplicants newly
slain by the word. Records of their progress appeared in the scores of
spiritual autobiographies that preserved and amplified the literal correlation between their authors' lives and the primitive lives of first-century
Christians.[86]

It was this movement that swept up Elaw in 1808, converting her from
Quakerism, the religion of her adopted parents. Like the captivity narrative, her story of her daily journey toward salvation recorded the pilgrim's progress across a blighted landscape—filled not with the perceived
terrors and treachery of Rowlandson's assailants (though Elaw, like Jarena Lee, more than once encountered Satan in physical form), but with
grueling physical challenges and the suffering widespread in nineteenth-
century America, particularly among the poor, white women, and both
men and women of color. Elaw informs her readers that of the twenty-
two children her mother bore before perishing in childbirth, only three
lived to adulthood. Her father died shortly after her mother. But by turning her life into a narrative of the pilgrim's journey, she found spiritual
meaning even in these tragic events.[87]

In her memoir, Elaw first elicits readerly identification with the universal experience of all Christians, exemplified in Bunyan's protagonist
as an Everyman. She suggests the extent of this universal, transhistorical application of the pilgrimage allegory when, defending evangelicalism, she explicitly invokes Bunyan: "It is worthy of extensive observation, that the vast variety of mental exercises and religious experiences
of all true and lively Christians, in every grade of society, in all ages,
and in all denominations and sections of the Christian Church, are . . .
uniform and definite a character . . . so widely spread an uniformity as
that which exists in the genuine pilgrim's progress of Christian experience" (*Memoirs* 73). Elaw was hardly alone in her choice of spiritual self-
fashioning. As William Andrews points out in his deft analysis of early
African American autobiography, "The central metaphor of the black
spiritual autobiographer of the late eighteenth and early nineteenth centuries might be summarized as: 'I am as Mr. Christian' (in *Pilgrim's
Progress*) was, a spiritual pilgrim in an unredeemed world."[88] In *The Pilgrimage of Ransom's Son,* the popular autobiography of Elaw's younger
African American contemporary, R. C. Ransom used this masterplot to
encourage identification by helping readers to frame their own personal

experience, their particular failings and strengths, within the universal pilgrimage template.

Elaw's narrative exemplifies the strong correlation African American and poor white evangelicals perceived between the material and spiritual realms. Just as Shepard's beleaguered retreat across England figured the flight of the righteous from the persecutions of the wicked, so the hardship of survival for the poor in the first half of the nineteenth century revivified the primordial connection between the word and the experience it represented. What white "settled" congregations might interpret as biblical metaphor, African Americans and uneducated white "field" audiences often received as literal. Black spiritual vocabulary, for example, systematically differed from white in employing the biblical tropes of liberty literally rather than metaphorically. Whereas the sermons written for middle-class white audiences referred to humanity's bondage to sin and appetite or its enslavement to pleasure and vice, black exhorters and diarists emphasized the actual connection between spiritual and physical freedom, between the shackled body and the stifled will. Black autobiographers such as Elaw, Lee, Sojourner Truth, and Richard Allen spoke of freedom from real toils, from lives born and bred in slavery, and from the chains of doubt, self-hatred, and despair such lives begot.[89] For black evangelicals, even those freeborn, bondage to sin and bondage in servitude—poverty or slavery—were, if not one and the same, sufficiently similar in a racially divided nation that physical servitude often meant a life of coerced sin: lying to avoid punishment, stealing to eat, Sabbath-breaking to labor, and casuistry to justify need and supply real want. The correlation between enslavement or servitude and the New Testament's admonitions against being "enslaved" or "in bondage" to lust, sin, or worldly pleasures collapsed the difference between spiritual and physical freedom, such that in spiritual journals, as in black sermons, the term "jubilee" came to signify not just the Resurrection, but emancipation.

Fugitive slave narrators such as Moses Roper, John Marrant, and James W. C. Pennington further codified the connection between the material and spiritual struggle for salvation, reminding their readers that even Bunyan must be read literally before he could be understood allegorically. (At times, however, literalist readerly identification became so intense that it overwhelmed the proper end of homiletic identification: understanding one's life within the universal Christian pattern. The slave narrative of James Albert Gronniosaw, for example, records how, given *Pilgrim's Progress* after his conversion, he so identified with Bunyan's protagonist that he "took the book to my lady, and inform'd her I did not like it at all, it was concerning a wicked man as bad as myself."[90]) By stressing the dichotomy between body and spirit, the spiritual autobiography, like its sermon counterpart, emphasized the spirit's autonomy—the soul's volition and hermetic purity—even when the physical body was coerced by another's bidding or polluted by another's agency.

Yet, in the American evangelical tradition, the body also spoke through the performance of text, as another form of interactive reading. In essence, typology itself was predicated not merely on the recognition—the "reading"—of sacred patterns in everyday experience, but on their enactment. In a modern approximation of the medieval morality play as a communal performance, African American Methodists and Baptists performed typological enactments at ante- and postbellum camp meetings. In her recent study of evangelical conversion and devotional experiences, Anne Taves demonstrates the vital role such enactment served in the formation of particular religious communities and in assisting their members to envision the correspondence between their particular histories and providential design.[91] For example, by reenacting the Old Testament narrative of captivity, emancipation, flight from Egypt, and arrival at the Promised Land from the Book of Exodus, African American Methodists and Baptists emphasized the sacred pattern of their captivity in the Americas. In what Taves refers to as "body narratives," these revival evangelicals performed a script that wove learned responses with extemporaneous actions, embodying sacred history through the enactment of biblical story.

Framing their experience as slaves within typological patterns, African Americans simultaneously historicized and dehistoricized American slavery. Not unlike the providential narratives revealed by Calvinists like Thomas Shepard, the typology that African American evangelicals enacted helped them envision how their experience transcended history. In so doing, they transformed themselves by reframing, within a narrative of salvation, conventional proslavery readings of biblical narratives that depicted African Americans as a spiritually debased and culturally degraded people. Reinterpreting the ascribed typologies that justified slavery through viewing Africans as progeny of the cursed Cain and Noah's son Ham—both of whom God allegedly "marked" with dark skin—black evangelicals transfigured their past by altering the providential meaning of their destiny. This typological rereading also transmogrified the conventional white Southern view. Figuring slaves as the Israelites in captivity, African American evangelicals transformed their status from spiritual outcasts to chosen people, a shift that represented Southerners as imperious Egyptians on the brink of ruin. More importantly, this typological reading generated new meaning for a history of otherwise inexplicable pain and sorrow, transforming slavery from a senseless atrocity—explained as a historically and geographically localized social phenomenon produced by particular colonial/imperial agrarian economic conditions—into a powerful eschatology with a rich web of sacred meaning and spiritual value. In this altered typology, African Americans could reinterpret their suffering as a Christian sacrifice in a historical struggle whose real significance lay not in this world, but in eternity.

The body narrative is homiletic in that it offers a pattern for emulation by enacting black history as sacred text. Only when performed with the appropriate spiritual orientation could biblical typology work a kind of *remedia* to transform African American history. As with the Sins' conversion in the medieval Paternoster plays (personified vices were often converted by the virtues they sought to corrupt), the new eschatology is triggered in the material world through an act of faith. Like medieval morality plays or the more modern Protestant drama of the Lord's Passion, performed first in 1633, the body narratives provided frames within which participants could organize their experience and shape their future responses.[92]

Such folk practices offer a caution against too narrowly construing the reading epistemologies of nineteenth-century religious communities or underestimating the interactive hermeneutic from which homiletic narrative continually emerged. When, for example, a careful historian like Nathan Hatch writes that "black evangelist Harry Hosier gave riveting vernacular dramatizations of the Bible" as evidence of the prevailing historical conclusion that nineteenth-century "popular preachers had little else to fall back on if their presence and charisma were unconvincing," he fails to credit the collaboration of popular audiences whose participation from a historical distance might too easily be attributed to the preacher's presence and charisma.[93] These audiences, in fact, were predisposed through their training in the allegorical structure of biblical typology to understand their lives in accordance with sacred patterns whose ends revealed their place in a predetermined eschatology.[94] To privilege the written record and the accepted active-speaker/passive-audience binary is to risk masking the racial and class diversity of alternative hermeneutic traditions that fostered and, in turn, were fostered by homiletic narrative.

Homiletic Fiction and the Novelization of Progress

As a critical structuring device of the nineteenth-century novel, the pilgrimage masterplot functions not only as a literary archetype but also as a pervasive social practice that saturated American oral and discursive culture. This archetypal masterplot can be traced across a diverse body of nineteenth-century American literature, from texts like the African American Methodist memoirs to the genteel classic of American children's fiction, Louisa May Alcott's *Little Women*. Critics of *Little Women* have long recognized its embedded pilgrimage structure derived from *Pilgrim's Progress,* but have tended to dismiss it as quaint or largely incidental to the novel's major purposes.[95] Yet reading *Little Women* within the larger tradition of allegorical pilgrimage masterplots offers an alternative view of the history and social function of the American novel.

While the pilgrimage narrative unified American Protestants and served as the basis for many homiletic practices, its application varied depending on particular interpretive communities and generic adaptations, a range reflected in Alcott's and Elaw's common grounding in *Pilgrim's Progress. Little Women* represents the initial stages of the novelization of homiletic narrative, but it also exemplifies a different branch of the holiness movement than the one in which Elaw and Lee were so deeply involved. The interdenominational holiness movement sought to make all time sacred, deemphasizing the traditional focus on the Sabbath as the sole day of intensive prayer, devotional reflection, and scriptural study. The movement stressed the emergence of a second stage in the conversion process known as sanctification, which Wesley, against the protests of Jonathan Edwards, emphasized as a spiritual state above the recursive sin-expiation-redemption cycles that marked evangelical life. As opposed to the conventional regeneration in which humanity remained burdened by original sin, sanctified individuals transcended their carnal corruption, a renewal marked by the desire to focus every hour of every day on God. These evangelical perfectionists were consumed by the idea of a constant communion with Christ, which they read into works like Edwards's *The Life of David Brainerd,* and Wesley's and

Whitefield's serialized journals. By the 1840s, many evangelical denominations boasted large numbers that embraced the doctrine. To the cha-
grin of conservative Congregationalists and Presbyterians, long losing
ground to popular religion, Charles Finney's Oberlin Seminary in Ohio
became an unofficial seat of the antebellum holiness movement, building a pietistic fervency coterminous with his congregants' experiences at
New York City's Chatham Street Chapel. After the Civil War, the movement continued to flourish, especially among the poor, as a calling to
spiritualize all aspects of social life. But a large middle-class population
also responded to the possibilities it offered for unifying the experiences
of interdenominational groups increasingly divided in the work place,
neighborhoods, and homes by postindustrial specialization that, in urban centers, further compartmentalized individuals and social groups
along demographic lines. In the increasingly unwieldy social makeup
coming to define the urban middle class, the normative Victorian attitudes governing Christian propriety, morality, and duty had absorbed
the visible emotionalism that marked holiness worship among the rural
and poor, transforming holiness fervor into an energized yet genteel piety that suffused ordinary life, raising the bar of middle-class moral conduct and social stewardship and integrating and spiritualizing such civic
values as benevolence, social intervention, and self-improvement into everyday routines.

The ministry of John H. Vincent, a Methodist minister and prolific
author on Christian education, offers but one example of how this new
popular theology flowed upward from the enthusiasm of camp revivals
into more refined and "respectable" postbellum Christian society. Vincent's interdenominational Chautauqua Association, cofounded with
Lewis Miller in 1873 as a motivational institute to train Sunday school
teachers, brought the primitive piety of revival evangelicals to emotionally temperate, denominationally identified audiences looking to infuse
youth programs with the immersion experience of camp meetings. Increasingly, after instituting its famed speakers circuit that showcased
the likes of Henry Ward Beecher, Jacob Riis, Jane Addams, Washington Gladden, and John Dewey, Chautauqua appealed to a broad cross-
section of middle-class audiences eager to embrace new methods for integrating education with uplifting spiritual entertainment. "Every day,"
Vincent mused, "should be sacred. . . . There should be no break between Sabbaths. The cable of divine motion should stretch through
seven days, touching with its sanctifying power every hour of every day.

Kitchen work, farm work, shop work, as well as school work, are divine."
Vincent articulated for many a sentiment that conformed to the pervasive interdenominational belief that a gentle savior was everywhere present, watching, guiding, and guarding. As he put it, "Things secular are
under God's governance, and are full of divine meanings."[96]

The focus in Christian fiction on the mundane duties of the young
was a measure of the holiness movement's impact on children's activities, recreation, and everyday decisions. Such focus also helped elide the
postbellum divergence between middle-class children's lives and those
of their working-class counterparts. The imputed duty of middle-class
children to develop moral character occasioned a language of labor, suffering, and sacrifice that shadowed reform narratives about the lives of
laboring-class children toiling in urban sweatshops for subsistence
wages. The pilgrimage template did double duty: first, it transformed the
material tropes of poverty, labor, and suffering into spiritual markers,
making the poor's affinity with the impoverished Christ and his lowly
disciples available to the socially privileged; and second, it represented
for the middle class the commensurability of their eternal fates with the
spiritual dangers imperiling lower-class children. Often cited in this context, the parable of Dives (Luke 16:19–31)—the rich man thirsting in per-
dition for his failure of charity when living—illustrated the steep spiritual price of wealth and leisure. Whereas poverty purportedly focused
the indigent on eternal riches—whether or not deprivation shortened
their lives—wealth could seduce middle-class children by drawing their
gaze from celestial rewards to earthly treasures. The proper exercise of
volition thus became key to pilgrims' daily progress, for if they made
the wrong choices, the ensuing day's trials would be so much the harder,
while keeping to the right path brought immediate rewards. Interactive
hermeneutic templates and pilgrimage typologies helped readers navigate the minefield of moral decisions, as they had taught earlier generations of readers to make sense of their daily sufferings through hagiographic identification.

Within this homiletic context and despite its having been boycot-
ted by some Sunday school libraries for its liberal Christian values, *Little Women*, long characterized as a secular story with moral implications, did more than convey Christian principles.[97] It was a template for
reader identification and imitation, and a lesson in the kinds of interpretive practices—applied at once to the literary text and to the text of
one's life—that we have seen throughout this chapter. If *The Pilgrim's*

Progress was the apotheosis of medieval pilgrimage allegory, as Barbara
Johnson has noted, and an originating source of the English novel, as
Michael McKeon and Leopold Damrosch have demonstrated, I would
argue that *Little Women* was to the late nineteenth century what *The
Pilgrim's Progress* was to the late seventeenth: a bridge text in the transition between homiletic heuristic paradigms and popular literary forms
for lay audiences whose tastes influenced the novelization, and, to an extent, the secularization, of homiletic literature.[98]

*   *   *

Between the late seventeenth century and the time Alcott wrote *Little Women,* homiletic practices among evangelical denominations had
proved remarkably adaptive. Faced with the encroachment of secular
culture—particularly the allure of popular entertainment for the young—
nineteenth-century ministers sought new ways to adapt the Christian
message and traditional pedagogy to new, popular narrative forms. In
this way, homiletic practice not only harnessed the authority of popular
culture, but also enjoyed the technologies that met the market demands
for particular kinds of literature. In the antebellum period, the novel finally overtook the sermon and religious tract to become the most popular genre in the United States as it had been for nearly a century before
in Great Britain. Christian education wasted little time pressing this literary form into the service of moral regulation. The novelization of the
sermon was a gradual process, emerging with the new modes of realism
in works by Mason Locke Weems and George Lippard, and later under
the rubric of Sunday-school fiction epitomized by Susan Warner's *The
Wide, Wide World* (1851; which the March sisters in *Little Women* read
to learn of *another* young girl guided by *Pilgrim's Progress*[99]). After the
Civil War, the homiletic novel emerged fully formed, and, as we will see
in the next chapter, its popularity breathed new life into traditional evangelical education and culture. *Little Women* marks a pivotal moment in
this narrative transformation.

   Published in October 1868 as a complete novel, what is now part I of
Little Women follows the lives of the four March sisters, whose father
has recently left to serve as a chaplain in the Union army, and concludes
with the family's Christmas reunion one year later when Reverend
March returns. Written in the ensuing year, the sequel, *Good Wives*—
published in April 1869 and now integrated as part II under the original

title—takes readers through three of the sisters' courtships and subsequent marriages and follows the illness and death of the fourth. Building on the popularity of what would become part I of *Little Women,* which is largely organized around allegorical frames and little attuned to temporal order, the sequel is plot driven, intricately keyed to narrative time, though Bunyan's allegorical structure persists. The scores of fan letters Alcott received, many offering direction for a sequel, are an ample index of the market demands that motivated Alcott to extend the original story.[100] Apart from economic considerations, these letters—an innovation in authorial celebrity—attest to the intensity of readerly identification with Alcott's fictional heroines, whose moral struggles and attempts to strengthen their faith resonated with readers in an age in which war, technological and scientific advances, immigration, and urbanization challenged traditional Christian values, rendering the first-century biblical parables increasingly remote and unreceptive to modern spiritual identification.

Unlike its sequel, part I drew on the childhood experiences of Alcott and her sisters and on practices emerging from the pedagogical theories of their father, Amos Bronson Alcott. Defending *Little Women* against the broad brush of sentimentalism that tarred the works of nineteenth-century women writers, Alcott insisted that it was "not a bit sensational, but simple and true, for we really lived most of it."[101] Although Bronson Alcott eventually broke with Congregationalism for Swedenborgian mysticism and transcendentalism, his daughters' childhood, like New England generations before them, was immersed in more traditional Protestantism.[102] Drawn from the Alcott sisters' childhood training in these homiletic practices—such as the many performances they enacted of *Pilgrim's Progress* for their approving father, who as a child had also performed Bunyan's allegory—part I reveals how devotional and hermeneutic exercises were integrated into fiction.[103] More specifically, it demonstrates how such pedagogy incorporated the novel in order to absorb its cultural authority and exploit its epistemological flexibility, even while supplanting its secular outlook with spiritual ends.[104]

From the first chapter, "Playing Pilgrims," *Pilgrim's Progress* structures the narrative, and though few readers today are sufficiently familiar with Bunyan's allegory to track the connections, we can be certain that Alcott could assume her readers' intimate familiarity with that text. The novel opens on Christmas Eve, 1861, with Mrs. March reading a letter from Reverend March to their daughters. In the course of the letter,

when he rallies his daughters "to do their duty faithfully, fight their bosom enemies bravely, and conquer themselves" (*Little Women* 8), he does
so in the language of Bunyan's allegory, emphasizing (as does Alcott's
choice of the family's surname) the broad evangelical view that the road
to salvation is a lifelong struggle, an embattled march toward the Celestial City. His exhortation produces remorse: each daughter confesses to
having done little to resist her "bosom enemy." Twelve-year-old Amy,
the youngest, remonstrates, "I *am* a selfish pig," her verbal emphasis indicating that she echoes a familiar judgment. The eldest, sixteen-year-
old Meg, reproaches herself for her vanity and "aristocratic" affectations
(26). The second sister, fourteen-year-old Jo—Alcott's professed alter
ego and the story's emotional center, with whom many readers identify—
confesses her terrible temper; once angry, she is implacable in her resentment.[105] Finally, the confession turns to thirteen-year-old Beth, the
third child in the family lineup. Her self-assessment occasions a debate
among her sisters, who are disinclined to believe her capable of a persistent moral weakness. Beth's insistence that her particular burden is envy
is undermined by the earnestness and childish innocence with which she
identifies what she envies most: "girls with nice pianos" (10). Her angelic
disposition and chronic illness reveal a nineteenth-century reality that
furnished a popular literary trope. Beth's pilgrimage, unlike those her
sisters undertake, is not destined to be long.

Like any program of reform, the sisters' self-improvement requires a
narrative frame that will enable them to conceptualize the abstractions
of moral failings; they must particularize individual faults into concrete
"burdens," the tangible "bundles" Bunyan's wayfaring Christian bears
on his back at the outset of his redemptive journey. Sensing her daughters' struggles to grasp the task of moral improvement, Marmee offers
them a familiar heuristic by which they might both concretize their failings and track their spiritual growth: "Do you remember," she asks, "how
you used to play *Pilgrim's Progress* when you were little things? Nothing delighted you more than to . . . tie my piece-bags on your backs for
burdens . . . and let you travel through the house from the cellar, which
was the City of Destruction, up, up, to the house-top, where you had all
the lovely things you could collect to make a Celestial City." Embodying young readers' naiveté about spiritual enactment and readerly identification in Christian homiletic practice, Amy concedes, "If I wasn't too
old for such things, I'd rather like to play it over again" (*Little Women*
9). Her declaration reflects a modern sense of age-appropriate role play-

ing in an increasingly secular world in which the ascendancy of an empirical epistemology had sharpened the ontological distinctions between
the material and the numinous and between the literal and the allegorical. Yet Marmee, whose role as moral counselor to her daughters extends to readers who identify with them, reproves Amy—and thus the
reader—explaining that the experiential key to homiletic reading depends on the ability to see the spiritual implications beneath the material:
"We never are too old for this . . . because it is a play we are playing all
the time in one way or another. Our burdens are here, our road is before
us, and the longing for goodness and happiness is the guide that leads us
through our troubles and mistakes to the peace which is a true Celestial
City" (10).

The sisters recall the childhood pleasure of playacting Christian's pilgrimage, little aware at the time that it predisposed them to see their
lives as a path advancing, literally, from birth to death and, allegorically, from eternal death to eternal life through redemption and good
works. In the course of the story, Jo recollects the satisfaction of "fighting Apollyon" (Christian's fiendish antagonist) and the subsequent suffering of having passed "through the Valley where the hobgoblins were."
Remembering the moment when "the bundles fell off and tumbled down
the stairs" (*Little Women* 10), Meg feels the moral satisfaction her struggle and its success had occasioned. What each recalls foreshadows what
lies ahead, as though her childish soul had cleaved to the lesson that answered its own moral weakness. Each recollection becomes a prescient
signpost along the spiritual path. Jo encounters her own wrath as Apollyon, nearly plunging her family into sorrow. After years of struggle,
Meg overcomes her desire for fashion, invitations to elite social events,
and the approval of wealthier peers, figured in the narrative as her "Vanity Fair"—the festive encampment that lures Bunyan's protagonist from
his spiritual course. Realizing the emptiness of flattering friends and social balls at which wealth and prestige measure merit, Meg marries not
one of her rich, though spiritually wanting, suitors, but a man of modest
means whose sacrifices for the March family and the nation in war have
earned him the pet name Greatheart (167), bestowed by the March sisters in honor of Bunyan's heroic Christian warrior in book II of *Pilgrim's
Progress*. Poignantly, Beth's memory of the Celestial City, "where," she
says, "our flowers and arbors and pretty things were, and all stood and
sung for joy up there in the sunshine" (9), presages her proximity to
death, as does her longing to see heaven. Echoing a sentiment popular-

ized by the short-lived Brainerd—who "felt the part of a *pilgrim* on earth
[and] longed much to leave this gloomy mansion" (*Life* 113)—Beth laments, "It is so long to wait, so hard to do; I want to fly away at once, as
those swallows fly, and go in at the splendid gate" (*Little Women* 141).[106]
To enter that city, she must forgo her worldly idealism and resign herself
to a "solitary struggle" against the imperfections of the temporal world;
she must learn "to say good-by to health, love, and life" and in doing so,
to "take up her cross cheerfully" (*Little Women* 373). Finally, too young
to recall her pilgrim role, Amy comes away with the most enduring homiletic lesson: a concrete idea of the abstractions of eternal reward and
punishment as the eschatological end of earthly pilgrimages. She recalls
the City of Destruction as the "cellar and dark entry" and the Celestial
City in the material form of cake and milk "at the top" (9).

The sisters' morality play demonstrates how homiletic literature pre-
pares the inexperienced for the real stakes of spiritual struggle by providing an enduring frame—viable, as Marmee reveals, even in adulthood—
by which to organize the messy business of living into a teleology that
keyed personal agency to crucial moments in the unfolding destiny
which that teleology engendered. As with biblical typology, such homiletic templates helped trace causality between the temporal and eternal,
and the personal and the universal, charting moral and spiritual maturation across time. In this context, Marmee reminds Jo in a lesson emphasizing Christianity as a lifelong struggle, "the troubles and temptations
of your life are beginning, and may be many" (*Little Women* 81).[107] Re-
prising her daughters' identification with the Christian narrative tradition by encouraging them to insert themselves into the frame of a homiletic template, she urges, "Now my little pilgrims, suppose you begin
again, not in play, but in earnest." Meg coaxes her sisters to embrace the
plan: "It is only another name for trying to be good," she explains the
heuristic's purpose to her sisters, "and the story may help us." Determined to transform their lives, they turn to Bunyan's allegory as a model
and structure for daily conduct. "We ought to have our roll of directions,
like Christian," Jo reminds her sisters. In response, Marmee instructs
them to "look under your pillows, Christmas morning, and you will find
your guide-book" (10). Thus Alcott's novel models one way heuristics
trained readers in inserting themselves within allegorical frames, to personalize contexts, responding to the interactive template beneath and
within novelistic representations, and, conversely, to furnish traditional
allegories with vivid, temporally specific realism.

Elaine Showalter has argued, rightly I think, that the "beautiful old story of the best life ever lived" that each daughter finds under her pillow on Christmas is a copy of *Pilgrim's Progress,* not the New Testament, as many critics have assumed.[108] Whichever text it may be, Alcott figures it according to Bunyan's model: it is, as Jo later asserts, "a true guide-book for any pilgrim going on a long journey" (*Little Women* 12). Meg then outlines the plan for their personal reformations: "Mother wants us to read . . . and mind these books, and we must begin at once. We used to be faithful about it. . . . I shall keep my book on the table here, and read a little every morning as soon as I wake, for I know it will do me good, and help me through the day" (13). Replicating the intensive reading mode that John Wesley ascribed to Thomas à Kempis's *The Christian's Pattern,* the sisters study their little books as a daily devotional exercise much like a modern-day book of the hours.[109] As seventeenth-century readers used contemplative almanacs and devotional works like *The Practise of Pietie* and *The New England Primer,* the sisters superimpose the imaginative landscape of *Pilgrim's Progress* onto the moral and spiritual topography of their lives. Drawing analogies between Christian's experiences and their own lives—much as missionaries in an earlier generation had with the life of Brainerd, who confessed to have patterned his own on that of Paul—each sister asserts a typological identification with Christian, who in turn sought to model himself on Christ, the archetype. Homiletic novels thus taught that living as Christian, in a modern *imitatio Christi,* means rendering oneself allegorically in an ongoing process of self-textualization.

Narrative Incrementalism

The allegorical narrative takes hold as each sister begins to pace her development within its discursive frame. Weeks after Jo resolves to face her Apollyon, after her resentment leads to Amy's near-fatal skating accident, her mother writes to her: "You say nothing about your trials, failures, or successes, and think, perhaps, that no one sees them but the Friend whose help you daily ask, if I may trust the well-worn cover of your guide-book. I, *too,* have seen them all, and heartily believe in the sincerity of your resolution, since it begins to bear fruit" (*Little Women* 120). Much like Rowlandson's progressive "removes," or John Bunyan's *The Life and Death of Mr. Badman* (1680)—in which he writes, "Here

therefore, courteous Reader, I present thee with the Life and Death of
Mr. *Badman* . . . that thou mayest, as in a Glass, behold with thine own
eyes, the steps that take hold of Hell"[110]—the pilgrimage frame allows
each sister to measure moral improvement or relapse as a journey incrementally unfolding, as steps to or from salvation. Implicit in this progress is the gradual change that will fit these pilgrims for the Celestial
City; explicit in the progress is the allegorical frame that allows readers
to conceptualize the abstraction of personal growth in relation to incre-
mentalized narrative. In his sermon "The True Christian's Life a Journey," excerpted as an epigraph to this chapter, Jonathan Edwards illustrates how this incrementalism links progress with spiritual growth or
decline:

> Some men spend their whole lives . . . in going down the broad way to destruc-
> tion. They don't only draw nearer to hell in time, but they every day grow
> more and more ripe for destruction; they are more assimilated to the inhab-
> itants of the infernal world. While others press forward in the straight and
> narrow way to life, towards Zion, and laboriously travel up the hill against
> the inclination and tendency of flesh, these run with a swift career down to-
> wards the valley of eternal death, towards the lake of fire, towards the bot-
> tomless pit.[111]

Marked by phrases that inflect spiritual maturation with time and
struggle—"draw nearer . . . in time," "every day grow more and more,"
"more assimilated," "press forward," "laboriously travel," and "against
inclination and tendency"—the pilgrimage template injects the morphology of Puritan incrementalism into the homiletic novel and, in turn, that
incrementalism intensifies the genre's implicit narrative of progress. As a
broad feature of the novel genre, the formal realism—the novel's replication of homogeneous time and space and the specificity of character development (tuned to themes of spiritual growth and salvific progress)—
further naturalizes incrementalism as an evidentiary marker of salvific
progress, heightening the homiletic novel's realism and thus its capacity
for readerly identification.

The structure of *Little Women* comes from an older heuristic tradition
that by the early nineteenth century was morphing into novelized homiletics. Scores of allegorical guidebooks led spiritual novices in transforming their own lives according to familiar typological patterns. In

his widely read "looking-glass" tales, for example, Mason Locke Weems parsed the sins of alcoholism, gambling, dueling, adultery, and murder into stages of spiritual declension, showing how vice escalates from minor infractions to cardinal sins, destroying individuals' moral resolution in incremental, thus recognizable, stages.[112] As the secular novel superceded the sermon in the early antebellum, religious educators like Weems began novelizing homiletic pedagogy, initiating new forms of realism meant vividly to replicate experience in an attempt to exercise the volition of the young while feeding their appetites for newly popular literary forms.

A notable example of a transitional tract in the novelization of Christian allegory is John Warner Barber's 1834 foldout, entitled "Bunyan's Pilgrim's Progress, from This World to That Which Is to Come: Exhibited in a Metamorphosis, or a Transformation of Pictures." Barber made a career of creating homiletic materials, including tracts updating Bible stories to make them relevant to the young. A gifted engraver and exhorter, his primary goal was "to preach the Gospel by means of pictures," training audiences in Jacob Abbott's mode of viewing, which, as we will see in chapter 4, was part of the visual tradition that would inspire Social Gospel advocates to integrate photography into conventional homiletic forms in an effort to train and motivate would-be reformers to charitable intervention. Barber's woodcuts of biblical scenes and emblem books, like similar works such as John Vincent's *Curiosities of the Bible* (1887), updated Puritan homiletic aids such as *The New England Primer,* and almanacs of spiritual meditation such as Patrick Ker's *The Map of Man's Misery: The Poor Man's Pocket-Book,* made homiletic manuals newly relevant to generations psychologically removed from the Calvinist focus on eternal suffering. Barber's work culminated in the best-selling *The Bible Looking Glass,* which sold two hundred thousand copies in the United States before and after the Civil War. His popular homiletic manuals, some coauthored with Reverend William Holmes, included *The Dance of Death* (1846), *The Book of Similitudes* (1860), *Religious Allegories* (1866), *Religious Emblems* (1866), and *The Picture Preacher* (1880). Many of his tableau engravings were allegorical images accompanied by explanatory narrative. As titles containing keywords like "similitude," "allegories," "emblems," and "looking glass" suggest, his works encouraged readers to see the world around them reflexively, in a double register, at once literal and allegorical, revealing

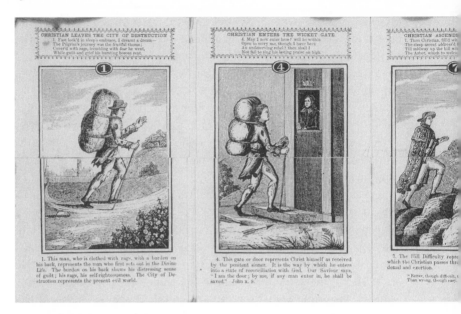

FIGURE 1. John Warner Barber, "Bunyan's Pilgrim's Progress, from This World to That Which Is to Come: Exhibited in a Metamorphosis, or a Transformation of Pictures,"1832. Barber's emblem book facilitates homiletic practice through a series of images that renders Christian allegory immediately accessible to young readers, who could then apply Bunyan's typology to everyday life.

in material forms, as through a glass darkly, faint reflections of eternal reality.

Barber's pocket edition of *Pilgrim's Progress* digests Bunyan's plot. The "slow chewing" that medieval devotional manuals demanded of readers was increasingly performed by homiletic texts for young readers unevenly trained in traditional hermeneutic reading practices. The tract opens accordion fashion into five folds, each revealing a key scene in Christian's journey. Each fold opens up in turn from the center with a top and bottom flap, which, when lifted, reveal new tableaux beneath (fig. 1). The image beneath the flap merges with the bottom half of one of the corresponding five folds to create a new tableau. In all, the tract depicts fifteen tableaux, from Christian's burden-laden departure through the Wicket Gate, to his crossing the River Jordan to enter the Celestial City (fig. 2). Each tableau incrementally interprets the allegory. In the first, for example, the caption beneath the image of Christian setting

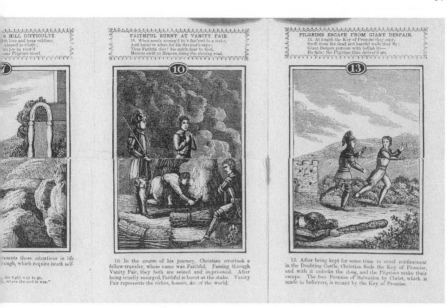

FAITHFUL BURNT AT VANITY FAIR.
10. When sorely scourg'd he's fast'ned to a stake,
And burnt to ashes for his Saviour's sake;
Thus Faithful dies! his spirit dear to God,
Mounts swift to Heaven along the shining road.

10. In the course of his journey, Christian overtook a fellow-traveler, whose name was Faithful. Passing through Vanity Fair, they both are seized and imprisoned. After being cruelly scourged, Faithful is burnt at the stake. Vanity Fair represents the riches, honors, &c. of the world.

PILGRIMS ESCAPE FROM GIANT DESPAIR.
13. At length the Key of Promise they espy,
Swift from the dead and hateful walls they fly;
Giant Despair pursues with hellish ire—
He falls: the Pilgrims then deliver'd are.

13. After being kept for some time in cruel confinement in the Doubting Castle, Christian finds the Key of Promise, and with it unlocks the door, and the Pilgrims make their escape. The free Promise of Salvation by Christ, which is made to believers, is meant by the Key of Promise.

forth informs the reader that the "burden on his back shows his distressing sense of guilt; his rags, his self-righteousness. The City of Destruction represents the present evil world." In the second vignette, beneath the picture of Christian bogged down in a roadside swamp, the caption reads, "But, as he hurries along, with more eagerness than caution, he runs into a miry Slough, called the Slough of Despond. The Slough represents those discouraging and desponding fears which often harass new converts."

Barber's schematic offered a template that illustrated the correlations between the events of readers' lives and the stations along the pilgrim's progress, helping readers extract a rudimentary structure from the older allegory in a cultural context that made identification with personified virtues and vices increasingly difficult.[113] Visual signposts demonstrated how particular and universal struggles corresponded, confirming for readers that they were on the path, as Alcott's epigraph in *Little Women* declares, "which saintly feet had trod." Using Barber's heuristic as an evocative mode of realism, they could see, with the clarity of snapshots, how their own spiritual development occurred through, and thus concurred with, as Barber's subtitle suggests, a "transformation of pictures."

3. After Christian sets out upon his journey, his two neighbors, Obstinate and Pliable, attempt to fetch him back by force; but not succeeding, he prevailed upon Pliable to accompany him, by representing to him the glories of the Celestial City, to which he is going. He proceeds with him till they both fall into the Slough of Despond. This unwelcome accident so discouraged Pliable, that he determines to go no farther; and accordingly gets out of the Slough, and returns to his own house.

6. When the Believer in a Divine light views the Redeemer's Cross, and discerns clearly the motive and efficacy of his extreme sufferings, the perfect freeness and sufficiency of this blessed way of salvation, he is relieved from his sorrow, the burden of his guilt is removed, and he embraces his crucified Saviour with faith and love. While he was here at the cross, three shining ones suddenly presented themselves before him with a beautiful garment, which signifies the righteousness of Christ, set a mark on his forehead, and gave him a roll, which denotes assurance of salvation.

9. After descending H enters the Valley of Hur proceeded far, before a the way, and disputed desperate struggle Chris pressed so hard upon despair of life; but at him a deadly thrust wit and gains the victory. severe trials and temptat children of God experi enemy of souls.

PLIABLE TURNS BACK.
3. Pliable floundering forced his passage through,
Regain'd the ground, and home again he flew;
But Christian struggled on without his mate,
And reach'd the side towards the Wicket Gate.

CHRISTIAN'S BURDEN FALLS AT THE CROSS.
6. No sooner had he spoke, than, strange to tell,
That moment from his back his burden fell;
Believ'd at once from all his guilt and pain,
He wept for joy, then gaz'd and wept again.

CHRISTIAN FIG
9. When, welcome spe
Christian must fight as
The valiant man by fa
Doth make him, thoug

CHRISTIAN IN THE SLOUGH OF DESPOND.
2. While thus with heedless steps he onward went,
In deep thought of his journey was intent,
At once he fell: all little did he think
So soon in miry clay and mud to sink.

CHRISTIAN IS SHOWN A PORTRAIT.
5. First view that picture hung against a wall,
That man a minister of Christ we call;
Grave are his looks, to Heaven he lifts his eyes,
Studies the best of books to make him wise.

CHRISTIAN ENTERS TH
8. The palace Beautiful w
Fse fellowship with Pil

2. After Christian had begun his journey to the New Jerusalem, his friends and neighbors endeavored to prevent his going; some mocked, others threatened, and some cried after him to return; but he is determined to proceed, being convinced, though fear is before, yet certain destruction awaits him if he abides in the city. But, as he hurries along, with more eagerness than caution, he runs into a miry Slough, called the Slough of Despond. This Slough represents those discouraging and desponding fears which often harass new converts.

5. Christian being admitted at the Wicket Gate, continues his journey till he arrives at the house of the Interpreter, who shows him a picture of a grave person with a book in his hand, the law of Truth written on his lips, the world behind his back, and a dazzling crown of gold over his head. This Portrait represents the true minister of Christ. Christian is requested by the Interpreter to take particular notice of this piece of painting, because the person it represents is the only person who is authorized to be his guide in any difficult or dangerous situation.

8. The Palace Beauti sent the privileges of C the ordinances of the admitted by the Porter, ful, and is introduced House, Piety, Prudence come him with joy. in the most agreeable m the Armory and armed fare, with the Sword of of Salvation, the Shield shod with the prepara Peace. (See Eph. vi. 1

FIGURE 2. John Warner Barber, "Bunyan's Pilgrim's Progress, from This World to That Which Is to Come: Exhibited in a Metamorphosis, or a Transformation of Pictures." The act of reading performs revelation, as the progress of images requires the reader to move between visible images and those hidden beneath the flaps.

Hill Difficulty, Christian
miliation. He had not
foul fiend met him in
his passage. After a
stian falls, and Apollyon
him that he began to
length Christian gives
h his two-edged sword,
This fight denotes those
tions which some of the
ience from Satan, the

12. The Pilgrims at length find a little shelter, in which they conclude to wait the approach of morning, but being weary and over come by fatigue, soon fall asleep. Here they remained till awakened by the voice of the formidable giant Despair, who with a fierce and malignant countenance drove them to the Doubting Castle, and there confined them in a dark and filthy dungeon. This may represent the case of those Christians who have wandered into forbidden paths, till they have sinned in such a manner, that they begin to despair and doubt of the mercy of God.

15. The Pilgrims in their passage through the river of Death, leave their mortal garments in the river: they are immediately clothed with immortality, and conducted by two ministering spirits into the New Jerusalem, the Paradise of God. As they enter the heavenly City they are transfigured and clothed with raiment shining like gold. Here they are welcomed by their dear Saviour and all the heavenly host with joy; here they are to dwell in the most perfect happiness for ever and ever. May we all be received in like manner into the kingdom of God.

TS APOLLYON.
ich can hardly be,
angel: but you see,
anding sword and shield,
s a dragon quit the field.

THE PILGRIMS TAKEN BY GIANT DESPAIR.
12. What could they do? to whom could they complain?
Resistance to a Giant was in vain.
Straight to the castle-yard he drove the men,
And lock'd them in a deep and dirty den.

PILGRIMS ENTER THE NEW JERUSALEM.
15. The river past, their heav'nly home is near,
When lo! two bright seraphic forms appear;
To Zion's hill with airy steps they soar,
With rapture fill'd, I wak'd and saw no more.

E BEAUTIFUL PALACE.
tacle! at hand appear'd
usent rear'd;
as justly nam'd,
lgrims greatly fam'd.

THE PILGRIMS IN BY-PATH MEADOWS.
11. Darkness came on, with thunder, lightning, rain,
Torrents pour'd down, the waters rose amain;
The storm terrific filled their souls with dread,
And vengeance seem'd just bursting on their heads.

THE PILGRIMS IN THE RIVER OF DEATH.
14. The river Death, the Pilgrims stand aghast,
At this hard trial, though is the last;
No heavenly crown of life can they expect,
Until they pass this dark and frightful deep.

ful is designed to repre-
Christian communion in
Gospel. Christian is
, whose name is Watch-
to the maidens of the
, and Charity, who wel-
After being entertained
anner, he is taken into
for the Christian war-
' the Spirit, the Helmet
l of Faith, with his feet
tion of the Gospel of
4—18.)

11. After Faithful was burnt, Christian made his escape, accompanied by a fellow pilgrim named Hopeful, who was induced to become a pilgrim by beholding the faith and conversation of Faithful during his trial and execution. The pilgrims proceed on their journey, and after some time find their way grown rough and difficult; for the sake of ease they turn into a forbidden path, which went through by-path meadows. After wandering about for some time, there came on a storm of thunder, lightning, and rain. This represents the believer under the hidings of God's countenance.

14. Death is here represented by a deep river separating the believer from his heavenly inheritance, as the river Jordan separated the children of Israel from the promised land. All that are born must die. However distant we may now think the day of our death, yet in a few years, and perhaps in a few days at most, we must go the way of all the earth, and these bodies of ours, though now so active, will moulder back to dust, and on the morning of the Resurrection will rise to eternal life, or sink in endless woe.

Popular homiletic templates like Barber's envisioned each moral struggle as a setback or victory, a step toward or from a spiritual horizon, in a progress that must be measured over time. This concept is at least in part constitutive of the nineteenth century's focus on incremental learning, on building a reservoir of experience in accordance with Locke's pervasive influence on education.[114] As we saw in the case of Jo and Laurie, incrementalism prevented individuals from becoming overwhelmed by the journey ahead or discouraged by moral relapses, easily perceived as judgments about one's spiritual status. Much as, after 1870, American Sunday schools shifted their focus from conversion to nurture through moral "impressions" that would less catastrophically lead pupils to accept Christian life, homiletic literature helped young readers understand their moral setbacks as part of the constant struggle that develops moral stamina and spiritual fortitude, *edifying* in its original sense.[115]

The March sisters' progress takes this shape. Throughout, the novel exhibits the holiness movement's focus on sanctification and deemphasis of the split between sacred and secular time, highlighting the incrementalism of moral change. Meg and Jo's employment, undertaken to help support their family during the war, for example, realistically illustrates the mundanity of spiritual vigilance and development: "Oh dear," Meg says of her pilgrimage's daily grind, "how hard it does seem to take up our packs and go on" (*Little Women* 34). Even late into the novel, Jo reveals to her mother that when confronted again by the demon she has repeatedly vanquished, "I read my little book, felt better, [and] resolved . . . *my anger*" (170; original emphasis).

Paralleling Bunyan's allegory, the narrative of the girls' journey reconfigures the Christian struggle as a representational portrait of everyday life. For a readership trained in homiletic practice, the novel reproduces a recognizable—if critically overlooked—mode of realism. Never is any aspect of the March sisters' development quick, easy, or complete. Even after their pilgrimages have progressed, and they have individually and collectively learned crucial moral lessons, they, like Bunyan's protagonist, stray from their spiritual paths, as in the chapter titled "Experiments" (then still a Baconian synonym for experience). After months of working to improve themselves, they need their mother, like Christian needs Evangelist, to assist them, by adjuring them to "take up your little burdens again; for though they seem heavy sometimes, they are good for us, and lighten as we learn to carry them" (*Little Women* 117).

Alcott's novel thus models how readers were to transpose the allegorical frame from the narrative to their lives, even as it reveals how the intensive mode of reading naturalizes the process of self-textualization. Even the original novel's calendrical cycle—from Christmas 1861 to Christmas 1862—recapitulates both the standard increment by which we measure secular time and the liturgical calendar that represents history in the repetition of specific sacred events in one-year increments. By offering a collective progress report on their journey, for instance, Beth illustrates how the sisters redact everyday events through the structure of Bunyan's allegorical stages: "I was thinking about our 'Pilgrim's Progress,'" she announces; "how we got out of the Slough and through the Wicket Gate by resolving to be good, and up the steep hill, by trying; and that maybe the house over there, full of splendid things, is going to be *our* Palace Beautiful" (*Little Women* 57; emphasis added). Key to how the universal and local converge in snippets of realism, homiletic incrementalism allows Jo and her pilgrim companion Theodore Laurence ("Laurie") to see their own moral progress as an imagined distance they have spiritually traveled in relation to time, the moral struggle, and the final destination. "I will have to fight and work," Jo says, "and climb and wait, and maybe never get in after all" (141).[116] Fifteen-year-old Laurie similarly assesses the difficulty of redemption as a function of temporal and geographical distance between points: "You'll have me for company. . . . I shall have to do a deal of traveling before I come in sight of your Celestial City." Beth encourages them to pace themselves by focusing not on the distant destination—the telescopic focus that perilously draws Bunyan's protagonist from his immediate path—but on the steady progress of each day: "'If people really want to go'" to heaven, she reassures Laurie, "and really try all their lives, I think they will get in; for I don't believe there are any locks on the door, or any guards at the gate" (142). Bunyan could not have anticipated the extent to which his allegory would advocate salvation through works, or foreseen how far the nineteenth century would go in overturning the Augustinian-Calvinist view of humanity's fallen condition and Augustine's insistence that destination—not the race well run—was the *sine qua non* of the pilgrim's journey. Among middle-class evangelicals after the Civil War, spiritual struggle and self-sacrifice betokened proper piety. Beth's revisionist theology not only prefigures the Social Gospel's focus on works, emphasized in her use of the term *try,* but also on the capacity of human volition and salvation for all who sought it, barely perceptible in what many critics have seen as Bunyan's fledgling Arminianism.[117]

In this context, Marmee, like Beth, also plays a crucial role in her daughters' journey. "We were in the Slough of Despond to-night," Jo declares early in the novel, "and mother came and pulled us out as Help did in the book" (*Little Women* 10). Marmee continues to direct the girls' pilgrimages long after their childhood play has been absorbed and naturalized into the normative Victorian expectations of morality, female propriety, and good character. In her note to Jo after Jo's encounter with Apollyon later in the novel, for example, she confesses to having faced the same demon years before, offering her ultimate triumph then as proof against Jo's failure now (120). Marmee's confession is a lesson in how homiletic cycles regulated spirituality for generations: her role as Help (or Evangelist) to her daughters' respective roles as Christian replicates the way in which Reverend March had once served as Help for her. The text thus models the appropriate mode of its own reading, demonstrating the typological cycle of homiletic narrative. It further underscores this literary reflexivity when Jo reads Warner's best-selling *The Wide, Wide World,* a novel which, nearly twenty years before Alcott's, incorporated *Pilgrim's Progress* as a masterplot. Like the March sisters, the story's young heroine uses the pilgrimage template to direct her own spiritual development. Through these mirroring devices, *Little Women* does for its readers what *Pilgrim's Progress* does for the March sisters; it provides a framework by which to quantify and pace salvific progress.

While each sister has moments of temptation, the novel portrays how small acts and good habits ensure moral stability and self-esteem, secure the good opinion of others, and, ultimately, the success of one's journey. After counseling her daughters to resume their burdens, Marmee reminds them of how incremental growth gradually brings rewards: "Have regular hours to work and play," she advises, checking their zeal to race across an imaginary finish line. "Make each day both useful and pleasant, and prove that you understand the worth of time by employing it well. Then youth will be delightful, old age will bring few regrets, and life become a beautiful success, in spite of poverty" (*Little Women* 118). *Little Women* portrays the sisters' progress as a narrative of gradual development, emphasizing the seemingly inconsequential words and deeds that mold character over time by building moral musculature. Representing moral change over time—particularly through its focus on real-

istic character development—the nineteenth-century novel served homiletic purposes well.[118]

Bifurcated Time

Alcott's novel provides a framework within which readers could understand and chart their own spiritual development, but homiletic fiction
also reminds readers that an essential element of their individual engagement in the universal struggle is their responsibility to reach out to other
pilgrims. In this context, not only does Alcott's novel dramatize the
changes reshaping American evangelicalism in the decades before and
after the war, it accentuates a profound shift in American Protestantism between the seventeenth and twentieth centuries—the emergence,
growth, and maturity of human volition, which arguably achieves its apogee with the rise of the Social Gospel, Christian socialism, and muscular
Christianity in the decades following the publication of *Little Women.*
This shift came so gradually that it is difficult to appreciate apart from
its negation—not absence—in colonial theology. Sacvan Bercovitch has
explored the allegorical character of Puritan hagiography—particularly
Cotton Mather's *Magnalia Christi Americana,* arguing that the Puritan self, from which emerged an American self, was multifaceted.[119] An
important thesis of his study was that early American literature represented the self as moving in and out of time: a concrete, static object one
moment, and a dynamic, evanescent subject the next. The self was a self-
in-progress, remade by degrees as a better Christian, just as God was
making North America the model of Christian piety. That self, like Alcott's little women, was also on a journey, a pilgrimage of sorts. It was, as
we have seen throughout this chapter, also a model, a standard: the self
as exemplar, alongside the self as pilgrim.

Homiletic texts such as *Little Women* cultivate the double vision we
have seen in the works of Shepard, Rowlandson, Wesley, Elaw, and others, allowing audiences to perceive themselves as forever in a transhistorical present, bearing the cross *with* their suffering Savior. Where
there is a double vision there is a double self. In a world of constant religious striving, where synchrony and diachrony woven together constitute
the framework for consciousness, time stands still for the static self and
ticks away the steps for improvement for the self-in-process or the self-
in-making. This conceptualization of personhood, with parallel devel-

opments in German Romanticism, took root in America in a wide range of literature, so that by the time Henry Adams drafted *The Education of Henry Adams,* he wrote with some certainty that "Life was a double thing" and that "he could not but develop a double nature," or as Oliver Wendell Holmes put it in his novel *Elsie Venner* (1861), one became a "double being" or derived a "double consciousness."[120] What homiletic works after Edwards do particularly well is draw a connection between volition and doubleness. Bercovitch's analysis of Mather's theology included little about volition, about *choosing* to be a certain self, for in the Puritan scheme, God directed the will. Even though human agency was creeping into the thought-world of early New Englanders by 1700, the official theological position was that Calvinists surrendered their will to God. In the interim between the first third of the seventeenth century and Alcott's day, decades of evangelical campaigning culminated in the revivalist admonition to choose spiritual rebirth. For homilists like Alcott, pilgrimage is a matter of choice. Each day it is a matter of choice, as the sisters move incrementally toward what they are becoming. The homily in this instance is about choosing each moment to remake the self. Living simultaneously in two moments, they stand inside and outside themselves. In the flowing together of diachrony and synchrony, each one is both a static object and a transhistorical subject. Volition is the pathway between the two.

Readers drew on allegory to invoke a spiritual world, affording those who engaged the narratives a glimpse of their part in God's design. This bifurcated perspective fostered a weak sense of anachronism, demanding that disciples recognize, if not achieve a perspective outside history. It reminded the faithful that they were in but not of this world, imagining the possibility for them to stand at the intersection of the temporal and eternal, simultaneously in secular and sacred time. Much as medieval art patrons had their likenesses inserted into works of sacred events, the faithful understood how the diachronic path of their lives passed through the sacred scenes of Christ's life, and thus imagined how their Savior's blood could flow from the cross not only forward but also back in time. Through this attenuated sense of anachronism, homiletic narratives immersed audiences in contemporary moral and social concerns, declaring that the challenges of their world corresponded with those of the spiritual realm.

Such a mode of reading is visible in the earliest novels. Contrasting the

March family's intense identification with Bunyan's pilgrim, Royall Tyler's novel, *The Algerine Captive,* for example, published in 1797, amidst the swelling rural revivalism preceding the Second Great Awakening, satirizes what he saw as the simple-mindedness of extreme religious devotees. The novel appeared at an important juncture in American literary history, when the didactic medium of allegory was losing ground to secular, novelistic realism. Through his protagonist, Updike Underhill, Tyler mocks the interactive model of homiletic discourse: reading *Pilgrim's Progress,* Underhill takes a penknife to an illustration in the text, gouging the eyes of Apollyon in order "to help Christian beat him."[121] In making Underhill's assault on a book the crux of his joke, Tyler highlights the widespread belief that the action of the faithful in this life had a concurrent impact on the invisible world beyond. Even in what Tyler presents as a ludicrous substitution of a book for a beast, Underhill's motive bespeaks the prevalent religious assumption that the temporal world corresponds with the spiritual. Tyler's depiction of the rural religious reiterates how literally, in his day, such believers understood Christian allegory, not unlike medieval believers' faith in the *remedia* agency of the Paternoster plays or present-day believers' confidence in scripture as a powerful prayer charm against evil.

Tyler's introduction lampooned the homiletic epistemology and worldview of Edwardsian ministers like Timothy Dwight, Joseph Bellamy, and Nathanael Emmons and post-Revolution Methodists who popularized love feasts, "ring shouts," and body narratives. To a reader outside the homiletic tradition, the intensity of readerly identification it encouraged seemed laughable indeed: "They wore themselves out fighting Apollyon," Tyler scoffs, or wearied themselves "trudging up the 'hill of difficulty' or through the 'slough of despond.'"[122] While novels laid out their fictive landscapes in a linear path commensurate with secular readers' perceptions of historical and homogeneous time and space, homiletic narratives cathected religious readers' identification with allegory, a typological script whose action unfolds simultaneously inside and outside historical time. To "read" narratives in this way is to see oneself as a historically grounded subject with transhistorical agency.

Thus Marmee recasts the sisters' spiritual development, not as Jo's misplaced romances of errant knights and distressed damsels, but as a moral struggle on the microlevel symbolic of the struggles concurrently taking place in increasingly larger realms. Battles against wrath, pride, selfishness, greed, and materialism were localized vices causally (and accumulatively) linked to the national conflict produced by the constitutive correspondences between micro and macro (moral and economic). The novel directly links the domestic familial and national not only in the Marches' double connection to the war through both Reverend March and Meg's future husband, but through the old man Marmee meets who has given the lives of all his sons to the salvific cause of nation and Christ. Framed as a spiritual contest patterned on Christ's sacrificial death "to make men holy" (as Julia Ward Howe's 1862 "Battle Hymn of the Republic" put it)—to which, in the *imitatio,* the human correlative was "let us *die* to make men free"—the corrective, like the cause, lay in the correspondence of the temporal and eternal. In a martial trope that collapses the Civil War with her own struggle, Jo redirects her penchant for chivalric romance back to its origin in medieval Christian allegory.[123] When she receives written "commendation" from her mother, she pins "the note inside her frock, as a shield and a reminder, lest she be taken unaware" (*Little Women* 120), a martial motif of Christian allegory (found, for instance, in Spenser's *Fairie Queene,* in which Red Crosse Knight bears the image of Una, the Protestant Church, engraved inside his shield). Like Bunyan's Greatheart, arrayed in the whole armor of God, Jo feels "stronger than ever to meet and subdue her Apollyon," a sentiment that is a moral adumbration of the Civil War's perceived spiritual ends. By strengthening the correlation between the individual's and the nation's battle for moral self-mastery, Marmee teaches her daughters, in degrees of relation, to see the correlation between spheres. When they take up Bunyan's allegory as the "guide-book" that they must "mind" to become pilgrims, they embrace the allegorical nature of a life lived in the simultaneity of temporal and eternal realms (12). The sisters perform in the belief that what one does on earth reverberates in the spiritual world, just as they acknowledge that, while historically localized, the interregional conflict between North and South, like the English Civil War in Bunyan's time, exemplified the recurrence of sacred history, and was even then shaping the spiritual destinies of untold millions and, as one dimension of the eternal psychomachia—epitomized similarly by the millennialist verses of Howe's poem and the *Left Behind: Eternal Forces* video game—weighing in on the great battle waging outside historical time.

Aside from the shift toward volition—predicated on the shift away from predestinarianism—what remains largely constant between Bunyan's and Alcott's times is the allegory's heuristic function within a particular hermeneutic reading practice. For the March sisters, *Pilgrim's Progress* illustrates how identification with Christian's salvific struggle must be perceived in both a personal and a universal register. Each sister must identify with Christian as a radically unique individual before transcending the personal to become an everyman—everywoman—herself.[124] Art historian Barbara Stafford describes the mechanism of this typological act requiring a middle ground between personalization and self-alienation by emphasizing its origin in the Puritans' analogical imagination, with its "double avoidance of self-sameness and total estrangement." Likeness can never be identical nor difference incommensurable; analogy must function within the logic of recognition, which encourages relation across distinction, bridging the perceived difference between ordinary individuals and those deemed particularly sacred, and ultimately between individuals and God.[125] For Alcott's readers, the personal register encourages the inexperienced to tailor their readerly identification to their moral faults, thus choosing the appropriate fictional type. The universal register encourages them to transcend the personal, to see their individual lives within the pilgrimage-template tradition of Christian allegory. Only through such identification can readers, in effect, textualize themselves, becoming, as the sisters do in turn, "heroines" (*Little Women* 164) in their own personal progress.

True to their view of *Pilgrim's Progress* as a "guide-book," the sisters carry it about with them. When Laurie finds them at work and reading Bunyan's allegory, Jo explains to him how their performance draws on their early homiletic training: "Well, you see we used to play 'Pilgrim's Progress,'" she tells him, "and we have been going on with it in earnest all winter and summer" (*Little Women* 140). Incorporating the spiritual into everyday activities, Alcott's pilgrims epitomize the commitment to spiritualizing time that characterized the middle-class transformation of the holiness movement from extremes of pietism to the pious pursuit of secular life. Like Sunday-school children at Chautauqua who were led on "pilgrimages . . . through the Park of Palestine, under the direction of experienced tourists" (*Chautauqua* 55–56), the March sisters learn how to transform local geography into the sacred landscape of pilgrimage. As Vincent encouraged the Chautauqua pilgrims to see "the lay of the land which makes the physical Chautauqua an allegory" of the spiritual or "upper Chautauqua," which "not all who visit the place see . . . and not all who become Chautauquans reach" (*Chautauqua* 50), so the Marches spatialized their faith, seeing their world in a series of double registers (the material and spiritual, temporality and spatiality, incrementalism and sacred historical cycles): "We call this hill Delectable Mountain," Jo tells Laurie, "for we can look far away and see the country where we hope to live sometime" (*Little Women* 141). In the way that Jo's allusion to the country where they hope to live sometime blurs the distinction between a neighboring village and the Celestial City, between this life and the next, or in the way that Mrs. March's directive to the sisters to enact Bunyan's allegory to "see how far you can get before Father comes home" (11) is also a Messianic reference to the second coming, Alcott's novel deliberately elides the distinction between sacred and secular, dramatizing how, among interdenominational evangelicals, the spiritual was coming to suffuse all aspects of life. As Vincent put it, "Away with the heresy that a man is stepping aside from his legitimate work as a Christian minister when he is trying to turn all secular nature into an altar for the glory of God!" (*Chautauqua* 89).

As the young March sisters personalize *Pilgrim's Progress* by inserting themselves into its narrative structure, so Alcott implicitly invites young readers to engage the moral action of *Little Women,* to become participants in a narrativized struggle against anger, selfishness, greed, and fear. By illustrating how the sisters read Bunyan's allegory, *Little Women* negotiates the difference between the universality of allegory and the specificity of novelistic realism. While the characters reflect the uniqueness of individuals, they are also universal (or national) in their facilitation of readerly identification. "There are," for instance, as the text tell us, "many Beths in the world, shy and quiet, sitting in corners till needed, and living for others" (*Little Women* 39). There are also impetuous but well-meaning Jos, spoiled but promising Amys, and envious but self-mastering Megs. Adapted from book II of Bunyan's narrative, Alcott's verse epigraph expresses the wish that reading the novel in the appropriate way might "make" young readers "choose to be / Pilgrims better . . . / for little tripping maids may follow God / Along the ways which saintly feet have trod" (xxii). The novel's heuristic design invites a radical identification with familiar cultural patterns still vestigially operant, though less visible today. This is the key to understanding the extraordinary level of identification with the March sisters that has typified the experience of countless readers, even when, as is true for many secular critics today, they can no longer locate the hermeneutic origin or spiritual implications of that identification.

Homiletic literature's capacity to co-opt new literary forms should caution us against assuming, as critics often have, that Christian allegory, with its explicit epistemology of reading, largely gave way to a modern implicit epistemology exemplified in the rise of the novel. More wish than fact, for example, Royall Tyler's spoof on religious reading practices prematurely celebrated the decline of homiletic allegory among secular, urban audiences, forecasting the market interest in the popular new literary genre by sharpening the contrast between the unfashionable rural penchant for allegory and the novel's urban vogue. The historical irony is that, rather than witnessing the displacement of homiletic allegory, the postbellum period saw the homiletic tradition's incorporation of the novel's form, revivifying the hermeneutic that Tyler mocked as a reading practice surviving only on the cultural margins. We can see this process not only in *Little Women,* but also in scores of homiletic novels in the 1880s and 90s, a phenomenon we will explore further in the next chapter. Similar to what Myra Jehlen refers to as a "zone of contest"—where competing civilizations use resources in distinctive and shared ways—spiritual works themselves became contested sites in which individuals from disparate worldviews, cultures, and doctrines interpreted and framed knowledge differently, even anachronistically.[126]

In fact, the secular novel's roots have frequently been traced back to Protestant texts, such as *Pilgrim's Progress* and Rowlandson's captivity narrative, and similar genres such as the spiritual autobiography or confession narratives. With the recovery of women's fiction and popular fiction in the last decades, scholars have begun to recognize how forcefully Protestant themes and structures dominated the form of much of American fiction. In texts running from William Hill Brown's *The Power of Sympathy* to Warner's *Wide, Wide World,* to Stowe's *Uncle Tom's Cabin,* authors combined the moral sentimentalism of eighteenth-century thought with Protestant themes of moral reformation. In this light, they provide an important counter to our tendency to read the novel as a secular form, even when an implicit Calvinist or evangelical worldview is evident. Similarly, critics often read sentimental culture as secular, or largely emptied of its religious content. While allowing for a religious structuring, however, these sentimental texts do not work primarily as homilies or evince a homiletic structure. Such texts display homiletic elements—exhibit religious themes, narrate spiritual truths and moral

lessons—but they lack the homiletic structure that fosters readerly identification as a script for agency and action in the social world. Rather
than directing readers about how to act in pursuing their own spiritual
pilgrimage—how to conduct their lives within a social realm defined in
empirically realist terms—their morally didactic plots direct readers to
sympathize with characters whose experiences and lives would seem
to lie beyond those of their putative readership. In *Uncle Tom's Cabin*
readers mourn the deaths of the unworldly Little Eva and Uncle Tom; in
Little Women they imagine themselves as Jo, an identification that per-
sonalizes the text, much as, we recall, eighteenth-century sermons personalized the hellish images they invoked. It has become a critical commonplace that the fundamental strategy of much sentimental fiction was
to make the other, the different—whether in terms of race, class, age,
or subjugation—similar enough to evoke their reader's pity or sympathy.
Although such works implicitly and sometimes explicitly call for political or social action, their tendency, unlike homiletic texts, is to endorse
the importance of feeling right above all. For all of Stowe's emphasis on
working to end slavery, for example, her final injunction to her readers in
Uncle Tom's Cabin is to ensure that their sympathies are "in harmony
with the sympathies of Christ."[127] Where the homiletic tradition builds
on the change in heart that takes place in the born-again tradition, by
the late nineteenth century, as we will see in the next chapter, it emphasizes the change in behavior that must follow the change in heart. Stress
is placed on acting in this world. Although, as Jane Tompkins has argued, critics have dismissed Stowe's and Warner's works as sentimental
because they emphasized feeling, the homiletic novel, as embodied in
Little Women, advocates a social realism begun in narrative and completed through the reader's agency outside the text.[128] While Stowe famously concludes in *Uncle Tom's Cabin* that what "every individual can
do" in the cause of social and moral justice is *"feel right,"* the homiletic
novel—in the Edwardsian homiletic tradition in which sense itself produced "immediate evidence" or authentic firsthand knowledge—taught
readers that the only moral response to *feeling* was *doing.*[129] Whereas the
temporal focus of Stowe's novel and Warner's works, as Tompkins points
out, is not of this world, in *Little Women,* while allegorical, the focus is
on temporal reality.

Yet the novel's formal realism—its use of proper names, its action in
homogeneous time, its attention to temporal and characterological spec-

ificity and causality, and its focus on the history of an individual without the dehistoricizing cues that gesture toward transcendent universals—did threaten readers' capacity to identify with allegorical figures. Religious writers like Alcott responded by creating heuristics to train readers to insert themselves within allegorical frames, to personalize contexts, responding to the interactive template beneath and within novelistic representations, and, conversely, to furnish traditional allegories with vivid, temporally specific realism. One place this happened was in Sunday school fiction, precursors to homiletic novels, like Susan Warner's *Wide, Wide World,* which incorporated the pilgrimage template into the fictional narrative. But a broad range of transitional heuristics also trained readers in basic practices of radical Christian identification that they could then apply to novelistic narrative.

The Novelization of Christian Duty

We have seen that Alcott's novel provides a framework within which readers could understand and chart their own spiritual development. But for all its emphasis on personalization and self-reflection, this framework does not invite readers to interpret everything in terms of their own soul's growth. Homiletic fiction reminds readers that an essential element of their individual engagement in the universal struggle is their responsibility to reach out to other pilgrims. In this context, Alcott's novel dramatizes the changes reshaping American evangelicalism in the decades before and after the war.

Nothing marked individuals' new sense of social identity—or fused that identity with a new ethic of salvific intervention—more than the shift away from the radical individualism that had been the focus of eighteenth- and nineteenth-century revival conversions and sanctification, exemplified by such models as Brainerd's and Elaw's Christ-centered pilgrimages. In this sense, Elaw, though just four decades older than Alcott, espoused a faith closer to Bunyan's than to Alcott's—an indication of the diverse ideological ends a particular homiletic template or metanarrative might serve, even in the same historical moment. The individual-focused conversion popularized at the great Cane Ridge revival in 1798 radicalized the born-again emphasis Methodists had placed on the new heart religion. Revivalists depicted conversion as a process in which the "old man fell" away like a dry husk, as the "new man" (Romans 6:1–19) emerged in the awakened sense of God's revulsion toward the unregenerate and Christ's love, glory, and sacrifice.

But in large part due to tragedies of the Civil War, the nation's devotional life transformed this radical individualism into an ethos of social connection. Prayers for nation and for soldiers, for the injured, sick, and dying, deemphasized the self, revivifying the sacrificial core of evangelicalism inflected by the social diffusion of disinterested benevolence. In the enormity of the war's suffering and sacrifice, personal salvation as the individual's primary concern came to seem cold and selfish to evangelicals increasingly invested in social reform. While revivalism's focus on internal change had undermined seventeenth-century Protestantism's emphasis on formal ritual, sacraments, and ordination, the Social Gospel for a time displaced what had heretofore been unassailable: baptism as the salvific trigger by which converts designated the birth of the new man.

Ministers such as Henry Ward Beecher, whose celebrity ultimately eclipsed his father's, stressed the collective, social nature of suffering and sacrifice. In his nationally published sermon "The Sources and Uses of Suffering" (1875), Beecher articulated a sentiment that must have stunned his audience, not least for the logic with which he dramatically altered views of battlefield death: "The sufferers in the great war were not those who bled on the battlefield. The drops that fell on the hearthstone were more and bitterer than those that fell on the field of battle. Not he who haply was a martyr in the cause of his country, but they that lived to mourn, suffered most."[130] Shifting the site of sacrifice from the battlefield to the home, Beecher transformed every American from spectator of tragedy to participant. Illustrating the correspondence of moral action between distinct spheres, he demonstrated the ineffable meaning of Reverend March's observation that "while we wait, we may all work" (*Little Women* 9)—which in the millennialist idiom of the Social Gospel came to mean performing the spiritual work of suffering with others. By suggesting that those who survived the war suffered more than those who died upon its "crimson fields," Beecher turned the individual's gaze back on the self.[131] But on the cusp of the Social Gospel, his emphasis was meant to awaken his following to the grieving around them, inspiring them to reach out to others connected to them through the common bonds of national suffering and sacrifice, to forge from the particular lives of the many a national typology. Such a typology caused no one

to marvel more over the capacity of the religious for sympathetic identification than William James: "Can there in general be a level of emotion so unifying, so obliterative of differences between man and man,"
he mused, "that even enmity may come to be an irrelevant circumstance
and fail to inhibit the friendlier interests aroused?" (*Varieties* 228).

The Civil War provided a fulcrum with which to lift the focus on
earthly suffering that had so suffused antebellum revivalism into
middle-class life, granting suffering a moral respectability that encouraged Christians to embrace hardship and calamity. While lending virtue to the surviving, the value placed on suffering had the advantage of
taking nothing from the dead. The Social Gospel pushed disinterested
benevolence to its logical conclusion, making communal salvation the
essence of individual redemption. At a time when social determinism
advocated a laissez-faire approach to poverty, the Social Gospel's sacrificial ethos countered by infusing reform with an interventionist ethic.

Alcott dramatizes this disinterested benevolence in Beth's sacrifice
for the Hummel family, an example of how Christian reform in humanitarian causes like abolitionism in the 1830s (in which Alcott's mother actively participated) informed the interventionist ethic that drove both the
Social Gospel and Progressive Era reform.[132] Beth's stewardship of the
Hummel children illustrates a trope of homiletic literature. Susan Warner's *The House in Town* (1872), for instance, a precursor to the homiletic
novel, models charitable visits, but the convention had a lengthy tradition in evangelical practice, epitomized in Legh Richmond's widely dis-
tributed tract, *The Dairyman's Daughter* (1809), in which middle-class
readers were treated to a dish of romantic fare intended to reprogram
class attitudes and foster resignation to one's social lot.[133] By the latter
part of the century, such charitable visits worked to different ends, and
merely bearing witness to another's suffering without physically sharing
in it was condemned, as we will see in the final chapter, as what religious
activists called—with frightening scriptural implications—"lukewarm
Christianity" (Revelation 3:15–17).

While in its theological sense disinterested benevolence in the late
eighteenth century had meant sacrificing for another for no salvific benefit to the self, by the mid-nineteenth century, as everyday life was increasingly valued in and of itself, it came to mean willingly embracing
pain for another, a sacrifice notwithstanding its presumed spiritual reward. This sacrificial ethic points up the radical ends to which the Social

Gospel pressed older forms of homiletic identification, the traditional *imitatio Christi*. In the course of her regular visits to tend the needs of the Hummel children, for instance, Beth nurses the dying Hummel infant, who, while cradled in her arms, "gave a little cry and trembled" (*Little Women* 177), and died. Taxed by her exertions to save the child and exposed to a deadly contagion, Beth contracts scarlet fever. While she survives the initial episode, the disease shatters her body's last defenses, and, never physically strong, she becomes vulnerable to other ailments. Her illness and need for constant care essentially reduce Beth to the condition of the Hummel infant she had nursed. Her symbolic transformation into a helpless child exemplifies the ultimate assumption of another's suffering—the radical identification advocated by the Social Gospel through homiletic novels by scores of authors like Charles Sheldon and Harold Bell Wright. In an identification so radical it integrates subject and object into a single suffering body, Beth's absorption of the infant's pain illustrates through typological identification how Christian imitation transforms the particular into the universal, the historical into the transhistorical, personal specificity into type. By "laying down her life for a friend" (John 15:13)—the credo of Social Gospel identification—Beth becomes a true type of Christ, illustrating why, for the emerging Social Gospel, the salvation of the individual was inexplicably linked to the salvation of all. No contemporary reader of *Little Women* would have missed the gravity of Beth's sacrifice, her "unselfish ambition to live for others" (184), no less a sacrifice for the good of society than was that of those who—like the old man Marmee meets in her Union charity work who gave all his sons to the Northern cause (43)—died or lost loved ones in the war.

By the time Alcott wrote *Little Women,* the war's death toll and the pervasive view of God as a loving, gentle father had largely shifted the emphasis from graphic depictions of hell to a focus on heaven, with its sublime and enchanting vistas. Even in their game of playing pilgrims, the March sisters' vision of hell seems little more than a vague construct, obliquely symbolized by the "cellar and dark entry," whereas heaven invokes a richly detailed description.[134] Literary representations of salvation reached their apogee just after the Civil War, as the catastrophic human loss refocused theological reflections among the grief-stricken away from hell's violence to the promised reunion with loved ones in the next world. Rich fantasies of the afterlife appeared in articles, pamphlets, novels, and sermons, but no works of literature did more to popularize this religious sentiment than Elizabeth Stuart Phelps's best-selling trilogy, *The Gates Ajar* (1869), *The Gates Between* (1871), and *Beyond the Gates* (1883), novels that dramatized the joy of celestial reunion. Anxious to preserve their relationships with loved ones beyond the grave, readers clung to Phelps's descriptions of dead friends and family members in close proximity to the living. The national fantasy sustained and was, in turn, sustained by an age given to spiritualism, as séances and stories of spiritual contact swept the country well into the twentieth century, consoling the grieving.[135]

Closer to Social Gospel attitudes of progressivism, social optimism, and millennialism than Phelps's novels, which peddled the theme of life as a proving ground for heaven, Alcott's novel resists an early and brief postwar trend in religious literature that focused on dramatic visions of a future glory at the expense of the present. *Little Women* instead emphasizes the possibility to alter social conditions, an investment at odds with emergent strains of social determinism. In so doing, it anticipates the maturation, in the next decade, of the homiletic novel as a dominant fictional paradigm for religious readers. This category of texts eschewed spiritual deferral. Energized by both postwar millennialism and Christian socialism, it pushed the theme of heaven on earth, emphasizing commitment to community as a panacea to the war's national fragmentation. While novelists like Harriet Beecher Stowe (particularly in *The Minister's Wooing* and *Old Town Folks*), John W. De Forest, John Fox, Jr., Thomas Nelson Page, and Thomas Dixon turned back in time—with disparate views of race, region, and class—to recover the lost thread of the nation's sacred destiny, authors like Alcott, Edward Everett Hale, Washington Gladden, Albion Tourgée, and Charles Sheldon, in opposition to the celestial escapism of Phelps's works, took wartime culture head on, resisting social complacency to struggle against injustice, poverty, and suffering. Drawing on sermons that had urged women and children to fight and suffer for their country behind the curtains of the nation's theater of war, these novels rallied all to soldier on in the new wars—many emerging out of the scientific skepticism and national pessimism wrought by four years of violence—against the social ills of poverty, vice, alcoholism, and unemployment. While novels like those in Phelps's trilogy encouraged readers to persevere by envisioning deceased loved ones peering out from behind a celestial barrier left ajar, novels by such authors as

Alcott, Sheldon, Wright, and Tourgée urged readers to embrace not the suffering of those who died, but of those who lived.

*   *   *

Increasingly, the forms of homiletic materials were adapted to meet the popularity and market demand for the new genre. In the next chapter, I will take up the homiletic novel, what Charles Sheldon, one of its principal architects, called the "sermon story," a label that identifies its goal of garnering a broader audience. More compelling among American readers than the rendition of Christian principles was the fictional incorporation of traditional structures of Christian hermeneutic practices. Rather than lecturing the religious on morality or instructing them in platitudes of Christian charity, these new narratives, through interactive, devotional practices, helped orient them to greater action.

"What Would Jesus Do?" Practical Christianity, Social Gospel Realism, and the Homiletic Novel

Let Christians help one another in going [on] this journey. There are many ways that Christians might greatly help and forward one another in their way to heaven: by religious conference and otherwise. And persons greatly need help in this way, which is, as I have often observed, a difficult way. Let Christians be exhorted to go this journey, as it were, in company, conversing together about their journey's end and assisting one another. Company is very desirable in a journey, but in no journey so much as this. Let Christians go united, and not fall out by the way, which will be the way to hinder one another, but use all means they can to help one another. This is the way to be more successful in traveling and to have the more joyful meeting at their Father's house in glory. —Jonathan Edwards, "The True Christian's Life a Journey towards Heaven"

Christ's thought, however slow to manifest itself firmly in the details of our social, political, and religious organization, has assuredly taken root in the novel. —George Parsons Lathrop, "The Novel and Its Future"

In the late 1880s, Reverend Charles Sheldon, minister of the Central Church of Topeka, Kansas, delivered a series of weekly "sermon stories" to his several hundred parishioners. Week by week through Kansas's long winters and sweltering summers, Sheldon riveted his parishioners with homilies depicting characters confronting the challenges his congregants faced daily as they struggled to maintain their religious values amid dramatic social, political, and economic changes. Over weeks and months, each sermon linked to the next in what became a larger, sweeping narrative; each Sunday, Sheldon delivered successive chapters in what ultimately became a full-length book. Sheldon's sermon stories enjoyed immense success not only in his own congregation but also in churches across the nation and beyond.[1] Through the rise of a new industry of popular religious pedagogy, the narratives he recounted to his Central Church members enjoyed sensational success, for he sent each freshly delivered sermon off to the *Advance,* a popular Chicago-based Congregational weekly. Ministers across the nation adopted the serialized chapters, reading them to their own receptive congregations just weeks after their initial delivery. When the series concluded, the entire collection appeared as a novel aimed at a broad national audience. Sheldon's novels appealed both to middle- and working-class congregations and were adopted as sermons by both white and traditionally black churches.[2] Beginning with *Richard Bruce* in 1891, Sheldon averaged a volume a year for more than thirty years, including *Robert Hardy's Seven Days, The Twentieth Door, The Crucifixion of Phillip Strong, John King's Question Class, His Brother's Keeper,* and then, in 1896, the publication phenomenon *In His Steps,* likely the best-selling novel of the nineteenth century.[3]

Sheldon's remarkable career exemplifies the rise of what I have been calling the "homiletic novel," a literary phenomenon that included a cluster of authors as diverse as Hjalmar Hjorth Boyesen, Florence Converse, Edward Everett Hale, Bradley Gilman, Jesse Jones, Elizabeth Stuart Phelps, W. T. Stead, Albion Tourgée, Katharine Woods, and Harold Bell Wright. This chapter will take us into a more popular reading culture than the one principally reflected in the readership of Alcott's genteel childhood classic. Perhaps more than any other body of religious works, the extraordinary popularity of the homiletic novel raises intriguing questions about the evolving nature, structure, and meaning of religious thought, experience, and pedagogy in the late nineteenth century. It also offers a new context for considering two far-better-known American literary modes: realism and naturalism.

My use of the term homiletic here will focus increasingly on the visual and literary strategies by which authors like Sheldon engaged religious readers in narrative enactments aimed at merging fictive settings with the reality of the readers' everyday lives. Influenced by the Protestant sermon traditions and homiletic realism that we have been examining, the homiletic novel aimed to facilitate private devotion, strengthen moral autonomy, and foster social engagement through particular acts of reading. It was to a nation of like-minded Christians what the sermon

had been to smaller, regional communities. Whether a fast day, election
day, or other occasional sermon, such as the jeremiad, sermons had from
colonial origins built community ties, reclaimed the perceived piety of
preceding generations, renewed ancestral covenants, and secured doctrinal alliances and ideological commitments among independent congregations and interdenominational faiths. As we saw in the preceding
chapters, evangelical cultures reaffirmed community, past and present,
through homiletic structures of religious performance. As a powerful
form of mass media before the advent of radio and television evangelism,
the homiletic novel also performed a kind of communal collective bargaining, allowing individuals to articulate the limits of moral and social
concession, addressing through dialogue, public praise, and proscription
what was acceptable, negotiable, or intolerable, and thus framing the
broadest features of national and communal Christian values. Largely
discussed in the subjunctive mood—as illustrated by the titles of numerous essays such as James A. Chamberlin's "If Jesus Were an Editor" and
Sheldon's "If Jesus Were Here Today," "If I Were a Teacher," "If I Were
President," and "What I Would Do If I Were a Farmer"—these conversations not only explored moral options but pragmatically defined the
stakes for the world around them.[4] In this context, the homiletic novel
announces its ideological partisanship in the postbellum struggle between, on the one hand, evangelical factions attempting to muscularize volition and, on the other, various strains of determinism, ranging
from a lingering predestinarianism to emergent forms of evolutionary
causality. Homiletic novelists worked to create a practical link to an otherwise abstracted God whose "menial services," William James wrote,
"are needed in the dust of our human trials, even more than his dignity
is needed in the empyrean."[5]

Through both form and content, the homiletic novel proved an effective antidote to two challenges plaguing most late-nineteenth-century
congregations: Christian resignation in the face of naked social need and
parishioners' enervating doubts about religion's relevance in a fast-paced
age of industry, mechanization, and scientific advancement.[6] Formerly
apathetic congregants were drawn back to the pews because sermon stories captured their interest and engaged pragmatic, local concerns. But
the homiletic novel and the rise of Practical Christianity in this period
are far more than just stories of new literary strategies and technologies generating interest and meeting practical needs. The movement ultimately engaged so many Americans because it offered answers to pro-

found questions about epistemology and human agency during an era in which mainline Protestantism seemed to cede idealism to empiricism and rationalism, offering little response to the modernist decentering of the core philosophic beliefs that had guided Americans' religious thought and experience for generations.

This Practical Christianity, as the larger fusion of Social Gospel efforts with pragmatic action has been termed, had antecedents in seventeenth- and eighteenth-century American Protestantism, where, as we have seen, ministers and exhorters like Jonathan Edwards, Thomas Foxcroft, and, later Jacob Abbott, Charles Finney, and Zilpha Elaw shaped homiletic pedagogy as a defense against a perceived declension in moral vigilance and the worldly encroachment it presaged. Coincident with pervasive socialist efforts and labor strife in the later nineteenth century, Christian socialists, first in New York and then in Boston and Chicago, retooled homiletic pedagogy as an offensive strategy against the socially enervating diseases of poverty, ignorance, and middle-class complacency. As Practical Christianity merged conventional tenets of Protestantism with a new ethos of active reform, and as the movement grew, it drew together the energies of both secular and religious reform organizations. Such renowned Social Gospel ministers as Lyman Abbott, W. D. P. Bliss, Richard Ely, Washington Gladden, Walter Rauschenbusch, Charles Sheldon, and Graham Taylor ranked among its religious leaders, and such visionary reformers as Jane Addams, Helen Campbell, John Dewey, Benjamin Flower, Ellen Starr, John H. Vincent, and Lillian Wald were among its prominent secular activists who had had religious formations. Breaking with nineteenth-century pedagogical conventions based on either rote memorization and repetition or the still popular clerical imparting of moral knowledge among formal denominations, homiletic practitioners of the Social Gospel sought not just to educate but to motivate. They traced their lineage not through the rationalism of Anglican, Episcopal, or Unitarian lines, but back to the origins of evangelicalism in the popular field sermons of Whitefield and the New Light revivalism of Presbyterians, Congregationalists, Baptists, and Methodists. The Social Gospel phenomenon would reach its apogee in the late 1890s and flourish up until the First World War.[7]

This chapter explores the rise of the homiletic novel, best exemplified by Sheldon's *In His Steps,* in order to trace the technological and theoretical roots and mechanisms of Practical Christianity as it emerged from older forms of evangelicalism and took shape in religious fiction in the decades following early postbellum homiletic novels, such as Alcott's *Little Women*. Of particular significance in this story is how its central mantra (and novel's subtitle), "What would Jesus do?" altered the discourse and practices of Protestant theology and social activism, becoming the catechism of the homiletic tradition and the rallying credo of an enduring national movement. Homiletic novelists broke from the rather narrow, instrumentalized view of fiction epitomized by earlier generations of religious leaders, who often advocated what I identified in the preceding chapter as Sunday school fiction.[8] These novelists projected a more expansive understanding of the multiple roles that literature could play in spiritual awakening, in the pilgrim's journey, in moral self-reformation, or even in individual and communal commitments to social intervention. In the pages that follow, I analyze homiletic novels within the broader currents of Practical Christianity to demonstrate the role that homiletic narrative and realism played in galvanizing human volition and agency and in the fusion of religious practice and nineteenth-century social reform.

A more thorough critical assessment of the homiletic novel still awaits literary scholarship because, despite the work of Michael Denning, David Hall, Janice Radway, Jane Tompkins, and others on reading communities and modes of reading, prevailing theories of genre lack a nuanced understanding of the psychology of highly specialized religious readerships.[9] Sheldon's novels—and others like them—may be "theologically sloppy, and literarily forgettable" or suffer from "abysmal literary quality," but only when viewed from our present critical perspective, from the implicit epistemology assumed by modern, secular reading conventions.[10] In his study of the nineteenth-century dime novel and laboring-class readerships, Denning observes that a principle force still shaping nineteenth-century secular, working-class "systems of reading" was the tension between "novelistic and allegorical or typological modes of reading."[11] If readers applied to dime novels the heuristic, interactive, imaginative capacities required by older modes of collective reading and orality, then we should not be surprised by the more complex interpretive practices that helped shape the homiletic novel as a hybridized form. Denning's attention to the interpretive modes of dime novel reading— collective rather than solitary, *intensive* rather than *extensive,* "a working through of books" rather than passive escapism through the "constant absorption of endless printed matter"—reminds us that the novel's history has been as much a resistance to the forces of modernity as a symptom of them.[12]

For religiously oriented readers of all classes, the moral authority of the homiletic novel derived not from the text's conventional literary aesthetic but from its function as a moral script for social and spiritual performance. Influenced by the Social Gospel, readers' interpretations of the struggles between moral temptation and suffering virtue, or between the greed of capital and the plight of the "undeserving poor," encouraged them to identify with oppressed groups.[13] While such narrative identification seems foreign to modern critical conventions, the historical record provides numerous accounts of how homiletic novels altered readers' lives. A recent example of one of the most well-known figures to engage homiletic literature in just this way is Ronald Reagan. Among the last generation born in the Progressive Era and in the waning years of the Social Gospel, Reagan repeatedly recounted how Harold Bell Wright's 1903 homiletic novel *That Printer of Udell's* had, in 1922, made him a "life-long practical Christian." Deep into his seventies, Reagan described how the novel changed his life through his lasting identification with a fictional character: "That book had an impact I shall always remember. . . . The term, 'role model,' was not a familiar term in that time and place. But I realize I found a role model in that traveling printer whom . . . Wright brought to life. *He set me on a course I've tried to follow even unto this day.*"[14] Reagan's identification with an exemplary protagonist (who also struggled up from poverty to become an elected national leader) speaks to the extraordinary function particular religious groups perceived narrative to serve. It also suggests the need for a critical reevaluation of prevailing assumptions about the homogeneous nature of nineteenth- and early-twentieth-century reading practices and genre formation.

To the set of values and practices that were coming to define literary studies near the end of the century, the homiletic novel proposed an alternative set of narrative strategies—or steps—in the process of Christian reading, creating a practical link between reading and doing, knowledge and action, representation and reality. In fact, as I argued in the introduction, literary realism and homiletic narrative traveled on parallel tracks, precisely because many of literary realism's narrative strategies were also derived from older Protestant forms. But secularized literary modes such as realism and naturalism, as we will see, tended to disengage the mechanism of activism so crucial to the tradition of hom-iletic fiction.[15] To recover these novels' function as their religious read-ership understood it, we need to reconstruct a set of reading practices derived from older sermonic and religious pedagogical traditions we ex-amined in the last chapter, and in so doing, trace the evolution of homi-letic forms from the Social Gospel back in time to those traditions and the forms they employed.

First, through invoking a kind of virtual reality, homiletic allegories like Sheldon's *In His Steps* denied readers a passive role, presenting in-stead real-life scenarios that demanded narrative participation, insisted on moral volition, and asked readers to apply discursive enactments to their own lives through imaginative exercises for structuring everyday reality. These texts encouraged readers to identify with characters, to engage in a dialogue about their decisions and their implications for per-sonal experience and social obligation. In many settings, readers' suc-cess or failure navigating the choices they made was revisited through congregational discussions. Nowhere is such a dialogue—or the interplay between homiletic fiction and lived experience—better illustrated than in the congregational roundtables following the delivery of each chap-ter of Sheldon's novelized sermons, in which audiences discussed their motivations for and duty to moral choices, and explored the implications for their own lives.[16] Such communal discussion evokes Denning's Bakh-tinian formulation of "multiaccentual signs" developed by V. N. Volishi-nov, class accents, that appear in narrative "centers," keywords, and plot formulae of dime novels that become for their diverse readerships *mu-table* arenas of meaning-struggle by the constituent components of au-thorship, genre, and readership.[17] Robert Darnton has, in a different context, extended this more or less Aristotelian triad to include editors, publishers, and distributors, in defining a "communication circuit," all the more applicable, as we have seen, in the interactive and identifica-tory networks comprising religious pedagogy largely outside the purview of Darnton's and Denning's respective studies.[18] (We have only to think of Mason Locke Weems, who wrote, printed, peddled, and promoted his novelized hellfire sermons throughout the mid-Atlantic and south-ern states.) In this communication circuit, then, we must not forget to in-clude the revelatory capacity living-word theology attributed to holy writ and the rich readerly practices many evangelical audiences brought to and found in homiletic texts.

From parishioners, to authors, to the *Advance* magazine, to the Chris-

tian presses, to subsequent revisions of Sheldon's novels based on localized congregational needs, such a communication circuit—evident in the
roundtables like those Sheldon himself led after initially drafting each
chapter—anticipated larger interfaith community gatherings that built
intersectarian alliances. Not by chance, such alliances came at a time
when national religious leaders such as Washington Gladden and Edward Everett Hale wrote novels promoting interdenominational Christian "leagues," or "Christian commonwealths," formed by the union of
disparate denominational churches, and, similarly, at a time when fellowship was being touted above doctrine as newly formed interfaith groups
from around the country participated in local, state, and national Sunday School Union conventions like those organized at Chautauqua to
meet the demand for religious education training.[19] Commensurate with
the ways homiletic texts fostered moral, spiritual, and doctrinal consensus, Sheldon's congregational collaborations conceived of texts as speaking with a multitude of voices, as sites of accumulative faith-based experiences, wisdom, and spiritual insight that might simultaneously register
at the level of congregations, regions, and the nation. While the secular
novel's promotion of realism tended to collapse the layers of allegory, the
homiletic novel's annexation of generic and homiletic conventions and
authorial collaboration in the moral contingencies it examined, tested,
and contested preserved the heuristic function of allegory, in which the
collaborative process itself embeds or encodes multiple possibilities for
readerly identification. As with Bunyan's allegory or Barber's and Alcott's revisions of it, the reader was invited to reconstitute the allegory
through an act of personalization that moved from impersonation to the
superimposition of typological patterns on generic forms, in effect transforming (and exploiting) the very universality that *genre* itself implies.

Second, as we saw in the preceding chapter, homiletic narrative fostered a double vision that helped Christians perceive their actions as having consequences in both the temporal and spiritual realms, a simultaneity that, in *The Heart of the World,* Sheldon refers to as the "ever present
now."[20] Following Romans 6:5–6 (for the Social Gospel the kernel of
Pauline theology), homiletic narrative promoted an identificatory theology that helped readers envision themselves "crucified *with* Christ"—
"planted together in the likeness of his death"—to be raised up "in the
likeness of his resurrection" (emphasis added).

The extremes of the identification this theology fostered can be seen
in a wave of cultural representations. Between 1896 and 1898, the pho-

tographer F. Holland Day, for instance, created a series of images of himself as Christ crucified on the cross. While blasphemous to more conservative Christians in his own time, Day meant no disrespect. On the contrary, his embodiment of Christ was the ultimate form of identification—the radical *imitatio Christi* we have been following, taken to its logical conclusion—the literalization of the slogan, "Be a Christ!" popularized in W. T. Stead's *If Christ Came to Chicago*. In the perfection that the Social Gospel promised followers, humanity became one with their Savior. "The Divine that is in you," Henry Wood proclaimed in 1893, "is *you*. The deific incarnation in Jesus is not lowered or disparaged, but all humanity, in varying degrees of unfoldment, is lifted towards it."[21] Even more measured forms of identification emphasized how events in the lives of the faithful perpetually intersected those in the life of their Savior. In his sermon "The Living Christ," for example, Reverend Alfred Cave told the International Congregational Council meeting in Boston in 1899 that "personal feeling with Jesus" was one of the "great Christian virtues." As with Paul's insistence that the "old man" is crucified *with* Christ, Cave asserted that "Wherever we are called to live and work, we are to be known as thinking *with* Jesus, and feeling *with* Jesus, and acting *with* Jesus."[22] For, as Stead proclaimed, "The Eternal is fashioning the world in which we now live. . . . The Passion and Cross are for us day by day and hour by hour, moment by moment. Nor will Jesus cease from dwelling amongst us—the living word made manifest in flesh."[23] Homiletic narrative built networks of reform, translating individuals into communities of action that read religious fiction as experiential templates for their own lives.

Homiletic Experiences

Evolving homiletic literary practices with long roots in the sermonic realism of the hellfire sermon intersected with another experimental form of American literary realism, a secular tradition grounded, like the homiletic novel, in a historically specific cultural matrix. By the mid-1890s, a robust market had developed for social narratives that pictured the brutal experience behind the statistical facts and figures of poverty. Sociological exposés of human suffering and urban blight recounted the criminal and pathogenic opportunism that preyed on destitution, starvation, and unprotected innocence. In these decades, scores of narratives emerged—real and fictional—whose authors thinly veiled themselves as narrators or protagonists donning disguises in order to transgress class boundaries and color lines and bear witness to social malaise. Collapsing the difference between real and simulated experience, these texts reveal an experimental discourse engineered to narrow the epistemological gap between life and narrative, between subject and object. Principal among the market's best sellers was what Eric Schocket calls the "class-transvestite narrative" (from Micaela di Leonardo's "status transvestitism" in Jack London's work)[24] and what, explicating their religious context, I will describe at length in the next chapter as the "virtual-tour narrative," wherein amateur sleuths, social reformers, gritty journalists, and fictional "insiders" led readers on simulated excursions into tenement slums, through refuse-strewn alleys, and along skid rows peopled by orphans, prostitutes, alcoholics, the dispossessed, the mentally ill, and the dying.[25] Largely operating as self-styled "sociologists," writers as divergent as urban reformers Benjamin Flower and Helen Campbell, the Princeton professor Walter Wyckoff, the soldier of fortune Josiah Flynt, and the famed early-career journalists Stephen Crane, Jack London, Theodore Dreiser, and Jacob Riis joined the ranks of social investigators advocating visceral knowledge through social immersion.[26]

Advertised as new realism or literary naturalism, this body of secular narratives emphasized the empirical basis of social knowledge and privileged physical detail. This secular narrative tradition and the nascent sociology that informed it drew from a Lockean empirical model that held that the apprehension of persons and phenomena was restricted to the agent's perception of their materiality, as measured by the senses. Yet, this literary movement also inherited from Locke a profound awareness of the limited nature of this sensory encounter. For such amateur sociologists as London, Crane, and Flynt, vast realms of reality—the deepest essence of the empirical referent—remained ensconced behind a barrier impenetrable to the senses. They thus sought to address the epistemological limits of empiricism through "experiments in reality" (a phrase popularized by the title of Wyckoff's study). These experiments attempted to move beyond the knowledge culled from sensory interactions with natural objects at a remove to a model of immersion in which material reality was observed in its natural environment.[27]

Critics have long recognized how this development in empiricism influenced a sociological model that also produced the literary movements of American realism and naturalism.[28] In the context of eighteenth-century England, Michael McKeon, building on the work of Ian Watt, traces a broader history of influence, demonstrating how the epistemological shifts prompted by Locke's *Essay Concerning Human Understanding* led to the rise of the novel in eighteenth-century Britain.[29] If we consider the transformative impact of Locke on Edwardsian theology and its accompanying homiletic practices, the missing component within accounts of the rise of American literary realism becomes clear. The narrative strategies attributed to an empirical thread emerged from the much older—yet still dynamic—tradition of homiletic realism. The "veracious narratives" of realism and naturalism jettisoned the homiletic's religious teleology while retaining its discursive strategies.[30] These strategies also registered the split between the subjective experience of empirical reference and the presumed reality beyond this reference. The strategy of creating an experiment in reality to deal with this split was the same in the homiletic realist mode as in its secular counterpart; the difference resided in investing that supplemental reality with a sacred or secular mooring. The secular class-transgressive investigations of London, Crane, and Flynt, like those of other less well-known investigators, indeed promoted social immersion as a method for acquiring authentic social knowledge—but it was knowledge for its own sake, rather than a means to social intervention. Even the metaphor of social immersion within these texts emphasizes the narrative's radically subjective, empirical, and deterministic focus, as when London describes his "descent" into the destitution of East London as a "vast and malodorous sea" that "had welled up and over me, or I had slipped gently into it"; or as when that subjective focus expands to include another with whom he identifies, an individual of the "finest grade," who is "being slowly engulfed by the noisome and rotten tide of humanity."[31]

Homiletic traditions, by contrast, offered a grand scheme for social salvation through acts of personal identification, wherein each life was connected to others. Even in his undercover investigation of the impoverished Eastside of England's capital, Jack London refused the pattern established a decade earlier by the Social Gospel investigators Sheldon, Walter Wyckoff, and Benjamin Flower. While Sheldon, Wyckoff, and Flower sought out opportunities to engage the less fortunate, to share rooms or travel with itinerants, London eschewed such intimacy, making daily excursions from a rented flat on the edge of the ghetto.[32] As we will see in the next chapter, Riis and Flower adapted the virtual-tour narrative from a sermon tradition, encouraging the reader's closer proximity to objects of inquiry by using the first- and second-person plural forms of address to simulate the intimacy and immediacy of a tour—part of the system of homiletic strategies comprising an aesthetics of immediacy. As witnesses on the ground, they measured authenticity less by graphic catalogs of human misery, depravity, and disease than by strategies of interaction with the suffering they encountered. London and Flynt borrowed the homiletic's class-transvestite narrative but used it to strip humanity of its artificial decorum. Influenced by an increasingly clinical aesthetic of urban sociology, they exposed poverty as a debasement, rendering the poor as brutes incapable of the psychological reflexivity required to motivate change from within and insensitive to psychological pain—hence impervious to aid from without.[33]

In London's *The People of the Abyss* (1903) or Josiah Flynt's *Tramping with Tramps* (1899), narrators penetrated the social "underworld" to glean demographic facts.[34] But according to religious critics like Christian Pragmatist Josiah Royce, their graphic and clinical descriptions of verminous tenements, contagion, poverty, and sin—relentlessly hellish inventories that, Royce admonished, overwhelmed readers with "one *damned* thing after another"—only served to captivate the senses through voyeuristic exercises aimed at helping readers codify their class identity. Vehemently denouncing such recreational prurience, Royce derided "the pretended literary wisdom . . . that patiently and lucratively prowls amidst ghastly facts, not for the sake of . . . real truth, but merely for the sake of emphasizing its own weak-minded bewilderment."[35] Where twentieth-century literary critics would read such rejections of realism as simply a repudiation of mimetic representation, this criticism, in fact, reveals a deeper epistemological critique of the possible disconnection between virtual experience and action in the world. For Christian critics, such lurid catalogs ensnared readers in the sensual world (much as Vanity Fair traps John Bunyan's wayfaring pilgrim), seducing them into exchanging spiritual reality for tangible materiality, the eternal verities of faith-based knowledge for the disenchanted, deceptive authority of modern secular epistemology. Twentieth-century critics have often misread the rejection of this kind of realism as a Victorian queasiness on the part of the religious, when in fact this critique was actually invested in the positive moral ends anchored in empirical reference.

Taking metaphysical capacities for granted (what Royce called "apperception" and "insight"), Christian socialists defied the limits to perception as understood within Cartesian dualism and the Lockean legacy of scientific empiricism, and thus the existentialism toward which the "sociological" works of Crane, Jack London, and Frank Norris tended.[36] While literary realism anatomized the experience of *reality* as though it were an ontological end in itself, Social Gospel advocates focused on the reality of *experience*. Naturalist definitions of realism, for instance, assumed that reality exists apart from experience—at least a single individual's experience—such that the authenticity and accuracy of an individual's perception must be evaluated in relation to a body of perceiving individuals (narrator, author, or reader), or measured against an implied omniscience. By contrast, anchored in Protestantism's revivified emphasis on individual volition and commitment to spiritual self-evaluation, the proponents of homiletics assumed personal experience to be the measure of reality. Put another way, William James argued that spiritual experience accounted for a reality apart from the one fin de siècle secularism and science increasingly advocated as our epistemic limits. Discounting science's dismissal of the spiritual as idealism, James argues that "the unseen region" beyond the "visible world"

> is not merely ideal, for it produces effects in this world. When we commune with it, work is actually done upon our finite personality, for we are turned into new men, and consequences in the way of conduct follow in the natural world upon our regenerative changes. But that which produces effects within another reality must be termed a reality itself, so I feel as if we had no philosophic excuse for calling the unseen or mystical world unreal. (*Varieties* 406)

Yet, James does not lose sight of the idea that access to this unseen world is deeply and inextricably tied to personal experience: "We belong to it," he asserts, "in a more intimate sense than that in which we belong to the visible world" (*Varieties* 406).

What might literary realism look like if we reconnect the form of its discursive strategies to the religious teleology of the homiletic tradition? It might look like any one of the many novels written in the last third of the nineteenth century by or about ministers entering the "social abyss." In the opening of Albion Tourgée's 1890 novel *Murvale Eastman,* the young Reverend Eastman steps behind the sanctuary of one of the city's most affluent churches, into the privacy of his office.[37] There, he removes the vestiary markers of his identity—garments distinguishing him as educated, middle-class, and employed—and dons ragged clothes that enable him to pass among the denizens of the city's "social cellar." Eastman's reconnaissance among striking workers—not, as often happened, to gather union strategies for management's mounting opposition to labor—allows him to discover firsthand the causes and consequences of social unrest. Initiated into the life of a laborer, he experiences the desperation of the poorest classes and witnesses the ruthless indifference with which disembodied capitalism discards sick and injured workers, thrusting their children from deprivation into lives of moral abandon. Yet not until a man dies in his arms does the abstraction of facts and figures give way to visceral knowledge of suffering and its moral imperative. Only then can Eastman comprehend the materiality of the wretchedness around him and assess his church's culpability in the cycle of urban despair. In this way, the homiletic novel advocated personal encounters with and intervention in suffering as the basis of authentic social knowledge, vicariously training readers for their own forays into social reform.

The year before Tourgée wrote *Murvale Eastman,* Charles Sheldon, newly installed as minister of the Central Church and still a stranger in Topeka, "dressed down" in his oldest clothes, donned a tattered jacket and hat, and walked out into the icy January winds. For more than two weeks, in a time of rampant unemployment, he scoured the city for a job. Determined to embrace the vagaries of a day laborer, he called at stores, factories, coal yards, and flour mills, rubbing elbows in bread lines with the city's working poor. His search occasioned meetings with the out-of-work, the elderly, dispossessed farmers, ghettoized African Americans, and children struggling to provide for families. His epiphany, like the fictional Eastman's, came neither from abstract concepts nor from poverty statistics marshaled by amateur sociologists like Flynt, but rather from "visceral knowing" through immediate personal suffering that rendered the investigator's body itself the site of class and racial integration.[38] In eight sermons drawn from these forays, delivered on consecutive Sundays in 1889, Sheldon turned his experience among the working poor into a sharp call for social intervention. In tones running the gamut of human emotions, he, like Tourgée's fictional Eastman, defined as his congregants' duty a personal intervention in the indigents' hand-to-mouth struggle for existence. From such undercover explorations emerged homiletic novels that deployed a range of discursive strategies in order to train ground troops for what he called a battle with poverty.

This was not simply an instance of life imitating art, or art life. Rather than codifying realism's empirical distinction between fact and fiction, the stories of Sheldon or of Tourgée's fictional Eastman seek to soften the lines between representation and reality, between simulated and lived experience, and between the deceptively "real" world and the seemingly intangible spiritual realm. In order to inspire meaningful action in the material world, they expose that world as a shadow show whose debasement of spiritual reality requires an epistemological reorientation and a renewed faith in humanity to correct. Thus, for example, in Sheldon's *In His Steps,* two wealthy, young sisters, Felicia and Rose, attend a stage play about the tragic life of the indigent living in an urban ghetto. (Like the contemporary theatrical adaptation of Hall Caine's *The Christian,* a "graphic account of a self-denying ministry . . . in the slums of London,"[39] or similar stage adaptations from Hjalmar Boyesen's *The Social Strugglers* [1893], such dramatizations of poverty were a popular tool in the homiletic arsenal of late-nineteenth-century social reform.) The narrative records the audience's reactions, which are similar to those evoked by the magic-lantern presentations of Riis and Flower: "The rags, the crowding, the vileness . . . the horrible animal existence forced upon creatures made in God's image were so skillfully shown in this scene that more than one elegant woman in the theatre . . . caught herself shrinking back . . . as if contamination were possible from the nearness of . . . scenery. It was almost too realistic. . . . In reality the scenes on the bridge and in the slum were only incidents in the story of the play, but Felicia found herself living those scenes over and over" (*In His Steps* 249).

After the final curtain, the sisters reveal to each other the impact the play has had upon them. Visibly shaken by the representation of poverty and suffering, Rose condemns the dramatic realism: "The slum scene was horrible," she tells her sister. "I think they ought not to show such things in a play. They are too painful."[40] The blurred distinction between representation and reality troubles Rose, who prefers to acquire knowledge without being made to experience suffering, which, as she reluctantly admits, is the inevitable ethical response to such "painful" scenes. More attuned to the purpose of the homiletic realism, Felicia acknowledges its function to move the reader or auditor beyond representation: "They must be painful in real life too" (*In His Steps* 250). In her response to the representation of poverty, Felicia distinguishes between

knowledge divorced from an ethical or moral response, and the process
by which knowledge mandates moral action: "And yet we never weep
over the real thing on the actual stage of life. What are the [shadows]
on the stage to the shadows of London or Chicago as they really exist?
Why don't we get excited over the facts as they are?" (*In His Steps* 244).
She thus draws the appropriate conclusion from the Social Gospel's pedagogical adaptations of homiletic realism, while demonstrating the ontological worldview—the spiritual sight—that allowed homiletic readers to glean experience from what a modern point of view might see as
merely representation. In the perspective of the homiletic novel, everything in the temporal world is representation, a shadow of a larger, universal reality.

   Homiletic novels stressed the difference between representation as
amusement and representation as an initial stage of intervention by com-
menting on the popular urban middle-class recreation of "slumming,"
in which middle-class individuals toured the tenement and ghetto districts as a form of amusement or social exploration. In both *In His Steps*
and Boyesen's *The Social Strugglers,* for example, groups of young people go on "slumming parties" as a form of social diversion.[41] Yet in both,
confronted by suffering in a personal way, having to intervene in an accident before them, the young recreational investigators are forced to confront their own sense of social distance and to avow their moral failing in
not having identified with the suffering of others. Because the principal
tenet of Practical Christianity was empathetic social intervention, the
homiletic novel self-consciously asserted the difference between knowledge for what Sheldon called "inert ends," and knowledge as a means to
strategic social transformation. Joining a national chorus of Social Gospel advocates, Sheldon resented the emerging trend in literature and science to explore poverty and accrue social knowledge as an end unto itself, and not as a means to the kind of personal discovery that foments
change.

   The profound legacy of homiletic discourse for secular realism becomes evident when we consider how, in the homiletic novel, descent into
the social underworld was predicated on this ethos of spiritual identification and intervention. Such radical empathy was motivated not only by
the desire to answer a theological question that preoccupied postbellum
evangelical Protestants—"Who was Jesus?"—but also by the desire, in
the context of contemporary life, to engage in a radical *imitatio Christi*
by asking, literally, what would Jesus do?

Who Was Jesus?

The second half of the nineteenth century witnessed a wave of historical works absorbed with the details of Jesus's life and suffering, including Henry Ward Beecher's enormously popular *Life of Jesus, the Christ*
(1871), numerous translations of David Strauss's *Life of Jesus* (translated
to English in 1846), Ernest Renan's *The Life of Jesus* (trans. 1864) and
The Apostles (trans. 1866), Philip Schaff's *The Person of Christ* (1865),
August Neander's *The Life of Jesus Christ* (trans. 1880), Joseph Holt Ingraham's *The Prince of the House of David* (1855), and Elizabeth Phelps's
The Story of Jesus Christ (1897). Fictional works such as Lew Wallace's
best-selling *Ben Hur: A Tale of the Christ* (1880) and *The Boyhood of
Christ* (1888), Henryk Sienkiewicz's *"Quo Vadis"* (trans. 1897), and Hall
Caine's *The Christian* (1897) wove realistic tapestries of first-century life.
Increasingly supplemented by archeology, ethnography, and emerging
historiography, such works depicted the Mediterranean world in evocative detail.[42] Attesting to the realism of a "new development" in spiritual
dramatization in 1904, Thomas Hughes celebrated the "graphic delinea-
tions of Jewish and Roman life in the days of Jesus Christ," promising
that "In witnessing such a play the Biblical student learns more of the environments and colorings of Hebrew life in three hours than he could in a
lengthened course of Biblical study," and the dramatic "presentation . . .
brings with it the highest form of inspiration."[43] Producing feasible, if fictional, narratives of Jesus's childhood and psychological profiles of Jesus
the man, these novels and dramas—not unlike Mel Gibson's blockbuster
film *The Passion of the Christ* (2004) or Martin Scorsese's *The Last
Temptation of Christ* (1988)—recreated the passionate immensity of his
struggles with temptation and the pain of his suffering for humanity.[44]

   This religious realism, pushed to new limits by the holiness movement, helped fuel the Social Gospel's injunction to imitate Christ, although, as we shall see, the historical particularity of these accounts
needed to be translated into that of readers' own lives. Like Stead's slogan "Be a Christ!" Sheldon's mantra "What would Jesus do?" depended
upon a presumptive familiarity with Christ's daily life, thoughts, doubts,
and spiritual resolve. In the words of Sheldon's narrator, this familiarity was "two thousand years' knowledge of the Master" (*In His Steps*
191). As an allegorical model of how to live as a Christian, Christ's life,
depicted in the broad emblematic strokes of the Synoptic Gospels—the
first three New Testament books—provided a sufficient roadmap to sal-

vation, particularly when, as God in human flesh, Jesus's life was less an example for daily living than a general exemplar for life. But in the Social Gospel's theology of imitation (as in the March sisters' pilgrimages), Jesus's life was to provide a detailed pattern for daily life, a guide to all social relations, and a constant moral structure for both spiritual conduct and secular life. Jacob Abbott, father of Sheldon's Andover mentor Lyman (and the homiletic theorist whose extensive model of reading we examined in the preceding chapter), expressed in his homiletic series for children how biblical historicism fostered identification with Christ in response to his historical identification with humanity: Jesus "dwelt among us, learning, in his own slow and painful experience, *what it is to be a human being* in the world of trial. . . . Remember, the Savior was once as young as you—exposed to such little difficulties and trials as you are" (*Young Christian* 39; original emphasis).[45] The narrator of *In His Steps* reveals the essence of true discipleship in a return to the past, asking readers to imagine themselves on foot to Damascus, in a village in Nazareth, on the banks of Jordan, or casting nets along the shore of the Sea of Galilee: "There is not a different path today from that of Jesus's own times. It is the same path. The call of this dying century and of the new one soon to be, is a call for a new discipleship, a new following of Jesus, more like the early, simple, apostolic Christianity, when the disciples left all and literally followed the master" (*In His Steps* 299).[46] Acknowledging the critique that Social Gospel Christians sought to live lives minutely patterned on elaborate suppositions, Sheldon had religious critics within *In His Steps* characterize those who asked "What would Jesus do?" as being "foolishly literal in their attempt to imitate the example of Jesus" (*In His Steps* 236). Yet the criticisms Sheldon had anticipated—his novel, as one critic wrote, was "too practical" in its literal application of Christ's life to everyday experience—were out of step with the cultural currents of Sheldon's diverse audience and the broader Social Gospel ethos of the time.[47]

Sheldon sets *In His Steps* in Raymond, a fictional city not unlike his hometown, Topeka. Although provincial, Raymond reveals the tremendous social complexities of a large civic infrastructure; it boasts competing newspapers, an uptown and a downtown, and a level of poverty and crime more typical of a metropolis like New York or Chicago than a city on the Kansas plains. A composite of American society, Raymond is a place where small-town Americans confront the facts and consequences of urbanization, industrialization, and immigration.[48] Alienated from the cyclic rhythms of production and rest that had structured rural life by seasons, Raymond's world of ghettos, tenement districts, and mass poverty conjures urban America's most pressing social problems, including how to enact civic reform from within inner-city neighborhoods and how to address disproportionate economic structures, overcrowding, sanitation, disease abatement, and the like.[49]

In His Steps opens with the arrival of a destitute man at the doorstep of Henry Maxwell, minister of Raymond's First Church, a name foreshadowing the congregation's emerging apostolic affiliation with the first-century church. Regretfully, Maxwell informs the destitute man that he has no work for him and directs him to what might be another opportunity down the road. On the following Sunday, the man turns up again, this time seated in the First Church congregation. After listening to Maxwell's sermon, he rises to question the minister about the sermon's meaning. "What I feel puzzled about," he tells the congregation, "is what is meant by following Jesus? Do you mean that you are suffering and denying yourselves and trying to save lost suffering humanity just as I understand Jesus did?" (*In His Steps* 14). In the ensuing discussion, the visitor reveals that he has lost his family to starvation and disease while living a brutal existence in a New York tenement. "I see the ragged edge of things a good deal," he tells them:

> Somehow I get puzzled when I see so many Christians living in luxury and singing, "Jesus, I my cross have taken, all to leave and follow thee," and remember how my wife died in a tenement in New York City, gasping for air and asking God to take the little girl too. Of course I don't expect you people can prevent every one from dying of starvation, lack of proper nourishment and tenement air, but what does following Jesus mean? I understand that Christian people own a good many of the tenements. A member of a church was the owner of the one where my wife died. . . . It seems to me sometimes as if the people in the city churches had good clothes and nice houses to live in, and money to spend for luxuries, and could go away on summer vacations and all that, while the people outside the churches, thousands of them, I mean, die in tenements and walk the streets for jobs . . . and grow up in misery and drunkenness and sin. (*In His Steps* 14–15)

Unfolding as a homily, the itinerant's story makes the case for the Social Gospel's principal complaint against organized Christianity: its social complacency in the face of human want.

As the visitor's interrogation culminates, he grows faint, lurching "in the direction of the communion table," then "falling heavily forward on his face, full length, up the aisle" (*In His Steps* 15). Within the week, he is dead. Sheldon represents the encounter with a homeless stranger as a defining moment both for Maxwell's ministry and his congregation. The following Sunday, the contrite minister poses the stranger's question to his congregation: "What would Jesus do?" (*In His Steps* 21). Adopting this seemingly simple theoretical position, he challenges his congregation to alter their lives according to its dictates. The soul searching the characters undergo, which begins in self-recrimination and remorse and ends with personal intervention, serves as a model for Sheldon's readers as well. The challenge goes to the heart of Social Gospel pragmatism: how to live an engaged life of faith in a modern age in which, as Henry Adams wistfully observed, the enchanted world of the virgin had given way to the technological sublimity of machine.[50] Believers, Sheldon writes in *Jesus Is Here!* his 1913 sequel to *In His Steps,* must ask the "fair and reverent question . . . what would be the attitude of Jesus as he faced the complex conditions of modern society?"[51] While it is easy to spoof the high seriousness and sentimental pull of Social Gospel rhetoric, it would be a mistake to overlook how powerfully the homiletic novels argued for a moral selflessness genuinely admired and emulated by a broad readership.[52]

The life-changing question that emerges from the visitor's death— "What would Jesus do?"—also announces the homiletic novel's stake in the century-long Trinitarian debates about the ontological nature of the incarnation. In other words, *who* was Jesus? The debate became particularly contentious in the years after the American Revolution, with the rise of Unitarianism and the popularity of a commonsense standard fostered by the Enlightenment.[53] Almost all late-eighteenth-century Calvinists (including Congregationalists, Presbyterians, Methodists, and Baptists) subscribed to the traditional three-person Godhead, labeling the emergent Boston Unitarian one-God-three-natures theology heretical. The difference between Trinitarians and Unitarians came down to the problem of how Christianity can be a monotheistic religion and at the same time acknowledge a Godhead of separate personages. In response, the Unitarians "insinuate[d]," in the words of the Trinitarian Congregational minister George Burder (1752–1832), "that we, who believe the Trinity, admit of more than one God."[54] Gradually the debate evolved into one about the nature of the Godhead, what Burder called the "Tri-Unity, or three in one," and none of the three garnered more disagreement than the person of Christ, less as a question of his heavenly form than of his earthly one, and his origin: "eternal in the father," whether created sometime before Creation, or born a "God-man."[55] By the antebellum period, the popular debate took up roughly three positions, all of which, of course, had been propounded by various Christian movements going back to the early church. As they were rudimentarily explained in nineteenth-century sermons and tracts, Christ was God in man ("Docetism"), Christ was man endued with divinity at his baptism ("adoptionism"), or Christ was thoroughly a man, embodying humanity's frailty ("Arianism," or "Socinianism").[56] Few theological debates better epitomized the enormous humanist shift taking place in American Protestantism: the question went to the core of human volition, whether or not individuals were, as Milton famously insisted, created sufficient to stand but free to fall. "Who Jesus was" became the key both to evangelical and Social Gospel plans for pragmatic intervention.[57]

If Christ was God incarnate, then his purpose of ransoming the world seemed a primitive blood sacrifice that, by confirming the doctrine of imputation (the transmission of sin from Adam to all descendents), left humanity to its futile struggle against its own fallen nature. If Christ walked among humanity as God, asking what he would do in any given situation would have no practical use, no "cash value" in everyday life, to use the phrase William James initially coined to illustrate the pragmatic value of faith in the absence of empirical evidence.[58] In this view, Christ's temptation in the desert and crisis of faith in Gethsemane and on the cross were empty gestures staged to affirm his status as the Messiah but hardly exemplary as exercises to which humanity could aspire. If, however, he sacrificed his divinity to experience the world's suffering—if, as Stead put it, he came "into our world . . . [as] one of us . . . that he might learn by experiment what the human condition is, in all its details"[59]—then his ministry could be read as blazing a trail to salvation, not with the strides of a deity, but with the steps of a man.

In this context, Jesus's trials were seen as having immense practical value, offering hope, inspiration, and a script for living to which the human will and spirit were equal, if, occasionally, the flesh was not. If Jesus was a man, his actions, while possibly superhuman, were emphatically not suprahuman. In his encounters with poverty and sin, the disorders of passion, ambition, guilt, and erotic desire had not been repelled by a divine barrier that, as traditional iconography envisaged, encased him in a protective nimbus of light, but had instead penetrated to the core of his finite being.

Both the desire to historicize Jesus and the continual effort to transform biblical literalism into evocative clips of narrative realism were part of a larger pattern of biblical criticism emerging after the Civil War. The question of who Jesus was came twinned with another question that went to the core of a debate pitting faith against empirical evidence: What was the status of the Bible and biblical history? William James analyzed that status by breaking it down into two parts: "What is the nature of it?" and "What is its importance, meaning, or significance, now that it is here?" (*Varieties* 13). By the 1890s, Social Gospel practitioners no longer questioned what their Protestant forebears had attacked only half a century earlier as a heresy coming out of German universities: the practice of historicizing the Bible and, more broadly, Christianity in an analytic method that came to be known as the "higher criticism." Sheldon's audience had come of age during the popularization of this new scriptural analysis that, by focusing on the Bible as a set of historical texts collected from divergent sources and shaped by centuries of exegesis, translation, canonization, and decanonization, challenged a view of the scriptures as sacred, divinely inspired, and infallible. Attempting to demonstrate the Bible's utility for daily life—its cash value—whatever its sacred status, James further refined the relevant issues: "Under just what biographic conditions did the sacred writers bring forth their various contributions to the holy volume? And what had they exactly in their several individual minds, when they delivered their utterances?" (*Varieties* 13). His questions highlight the "individual minds" and specific "biographic" details of the authors' lives, precisely the level of realism homiletic authors and readers were seeking.

The higher criticism gained in popularity in the United States after the Civil War, an important juncture when emerging scientific determinism sought to explain the national crisis not as an irresistible conflict between human values and godly morals but as the irresistible impulses of social, economic, and evolutionary forces. While Ann Taves has recently demonstrated how science and religion collaborated in the late nineteenth century, an either-or mentality persisted among many evangelical Christians.[60] Fueled by an accumulating fossil record, the growth of industry and technology, increased cycles of economic boom and bust, and the rise of socialism and unprecedented labor unrest, tensions between science and religion, between faith and empirical evidence, increased, further solidifying the debate over scientific determinism and the ability of biblical exegesis to absorb contradictions that both threatened biblical literalism and pitted a mechanistic depiction of human instinct, survival, and evolution against humanity's volitional and rational capacities.[61] Writing in 1875, John W. Draper described the task before the religious in his enormously popular *The Conflict between Religion and Science:* science, he writes, "insisting that human affairs present an unbroken chain, in which each fact is the offspring of some preceding fact, and the parent of some subsequent fact, declares that men do not control events, but that events control men."[62] While many Protestants achieved an acceptable balance between science and religion in their lives, others worried that to accede to the authority of science was to concede volition, humanity's capacity to alter the world, to alleviate the terrible suffering increasingly visible in the closing decades of the century.

Christians who supported social evolution bore the brunt of the fury. Social Gospel adherents insisted that those believers who credited Social Darwinism or Spencerian class theories did so for one of two reasons. Either they embraced scientific determinism in an effort to explain suffering and justify their own apathy and social neglect, or, worse, they did so to evade the democratization of salvation—the individual's capacity to seek redemption—in effect reconstituting an election of the social elite. Either way, the doctrine of determinism was a blatant denial of the capacity of human will. Thus, for instance, the Christian philosopher Josiah Royce, in sympathy with William James, was appalled less by organized religion's lack of concrete action to alleviate poverty and suffering than by Christianity's myriad rationalizations for such inaction. In "The Problem of Job," he summarized the two most prevalent rationalizations. The first argued that our vision is finite, and "the wretch doomed to pangs now unearned, sinned of old."[63] The second suggested that suffering is a misconception, that "since God's world, the real world, in order to be perfect, must be without evil, what we men call evil must be mere illusion—a mirage of the human point of view." Neither perspective was tenable for Royce or the broader Social Gospel movement. Royce argued that by viewing suffering as the inevitable moral effect whose cause was invisible to immediate perception, determinists put all individuals in "a sin-tight container," rendering their suffering hopelessly inaccessible to intervention from without.[64] In its denial of a cooperative social remedy, such a view, for Royce, proffered a sponge of vinegar where a drink of water was wanting. On the other hand, by backing a blind faith that all worked together for the glory of God—a logic James rebuffed as the Christian's "moral holiday"—the second rationalization implied, for Royce, not merely a gulf between individuals but a vast distance between God and humanity.[65] By naturalizing humanity's passivity in a mechanized universe, advocates of this view recapitulated the Deistic universe-as-clock analogy, mounting instrumentalism as a placeholder for an absent God.[66] Thus, failure to exercise volition was to give in to the logic of Social Darwinism or to reinstall predestinarianism, both of which the Social Gospel mocked as "laissez-faire determinism" for their promotion of a negative freedom that advocated allowing individuals to rise or fall, starve or prosper, according their "natural" abilities.[67]

In this context, higher criticism's historicizing, and its use of sociology and anthropology, would, on the face of it, appear to have supported only the interests of the natural sciences and emerging narratives of geological time and social evolution. Yet one of the profound ironies of higher criticism is how, by historicizing, and thus humanizing Christ, it also played to the interests of Social Gospel ministers intent on muscularizing volition. After all, only if Jesus were born into the world as a man could he both provide a model for human emulation and validate human volition. What purpose would Christ's humanity serve the sinning world if humanity itself were irrevocably enslaved to natural drives, subject either to evolutionary or religious determinism? What ameliorative effect could a rejection of predestination and a weakening of original sin have, if humanity were freed from one form of fatalism only to fall captive to another? That Christ had been born into the world a man who, through mortal means, overcame humanity's moral and spiritual frailty clearly bespoke the power of the will, despite mounting evidence to the contrary on the part of social and biological determinism.

Numerous books appeared in the last decades of the fin de siècle promoting the hidden, untapped reserves of human will, a self-help tradition that would culminate thirty years after the Social Gospel era in the New York City ministry of Norman Vincent Peale and his monumental 1952 bestseller, *The Power of Positive Thinking.* In 1893, for instance, in *Ideal Suggestion through Mental Photography,* the homiletic novelist and Social Gospel proponent Henry Wood touted the will's power above all other human capacities: "I will," he trumpeted in the idiom of Bunyan's allegory, "is a projectile that hits the mark, a power that 'removes mountains.' Doubt is disintegration. It leads into the Slough of Depond. . . . 'I will' is the pilot that grasps the helm and steers the hu-

man craft Godward."[68] In response to social Darwinism's implication
that the Civil War resulted from inevitable forces beyond human control,
postbellum Social Gospel evangelicals retooled the faculty of volition in
earnest—beginning by rejecting deified incarnation.[69]

The competing worldviews represented by an older acceptance of divine truth and the scientific orientation of the higher criticism finally
shared a common interest in Jesus, and a middle way opened up that
both preserved his sacred aspect and portrayed him as a historical figure
who, like other men, daily lived with contradictory impulses and human
emotions, desires, and needs. The higher criticism could thus enhance
the pragmatic value of biblical narrative, James had asserted, if readers
could "allow that the book may well be a revelation in spite of errors and
passions and deliberate human composition, if only it be a true record of
the inner experience of great-souled persons wrestling with the crises of
their faith" (*Varieties* 14). In that spirit, Social Gospel Christians imagined living in the perpetual presence of Jesus, not in the awe-inspiring
robes of a Messiah but, as one of Sheldon's readers put it, as an "intimate
and concerned personal friend."[70]

Christian activism was thus rendered not only spiritually necessary
but also practical and effective, and its driving mechanism was identification. Embracing Paul's injunction that the faithful make their "bodies
a living sacrifice" (Romans 12:1)—that is, that they *live* (rather than die)
sacrificially (Social Gospel reformers outpaced other Calvinist denominations steeped in the tradition of "Bible Onlyism"), a supercharged
sola scriptura given new legs by the Stone-Campbell movements—by the
extreme to which they pushed biblical literalism in order to place the
themes of sacrifice and suffering at the core of Christian activism. As
one observer of Henry Maxwell's theology explains to a visitor, "So far
as I can understand, the idea that is moving him on now is the idea that
the Christianity of our times must represent a more literal imitation of
Jesus, and especially the element of suffering" (*In His Steps* 237). Sheldon dramatized the desire to forge allegiances through suffering, as Jesus had done, by making his auditors' bodies living testaments to another's pain: "There had sprung up in them a longing that amounted
to a passion, to get nearer the great physical poverty and the spiritual
destitution of the mighty city. . . . How could they do this," his narrator
asks, "except as they became a part of it, as nearly as one man can become a part of another's misery? Where was the suffering to come in,
unless there was an actual self-denial apparent to themselves . . . un-

less it took this concrete, actual, personal form of trying to share the deepest suffering and sin of the city?" (*In His Steps* 223). By presenting the doctrine of atonement as "concrete, actual, and personal," the homiletic novel's insistence on willed, realistic empathy and sacrifice offered a powerful, emotionally compelling panacea to mainstream Protestant indifference. Suffering became the primary mechanism for such identification, the epistemological bridge that Sheldon, like Alcott before him, promoted through the homiletic novel between subject and object made "concrete," "actual," and "personal" in the visceral experience of another's pain. But it also prompted individuals to cross social barriers. As W. T. Stead assessed the value of Christ on the Chicago streets in 1894, "It is not as the Judge of all the earth, nor as the Second Person in the Divine Trinity, that He appeals to the common people. Christ is to them the Man of Sorrows, who was tempted in all points even as we; *the Divine tramp*."[71] "What would Jesus do?" became a passport into otherwise remote worlds of destitution and despair.

Ultimately, Social Gospel advocates based their imitation of Christ on Matthew 25:35–40, where, in a scene imagining the day of reckoning, Jesus warns that he will measure the worth of each soul by its social response. "For I was an hungered, and ye gave me meat: I was thirsty, and ye gave me drink: I was a stranger, and ye took me in: Naked, and ye clothed me." As Phelps insisted in her 1868 bestseller, *The Gates Ajar,* the righteous learn from Jesus after the fact "what, in the unconscious ministering of the lowly faith which may never reap its sheaf in the field where the seed is sown, they had not . . . the comfort of finding out before,—'I was sick and in prison, and ye visited me.'"[72] The possibility of Christ's passing among men as a stranger, a beggar, a starving child, or a social outcast—arriving "as a thief in the night" (1 Thessalonians 5:2)—fired the imagination of Social Gospel authors. By this lesson, Jesus was perceived to have modeled the undercover investigation as an engine of social intervention. In the most quoted of Social Gospel verses, he condenses his gospel into a simple edict: "Inasmuch as ye have done it unto one of the least of these my brethren, ye have done it unto me" (Matthew 25:40).[73]

Resilient and rhetorically powerful, this trope passed between religious and secular texts. Riis's *How the Other Half Lives* (1890), Stead's *If Christ Came to Chicago!* (1894), Milford Howard's sequel *If Christ Came to Congress* (1894), Edward Everett Hale's *If Jesus Came to Boston* (1894), and London's *People of the Abyss* (1903), for instance, are all prefaced with James Russell Lowell's "A Parable," a reprise of Matthew 25:35–40. Relating Christ's incognito visit to a modern city, the poem begins: "Said Christ our Lord, I will go and see / How these men, My brethren, believe in me."[74] It concludes where Sheldon's novel starts: with Christ rebuking his followers for having turned him away. Disputing this claim, they ask when they had done so, and Christ replies that he was the freezing child on the corner and the old woman who begged bread at their stoop. An even rawer literary depiction of an all-too-human Christ undoubtedly caused *Atlantic Monthly* to censor a remarkable passage in Rebecca Harding Davis's 1861 publication of *Life in the Iron-Mills,* in which the young, downtrodden immigrant iron-mill worker Hugh Wolfe takes refuge in a Protestant church:

> Years ago, a mechanic [Jesus] tried to reform in the alleys of a city as swarming and vile as this mill town, who did not fail. Could Wolfe have seen him as He was, that night, what then? A social Pariah, a man of the lowest caste, thrown up from among them, dying with their pain, starving with their hunger, tempted as they are to drink, to steal, to curse God and die. Theirs by blood, by birth. The son, they said, of Joseph the carpenter, his mother and sisters there among them. Terribly alone, one who loved and was not loved, and suffered from that pain; who dared to be pure and honest in the devil's den; who dared to die for us though he was a physical coward and feared death.[75]

While such a desperate depiction of Christ tempted to drink, steal, and curse—or, on the eve of a war marketed in the North as martial Christianity's greatest campaign, a messiah beset by cowardice—would undoubtedly have upset the *Atlantic Monthly*'s well-heeled readers (no doubt including the *Atlantic Monthly*'s future editor and Social Gospel advocate, William Dean Howells) had it not been altered, this passage epitomizes the perceived value placed on Christ's total incarnation. The last lines of the unpublished passage is a rhetorically powerful instance of the trope of Jesus as undercover investigator: "If He [Jesus] had stood in the church that night, would not the wretch [Hugh Wolfe] in the torn shirt there in the pew have 'known the man'? His brother first. And then, unveiled his God."

In this context, the trope drew its most poignant irony from the tragic consequences of missed opportunity, the word unspoken, the deed undone, a failure with cosmic consequences for the individual's destiny at the intersection of the temporal and eternal. In a more radical version of this failure, for instance, W. E. B. Du Bois published a short story in the December 1911 issue of *Crisis* titled "Jesus Christ in Georgia," in which the Lord returns to a twentieth-century Georgia community in the person of a "Mulatto" man, only to be turned away by the white community. In 1920, Du Bois revised the story for his collection *Darkwater,* as "Jesus Christ in Texas." Far removed from the simple doctrines of the early church and blinded by racism and xenophobia, the white Texas community fails to recognize Jesus, though their African American servants recognize the black Messiah. At the story's ironic climax, the white Texans lynch the "olive skinned" Christ in the name of their white Savior.[76]

The trope of Christ as undercover investigator transforms Mark Seltzer's vision of the realist novel in its relation between authorship and systems of social control. If, as Seltzer argues, the realist novel is based on a fantasy of surveillance through the totalizing vision of the omniscient narration—which, following Seltzer's Foucauldian paradigm, becomes a policing regime—the homiletic novel naturalizes what Seltzer calls the "criminal continuity" between authorial vision and social control as part of the reader's projected self-transformation as an agent of social, moral, and spiritual reform.[77] The moral and social control at the core of spiritual obligation is transformed here from the affective mechanism of fear, from the punishing, omnipotent, all-seeing God of Calvinism, to that of a devotional, sacrificial piety. That devotional piety was sustained by the possibility of being trebly Christlike: at once imitating and serving the Savior. Christians could render aid to the suffering (as Christ had done); they could also literally assist Jesus imagined as literally embodied in the poor, whose visages more closely bore the impress of him as the divine tramp. The final, transcendent possibility of this radical *imitatio Christi* was, like Alcott's Beth, the sacrifice of one's own life in a social cause, the Social Gospel credo enshrined in John 15:13: that, like Christ, one lay down one's life for another.

The image of Christ as class transvestite also points up what many perceived and peddled as a powerful model of social declassification and deracination. If the trope could cut with bitter irony, as it does in Du Bois's story, it could also hold out a millenial vision of a society free from social caste and class hierarchy. In many ways, it was this vision that gave purchase to the popular depictions of first-century Christianity, encouraging ministers such as Sheldon, Lyman Abbott, Edward Everett Hale, and Washington Gladden—all representing congregations with remarkably different socioeconomic and geographical backgrounds—to play up the itinerancy and plebian status of Christ's fishermen disciples. Similar to the way in which Denning draws on Alfred Habegger's work on realism to argue that working-class readers interpreted fictional worlds politically— not as realism, but as microcosmic allegories of class struggle, "master plots" inflected with the "artisan variant of republican ideology" brought to the fore by the then "new labor history"—readers like Ronald Reagan perceived in homiletic novels allegories not of class struggle, but of moral battle within social microcosms that corresponded to the larger struggle occurring outside time.[78] Denning reasons that in the dime novel's masterplots (principally "two contradictory narrative formulas— the romance of contests and battles and the story of education and self-improvement"), the outlaw, hobo, street kid, or detective protagonist is repoliticized (decoded) as a participant within familiar vignettes of industrialized class struggles.[79] In contrast, homiletic readers—whose training within Protestant heuristic tradition laid the groundwork for their typological understanding—were encouraged to see how characters (drunks, prostitutes, corrupt politicians, and the like) who struggle for spiritual redemption, pulling themselves from the thrall of alcohol, gambling, greed, poverty, and secularism, were absorbed into the cooperative fantasy of a spiritual commonwealth or transfigured in death, thus transcending, in either case, the ideological and material markers of class and race, a transcendence that in itself became an index of salvific status.

In this sense, the impoverished stranger at Reverend Maxwell's door is none other than Jesus, and few homiletic readers would have missed the sobering irony of an otherwise vigilant minister having turned the Savior away—or the symbolism of the stranger's gesture of clutching at the communion table as he collapses to the floor. The affinity between the homeless tramp, his last breath an utterance of forgiveness, and Jesus, the outcast whose sacrificed body the communion signified, emblematizes the Social Gospel's view of the poor as closer to Christ than the privileged. Unblinded by material reality, the poor would not mistake the shadows of this world for the eternal substance of the next. In his lectures to a middle- and upper-class Edinburgh audience, William James demonstrates just how far flung such views had become among the economically privileged: "The laborer who pays with his person day by day, and has no rights invested in the future, offers also much of this ideal attachment. Like the savage, he may make his bed wherever his right arm can support him, and from his simple and athletic attitude of

observation, the property-owner seems buried and smothered in ignoble
externalities and trammels, 'wading in straw and rubbish to his knees.'
The claims which *things* make are corrupters of manhood, mortgages on
the soul, and drag anchor on our progress towards the empyrean" (*Varieties* 255).[80] Thus, immersed in suffering, indigent classes enjoyed greater
affinity with Christ. As Benjamin Flower reminded his readers in "Jesus
or Caesar," "It is . . . noteworthy that He chose to place Himself as the
incarnation of the oppressed, the suffering, and the needy."[81]

In accordance with the doctrine of atonement, homiletic authors promoted suffering as a means of achieving the affinity with Jesus that the
destitute were perceived to share. Sheldon's novel, for instance, repeatedly recalls 1 Peter 2:21, the verse from which it takes its title and from
which the characters draw their inspiration: "For even hereunto were ye
called, because Christ also suffered for you, leaving you an example, that
ye would follow His steps." Revealing the credo of Maxwell's church,
one observer writes to a correspondent that they "seem filled with the
conviction that what our churches need today more than anything else is
this factor of joyful suffering for Jesus in some form" (*In His Steps* 237).
Broadly speaking, the homiletic novel produced readerly identification
with protagonists who themselves identify with the plight of the poor.[82]
Much as the remarkable black exhorter Zilpha Elaw had celebrated the
dignity of African Americans half a century before—because, in contrast to white Christians with their "high-toned sensibility," their black
"brethren" exemplified "Christian morals [of] the apostolic era"—Social
Gospel authors idealized the "primitive" simplicity of those who, in *The
Narrow Gate,* Sheldon called the "wretched of the earth."[83]

In the various fictional portrayals of Jesus's undercover appearances
as beggar, child, worker, and black man, homiletic fiction imagined an
alternative model to the one Denning identifies as class accents, the keywords and plot formulae, we recall, that serve as mutable arenas of readerly contestation. By demonstrating how sociological categories (race,
gender, class, and the like) focused individuals on material markers or
the empirical references of subjective experience, the homiletic novel
crafted symbolic resolutions that—rather than negotiating antimonies
internal to specific class structures or neutralizing threats from without,
as Denning describes the cultural function dime novels served—sought
instead to transcend such distinctions altogether, projecting universal
Christian characteristics like spiritual autonomy in the face of peer pres-

sure, moral rectitude, disinterested benevolence, and self-sacrifice. The
power of this formula over readers could be considerable, releasing them
from the class moorings that Denning's study identifies as the basis of
the reader's decoding. It sought to release them as well, at least in the
theory of this identificatory theology, if not from gender, then from the
strict postbellum constructions of it. Female characters in *In His Steps*
who are initially bent on public, secular careers are not reined back into
a quasi-private domestic sphere. In the course of the plot, Sheldon has
them come to recognize how the public sphere is as much appropriate to
their capacities and virtues as it is for their male counterparts. Their aspirations for public careers, like those of the male characters, are channeled toward social venues to assist the poor, would-be converts and
those afflicted by terrible addictions.

As we have seen, many homiletic texts similarly troubled the simple
binaries of postbellum race constructions. In much the way Christ became identified with the poor, he also became identified with the racially
oppressed. Two years after suggestively using Christ's ambiguous racial
markers to indict southern racism, W. E. B. Du Bois made the connection explicit between Christ and turn-of-the-century African Americans:
"Jesus Christ was a laborer and black men are laborers; He was poor and
we are poor; He was despised of his fellow men and are despised; He was
persecuted and crucified, and we are mobbed and lynched." If his white
readers missed the direct connection with the Christ-incognito trope, Du
Bois reiterated the point in precisely Stead's idiom: "If Jesus Christ came
to America, He would associate with Negroes and Italians and working
people."[84] Like the black churches of Wilmington, North Carolina, African Americans read Sheldon's novels and embraced the responsibility of
their characterological actions within an imaginary landscape in accordance with the "What would Jesus do?" premise. All these phenomena
demonstrate the active process in which homiletic works were in effect
revised by a broad range of readers along the lines of Sheldon's own congregational roundtables. It is this appeal among the broadest conceiv-
able audience that made the homiletic novels at times resemble sacred
texts more than they did popular secular novels.

As these examples indicate, in venerating the needy, the homiletic
novel steadily enlarged its scope. Initially concerned with urban blight,
it eventually extended its reach to embrace poverty and suffering wherever they occurred. The rustic lives and folkways of the Appalachian

and Ozark people, for instance, struck evangelical readers as living homilies snatched from the past—from the slopes of ancient Palestine or
the Judean hills walked by the Psalmist's shepherd-king. Novels such as
John Fox's *The Little Shepherd of Kingdom Come* (1903) and *Heart of
the Hills* (1913) and Harold Bell Wright's runaway seller *The Shepherd
of the Hills* (1907) popularized the theme of impoverished hill folk struggling to preserve their primitive piety against the encroachments of modernity. Authors like Wright also linked Jesus's crippling climb to Calvary with disability, locating divine majesty in the broken body of an
asthmatic or the "feeble mind" of an autistic child, a folk theology that
would, in part, one day arm fundamentalist evangelicals against abortion, death-with-dignity advocacy for those in vegetative states, and even
stem cell research—the most radical gloss of all on "the least of these"
in Christ's admonition to be stewards of the most vulnerable. The homiletic novel produced readerly identification with protagonists who themselves identified with victims of suffering, even as they sought to alleviate it.

For Maxwell and his congregation in *In His Steps,* the suffering stranger's reenactment of Christ's death—their indifference "crucified" him,
one character insists (*In His Steps* 61)—casts them in a biblical drama.
Experience thus emerges from literary representation (the biblical account), to be reframed as another form of representation. Like the older
homiletic forms such as the religious allegory and spiritual autobiography that we considered in the last chapter, the homiletic novel exposes
an endless cycle of representation by construing all experience, narrative
or lived, as a recurrence of divine paradigms. In homiletic practice, the
literary and the dramatic parse knowledge in performable, albeit simulated, increments of experience; for its readership, homiletic fiction was
no less nor more real than unmediated experience. Phelps's protagonist
in *The Gates Ajar* encapsulates this vision, distinguishing between a realism predicated on spiritual truth and one based on material evidence:
"That is the reality," she muses, "this the dream; that the substance, this
the shadow."[85] The association of the Raymond pauper's suffering with
Christ's, his death with the Crucifixion, presupposes a perspective that,
when translated into the Social Gospel's ethic of intervention, was (in
Flower's words) "to give immediate relief or succor to the starving and
shelterless Christ of the present hour."[86] In this context, would-be reformers struggled to overcome detachment and doubt, to alter the social
world and thus to shape the course of their own and others' salvation.

Homiletic Audiences

The last two chapters traced how American Protestantism harnessed the power of sensation, creating interactive experiences of sin and punishment to inoculate the innocent against temptation. The emergence of what I am calling a theology of inoculation unified the material and the spiritual, the personal and the universal, through a series of narratives designed to proliferate a homiletic pedagogy that taught readers to interpret their own lived experiences according to spiritual templates. The novelization of homiletic realism, I have been arguing, grows out of these traditions. This genealogy is perhaps nowhere more visible than in the way the homiletic novel draws on the Puritan sermon tradition, from which the homiletic practice of audience interaction and agency developed. In the remaining sections of this chapter, I focus on this Puritan heritage to propose an analogous genealogy of the homiletic audience. Not only do narrative forms, shaped by a particularly American formation of Protestantism persist across a long, historical durée, but the reader's, listener's, and viewer's relationship to these forms persists as well. This seems counterintuitive from a modern perspective that privileges the passive and often secular receptivity of listening to a lecture or absorbing a text. We are not critically equipped to think of reading or even listening as a vitally active process. Yet the Puritan sermon tradition fostered expectations of audience interaction and agency not only through such identificatory mechanisms as narrative personalization and characterological impersonation as we have seen, but also through a particular culture of audition that would become embedded in the homiletic novel as the site of negotiation and conflict for local and national congregational roundtables—or, more abstractly, as the object at the core of our expanded definition of Robert Darnton's communication circuit. Far from passively absorbing or observing, homiletic readerships were trained in rigorously interactive programs of response.

In the generation before Sheldon, Henry Ward Beecher's sermons epitomized a growing pattern among Civil War–era evangelicals to stimulate individual forays into social activism. Beecher and his contemporaries staged numerous theatrical spectacles designed to provoke action as much as to impart insight, often in churches newly articulated to enhance a connection between the minister's dramatic presentation and audience participation.[87] At a Sunday service on February 8, 1860, for example, he led a nine-year-old African American girl onto the plat-

form. His voice cracking with emotion, he identified the child as a fugitive slave. In the graphic language that had secured his reputation as
the silver-throated orator, Beecher foreshadowed the brutality awaiting
the fugitive should she be returned, painting for his congregants scenes
of frothing hounds, the cracking whip, and the captive's bleeding lacer-
ations. With its imaginative and physical reality, the sermon stirred the
congregation to a pitch of zealous fury and resolve. Beecher then simulated a slave "auction," inviting congregants to purchase the child's
physical—and thus her spiritual—freedom. Parishioners leapt up, crying
and sobbing, to "bid" on the fugitive, accumulating money for the freedom fund.[88]

Beecher's sensationalistic drama, while unwittingly reifying racialized
power structures, also demonstrates how Protestant pedagogy yoked an
emphasis on social charity to an experiential ethic of intervention.[89] In
so doing, it illustrates the revolution occurring in popular evangelicalism
between the field revivals comprising the Second Great Awakening before 1835 and the late antebellum period. Beecher's and his congregant's
dramatic performance crystallizes how, among more liberal evangelical
camps, the intense inward focus on the individual's conversion and salvation began, alternatively, to turn outward toward a broader focus on the
social, on the salvation of community that the impending national cata-
clysm of the Civil War would finally galvanize into the Social Gospel's
interventionist credo. Among increasingly liberal evangelical congregations, the pilgrim's progress was no longer linked seamlessly to a unified
corporate identity but rather directed outward to the socially and politically marginalized and oppressed, rendering practices of social reform
integral to Christian identity. Had freeing a fugitive slave been his only
concern, Beecher could simply have requested money from a congregation renowned for charity. Instead, he sought not just to fix a problem,
but also to immerse his congregants in the personal trauma of a social
ill—to connect them to another's suffering and their agency to social relief. He believed that once his parishioners personally encountered human pain, they would be transformed from observers—voyeuristically
prowling among ghastly facts—to social activists.

This sermonic strand of sensationalistic drama and social reform inculcates homiletic patterns of religious realism within the novel, thus
opening up an imaginative space in which reader and text collaborated
in applying Christian allegory to social reality. The intellectual and
metaphysical traditions of Anglo-American Protestantism had always

attached knowledge to form, creating an epistemic scaffolding designed to reach beyond the ken of the senses to the invisible mystery of the divine, visibly represented both within the reader's typological imagination and through narrative forms. The sermon's use of logic, the division and categorization of all knowledge into interlocking parts, and even the complex heuristic systems that required specialized reading (or hermeneutic) practices were predicated on the unquestioned assumption that specific forms like the sermon, allegory, or religious emblems were embedded with specialized theological knowledge, such that, when properly opened and interpreted, these forms rendered a particular spiritual meaning.[90] The clearest example of the relation between form and knowledge—and how the reader approaches the former to achieve the latter—are the sophisticated mnemonic systems in which spatial paradigms were freighted with information that could, through the specialized process of reading and picturing (i.e., Barber's "transformation of pictures") that we earlier examined, or the architectural paradigms we will come to in the next chapter, be later retrieved, allowing congregants to explore or rehearse biblical truths at their leisure, unmediated by clerics or creed.[91]

To understand this process, we must briefly revisit an earlier Protestant homiletic practice that had been abandoned by revivalist ministers, while also recalling from chapter 1 Jonathan Edwards's need in "A Divine and Supernatural Light" to rationalize spiritual experience by routing it through Locke's sensual epistemology. Seventeenth-century sermon design—used by many formalist Presbyterians, Baptists, Methodists, and Congregationalists until late in the nineteenth century—utilized a classical rhetorical anatomy adapted from scholasticism, predicated on an affinity between form and the experience it embodied. By dividing sermons into five components—invention (*inventio*), arrangement (*dispositio*), style (*elocutio*), delivery (*pronuntiatio*), and memory (*memoria*)—ministers employed a linguistic algorithm that matched biblical wisdom to daily trials, then framed that lesson in a style calculated not merely to tickle listeners' ears but to penetrate their hearts. In the idiom of early modern faculty psychology, the sermon sought to lodge itself at the core of the conscience: rendered compelling by the affect it produced in the passions and the imagination, tested and tempered by the faculty of reason, it would reveal itself in naked simplicity to the understanding, the seat of knowledge. Once the new knowledge had passed sequentially through the initial faculties, the will, or faculty of volition, could use the new knowledge to direct moral conduct through the dictates of spiritual enlightenment. Feeding information into this complicated rhetorical equation, Puritan divines synthesized and categorized biblical exegesis, spiritual instruction, and the moral challenges of daily life into digestible units of knowledge.

In the Puritan sermon, the display of methodology was at least as important as content and meaning, adhering closely to the scriptural precept and Protestant mantra to "prove all things, [and] hold fast to that which is good" (1 Thessalonians 5:21). Sermon design created a forensic technology that verified its own theological accuracy. Implicit in this early pedagogy was the skeletal structure of what became nineteenth-century Practical Christianity's fully fleshed—often novelized—pragmatic theory of active and engaged learning. By directing auditors through the same finite number of steps, the sermon reiterated the process of its compositional development and knowledge acquisition, reducing the reader-auditor's passivity by locating him or her in the minister's authorial role. Such a role is not, however, an instance of postmodernism's reauthoring paradigm, in which the indeterminism of signification and rejection of universals results in the reader subjectively reauthoring the text. Rather, within the particular hermeneutic practice of the homiletic, the reader performs in the belief that, because knowledge is objective and truth universal, they reside in and are rendered visible by forms structured by, and anchored within, the cosmic design.

In the engaged hermeneutic of this older heuristic practice, the sermon was not a decree handed down from on high. Rather, it provided a built-in fact-checking system whereby the audience should quite literally audit the sermon in both senses: hearing and taking account. Each section, from invention to application, laid out the argument in progressive stages that congregants were to examine, try, and test. The sermon's forensic division engaged auditors in a step-by-step rhetorical equation whose sum was greater than its parts, allowing them to transcend the materiality of facts and figures and achieve a higher, spiritual knowledge. In this way, the steps of the equation initiated a supervised process of active engagement with spiritual truths, accruing knowledge, and applying learning. This is a consummate example of the *intensive* reading practice that distinguishes the allegorical from the *extensive,* novelized mode of reading. Assuming that knowledge is embedded in form, which one must open in order to access and interpret that knowledge and finally apply it to daily life, the Puritan commitment to systems and forms bequeathed this "auditing function" to the nineteenth-century sermon and, through it, to the homiletic novel.

By preserving the crucial relationship among form, hermeneutics, and readerly psychology, the homiletic novel revitalized the heuristic frame and function of its sermonic predecessor. Sheldon represents this process on the cover of *In His Steps* as a staircase leading readers from Bethlehem to Calvary (fig. 3). His titular pun announces the novel's pragmatic purpose as a template for translating the reader's life into a series of steps along the footpath to salvation. An important structure of the homiletic novel—evident, as we will see in the next chapter, in religious reform narratives as divergent as the sermons of Henry Beecher and the "lay sermons" by Jacob Riis—spatialized timelines encouraged readers to measure spiritual decline or ascent in increments. Like the modern self-help step systems they influenced, Lyman Beecher's *Six Sermons* (1827), T. S. Arthur's best-selling *Ten Nights in a Bar-Room* (1854), and Sheldon's *Robert Hardy's Seven Days* (1898) illustrate—as we saw with Mary Rowlandson's "removes," or the vividly episodic teleology of Thomas Shepard's and Zilpha Elaw's autobiographies, or John Barber's and Louisa May Alcott's staged spiritual progressions—how spatialized incrementalism creates the tableau of progress toward a personal and social redemption. Such incrementalism also demonstrates how narrative movement through progressive stations renders individuals' lives antitypes of both Old Testament and New World types, all leading directly to the messianic archetype, whose exemplary life was likewise measured out in the steps of a man.[92]

Sheldon would have encountered these Calvinist pedagogical strategies at Andover, which, in the 1870s, remained a center of conservative theology and homiletic technique in the tradition of Jonathan Edwards. In the heat of the revivals around Northampton between July 1740 and August 1741, for instance, Edwards had preached a series of seven sermons that keyed incremental development less to the anomalies of individuals' particular spiritual growth than to humanity's general development. By exposing the moral weaknesses and spiritual strengths of various age groups in this sermon series, he revealed how a natural, age-related development imposed its own form of incrementalism on the individual's broader spiritual growth. Beginning with a sermon aimed at children from ages one to fourteen, Edwards wrote two sermons target-

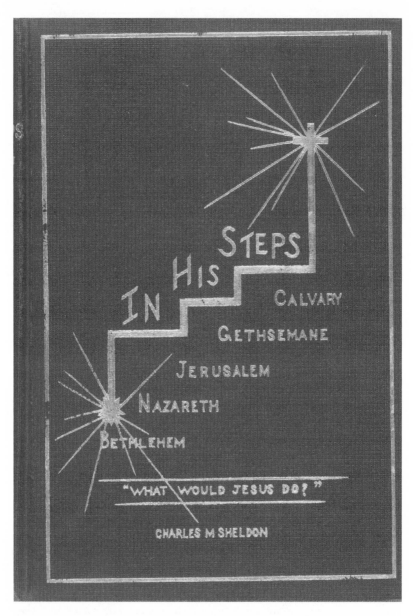

FIGURE 3. Charles Sheldon, the cover of *In His Steps: "What Would Jesus Do?"* 1896. Sheldon's cover features the stations of the cross in the form of a staircase, illustrating how the novel scripts a modern typology out of a traditional pilgrimage.

ing those between the ages of fifteen and twenty-five—the popular "The Danger of Corrupt Communication among Young People" and "Youth Is Like a Flower That Is Cut Down"—one sermon for those between ages twenty-six and fifty, and one for those over fifty.[93] This sermon strategy was just one of several that Edwards's generation bequeathed to his homiletic heirs.

As we saw in chapter 1, Edwards had endeavored to make the spiritually young feel the consequences of sin through simulation, so that knowing and doing become one and the same. As Perry Miller demonstrated, this pragmatic link between thought and deed was a part of Edwards's legacy: "The process from the form of the perception to the act of the will became, for the Edwardsian psychology, not what it had been in the scholastic physics of his predecessors. . . . It became an instantaneous and single moment. To perceive became to do."[94] To offset the risk that they would blindly stumble over the edge of a moral chasm, he advocated the imitation of experience through visually oriented sermons requiring auditors to transpose themselves into the narrative frame. There, they engaged in what-if scenarios, detailed hypotheticals demanding that they identify mimetically with situations and characters in order to examine and try what, in his notorious Enfield sermon, he likened to humanity's tenuous hold on mortality.[95] Here lay the principle behind the relationship between experience and literature that informed homiletic engagement and sermonic realism. Ministers trained in this tradition believed the study of sin must be visceral, as with the hellfire sermon or the modern-day hell house. If homiletic literature was to have a psychological impact, it had to convey the idea of sin and its consequences in the immediacy of sensuous experience. As Perry Miller observed, "If a sermon was to work an effect, it had to impart the sensible idea in all immediacy; in the new [Lockean] psychology, it must become, not a traveler's report nor an astrologer's prediction, but an actual descent into hell."[96]

The written word when transformed through the appropriate hermeneutic practice had, with vivid realism, to open the maw of hell, that parishioners might see it gaping before their eyes. This is an example of the particular habits of imagination that allowed homiletic readers to see their lives unfold in Barber's "transformation of pictures" or, more recently, to accept the characterological impersonation demanded by the *Eternal Forces* video game as plausible modes of realism. At Andover, Sheldon would have learned the importance of making sermons vivid

occasions for interactive engagement—portals transporting his parishioners into a virtual reality—not vehicles for abstract precepts, passively
consumed.

Sheldon's training reflects the Edwardsian homiletic principle in Jacob Abbott's 1832 homiletic manual, *The Young Christian,* in which, as
we saw in the preceding chapter, Abbott compares a father's cold reading of a scriptural passage to his children against a homiletic rendering of
that same passage. The lesson bears reiterating here: "Suppose that this
same father could, by some magic power, show to his children the real
scene which these verses describe. Suppose he could go back through the
eighteen hundred years which have elapsed since these events occurred,
and taking his family to some elevation . . . from which they might overlook the country of Galilee, actually *show* them all that this chapter describes" (*Young Christian* 230; emphasis added). What Sheldon would
have learned from his seminary training, then, was the importance of
this vivid homiletic showmanship.[97] As Abbott advised, the experiential
or "experimental" was the most compelling evidence for a "strong and
lasting impression upon the mind": "Experimental evidence . . . is the
most convincing of all. It is direct. There is no laborious examination of
witnesses to bring the truth to us—no groping in the dimness of ancient
times, and straining the sight to ascertain the forms of objects and the
character of occurrences there. All is before us. We can see distinctly,
for proof is near. We can examine minutely . . . for it is constantly recurring" (*Young Christian* 173).

Many before Henry Ward Beecher's generation borrowed the ac-
tion-oriented strategies of their evangelical predecessors to dramatize
personal agency as a function of salvation. Charles Grandison Finney,
for instance, had instituted the "anxious" or "mourner's bench," which
encouraged sinners to catalyze the conversion experience by visibly
bracketing—thus heightening—its emotions. The great populist preachers Lorenzo Dow and Barton Stone, the father of the "Christian Movement," prescribed the "jerking exercise," advising would-be converts
to writhe and shake in anticipation of being ravished by the indwelling
spirit, in the hope that effect might drive cause, that physical signs of
anguish might induce the emotional distress required to break the sinner's recalcitrant heart. And the evangelical temperance movement used
a horse-drawn wagon laden with new converts to sobriety, both to stage
and thus contractualize before witnesses erstwhile drinkers' cold-water

pledge and to demonstrate memorably the recidivist's having "fallen off the wagon" bound for glory. Operating in conjunction with the sermon's visual language and attached to its interactive auditing function, these homiletic dramas—often referred to as "new measures"[98]—linked narrative and experience, personalizing the sermon's spiritual realism, much as, in the century before, the hellfire sermons of Solomon Stoddard, William Cooper, Thomas Foxcroft, and Edwards had, through a new mode of homiletic realism, encouraged the young to imagine themselves at the Judgment and in the flames of eternal damnation. But it was Beecher's generation, on the cusp of the Social Gospel, that turned such strategies from personal introspection to social intervention, transforming the individually focused conversion experience into a communal awakening toward social salvation and a more public, pragmatic ethic of participation.

Sheldon's readers—like those of Hjalmar Boyesen and other homiletic authors who depicted moral lessons advocated in religious theatrical productions—would have been familiar with theater as a form of religious pedagogy, not only in dramatic productions such as the theatrical adaptations of *Parsafal,* Lew Wallace's *Ben Hur,* and Wright Lorimer's *The Sign of the Cross* and *The Shepherd King,* but also in churches like Henry Ward Beecher's Plymouth Church that drew on the performative template established at Chatham Street Chapel, the erstwhile New York City Chatham Theatre that religious philanthropists Lewis Tappan and William Green converted into a revival hall in 1832 for the famed Charles Grandison Finney.[99]

Like the sermons from which they borrowed their narrative strategies, Sheldon's novels provided virtual exercises and steps of graduated difficulty to strengthen Christians' moral muscularity—their resolve, judgment, and will. Through controlled exposure, the texts forearmed their audience against sin by simulating experiences that would prepare them for their ground duty in salvation's army as it morally rearmed the nation. In *In His Steps,* Sheldon critiques the modern conception of reading as a passive exercise disengaged from life and the world when he has a visiting minister, witnessing the changes among Maxwell's congregation, confess to another, "You and I belong to a class of professional men who have always avoided the duties of citizenship. We have lived in a little world of literature and scholarly seclusion, doing work we have enjoyed and shrinking from the disagreeable duties that belong to the life

of the citizen" (*In His Steps* 192). From within the hermeneutic tradition
in which Sheldon's novel operates, literature and experience cooperate
to form pragmatic models for social engagement.

The need to locate the catalyst of agency had become the holy grail
of Progressive reform in its struggle to overturn the moral inertia, social entropy, and political torpor of what was widely viewed as the greed-
driven fatalism of the Gilded Age. William James, influenced by the legacy of Edwardsian homileticism, offered one solution. Capturing the
optimism circulating in both religious and secular reform currents, he
used pragmatism to shore up faith against the assaults of relativism by
making belief, through the catalytic of thinking, the origin of action.
In his "Philosophical Conceptions and Practical Results" (1898), he extracted the Edwardsian core of Practical Christianity: "Beliefs," he announced, "are really rules for action; and the whole function of thinking
is but one step in the production of habits of action."[100] In his assessment of Christianity in 1901, James, like Sheldon, repeatedly returned
to experience as the only test of faith. In so doing, he, like Sheldon and
other homiletic authors, was turning back to what he called Edwards's
legacy of "empiricist criterion" (*Varieties* 25). James boiled down Edwards's *Treatise Concerning Religious Affections* (the theology begun,
we recall, in his sermon "Divine and Supernatural Light") to this "thesis": "By their fruits ye shall know them, not by their roots." In emphasizing experience as the practical and proper end of all religious training,
James follows Edwards closely, quoting his *Treatise:* by "forming a judgment of ourselves now, we should certainly adopt that evidence which
our supreme Judge will chiefly make use of when we come to stand before him at the last day. . . . There is not one grace of the Spirit of God, of
the existence of which, in any professor of religion, Christian practice is
not the most decisive evidence. . . . *The degree* in which our experience is
productive of practice, shows *the degree in which our experience is spiritual and divine*" (*Varieties* 25; original emphasis). Like Edwards before
him and Sheldon and other contemporary homilists of his day, James argues that spiritual knowledge can only be empirically verified by action.
Commensurate with the outcome Edwards achieved by harnessing the
faculty of the senses to that of the will, James made knowing and doing
one and the same thing.

This is how any narrative that shapes action—and thus experience—
decisively operates as a mode of literary realism. The Social Gospel's homiletic principle revivified its own genealogy when it declared

the belief that knowledge untried by experience could never navigate the perilous landscape that impeded the pilgrim's progress. In a similar legacy, the homiletic novel attempted to provide the narrative machinery—through the steps of reading, imagining, community dialogue, and revision—that might translate belief into action. Sheldon's Topeka congregation inherited this practical reformist orientation. In 1892, the congregants organized a kindergarten in Tenneseetown, Topeka's African American ghetto, where Sheldon had lived for several weeks to determine how to alleviate segregation-imposed poverty.[101] Through constructing a building, teaching elementary and Sunday-school classes, and staffing a nursery, Sheldon's followers worked to integrate the black community with the white congregation. As with Beecher's simulated slave "auction," the Tennesseetown experiment was not meant simply to intervene in the suffering of a marginalized population, but to construct a radically alternative, shared social reality that transcended the individuation on which race and class were predicated. Sheldon noted the dramatic change this experience had on his young congregants, most particularly in their worship: "I have often thought that in the singing of those songs where the black and white unison rose together in the heart of that American Africa, my young people came to feel the oneness of the human family more deeply than in all the work they did for the welfare of those brothers and sisters of ours."[102] Yet the historical record also records the difference Sheldon's program of integration had among the African American community. The effects of this movement were far reaching, extending even to early civil rights struggles. The son of one of Sheldon's kindergarten students, for example, would litigate the initial stages of the antisegregation case that, in 1954, became *Brown v. Board of Education of Topeka*. Charles Sheldon Scott, as his middle name attests, was a product of the educational system established through interventions first imagined in a homiletic novel.[103] Like Reagan's life-altering reading of Wright's novel, this incident concretizes how lived experience is manifested beyond the symbolic acting out of texts. In this regard, the rich archives of religious materials in the United States—often collected with little regard to any specific ideological content—provide unique, largely untapped possibilities for reconstructing localized nineteenth-century cultural life.

In the cycles of fiction and experience that the homiletic novel generated, the Tennesseetown experience in turn became the material for another of Sheldon's novels, *The Redemption of Freetown* (1899), which inspired religious communities around the nation. In the late fall of 1897, for instance, a group of Presbyterian Theological Seminary students began the John Little Mission in Louisville, Kentucky, among a large black community that had been ghettoized in the eastern part of the city. They organized Sunday school classes and worship services in neighborhoods lacking both facilities and spiritual leaders. Following a plan mapped out in the plot of *In His Steps,* they also offered courses in domestic economy for young women and vocational courses for men, organizing recreational activities for the community's young.[104] The seminary graduate Ferdinand Schureman Schenck advocated tenement visiting in New York City, wedding religious principles to ethical action. Drawn from the homiletic novel, his program that organized congregants into a relief society culminated in *The Sociology of the Bible* (1909), his manifesto defending the interventionist credo of the Social Gospel. It is in this context that religious historian Peter Williams suggests the extent to which the Second Great Awakening distantly augured new formations of power and authority that spilled over from religious organizations, altering traditional power relations within broader cultural and political forums.[105]

In the case of the homiletic novel, specific authors and religious templates were adopted and "revised" by diverse communities—among them communities such as several African-American congregations in Wilmington, North Carolina, that, as Ralph Luker records in *The Social Gospel in Black and White,* adopted *In His Steps* for their evening sermons and exhorted their audiences to accept its homiletic credo, "What would Jesus do?" as the basis of their daily decisions.[106] Rather than a one-to-one correspondence between characters and thematically depicted cultural differences and tensions, homiletic novels fostered diverse social representations that stand in for different readerly values, and that are claimed, contested, repudiated, and accepted. Yet the "terrain of negotiation and conflict"—to borrow the phrase Michael Denning applies to the dime novel—that homiletic novels catalyzed was less about the "proper accents of the popular" than about perceived supratemporal spiritual concerns that homiletic readers like Sheldon's congregants perceived to transcend class and race as the debased markers of the postlapsarian world.[107] As Sheldon repeatedly argued, "In the largest and truest sense there is no 'negro problem' any more than there is an 'Anglo-Saxon problem.' The only problem is the 'human problem.' And it is all capable of being resolved in simple terms which apply equally to every race and condition."[108] When a black man that Sheldon sent to the Topeka YMCA was refused admittance, the editor of *The Unitarian,* to whom Sheldon reported the incident, scolded the "so-called Christianity of our time": "If Jesus taught anything, he taught human brotherhood—that before God there is no rich or poor, no black or white."[109] As with Mason Locke Weems's early-nineteenth-century graphic novelized sermons— for which he carried signed testimonials from individuals whose lives these narratives had transformed—we should thus see Sheldon's ministerial activities and authorial efforts within the same dialectic of experience and literary realism, as stages in the hermeneutic cycle of homiletic engagement.[110] In offering pragmatic guides for action and framing a collective vision—and in the Edwardsian legacy of moral inoculation— his texts were scripted, cast, blocked, rehearsed, and produced in steps meant to soften, if not elide altogether, the distinction between imagination and experience, fiction and reality.

Enacting Allegory

While Sheldon's homiletic novels drew on interactive pedagogies innovated in Beecher's generation, they also used an older heuristic tradition of allegory to extend that interactive ethic from isolated instances, like Beecher's slave "auction," into daily habits of social intervention. Every anecdote, parable, and plot in homiletic texts allegorized deeper religious values and histories. This allegorical model has become largely invisible because secular novelistic conventions, combined with our current understandings of reading, foreclose the likelihood of alternative readerly epistemologies. As Denning observes, whereas readers in the novelistic mode take households, families, and individuals as "typical," "with thoughts, psyches, and motives acting in an everyday way," the allegorical mode sees such individuals or groups "as microcosms of the social world" or as social groups or types, acting within "a master plot, or body of narratives . . . shared by a common culture."[111] The homiletic novel provided its readers such a typological script, where action unfolds simultaneously within and outside historical time.

In the plot of *In His Steps,* this typological model becomes especially associated with what Sheldon called the "Raymond pledge," a commitment his characters make to do nothing without first asking, "What would Jesus do?" Acclaimed singer Rachel Winslow, for instance, turns

down a lucrative career with a national musical company to sing instead
for tent revivals, hoping her renowned voice will prepare the hearts and
inspire the souls of those seeking the word of God. Edward Norman, the
editor of Raymond's *Daily News,* decides to purify the town's paper by
dropping all sports coverage and all advertisements for products such
as alcohol, tobacco, and women's undergarments. While the Raymond
Daily News becomes famous in Christian circles throughout the country,
its declining ad revenue threatens its operations. Learning of the newspaper's struggle, Virginia Page, a wealthy heiress and attractive socialite,
decides that answering the gospel's challenge for her would mean fund-
ing the paper out of her own capital, which she then does. Ultimately, she
establishes a settlement house in the heart of Raymond's ghetto, based
on the theories and designs advocated by the British philanthropist Ar-
nold Toynbee and the Chicago reformer Jane Addams. The gradual de-
pletion of Virginia's finances—like those of other characters who sacrifice careers, business deals, and even their homes—in her pursuit of
the pledge to follow Jesus coincides both with Christian socialism's appeal to redistribute wealth and its desire to conform literally to the likeness of Jesus, who, as Flower phrased it, "chose to place Himself as the
incarnation of the oppressed, the suffering, and the needy."[112] Such concern about "acquisitiveness," William James noted, while "not exactly
the sentiment of humility, though it comes so close to it in practice," illustrated an emergent ethos of individuals "refusing to enjoy anything
that others do not share" (*Varieties* 260).

   Throughout Raymond, many alter the course of their careers and
lives as they make the question "What would Jesus do?" the basis for
their actions. Sheldon himself demonstrated locally how homiletic realism could shape lived experience. Following his character Edward Norman's plan for purifying the Raymond *Daily News,* in 1900, Sheldon
contracted with Frederick O. Popenoe, editor and owner of the *Topeka
Daily Capital,* to turn the paper into a daily Christian newspaper for one
week. The idea initially appeared in Sheldon's first homiletic novel, *Richard Bruce* (1893), which Sheldon read before his congregation in 1891. In
the story, the revered minister John King plants the idea in the mind of a
young journalist for a Christian newspaper that would be issued simultaneously in Boston, Chicago, New York, Philadelphia, and San Francisco.
In another instance of how homiletic realism linked narrative and experience, Sheldon's edition achieved unprecedented success, appearing

in Chicago, New York, and London, selling several hundred thousand copies each day. The experiments emerging from the homiletic novel helped shape a broader public discourse, dialectically shaping communal values. Sheldon's edition also inspired the antagonism of Topeka's other daily newspaper, the *State Journal,* which enlisted the famed editor of the *Atchison Globe* and secular journalism advocate, Ed Howe, who countered with secular editorials to oppose the enterprise with views that saw print in newspapers around the country. Evincing the extremes such a discourse could provoke, even when framed by satire, the *Atchison Champion,* a weekly that ran daily during the Sheldon experiment, announced that for the week of March 13—the week of Sheldon's run—it would issue its paper, not as Jesus would do, but rather, "as the devil would run it."[113]

Many of Sheldon's readers also took the Raymond pledge, gathering weekly to discuss their own struggles to meet the demands of such a radical *imitatio Christi.* In so doing, they typified widespread readerly identification with the characters and plots of homiletic novels, which compelled direct action in the world. Such a heuristic structure of reading was, as we have seen, an illustration of living-word theology, an absolute that could only be "interpreted" through experience, not through rationalism.[114] As with bibliomancy—the pervasive practice of opening the Bible to a random verse, trusting that the action is divinely guided—participatory reading assumes that religious allegory, like scripture, reveals truths not only universal but particular to individual lives. Practiced by Christians for ages (Augustine linked his conversion epiphany to this practice), bibliomancy is an instance of the "living word made manifest in the flesh" of the auditor's experience.[115]

For the Social Gospel, such an interpretive capacity loosened the stranglehold of an increasingly empirically verifiable ontology, allowing readers to see through the veil of history to the recurring patterns underneath. On the double-sided frontispiece of Stead's *If Christ Came to Chicago!* for instance, the recto illustrates Christ in flowing robes angrily overturning moneychangers' tables in the first-century temple (fig. 4), while the verso (the front cover of some copies of this edition) reveals him in a Gilded-Age club, upsetting the tables on which businessmen barter commodities (fig. 5). The images are not intended to be seen as historically separate, but as a simultaneous event, Christ present in both moments. By collapsing the diachronic register, the homiletic text of-

FIGURE 4. William T. Stead, *If Christ Came to Chicago! A Plea for the Union of All Who Love in the Service of All Who Suffer,* 1894. This image depicts Christ driving the money-changers from the temple (Matthew 21:12).

fers a newly relevant perspective, inviting viewers to shape themselves as self-sacrificing antitypes in accordance with Stead's exhilarating slogan, "Be a Christ!"

When William James assessed this sacrificial ethos to determine what motivated an increasingly popular ideology so seemingly contrary to self-interest, he found what he imagined to be a mechanism of motivation beyond blind faith. "Obedience may spring from the general

FIGURE 5. William T. Stead, *If Christ Came to Chicago! A Plea for the Union of All Who Love in the Service of All Who Suffer,* 1894. This contemporary image applies the same biblical passage to show Christ condemning modern capitalists. Together, figures 4 and 5 create an eschatology that emphasizes the connection between scriptural and contemporary events, registering the simultaneous effects of divine and human agency in the world.

religious phenomenon of inner softening and self-surrender and throwing one's self on higher powers. So saving are these attitudes felt to be that in themselves apart from utility, they become ideally consecrated." The belief in Jesus as a man tempted by human weakness fostered the urge to sacrifice for others. James ventriloquizes Social Gospel evangelicals: "In obeying a man whose fallibility we see through thoroughly, we, nevertheless, may feel much as we do when we resign our will to that of infinite wisdom. Add self-despair and the passion of self-crucifixion to this, and the obedience becomes an ascetic sacrifice, agreeable quite irrespective of whatever prudential uses it might have" (*Varieties* 250).

As Sheldon's characters take the "Raymond pledge" and enact it in their own lives, they choose from a smorgasbord of modern social problems, but, as with Stead's diptych, such problems appear palimpsestically embedded in human history, such that historical epochs are perceived to unfold simultaneously as though in synchronic time. Thus, Sheldon's "ever present now" became, in the words of one protagonist, a temporal compression he refers to as an "everywhere presently now."[116] Through collective acts of narration, the homiletic novel, begun on the page and completed in the imagination, helped readers to order the technologically evolving and morally unstable world around them. It is this continual reiteration of the universal struggle between the forces of good and evil that, for the Social Gospel (and for evangelical Christians today), made the question "What would Jesus do?" so relevant in each age. Like Updike Underhill's emulation of Bunyan's Christian—his attack on the image of Apollyon with a penknife in Tyler's *Algerine Captive*—homiletic readers were supposed to be undeterred by anachronism, and were expected to superimpose their own actions upon the scripted lives of Christian characters in the homiletic novels they read. In so doing, they would reenact Edwards's homiletic legacy, seeing themselves as agents "in the universal design, which is never fixed but dynamic, which is not a contemplative exercise, but a pattern in time," requiring for its fulfillment the recursive Christian cycles of struggle, failure, and success.[117]

In its function as an imaginative arena for individual and communal action, the homiletic novel tacitly serves, in the way Janice Radway has shown of romance novels, the function of a social contract between authors and specific religious audiences. Using traditional homiletic strategies newly incorporated into the novel form, religious authors directed their readers in the proper use of this homiletic heuristic.[118] This readerly involvement, historically assumed in Protestant reading practices, had implications for the structure of homiletic fiction. Contrary to the conventional novel's focus on two or three major plot lines, homiletic novels tended to generate multiple plots. Closer to the conventions of allegory than to those of the novel, Sheldon's stories and those of other homiletic authors offered character types and social roles that had to be filled by the reader's engaged imagination, reinforcing the experiential basis of religious realism. Mothers, fathers, children, heiresses, widows, professionals, farmers, homemakers, laborers, and ministers all people his stories. By turns, each character takes the spotlight, seeking ways to express commitment to Christ through commitment to humanity. When primary plots abruptly end without resolution and protagonists, in the midst of what Sheldon called a "crisis of character" (*In His Steps* 231), disappear from the novel's pages, new protagonists and story lines emerge, and the text sets the stage for another series of moral contests.

The homiletic novel's fragmentary narratives and focus on blindness and insight also recall the striking overlap of sermon with the emergence of gothic literature, which, in light of the discussion of Edmund Burke in chapter 1, we might more usefully think of as the Calvinist sublime. If the narrative breaks in homiletic novels imitate the disruptive sensationalism produced by eighteenth- and nineteenth-century image-driven sermons, they also resemble narrative breaks associated with gothic fiction, famous for its patterns of narrative interruption: stories begin in media res (often with the narrator finding a lost fragment of an older story), narratives abruptly terminate as narrating heroines swoon or plunge into the darkness of underground vaults, and villains die in the midst of crucial confessions upon which the plot mystery hangs. Such narrative ruptures are symptomatic of the narrator's epistemological blackout that then becomes the reader's psychological blackout, figured through conventional gothic tropes of fainting, terror-induced trances, subterranean falls, suddenly extinguished lights (or any form of sudden sensory deprivation). Yet homiletic novels also voice such tropes of psychological rupture as epistemological affirmation rather than blackout, marking the onset of conversion experience. The narrative breaks produced by sermons— trances, fits, and stupors; pew dramas, anxious benches, and jerking exercises; evangelical fervency, baptism as a symbolic death, and enthusiasm's cycles of mania and depression; and abrupt, life-altering breaks with vice, vocations, and family—are all important signposts along the pilgrim's proper path, and as such, are indexes of the supplicant's regenerative experience that, because it was physiologically or psychosomatically registered in the body, demonstrates the intended role of homiletic literature's aesthetics of immediacy.

While gothic is traditionally associated with romance rather than realism, in early Calvinist religious pedagogy, this experiential psychological regeneration did not merely imitate a particular reality, but rather attempted to reproduce it. As the Social Gospel increasingly turned from an emphasis on the individual as part of a uniform collective to the individual as agent of social reform, these violent conversion ruptures became a collective experiential component of homiletic literature in the form of the narrative breaks whose resolutions depended on communal acts of readerly engagement. *In His Steps,* the consummate example, does not bring protagonists' stories to resolution. Rather, it defers that resolution to provide a catalyst for discussions among members of reading communities and congregations across the nation, as they exercise both their spiritual faculties and volition in determining what Jesus would do, further instilling the appropriate habits of imagination required for homiletic reading.

By their abruptly terminating plots and refusal of moral closure, homiletic novels further dramatize the tension between novelistic and allegorical modes of reading, resisting what Fredric Jameson has described as the novel's modern reification of commodified literature. While in this novelized reading mode, as Jameson argues, readers "read for the ending," seeking "consumption satisfaction," the homiletic novel denies normative presumptions.[119] Its narrative breaks and indeterminate conclusions offer homiletic training for intervening in the social world. Consequently, these novels fail as novels in the Jamesonian sense. Yet they are not "*designed* to fail," to borrow Michael Davitt Bell's contested description of Henry James's purpose to subvert Howellsian realism; instead, they fail in order to foster homiletic realism.[120] If as Bell argues, James's performative intent was to expose realism's instability as a response to the demands of authorship and representation, the homiletic novel conversely exposes the competing ambitions for moral closure, on the one hand, and, on the other, the imposition of readers' moral agency as a constitutive element of the plot's extratextual continuation through their subsequent moral agency embodied in the text's insistence on readerly interaction. That insistence is never more clearly inferred than in Sheldon's use of the subjunctive mood: "What would Jesus do were he I?" Or "What would I do were Jesus here?" It is this transposition of the reader into the novel's action—and thus the extension of the novel's imaginary field into the reader's reality—that constitutes a mode, perhaps a hyper-mode, of discursive realism.

By reproducing the epistemological transition from empirical senses to spiritual sight, homiletic novels simulate the evidentiary crisis of the reader's sudden shift from material knowledge to initial blindness (often figured by Paul's conversion) in the spiritual world, where the senses have little traction. In the assumption that effect might drive cause (much as in the "jerking exercise" or "anxious bench" devised by Dow, Stone, and Finney), the novel's narrative ruptures produce sensory deprivation, the condition believed to sharpen the spiritual faculties. Through such deprivation, homiletic readers were meant neither to achieve spiritual self-fulfillment nor merely to practice devotional autonomy. They were meant instead to construct themselves as radically incomplete subjects in order to understand spiritual enlightenment and true piety as an open-ended ideal that must be practiced through constant struggle and hardship, achieved and lost in successive waves of failure, success, stasis, and growth. For Social Gospel converts, like their evangelical forebears in the antebellum "harvest fields" of camp revivals, sight became an inward organ, as initiates learned the meaning of the Social Gospel's Pauline credo, "We walk by faith and not by sight" (2 Corinthians 5:7). As William James succinctly puts it, "The absence of definite sensible images is positively insisted on by the mystical authorities . . . as the *sine qua non* of a successful orison, or contemplation of the higher divine truths" (*Varieties* 52). These images must crystallize and fade with the individual's cycles of faith and doubt. For the spiritually muscularized, it was this spiritual sight—the key to the Edwardsian epistemology, as we have seen—that revealed in the face of the tramp the visage of the divine.

* * *

Following the devastation of the Civil War and the apex of the industrial revolution, American evangelicals had become increasingly disillusioned with the relevance of the Bible and scriptural wisdom to their lives, so different, so seemingly advanced in relation to the primitive lives and spiritual needs of first-century Christians. The Bible described the first disciples in agrarian and pastoral metaphors—as seed, wheat, or chaff; as tilled fields, rocky soil, and the "wayside" where the seeds of Life sprout and grow, or wither and die; as sheep, goats, fish, flocks, and lambs; as vineyards and vines; and as fishermen, husbandmen, shep-

herds, and the like. In a Progressive Era marked by unprecedented economic growth and technological advances, biblical analogies and parables seemed crude at best and dead at worst. By tying readers' lives in
the nineteenth century to the life of Jesus, works like *In His Steps* modernized biblical typology, locating the origins of sacred history in the
New Testament rather than Old, and updating New World hagiographies
to mirror more closely the heroic and inspirational ideals of the present
age. But the real-life representatives of the primitive apostolic church
were not lost in the works of Sheldon and his cohorts who typologized
the suffering of society's poor as the late-nineteenth-century version
of the pastoral disciples of Christ. While homiletic realism reconfigured
the story of Christ to accommodate an emergent market culture, it also
represented those not benefiting from that culture as left over in a primitive and pietistic Christian past. Homiletic realism thus allegorized the
split between the rich and the poor as part of a modern-day typology, reinfused with a social reform imperative: to live in the steps of Jesus was
to address the spiritual needs of first-century Christians through social
programs for modernity's poor. Homiletic realism thus unfolds a narrative structure of typological fulfillment through self-other identification.
Referring to the "apostolic life" as the "Christ-principle" in 1893, the
Social Gospel advocate Henry Wood encouraged this identification: "If
life were ever inspired it should be inspired now, for the Christ spirit and
quality are as truly living as when incarnate in Jesus of Nazareth."[121]

In nothing did the homiletic novel demonstrate older reading practices so well as in its interpretation of the temporal world as a sign system of divine meaning relevant to the individual's spiritual needs. As
readers developed their roles within the novel's allegorical frame, they
learned to see their agency and action as playing a vital part in the Man-
ichean drama of good and evil. If the homiletic reader's life begins to resemble Christian's journey in *Pilgrim's Progress,* Red Crosse Knight's
crusade in Spenser's *Faerie Queene,* or even Updike Underhill's in Tyler's *Algerine Captive,* it does so for good reason. The homiletic novel
unfolds as a modernization of religious allegory, the advent of a new typology that, taken together with Edwards's spiritual sight as the source
of religious realism, reinvests the Protestant emphasis on scripture, by
reinvigorating the New Testament with fresh relevance for daily living.

As we saw in the last chapter, in much the same way that Ann Taves
describes how African American evangelicals had incorporated them-

selves into sacred historical narrative by enacting biblical typologies through ante- and postbellum tent-revival dance and drama, audiences of homiletic sermons and novels imagined through narrative enactment the ways in which their own lives revealed sacred themes drawn directly from the scriptures.[122] The homiletic novel required that readers fill in the complex narrative shell with personal and historically localized details, making the act of reading inseparable from the task of their own textual incorporation. As readers' homiletic enactment matured, the personal specificity with which they initially freighted the allegory gave way to the universal truths revealed by typology. The reader's act of transforming personal experience into a moral lesson—as a mark of God's favor or the sting of his chastening rod—does not so much eradicate as reorient the particular as an index of historical specificity. Through the patterns of biblical typology, historical particularity becomes a symbolic structure through which universal and eternal truths emerge. Rendering their lives as a spiritual allegory, readers experienced human will as divine grace, bringing the transcendent into history and historicizing the universal. The act suggested the most intimate and distinctive aspects of the individual, as well as the presence of a universal or transpersonal force. Shaped by the sermon's homiletic pattern, religious realism emerged as a powerful vehicle for transmitting pragmatic faith into churches throughout the nation, redesigning the novel as an interactive tool for civic training.[123]

In the tradition of Christian allegory, Sheldon demonstrated for his readers how the Christian is an "Everyman," helping them to recast their personal experience through the template of homiletic typology to render the spiritual teleology visible. The homiletic novel helped individuals imagine how they might organize and structure events in their lives—successes, failures, and setbacks—into what Northrop Frye, in his study of medieval allegory and romance, called an "and-then narrative," turning seemingly random events into a chain of meaningful links so as to invest all action with spiritual agency.[124] Narrative, after all, unfolds in what Royce called the "space of experience," suggesting why, as we saw with Edmund Burke in chapter 1, narrative exceeds all representational forms in its capacity to evoke sensation, and thus experience. "That is why," Royce writes in "The Temporal and the Eternal," "narrative is much more . . . effective than description . . . and why, if you want to win the attention of the child or the general public, you must tell the

story rather than portray coexistent truths, and must fill time with a series of events, rather than crowd the space of experience . . . with . . . un-
dramatic details."[125]

Even in secular and political realms, Sheldon's contemporaries used
homiletic frames to much the same end, demonstrating the way in which
Christian idealism fed secular currents. Theodore Roosevelt repeatedly
cited Bunyan's *Pilgrim's Progress* as a metaphor for the slow but steady
progress of reformers across a blighted urban landscape filled with physical and moral snares for the unwary. Giving the name "muckraking"—
from Bunyan's allegory—to the reformist press, for example, progressive
reformers like Roosevelt harnessed an already existing homiletic tradition to name and frame moral conduct as a particular course of political
agency and action. Roosevelt's appropriation of an allegorical tradition
of moral conduct helped not only to target a religious, reform-minded
demography, but also to concretize a particular mode of pragmatic reform within a field beset by an ambiguous set of moral options and motives. By tapping a preexisting hermeneutic that had long drawn on spatial metaphors and reshaping the homiletic realism vestigially attached
to late-nineteenth-century moral categories, urban reformers articulated
a category of action and initiated a standard of ethical behavior for tens
of thousands already predisposed to see reform in the religious terms
of the nation's moral rearmament. As with Theodore Roosevelt's 1912
avowal to "do battle for the Lord at Armageddon," George Bush's unfortunate reference in 2001 to the struggle against terrorism as a "crusade"
or his 2003 State of the Union address identifying the nation's "calling as
a blessed country" demonstrates, even in the current age, how in times
of crisis, the threadbare teleology of manifest destiny can take the shape
of a powerful millennialist eschatology.[126]

In Sheldon's era, as in our own, reformers' promotion of allegorical traditions of morality helped galvanize religious audiences. As we
will see in the next chapter, at a time just before the Pentecostal movement's born-again focus redirected evangelicalism from the social back
to the individual among emerging charismatic and, later, fundamentalist evangelicals, novelists like Harold Wright and politically minded reformers like Jacob Riis, John Dewey, and Roosevelt advocated Social
Gospel pragmatism as an antidote to both the moral relativism that enervated volition and the religious determinism that justified social indifference. Not merely an illustrated catalog of prescriptive admonitions,
then, the homiletic novel sought to intervene in moral development by

engaging readers in vigorous ethical action. By selecting localized problems that resonated in communities across the nation, homiletic novelists focused congregants' attention on specific social and moral problems while bringing the creative resources of thousands of communities to bear on these problems.

In His Steps has never been out of print. From Sheldon's day to our own, it has sold tens of millions of copies.[127] In the year following its 1896 publication, sixteen different publishing houses printed the novel, at prices ranging from five to fifty cents. By 1902, the novel appeared on publication lists for nearly a hundred publishing firms in the United States, Britain, and Europe. Newspapers and magazines from around the world continued to serialize it, making it a featured staple of the American Press Association, a supplier for more than half the nation's 16,000 newspapers. It was translated into more than twenty languages before the turn of the century, and has been continuously revised and updated by ministers to reflect the milieu of subsequent generations, making the example of Christ's steps newly relevant to each historical moment. Initially, revisions of the novel "corrected" Sheldon's Social Gospel message. Mrs. J. B. Horton's *In His Steps; or, The Rescue of Loreen,* for example, revised an episode of *in His Steps* to suit more orthodox theology. The setting of the novel has been updated to reflect a wide variety of ideologies, cultures, communities, and time periods. Even today, *In His Steps* remains the focus of annual youth gatherings, continuing to reinforce the homiletic patterns in such popular phenomena as the WWJD—"What Would Jesus Do?"—movement. By wearing bracelets or posting bumper stickers bearing the abbreviation (or one of its many spin-offs, such as the environmentally concerned "What Would Jesus Drive?" or the antiwar bumper sticker, "Who Would Jesus Bomb?"), or even by sporting the politically naïve Christian rock slogan "Do the Jew," an injunction to emulate Christ, evangelical Christians attempt to engage their faith in the world they inhabit.[128]

That *In His Steps* and the scores of novels it represents have faded in academic historical memory and have lacked intensive critical analysis makes current scholarly understandings of nineteenth-century religious, intellectual, and literary history notably incomplete. When contextualized within the *longue durée* of homiletic traditions and practices, and when read against broader currents of social reform, *In His Steps* and its many counterparts illuminate how homiletic novels, infused by pragmatism and lessons of practical Christianity, reinvested Protestant cul-

ture with a revitalized antebellum biblical literalism from which a new
kind of literary realism emerged. But the homiletic novel also reener-
gized Protestantism with a strange mix of practical application, liberal-
ism, and otherworldly spiritualism, sparking a fury of social activism that
would become hallmarks of the Progressive Era and have reverberations
that last to the present day. In the final chapter, we will turn to other
quasi-literary forms that took up the homiletic novel's call for action. In
so doing, we will examine how the literary influenced the social, even
as it absorbed new visual technologies that revivified the homiletic sermon's Edwardsian legacy (and the original meaning) of sensationalism,
seeking through new modes of experiential simulation to train reformers
for their descent into urban reality.

Cultivating Spiritual Sight: Jacob Riis's Virtual-Tour Narrative and the Visual Modernization of Protestant Homiletics

If you love and serve men, you cannot, by any hiding or stratagem, escape the remuneration. Secret retributions are always restoring the level, when disturbed, of the Divine justice. It is impossible to tilt the beam. All the tyrants and proprietors and monopolists of the world in vain set their shoulders to heave the bar. Settles for evermore the ponderous equator to its line, and man and mote and star and sun must range with it, or be pulverized by the recoil. —Ralph Waldo Emerson, *Lectures and Biographical Sketches*

And for morality life is a war, and the service of the highest is a sort of cosmic patriotism which also calls for volunteers. Even a sick man, unable to be militant outwardly, can carry on the moral warfare. He can willfully turn his attention away from his own future, whether in this world or the next. —William James, *The Varieties of Religious Experience*

On scores of occasions between 1888 and 1915, hundreds, sometimes thousands of Americans gathered in churches, guildhalls, theaters, and other venues to see progressive reformer Jacob Riis expose the misery of urban poverty. Projecting images on wide screens in darkened halls, Riis recreated New York tenement neighborhoods for his rapt audiences in ways that allowed them to explore urban despair and translate social knowledge into personal experience liberated from their fear of crime, contagion, and other perceived ghetto hazards.[1] In his most popular "magic-lantern"—or stereopticon—presentation, Riis introduced Tony, a first-generation Italian boy born in New York's eastside Bowery district. Using photographic images and speaking in the present tense and first-person plural form of address, Riis created the illusion that Tony himself stood before them. While Tony always began life as a "lad of promise," the subsequent details varied. Riis offered divergent narratives to provoke his audiences' empathy and outrage, sometimes depicting Tony as having been orphaned at birth, while at other times, as having been abandoned on the street at age two by his mother's death. In more distressing versions, five-year-old Tony was said to have fled a crowded, one-room apartment to escape his drunken father's daily beatings.

Of the many Progressive Era reformers who fought poverty and urban despair, Riis's legacy endures because of his powerful 1890 study, *How the Other Half Lives.* This illustrated text compiled and distilled his stereopticon lectures, offering readers today a hint of what his turn-of-the-century performances must have been like. But while Riis's text and photographs endure, modern readers have largely lost sight of their visual strategies and narrative forms, and the modes of reception through which his audiences gleaned their meaning. Understanding Jacob Riis's deep appeal for late-nineteenth-century audiences requires that we expand on the questions of race, class, and politics that are of concern to recent critics, to include the dynamics of homiletic realism in American religious history. Riis emerged as a product of, and catalyst for, late-nineteenth-century Social Gospel activism, and his lectures, delivered across the nation, drew directly on longstanding pedagogies of Protestant homiletics. Born in Denmark in 1849, Riis immigrated in 1870 to the United States, where, after a period of indigence, he began a career as a police reporter. By the 1880s he had become a passionate critic of urban neglect. His upbringing—within Reformation-old traditions of Scandinavian Protestantism, often overlooked in his biography—aided his seamless immersion into America's largely Calvinist tradition. Until his death, he attended Protestant churches throughout New York, including Brooklyn's Plymouth Church, where beginning in 1847, the renowned Henry Ward Beecher preached for nearly half a century, until his death in 1887.

From his first forays into social activism, Riis's approach to progressive reform drew on Social Gospel's central thesis, which questioned Christians' indifference to poverty and despair in their midst. Riis, of course, has stood as one of the most significant exemplars of the social reform movement's secular wing, and the close parallels between his work and that of Henry Ward Beecher significantly underscore the shared ideologies and narrative strategies between both religious and secular social reformers. As such, Riis's work in New York during the height of the Social Gospel movement provides a window into the gradual transformation of homiletic literature, both in its production of new kinds of social reality—linked to the Social Gospel's theological shift away from the obsessively introverted and individual-oriented conversion that marked antebellum evangelicalism and the advent of new visual technologies—and in its feverish advocacy of human volition. What I call Jacob Riis's "virtual-tour narratives" of New York tenements mark a transformative application of Christian social activism and homiletic pedagogy. In an era preceding the rise of modern cinema, drawing on the new and dazzling technology of slide projection, Riis initiated a technologically advanced visualization of Protestant homiletics, the religious pedagogical tradition we have been examining in which eighteenth- and nineteenth-century preachers summoned vivid imagery to crystallize moral issues, illustrated metaphysical abstractions through allegory, and employed spatialized logic and mnemonic organization to help audiences conceptualize and engage a kind of virtual experience. Coming down through Edwards's theological offspring of the New Divinity School and the broader New Light revivalists, the midcentury sermons of Jacob Abbott, Lyman and Henry Ward Beecher, and Charles Grandison Finney, among others, and the innovative homiletic narratives of the following generations—epitomized, as we saw, in the work of John Warner Barber, Louisa May Alcott, Albion Tourgée, and Charles Sheldon—transported audiences into detailed hypothetical encounters with moral dilemmas and sin itself. Inspired by this hell's-plot tradition—a genealogy bookended by the personalized sermons of Edwards's generation and the modern-day hell house—and speaking to audiences trained in the interactive and performative culture of homiletic reading, Riis's lectures combined the still-novel technology of photographic projection with vision-oriented homiletic pedagogy to stimulate and direct audience engagement.

Riis forced Christian audiences to confront the dangers and moral challenges of their rapidly urbanizing world. Wedding the sermonic allegory to both the stereopticon's three-dimensional projection and the perceived autoptic realism of pre-turn-of-the-century photography—the correlation between image and reality that John Dewey, in his Kantian phase of Social Gospel advocacy, mocked as the "kodak fixation"[2]—Riis simulated the physical spaces and metaphysical contours of what reformers referred to as the nation's "social cellar."[3] Drawing middle-class audiences into this social cellar, Riis sought to evoke their concern, making "their hearts 'burn within,'" as *Wesley Magazine* assessed one audience's reaction, by awakening them to their own culpability in human misery.[4] He illuminated the social questions at stake and surveyed the opportunities for Christians to alter not only his specific subject's world but also that of the poor everywhere. Tony, for instance, became an allegorical figure of youth's possibility and the implicit social promise that childhood signified during the Progressive Era.[5] Riis thus used Tony's story, like those of other orphans in his "underworld" pantheon, to emblematize the social rewards of charitable intervention timely met and the dire consequences when ignored.[6] With each plot twist, he underscored how tragedy might have been averted, deploring the part that "we" have played in Tony's plight by "our" indifference to the conditions in which he lived. Tony became a talisman of the momentous task standing between the faithful and the approaching millennium, which many believed their labor would occasion—one form taken by the Progressive Era revivification of human volition. The Social Gospel promise of a utopian period of social regeneration that would culminate in the world's salvation generated an optimism that flowed generously into the broader culture, replenishing Christian hope even in humanism's secular currents.

Riis's lantern lectures, often described as a new tool of social reform, in fact modernized similar virtual-tour experiences that the Beechers and other evangelical Calvinists had cultivated earlier in the century. It summoned the imaginative capacity of those trained in living-word theology and Edwardsian second sight—the ability to see the immutable through empirical references in daily life—and those prepared to expect the revelation of knowledge through personal experience simulated in a range of spiritual-progress narratives. Deploying the homiletic conventions of visual language, allegorical tropes, religious tableaux, and first- and second-person plural narration, all coming down through the revival sermons of the First and Second Great Awakenings, to invoke audiences' senses through an aesthetics of immediacy—heightened by anxiety, suspense, surprise, and the power of suggestion—Riis simulated excursions into New York's tenement slums. In darkened rooms loomed large-as-life images of poverty, vice, and the destitute that introduced a new dimension to the exhibition space. In conjunction with narratives that, according to the *Brooklyn Eagle,* combined "knowledge and imagination surcharged with feeling," Riis's photographic images, drawn from his personal archive, created a spatial dimension in which, like the personalization of narrative demanded in "New Light" sermons and homiletic novels, allegory and reality merged.[7]

This virtual world was allegorical for the double narrative it provided. While it offered a literal presentation of tenement life, a journalistic report featuring stark images, demographic analysis, and statistical facts, it also, like the typological narratives of colonial Protestants we saw in chapter 2, possessed an alternative narrative embedded within a tradition of Christian hermeneutics, and invoked by the themes of awakening, atonement, redemption, nativity, hell's harrowing, and, above all, pilgrimage.[8] Additionally, audiences familiar with homiletic practice recognized and developed the parallels between the tenement life depicted in the lantern lectures and Riis's repeated allusions to biblical parables, pilgrimage tropes, and the popular Christian allegories of the New Light sermon tradition, and the allegories of Bunyan, Dante, Edmund Spenser, and John Milton, among others.[9] In this allegorical space, Riis engaged audiences in the virtual immediacy of temporal experiences with spiritual consequences. He directed them along prescribed paths, through confining corridors, windowless rooms, crowded dives, and refuse-strewn streets. Introducing sights and sounds of suffering, he also evoked the fetid stench of tenement environs, intoxicating fumes that enervated mental and physical health. While literal, the landscape was also metaphysical: its contagion the cause of moral decay, its baffling contours the snares encumbering the spiritual journey, and its suffering denizens, lost members of Christ's fold, who, like Bunyan's Christian sinking in the Slough of Despond or imprisoned in the dungeon of Doubting Castle, had lost their way. For those stuck in the literal, Riis rhetorically prodded the slippage between the literal and allegorical: as he narrated his audience's descent down steep stairs into damp, verminous cellars, among families crowded into single rooms, he announced in the immediacy of the first-person plural, "We've descended into the underworld" (*Other Half* 44).

Taking up the particular strategies by which Riis engaged audiences in the reality of urban poverty, this chapter continues to unfold an alternative genealogy for the formal and thematic conventions that have come to define literary realism and its generic offshoot, naturalism. With other scholars of realism, I propose a connection between the discursive strategies and journalistic techniques of Riis and his more literary contemporaries, but from the perspective of this study, the heuristic investment of Riis's work, rather than a secular literary tradition, is the bridge between Riis and the homiletic novels of the postbellum era. Recent critics tend to view realism in the 1890s as an urban style focused less on mimetic representation than on a close-up perspective (primarily the narrator's) that, though experimental, remained deeply committed to the empiricism and immediacy of personal experience. To the detriment of urban reformers such as Riis, Helen Campbell, and Benjamin Flower—all using photographs (many taken by Riis) in their essays and lectures—critics of realism usually identify these authors' works within conventions of sentimentalism, against which they weigh the merits of literary realism.[10] In his study of Stephen Crane, Alan Trachtenberg qualifies the realism of Crane's urban tales in contrast to Riis's sentimental strategies, which, in his view, were largely "devices to preserve distance—devices of picturesque perspective or sentimental plot that protected the reader from the danger of a true exchange of point of view with the 'other half.'" Following Trachtenberg, Maren Stange, and others, Russ Castronovo insists that "through repeated and strategic use of foreground in photographs, Riis's shots accentuate the distance between the viewer and subject."[11] June Howard similarly makes Riis's *How the Other Half Lives* the epitome of a *fin de siècle* tradition of class identification in relation to the cultural abjection of the poor. Yet these critics overlook a religious tradition grounded in its own sense-based psychology that existed alongside but in explicit opposition to the increasingly secular and skeptical epistemology of modernity. Social Gospel audiences would have perceived the sensory encounter as springboards to transcendent knowledge and thus to spiritual enlightenment. The discursive strategies of the homiletic tradition thus invested Riis's aesthetic with a spiritual epistemology that instrumentalized such extrasensory capacities of intuition, empathy, instinct, and revelation. Riis's realism thus emerges as an aesthetic site that adjudicates the deeply contested threads of science, religion, psychology, and philosophy, allowing the seemingly sentimental plot to sit alongside the real and the transcendent to coexist with the empirically immanent.

In a work cited by William James, Henry Wood aptly articulated the deep ambivalence reflected by the emerging social sciences. In his 1893 *Ideal Suggestion through Mental Photography,* Wood describes the ontological and epistemological rent dividing the "new age": "Two great groups of forces are striving for mastery. On one side is arranged '*real-*

ism,' pessimism, and the Without; and against them, *idealism*, optimism, and the Within. . . . [This] general cleavage is running through religious denominations, therapeutic systems, governmental and economic theories, temperance, and ethics."[12] Sharing that ambivalence—while like Henry Adams also nostalgic for the certainty of old verities—James assessed the conflict for a new professional class unsure of the capacity of either religion or science to account for, much less represent, reality: "The claims of the sectarian scientist are . . . premature. [Spiritual] experiences . . . plainly show the universe to be a more many-sided affair than any sect, even the scientific sect, allows for. What, in the end, are all our verifications but experiences that agree with more or less isolated systems of ideas (conceptual systems) that our minds have framed? But why in the name of common sense need we assume that only one such system can be true?" Concluding that neither faith nor empiricism is wholly right nor wholly wrong, he parts truth in the middle: "What is certain now is the fact of lines of disparate conception, each corresponding to some part of the world's truth, each verified in some degree, each leaving out some part of real experience" (*Varieties* 105).

Seen from this perspective, Riis's "realism" requires modern critics to reassess the values that underlie conventional definitions of realism: the disdain for spiritual faith and teleological worldviews, cynicism toward Progressive Era faith in social intervention, and a "scientific" determinism that naturalizes social constructivism as an ontological certainty. It also requires care in not projecting our own cultural and political certainties on an age that we assume to be as polarized as our own between secularism and spiritualism, science and belief, and empiricism and faith. Such neat categorization seems appropriate from a historical distance, but at the turn of the twentieth century, these seemingly oppositional domains were more fluid, and the partisanships more multifaceted, ideologically contradictory, and fragmented. I argue that the aesthetic innovations of literary realism emerged not only from a cosmopolitan embrace of scientific empiricism but also from the superimposition of the visually oriented homiletic tradition onto new discursive and visual forms. It is from this perspective, taken together with the homiletic practices of readerly identification, that we can understand how it is that readers in Alcott and Sheldon's day could understand *Little Women* and *In His Steps* within a tradition of realism. Within this context, we can also better comprehend the extraordinary claims of readers, like Ronald Reagan or Sheldon's young congregants laboring to unify Topeka's black and white communities, who found in the protagonists of homiletic novels exemplary patterns for molding their own lives.

As we examine more closely the Progressive Era in which Christian and secular reform intersected, particularly in urban centers such as New York City and Chicago, this final chapter brings together the initial three. The homiletic materials and cultural histories explored in the preceding chapters illuminate how Riis's social activist realism was grounded in a particularly American Protestant tradition: the Edwardsian revision of Locke's sense-based epistemology to account for second sight; the steady muscularization of human volition, from its ebb after the English Reformation to its high point with the nineteenth-century emergence of a radically reformist milieu; and, finally, the gradual novelization of homiletic heuristic practices and the postbellum flowering of the homiletic novel. With Riis, then, we come to the culmination of a tradition that has continuously engaged with material experience in order to access spiritual truths and foster moral behavior, a tradition bridging secular literary forms and popular religious practices and the highest levels of theological and metaphysical theory. Because the brand of 1890s urban reform exemplified by Jacob Riis's work has in the critical tradition been the most decisively situated in the secular realm, I will revisit the homiletic theory outlined in the introduction in order to establish Riis and his cohort's immersion in that tradition.

Homiletic Theory in Social Gospel Reform

Riis's audience brought to the virtual-tour narrative an aesthetics of immediacy, or a particularly Protestant way of seeing and narrating social reality in visual, oral, and literary texts. As we saw with Barber's *The Pilgrim's Progress* as a "transformation of pictures" and Vincent's "upper" and "lower" Chautauqua, or *Little Women, In His Steps,* and *That Printer of Udell's,* homiletic texts employed allegorical frames to create social environments immediately present to viewing auditors in which individuals imagined possibilities for personal intervention. Readers of homiletic narrative understood Riis's stories of Tony and others not to be just tales particular to a time and place but representative of universal experiences—religious metanarratives and biblical typologies—with realities and consequences both within and outside historical time. Homiletic allegories transformed individuals into communities of action expected to engage with religious material as experiential templates or moral scripts for their own lives. As Tony's plight came to represent the plight of suffering children, the audience's feelings of sympathy and outrage evoked by his misery encompassed larger questions about social despair and want, leading to moral standards for social intervention. Through Tony's story, audiences began to wrestle with the tragedy of alcoholism, starvation, pathogenic infection, the oppression of Gilded Age capital, the despair of sweatshop labor, and the horrors of tenement life.[13]

Like the scores of Social Gospel narratives seeking to build coalitions of reform, Riis's magic-lantern talks drew on the strategy found in the homiletic novel of denying readers the role of passive onlooker. The magic-lantern talks also augmented these strategies by presenting a virtual reality that demanded their narrative participation and volition in moral choices. Far from mimetic representations of a social reality to be taken at face value, Riis's photographs functioned as religious tableaux for audiences that believed in revelatory power as a kind of second sight, an unmediated access to the divine that we have been tracing from Edwardsian theology. Many Progressive Era audiences saw the plight of the urban poor only as it became personal through virtual representation. The photographs capture the epistemic intersection between knowledge and form that, as I explained in the previous chapter, originated in the Puritan sermon. And like the sermon, the magic-lantern lecture depended on audience interaction, inculcating within its listeners the experience of post-Lockean Calvinism that, in this case, transformed the formal hermeneutics of knowledge into the initial stages of social action. The tableaux of urban despair Riis staged were the shadows cast by the union of allegory and new visual technologies, to which only the sympathetic identification of middle-class Christians could lend substance. In this act of identification, the cleavages between audiences' lives and the blighted tenement landscapes gave way through mutual bonds of suffering in which one person accepts another's suffering as his or her own.[14] In the projected images of Tony and his world, for instance, the suffering of photographic ghosts was taken on by the feeling flesh of middle-class spectators. Constructing his virtual-tour narratives around images of widowed mothers, dying fathers, homeless children, culturally unmoored immigrants, the aged, and the mentally ill, Riis elicited his viewers' emotions in a manner unavailable to the more rational, disenchanted political texts of Progressive Era reform. This was not emotionalism produced by sentimentalism—what critics have seen as the pandering of de-based religiosity—but rather feelings understood as a faculty of perception; knowledge gleaned by the "the sense of the heart" at the core of Edwards's revision of the Lockean epistemology, to which nineteenth-century evangelicalism was heir. In exposing such personal, familial, and emotionally saturated imagery, Riis transformed his audience's most intimate emotions into a ritualized expression of community demanding the deeply personalized intervention he referred to as reform by "vital touch."[15]

Steeped, as they are, in a secularized epistemology, contemporary literary and visual arts critics lack the tools of analysis that might best explain the specific ways that evangelicals, then as now, rely on specific kinds of virtual experience as a legitimate substitute for actual experience. In the course of this study, we have seen how the mechanism for virtual experience—recreated through various modes of verbal and discursive simulation acting on the religious's analogical habits of imagination—emerged among Edwards's generation to solve what they perceived as a terrible conundrum: how to inoculate the inexperienced against the experiences of evil without which, paradoxically, they could not recognize the dangers of such experience. While rooted in Reformation Calvinism, this conundrum was exacerbated by the experiential drive of the Lockean epistemology, which prompted a significant theological disruption in Calvinist metaphysics. Colonial Calvinists believed the young and inexperienced to be caught on the horns of a dilemma: not only knowledge but also experience of sin was the only mechanism for developing moral and spiritual defenses. If the young had no knowledge of how to avoid, much less recognize, sin without the experience of sinning, they were, for all intents and purposes, damned by their own innocence. Calvinists from the Reformation through the nineteenth century firmly believed that any exposure to sin came at a steep price. As with public health announcements that caution the young today about drug use, religious educators believed that the first experience might not only lead to addiction or habituation, but also serve as a gateway to escalating vice.

If a Lockean epistemology predicated on the absence of innate ideas and moral faculties produced the conditions for experience-based learning, it logically followed that sense-oriented pedagogies could instill the knowledge required to build moral and spiritual defenses, not through real encounters with sin but through their virtual simulation. Thus, spiritual guardians turned back to pre-Reformation literary strategies and innovated new discursive forms in an effort to provide the young with a semblance of evil and its devastating consequences. Despite present-day critical assumptions about the capacity of representation to create the sensation of experience—remorse, anxiety, fear, gooseflesh, and the like—constituting what Edwards called "immediate evidence" and William James, in his reading of Edwards, "immediate intuition," such virtual experience underlies much Protestant pedagogy. Today such pedagogy includes the hell house, the *Eternal Forces* video game, and the Holy Lands theme park in Orlando, Florida, in which the faithful virtually tour first-century Rome, where they finally follow their Savior in real time to Calvary to witness a brutally realistic dramatization of the crucifixion. In his 1904 essay "A World of Pure Experience"—the centerpiece of his study on "radical empiricism"—James expressed the epistemological value of simulated experience, a traditional staple of homiletic pedagogy:

> The towering importance for life of this kind of knowing lies in the fact that an experience that knows another can figure as its *representative,* not in any quasi-miraculous 'epistemological' sense, but in the definite practical sense of being its *substitute* in various operations, sometimes physical and sometimes mental, which lead us to its associates and results. *By experimenting on our ideas of reality, we may save ourselves the trouble of experimenting on the real experiences* which they severally mean.[16]

Simulated or "representative" experiences, James asserts, "form related systems, corresponding point for point to the systems which the realities form; and by letting an ideal term call up its associates systematically, we may be led to a terminus which the corresponding real term would have led to in case we had operated on the real world."[17] At the core of late-nineteenth-century Pragmatism lay the substitutionary principle of inoculation theology, the simulation of an experience that can empirically substitute for another. Terms such as "figure," representative," "substitute," and "corresponding" articulate the proximity of James's Pragmatism to a religious tradition predicated on a system of embedded substitution: Adam's posterity for Adam, Christ's death for human life, type for antitype, the sacrament for Christ's body—and, in Social Gospel theology—the sacrificing steward for the suffering poor. For the faithful, substitution mediated not one set of corresponding realities, but, as

James's language of doubling suggests, two. Experiences in what James calls the "real world" correspond to the spiritual world no less than his simulated experiences are "representative" of those in everyday life. It is from this perspective that Riis's virtual tour operated within a structure of realism.

In no instance did Riis press his audience to greater participation in the experiences of tenement life than in his effort to promote their identification with Tony's and others' suffering. Identification with personal tragedy had become central to the Social Gospel's strategy for reinvigorating Pauline scripture in Protestant life. By declaring with Paul that all are "crucified on the cross with Christ" (Romans 6:6), and embracing the immediacy of his injunction that the faithful make their "bodies a living sacrifice" (Romans 12:1), Social Gospel reformers placed the themes of ongoing sacrifice and suffering at the core of Christian activism. Through the narrator in one of his earliest homiletic novels, *The Crucifixion of Phillip Strong* (1894)—in part drawn from the virtual-tour narratives of urban blight and reform that Riis and Benjamin Flower published in the *Arena,* the unofficial organ of Christian socialism— Charles Sheldon dramatized the desire to build soul-sustaining alliances by making the body a living testament to another's pain. Urging his congregation to acts of personal intervention in the slums of the fictional Milton, the young Reverend Strong makes an appeal to his audience: "I solemnly believe the time has come when it is our duty to go into the tenement district and redeem it by the power of personal sacrifice and personal presence. Nothing less will answer.... [For] out of the depths of the black abyss of human want and sin and despair and anguish and rebellion in this place ... rings in my ear a cry for help that by the grace of God I truly believe cannot be answered by the Church of Christ on earth until the members of that Church are willing in great numbers to give all ... as it looks for the heart of the bleeding Christ in the members of the Church of Christ."[18] Sheldon's epistemological bridge—a "personal presence" that assumes, as a character in *In His Steps* similarly advocates, "part of another's misery" by taking the "concrete, actual, personal form of trying to share the deepest suffering and sin of the city" (223)—like Riis's own advocacy of tenement visitation and poverty intervention, coincides with William James's conclusion in his study of radical empiricism that "The objective nucleus of every man's experience [is] his own body," "a continuous percept."[19] In a mature form of empathy inchoately emerging from Edwards's Lockean revision in the century before, the

Social Gospel encouraged its adherents not merely to sympathize with the suffering—not merely to "feel right," as Stowe put it three decades earlier—but, in the most literal form of the *imitatio Christi,* to feel their pain bodily through an alliance of collective suffering.

Mainstays of Social Gospel literature, Sheldon's novels illustrate the injunction that the faithful become Christlike by becoming a "living sacrifice" for the social world, the homiletic catechism of muscular Christianity's interventionist creed. Pauline theology not only made suffering the mechanism of identification, the epistemological bridge between subject and object made "concrete," "actual," and "personal" in the visceral experience of another's pain—in the continuous percept of the agent's body—but it also underscored the stakes between worldly and spiritual priorities by contrasting the insignificance of the individual's historical localization with the universal and eternal significance of Christ's sacrifice on the cross. By then collapsing this difference, homiletic allegory helped Christians cultivate a double vision that allowed them to perceive themselves forever in a transhistorical present, or eschatological time, bearing the cross *with* their suffering Savior.[20] Christian socialists came to see ghetto existence as an allegory of the larger struggle between good and evil. Far from reducing the poor to abstractions in a moral lesson, diminishing their dignity, or denying their misery, this view made the measure of humanity more than the sum of its materiality—its perishable body and limbs. Imperiled bodies bespoke imperiled souls, a condition exacting the steepest price of all: eternal death. In the service of second sight, homiletic realism and instruction attacked the middle class's abject fetishization—its captivation with filth, disease, poverty, and the external markers of otherness—to promote instead sympathy and engagement with material instances of suffering.

The critical failure to make this distinction results from a lack of attention to a rich discourse already present in the postbellum era on the danger of viewers' separating themselves from the objects of their gaze. Henry Wood, for example, warned his Christian readers about focusing on lurid images, photographic or literary:

It is only ignorance and weak self-limitation in man that gives the reins to thought, and allows it to carry him as a captive into all the morbid negations and inversions that open to his distorted gaze. Perverted thought so abuses its sacred office that it goes out of its way to seek out the bitter, the misshapen, and the abominable. It almost revels in the unnatural and chaotic. It builds its

subjective structures from its ruling consciousness, and subjectivity and objectivity act and react each upon the other. It often feeds upon "realistic" and
debasing fiction, under the delusion that it is "artistic." It entertains sensuous
mental pictures, though worldly policy and outward respectability may re-
strain their external expression.[21]

Rather, in the homiletic tradition, Wood emphasizes the ability to see
what lies beyond the sensual trappings of the merely "realistic," to the
spiritual "Real" that "displaces" "the shadows, morbid pictures, images,
dreams which have only a seeming life."[22]

The cultivation of this double vision—the ability to see behind the
shadow to the spiritual real—became another component in the homiletic aesthetics of immediacy. Homiletic narratives drew on readers' sentimental perceptions to invoke a spiritual world, affording those who
engaged the narratives with a glimpse of their part in God's design.
Protestant readers in this tradition brought to and took from the texts
they encountered visions of a spiritual world through second sight. As
we have seen, this double vision weakened the modern sense of anachronism, eliding the sense of temporality as a fixed, calendrical progression, and restoring a sense of layered sacramental or eschatological time.
In such a view, sacred events were understood as distinct from secular
history, occurring and recurring in sacred patterns understood through
a rich typological tradition. This double vision encouraged the faithful to achieve a perspective outside their own historical localization—
to see the events of secular history and its causality as simply shadowing
eternal realities. In the Platonic tradition inherited through Augustine,
Protestant homiletics fostered an epistemological reorientation in order
for the faithful to see the material world as a dark glass that simply obscured the immutable behind it. For the religious, such a view stripped
humanity of its value-laden trappings—social markers that created ontological difference—exposing poverty, destitution, and urban blight as a
deception veiling God's image stamped on the impoverished, the ethnic
"other," the chronically sick, and the mentally ill.

The earliest homiletic frames reveal the tie between double vision and
spiritual growth, even as they alert us to the iconographic conventions at
play in Riis's atavistic use of photography. Such a vision motivated medieval art patrons to have their likenesses inserted into the sacred scenes
illuminating their Psalters and Protestant books of the hours, and informs the Protestant practice of including deceased loved ones in fam-

ily portraits, or still later, the practice of daguerreotyping lifeless children in their parents' arms—acts symbolizing the family's triumph over death at the end of time. Resurrection ultimately became synonymous with reunion, a homiletic precept that predisposed Riis's audiences to see the eternal nature of the social emblematized in his photography.[23] In this context, Riis's images of the poor were meant to remind viewers that they, too, were a family of sorts. "Awakening" to this complicity, Riis's audiences felt remorse for their previous indifference to poverty. Only then did Riis's photographs evoke biting irony. In his poem about Christ's return to a modern city—the epigraph of *How the Other Half Lives* and many of Riis's lectures—James Russell Lowell depicts the Lord shaming a Gilded Age crowd who have been indifferent to the suffering around them. As Christ points to "a haggard man, / And a motherless girl, whose fingers thin / Pushed from her faintly want and sin," he bitterly rebukes the proclaimed followers for the failure of their Christian stewardship: "'Lo, here,' said he, / 'The images ye have made of me!'" (*Other Half* xviii).

Infused with the aesthetics of immediacy, homiletic narratives immersed audiences into the contemporary world's social concerns, declaring that challenges of their world corresponded with those of the spiritual realm. Social Gospel homiletics demanded that the religiously committed draw on their spiritual vision—their second sight—to address human need. Riis's inclusion of new visual technologies enriched the core structure of homiletic pedagogy by literally adding sight to the tools used to cultivate spiritual vision. With photographs of dark interiors, saloons, street scenes located in or near the infamous Five Points district, and haunting family portraits, Riis drew his audience into Tony's world. They witnessed his struggle against poverty, hunger, sickness, freezing winters, violence at the hands of hobos and police, profiteers, and Tammany Hall graft and greed. They followed him into beer dives where "inhuman brutes" tempted him to drink and "kicked and cuffed" him, passed into narrow airshafts where he played with other "street Arabs," and toured rat-infested rooms filled with the "fumes of death," the noxious air to which reformers attributed high mortality rates. The virtual tour Riis provided was an exploration not simply of tenement conditions in the material world but also of the allegorical perils that impeded the poor's progress toward salvation. As they followed Tony through his daily trials, audiences experienced through the tableaux of narrative and image not the stations along the winding path to Calvary, but those along the broad way to destruction. Using photographs to chronicle Tony's childhood struggle, Riis would conclude by describing how he died suddenly by violence, wasted away body and soul from alcoholism, or lingered on the edge of death for days before succumbing to consumption, typhus, scarlet fever, or cholera. On rare occasions, much to audiences' delight, Tony would rise in Algeresque triumph from a youth of indigence and crime to the status of "redeemed citizen."[24]

When located within the multimedia format of the Social Gospel homiletic, Riis's virtual tours become more complex and dynamic than scholarship has generally suggested. Many scholars have treated his work solely as sociological exposés, focusing almost exclusively on its use of racial taxonomies rooted in turn-of-the-century ethnography to produce the forms of objectification that comprised middle-class identity formation. Typically, they situate Riis within secular reform, largely analyzing his photographs in *How the Other Half Lives* as prurient exercises that rendered tenement life as exotic spectacle.[25] In *The Real Thing,* for instance, the cultural historian Miles Orvell contrasts the photography of Riis with that of Alfred Steiglitz, Paul Strand, and Walker Evans. He argues that counter to Steiglitz's and his followers' development of an aesthetic marked by an interest in creating new structures of meaning by juxtaposing incongruent or dissimilar objects, and counter to the frontal directness of Evans's Depression Era photography, Riis—a representative, for Orvell, of Victorian photography's interest in aesthetic illusion and general types—simply constructed sympathetic yet stylized and voyeuristic portraits of the lower classes.[26] Such interpretations, however, shear Riis's book from the rich web of extratextual meaning that linked it to the more ephemeral pedagogy of his stereopticon lectures. Viewing Riis's photographs as visual artifacts *qua* visual artifacts—possessing an internal structure of meaning apart from any external context—creates a false category. The photographs Riis selected from among his magic-lantern lectures for *How the Other Half Lives* and for Helen Campbell's *Darkness and Daylight; or, Lights and Shadows of New York Life,* for instance, were meant to be contextualized through narratives, even occasionally containing linguistic components within them. Disengaged from the homiletic context and religious reform, Riis's images become open registers of sentimentality, icons of alien suffering, and ripe sources of class identification vulnerable to misinterpretation.

Departing from this critical consensus, I read *How the Other Half Lives* as a synthesis of Riis's stereopticon lectures. The compression of his virtual-tour narratives into book form has rendered Riis's homiletic strategies and the visual and rhetorical nuances of interactive lectures—lay sermons—tailored for disparate audiences less visible to present-day readers untrained in a traditional evangelical hermeneutic. This shift in reading epistemology is compounded because criticism of Riis's work has dislocated it from its context within homiletic technologies of a particular Protestant vision of social activism, tradition of sermonic realism, and emergence of evangelical voluntarism. In demonstrating how Riis's images drew upon a specific Protestant tradition of aesthetics and, in particular, how they modernized a homiletic practice honed by Henry Ward Beecher, we can gain valuable insight into how Social Gospel reformers galvanized humanist ideals around atavistic inoculation strategies to bridge not experience and sin, an early function of homiletic exercises, but the fears and facts of social difference for their audiences. Riis's virtual-tour narratives helped viewers surmount fears of tenement districts by disrupting their middle-class habit of viewing poverty as the result either of biology or moral stigma rather than environment. As he guided them to organize the indistinct features of poverty and depravity into systematic categories understandable through cause and effect and ripe for social analysis, his audience began to see individuals like Tony as sojourners in the faith and as members of the national family and broader humanity. In modernizing homiletic instruction, Riis intended to bridge the epistemological and geographical gaps that separated middle-class reformers from the individuals they sought to know and help.[27] His virtual tour became muscular Christianity's most technologically advanced reconnaissance into previously frightening corridors, and the analysis embedded in his texts trained Protestant ground troops for what he proclaimed was a "battle with the slums."[28]

Homiletic Allegory and the Architectural Frame

Describing his magic-lantern lectures and 1890 tenement study as "fit topics for any sermon," and in titling talks and chapters in *How the Other Half Lives* "The Awakening" and "The Harvest of Tares"—a Social Gospel maxim—Riis signaled his debt to the homiletic tradition as it was revitalized by his intellectual and religious mentors, Henry Ward Beecher and Lyman Abbott, Beecher's protégé.[29] He drew directly on this heuristic tradition and, in particular, on its use of allegory. The narrative structure of allegory shaped most homiletic texts, for the double vision it afforded, like the synthesis of the stereopticon's plates, offered a medium through which ministers could unify the material and spiritual realms, even as the medium's representational capacity in a double register simultaneously emblematized divergent ontological registers. Every anecdote, parable, and plot within homiletic texts allegorized deeper religious values, experiences, and histories.

Understanding Riis's work requires that we recall that nineteenth-century Protestant reformers expected audiences to engage homiletic texts in an *intensive* rather than *extensive* reading mode, an explicit rather than an implicit reading epistemology. As we saw in the last two chapters, secular novels lay out the fictive landscape in a linear path commensurate with secular readers' perceptions of life, and historical and homogeneous time and space. As with the character of Updike Underhill in Royall Tyler's *The Algerine Captive* and the March sisters in *Little Women,* readers' identification with allegory, on the other hand, reoriented their lives according to a typological script where allegory functions to link the personal to the Christian universal and to permit a lived experience of unified historical and biblical time. Riis himself repeatedly borrowed from the still popular *Pilgrim's Progress* to signal to his audience how to engage the material through the appropriate interpretive epistemology. By way of promoting self-help charity rather than "alms," Riis argues for helping the poor work themselves out of the "slough of despon'."[30] To read allegories in this way is to see oneself as a historically grounded subject with transhistorical agency. It is also to recover the older, interventionist gloss on "vicarious" living: "to substitute" oneself "in place of" another, a paraphrase of John 15:13, the interventionist mantra of Christian socialism.[31]

While allegory gave way in secular culture to narrative realism, it remained a central component of homiletic realism. Like ministers' use of vivid realism in eighteenth- and nineteenth-century sermons to evoke sensation, the allegorical frame had long provided an effective way to address one of homiletic pedagogy's key concerns: how to forearm Christians against sin through experience.[32] In his virtual-tour narratives, Riis adapted this tradition to the purposes of urban reform. In seeking to provide controlled experiences that, while protecting audiences from the hyped perils of the slum, generated authentic social knowledge, his magic-lantern narratives hearkened back to the century before, when ministers like Jonathan Edwards endeavored to make children feel the

consequences of sin through simulation: to know by doing.[33] Edwards
bequeathed to his theological descendents the mandate to provide a visceral knowledge of sin without endangering the spiritual pilgrim's moral
purity. Like Milton, he reiterated for his heirs of "New Divinity" the belief that a fugitive and cloistered virtue, unexercised and unbreathed,
could never compete for the immortal garland any more than knowledge untried by experience could navigate the perilous landscape that
impeded the modern-day pilgrim's moral progress.[34] Riis's multimedia
allegories of urban wastelands and indigent classes, however, emerged
with a difference. In the full bloom of the Social Gospel, his virtual-
tour narratives implemented the inoculation theology I have been tracing not to aid middle-class audiences in building resistance to moral contagion *through* fear, but to build resistance *to* fear, the fear of moral and
physical contagion associated with the lower classes, immigrants, and
tenement squalor. Counter to the Edwardsian tradition of employing
homiletic realism to anathematize children to sin through imaginative
encounters with physical and spiritual decay, Riis reversed the conventional homiletic process of instilling fear that he might encourage the
reform minded to enter the urban houses of hell to intervene in human
suffering.

Like other descendents of Edwards's New Light theology, Henry
Ward Beecher and Lyman Abbott experimented broadly in the homiletic tradition to perfect an empirical pedagogy that would give congregations a firsthand experience of the wages of sin, while sparing them
its steep price—that they might, as Beecher put it, "see the *end* of vice
before they see the beginning" ("Strange Woman" 206). As the leading popular homiletic theorist in the Edwardsian camp, Jacob Abbott
summed up the problem in his 1836 homiletic manual, *The Way to Do
Good; or The Christian Character Mature.* An elder contemporary of
Henry Ward Beecher and the father of Lyman, Beecher's assistant and,
later, Riis's Plymouth Church minister, Abbott devised his homiletic
manuals to provide a direct bridge between Edwards's sensational theory of language and the emphasis Riis's urban reform coterie placed on
the simulation of experiential knowledge through discursive and pictorial modes of realism. Following Locke, from Edwards to Barber, Alcott,
Sheldon, and beyond, experience had been seen as the key to authentic
knowledge and thus the capacity to direct the will according to the dictates of enlightened knowledge. Such experience had to be inculcated in
the audience through a series of mediating practices. As with medical in-

oculations to neutralize disease, homiletic technologies worked to simulate moral contagion with vivid but virtual realism, providing, in theory, experiences for which the consequences were attenuated.

The Edwardsian legacy had insisted on a mediated phase to particular kinds of real-life experience, so that the novice's first encounter with the seductive dangers of sin, vice, and depravity, the realities of *this* world, did not come at the expense of salvation in the next. Jacob Abbott had rebuffed the practice of countenancing sin for the sake of experience: "It is often said that the young must be exposed to the temptations and bad influences of the world," he writes in *The Way to Do Good,* "in order to know what they are, by experience, and learn how to resist them. 'They must be exposed to them,' say these advocates of early temptation, 'at some time or other, and they may as well begin in season, so as to get the mastery over them the sooner.'"[35] Like Henry Ward Beecher, Jacob Riis, and Sheldon, who, we recall, spent weeks living incognito among the poorest classes of Topeka, Kansas, the elder Abbott believed that true knowledge was born of experience, not admonition or precept, but he, like the colonial generations before him and the postbellum after, also believed that the act of sinning dangerously habituated the innocent to a "vicious" life.[36] The homiletic tradition was meant to help the young experience the ailment born of sin without actually contracting a disease that led to moral death. With a pedagogy suitable to the experiential tenet of his regenerative pedagogy—and founded in Edwards's and Mather's smallpox inoculation campaigns—Beecher wished to use a preventive medicine to inoculate his parishioners against a lethal disease. Without a controlled infection, they could never develop immunity to moral contagion.

Few texts better depict the homiletics' use of allegory to simulate virtual experience than Beecher's famous children's sermon "The Strange Woman's House," a precursor to homiletic dramas like the hell house. Based on a homily taken from Proverbs, he initially delivered the sermon on Christmas Eve 1843 but revised the text in 1847, before his move from Indianapolis to Brooklyn. The sermon begins with a small boy encountering a beautiful cottage amidst a pastoral landscape. Despite repeated parental admonitions about the danger of this particular house and its sole proprietor, the "strange woman," the surrounding garden's beauty and the home's alluring domestic felicity beckon the child. He suppresses his mother's warning to avoid the house, convinced he could turn back at any time. Pausing briefly to reflect on the security of his home, his happy domestic circle, he enters the house, from whence, Beecher ominously declares, "there is no return" ("Strange Woman" 199).[37]

Beecher's homiletic tour of hell had numerous precursors—most notably for readers today, Dante's *Inferno,* or John Bunyan's *The Life and Death of Mr. Badman,* in the introduction to which Bunyan recalls, "As I was considering with my self, what I had written concerning the *Progress* of the *Pilgrim* from this World to Glory, and how it had been acceptable to many in this Nation: it came again into my mind to write, as then, of him that was going to Heaven, so now, of the Life and Death of the Ungodly, and of their travel from this world to Hell."[38] Yet the narrative structure of Beecher's heuristic is more remarkable still, belonging to a range of interactive colonial Calvinist pedagogies. Largely in response to shifting epistemological perspectives and spiritual habits of imagination, the virtual-tour narrative anticipates new media forms, registering their potential to increase homiletic realism's aesthetics of immediacy. Yet these new forms still rely on a deep architectural structure to organize knowledge in units of information applicable to, and thus verifiable by, participants' everyday experience. As we have seen, the virtual-tour narrative as a participatory exercise of spiritual contemplation took a number of forms in Christian tradition, including the medieval Corpus Christi cycle, in which audiences literally toured scenes spatially arranged in the narrative progression of the passions that they might experientially, albeit virtually, encounter the emotional immensity of Christ's path to Calvary. Physical movement from one vignette, emblematically depicting the progression from one station of the cross to another, reiterated for audiences immersed in the *Devotio Moderna*—largely, we recall, through Thomas à Kempis's *Imitatione Christi* and later John Wesley's translation *The Christian's Pattern*—the applicability of the pilgrimage template as a way to frame and narrate each day's routines as an integral part of the individual's spiritual walk. It was, in a sense, the revivification of this intense focus on the spiritualization of each moment through eighteenth- and nineteenth-century Wesleyan perfectionism—channeled through national figures such as Charles Finney and Zilpha Elaw, among others, and, later, through the holiness movement's stress on sanctification in the work of figures like John Vincent—that renewed the demand for medieval narrative structures that might help frame and thus pace the continuity of time in incremental stages of spiritual growth. The narratives of self generated from this progress-in-stages further assimilated and personalized the perceived universality of religious ordinances and sacraments like baptism and communion and the anticipated markers of regeneration, such as moments of contrition, confession, expiation, piety, and charitable work.

One exemplary interactive pedagogy paralleling the pilgrimage template in its use of an architectural paradigm that marked progress in relation both to spiritual development and time was the cemetery tour. The pilgrimage template of spiritual growth and edification was a constitutive pedagogy in the American colonies not only as the allegory of New World migration that we have seen in Shepard's autobiography but also as the virtual-tour heuristic of colonial cemetery walks. The architecture of the cemetery tour was a precursor of Beecher's and Riis's homiletic heuristics for its use of space to structure knowledge and to catalyze homiletic habits of imagination toward an interactive spiritual experience. The space of the cemetery unfolded a specific though largely predetermined narrative outcome, but the heuristic practices applied to this space illuminate the transitional link between Beecher's use of visual rhetoric to embody a vividly evocative reality and Riis's use of visual media—etchings, photographs, and stereopticon projection— to intensify homiletic realism. Sally Promey has recently shown the extent to which colonial Calvinists used the typologically structured space of the cemetery as an interactive exercise in homiletic realism. Ministers like Edward Pearse and John Cotton, for instance, encouraged their flocks to visit the graveyard often. The author of *The Great Concern; or, A Serious Warning to a Timely and Thorough Preparation for Death* (1678), Pearse counseled his readers from his own deathbed to "Be much and frequent in the Contemplation of Death and the Grave. *The Meditation of Death is Life. It is that which greatly promotes our spiritual life;* therefore walk much among the Tombs, and converse much and frequently with the thoughts of a dying hour."[39] Walking much among the tombs meant contemplating one's eternal fate at the portal closest to the spiritual world, what Pearse, with an ambiguity that underscores individuals' agency in determining their eternal destination, called the "Gate or Door that lets Men out into Eternity."[40] On the tombstone of Robert and Mary Riddle in the eighteenth-century Chandler Hill Cemetery in Colrain, Massachusetts, for example, one finds the warning, "All you advanced in years, you healthy and robust are Touring around the graves and soon must turn to dust."[41] Nearby, the gravestone of David Lyons announces, "Behold fond man! See here thy pictur'd life." Agnes Willson's stone warns, "When you these lines do read and turn to walk away,

Oh don't forget you must apear [sic] at the great Judgment Day." For Calvinist ministers, the cemetery was a powerful reminder of a time when human agency was at an end. Death, Pearse warned, was "a determining thing [that] concludes the Soul for ever under an unalterable state of Life or Death, of Happiness or Misery."[42]

While still freighted by commemorative scripts, memorial rituals, and spiritual symbols today, seventeenth- and eighteenth-century cemetery visits inhabited a greater range of signifying practices that, through the typological imaginations of the faithful, occupied visitors in sustained interactive eschatological dramas. As Stanley French and Susan-Mary Grant have demonstrated, even as late as the postbellum era, the graveyard—"cemetery" coming into vogue at this time for its connotation of sleep—was deemed, in French's words, an "enchanting place" of "instruction." Grant further explains how, as part of the "new park cemetery movement," both "locals and visitors" were "furnished with guidebooks," and "encouraged to admire [the] new 'Gardens & Graves,' and to derive spiritual solace from them."[43] Yet even this latter-day culture of cemetery as an instructive touring had, in comparison to its colonial origins, lost much of its sacramental and devotional context, its efficacy as a renewable source of spiritual introspection. Promey has demonstrated how "walking among the tombs" was for colonial Puritans something of a Heraclitean stream, an ever-shifting chain of tableaux and thus a renewable and increasingly spiritually challenging pedagogy: one never walked through the same graveyard twice. Differences in time of day, seasons, changes in weather or visitor's material or spiritual conditions, newly interred bodies, and the irregular emplotting of colonial graveyards—uneven rows, family plots that wound along the contours of knolls and ravines, new graves wedged among the old—all combined to defamiliarize the space. Those disengaged from the interactive hermeneutic might find their complacency shaken, John Cotton warned his parishioners, by suddenly encountering the skeletal remains of the dead, freshly washed from the ground or rooted up by run-a-gate swine.[44]

A kind of hologrammatic tour, cemetery paths passed among gravestones indicating the interrelation between past, present, and future. Stones simultaneously marked ancestral burial sites, the viewer's immediate present in his or her relation to the deceased, and the spot where those buried would one day emerge fully embodied to stand before the Judgment bar. By invoking sets of parallel binaries, including life and afterlife, the temporal and eternal, the earthly and the celestial, cemetery tours reiterated, as they reinforced, the fundamental analogical binary at the core of Puritan hermeneutic practices, the perpetual oscillation between the literal and the figural. In this way, cemetery tours were interactive devotional texts. Alphabetically scripted and emblematically encoded in symbols decoratively framing the stones' face—and emotionally registered according to individuals' psychological moods provoked or intensified by the tour itself, and according to their spiritual and experiential capacity—gravestones illustrated how intensive reading required an imaginative engagement with diverse symbolic registers and shifting readerly modes.

The cemetery hermeneutic transformed the physical space into a metaphysical realm through an unstable doubling registered not only in symbols dimensionally embedded in the stones but also figurally lodged in the flickering doubleness of a vocabulary of spiritual transition, made up by the dual meaning of terms such as life, death, rest, sleep, pattern, copy, model, and type. Properly attuned to the graveyard's insistent eschatology, rows of tombstones visually evoked a sleeping village awaiting resurrection, Judgment, and salvation or eternal suffering. Unkempt plots bespoke extinct or migrant family lines; fallen trees and areas shadowed by elm and oak canopies made visitations unfamiliar, an obstacle course perpetually reiterating the constitutive influence of the physical and spiritual on one's religious pilgrimage. Stones marking the resting place of venerated saints, loved ones, the newly interred, ancestors, and apostates all contributed to ever-shifting patterns of contemplation that meted out different levels of devotion and spiritual anxiety. Thus not only were cemeteries not systematically emplotted, but the tourist's shifting perspective worked against an emplotted narrative, a stable typology, ensuring—as with the impersonation of the hellfire sermons discussed in chapter 2—the personalization of the virtual-tour experience. Redacted through personal introspection—shaped by a sense of guilt, spiritual inadequacy, salvific assurance, hope, and the like—such variables accommodated an inexhaustible combination of psychological moods and spiritual states, dishing out to visitors helpings of hope, inspiration, grief, shame, and despair. Scripts etched into the headstone comprised only one part of the complex eschatology that graveyard tours unfolded through the individual's interpretive engagement variously shaped by personal experience, particular routes through the cemetery, and the ephemera of psychological mood, sectarian mindset, and spiritual outlook. The graveyard, as Promey reminds us, was an emotionally and viscerally charged territory, where assertions of spiritual metamorphosis took place in the context of hard, cut and inscribed surfaces interacting with light and weather, where visitors might be enjoined to contort their bodies and endure physical discomfort to maximize vision, where the sight of one's own shadow cast on stone elicited both spiritual identification with the deceased saint and thought of impending bodily dissolution, where one was on occasion confronted with turned up bones and standing water, where it was sometimes very hard to ignore the sensory realities of rotting bodies.[45]

Nowhere in daily life was perspective so clearly and insistently bifurcated between the carnal and the spiritual, the imminent and the eternal than in the cemetery, where gravestones attested to the division of body and soul, flesh and spirit, old and new man, sinner and saint. The recurrence of a common death date throughout the cemetery bespoke the possibility of community extinction, the ravages of contagions—smallpox, cholera, yellow fever, diphtheria, plague—that swept towns and regions in waves, spiritually devastating to the young who were least prepared for the "dying hour." Clusters of family stones encouraged the living to look within for signs of their own salvific legacy. Like medieval images in which patrons had their likenesses inserted into the sacred scenes of Christ's life, family plots bore testimony of an afterlife reunion. The temporal gaps between adjacent gravestones coexisting in the immediate present forced Calvinists' analogical imaginations into an eschatological frame, fostering a typological perception of simultaneous action in and across the lived experience of biblical time.

Graveyards might reflect the sanctity and spiritual closure associated with deathbed scenes. Perceived as a time when the righteous possessed acute spiritual sight, deathbed scenes, as Sarah Rivett has recently demonstrated, were occasions when dying saints were accorded salvific confirmation and occasionally glimpses into the spiritual world.[46] Gravestones preserved these moments: they might record insight pregnant with the augury of those for whom the spiritual veil had been lifted. They offered snippets of scriptural wisdom and proffered freshets of hope to the spiritually struggling. They also warned of the dire consequences of one's tarrying too long in salvific preparations. "Touring around the graves," as the Riddles' gravestone put it, generated a personalized narrative through its approximation of homiletic reading practices. Inextricably tied to Calvinist hermeneutics, the graveyard walk performed a personalized, spiritual narrative that was also allegorically linked to a typological narrative. Like the levels of medieval allegory, these narratives generated from cemetery visitation fluctuated between registers of meaning. As the narrative logic moved from the material to the spiritual, from the perceptible world beneath to the corresponding structures of the invisible above, the graveyard typology experienced the literal as the virtual domain of the spiritual.

Headstones enjoined visitors to examine themselves to discern the status of their own faith interpreted in degrees of relation and correspondences. The graves of revered saints encouraged those touring to see their lives within typological frames. Much like the "spiritual pilgrimage" in which John Vincent led the young through the "upper" and "lower" levels of the Chautauqua grounds—a visible bifurcation determined by each child's capacity to discern its double register—the cemetery tour keyed physical movement across a literal landscape to an invisible spiritual topography (*Chautauqua* 50). Its mode of homiletic realism depended upon the touring party's apprehension of the dialectical relation between the material and the spiritual, between the shadowy, earthly similitude and its immutable reality beyond. In nothing was the binary between the carnal and spiritual brought home so nearly for visitors than in the emphasis of grave symbology on the tenuous union of body and soul. The architecture of the graveyard—the stone's embossed frame and recessed face, the shadowy play of seasonal light, the progression of saints visibly marked with a personalized stone, and the parceled topography of the grounds—constituted a palpable material link between the visible and the invisible, the personal and the typological.

The cemetery tour sets up an architecturally structured experience that is reproduced in Henry Ward Beecher's sermon for young boys. The beautiful cottage belonging to the strange woman in Beecher's sermons sits on a pastoral landscape that, we might imagine, exists as a palimpsest of the Puritan graveyard, for, as Beecher intones, it leads to the "chambers of death," a phrase whose meaning simultaneously registers the material and the spiritual, the literal and the metaphoric. Visually and epistemologically, this sermonic use of architecture echoes the heuristic tradition descending from seventeenth-century New England, and circuitously from older medieval heuristic and mnemonic traditions, such as the memory theaters made familiar by the work of Frances Yates and, more recently, Mary Carruthers.[47] But this migration of architectural type, from tombstone to house, from cold walks among seventeenth-century stones to the ominous inversion of the nineteenth-century hearth, does not simply reflect the adaptation of Protestant homiletics to the tropes and metaphors of contemporary culture. For in the Calvinist method of Ramistic logic, the Puritans used the figure of the house to illustrate the discrete categories of knowledge. In this memory system, students learned to use floor plans as schematic figures to separate, classify, and regulate the seven arts of learning. As an elaborate forensic and mnemonic figure, each room of the house embodied a general order of knowledge, and each part of each room with a more particular knowledge that seventeenth-century divinity students could retrieve by mentally touring the space.[48] In Beecher's sermon, the house's structure draws on this heuristic schema by constructing the ontological categories of sin as rooms depicting the various stages of a child's moral fall.

Beecher began his moral instruction by inviting his audience into the house's allegorical frame.[49] He beckoned: "Enter with me, in imagination, the strange woman's House, where God grant you may never enter in any other way" ("Strange Woman" 199). As he led his listeners deeper into the house of hell, he directed their attention to their surroundings: "The floors are bare, the naked walls drip filth, the air is poisonous with sickly fumes, and echoes . . . with misery. . . . On your right hand, as you enter, close by the door, is a group of felons . . . with swollen faces . . . bloated lips" ("Strange Woman" 201–2). Beecher added sound and smell, filling out the sensuous reality of his audience's experience beyond the Edwardsian model. He imitated groaning doors, "wretches gasping for breath," and creaking floors. "Its air represses every sense," he would tell his audience. "Its sights confound our thoughts, its sounds pierce our ear and its stench repels us; it is full of diseases" ("Strange Woman" 203). Attuned to the homiletics' Lockean imperative of teaching through a direct sensory encounter—marked in Abbott's reminder that the senses are "the great avenues to knowledge" (*Way* 299)—Beecher's allegory further collapses the formal distinction between lived reality and divine knowledge through a religious pedagogy that creates a virtual experience in the child's imagination. Beecher's sermon incorporates the Ramistic house as a frame for incremental knowledge into a new rendition of an old heuristic that allows young listeners to hear, see, smell, and ultimately feel sin and its attendant consequences.

The architectural frame that had once marked the necessity for memory systems to store incremental knowledge transformed in the nineteenth century into new discursive and visual heuristic forms. These forms were designed to render this knowledge immediately as experience, thus reducing and eventually eliminating pedagogical reliance on memory. The architectural trope of the house also informed domestic science promoted and theorized by Beecher's elder sisters Catharine Beecher and Harriet Beecher Stowe. In their textbook on domestic economy, for instance, the Beecher sisters freight the various spaces of the house with different kinds of domestic and moral order and knowledge—disciplined through a program of homilies, such as "a place for everything and everything in its place." Their principles of domestic economy employ the trope of the home as a space of moral reform as well as learning, helping an uncouth, uneducated immigrant class of young women transform into their new roles as republican mothers for a nation in need of moral leadership.[50] But while older mnemonic systems required memory repetition and elaborate spatial organization, its structural descendent provided simpler allegorical scaffolding for moral hierarchy, a spatially oriented catechism. Henry Ward Beecher, for instance, anchors a moral hierarchy in each "ward" of the house (or city), giving a vertical dimension to the narrative structure that resembles Dante's descending spiral through the fixed circles of morality. Touring listeners through the "the house of licentiousness," he warns that because sin initiates moral decline, the strange woman's "house is the way to hell, going down to the chambers of death," disease, and destitution ("Strange Woman" 199). His repetition of the phrase a "metropolis of base stories" puns on "story": in an idiom familiar to his audience, the word signifies each ward's narrative and the house's vertical dimension.[51] Among an audience familiar with homiletic practice, it was descriptive shorthand for an allegorical structure.

Descending from seventeenth-century Puritan heuristics and knowledge structures, Social Gospel literature capitalized on the relationship between architectural divisions and allegorical levels, between twin purposes of built environments and the emblematic rendering of moral and spiritual knowledge. In *Civilization's Inferno,* what he subtitles *Studies in the Social Cellar,* for example, Benjamin Flower stratifies urban society into the levels of a multistoried house. Emblematized as a pictorial allegory, the book's frontispiece (fig. 6) renders the social levels of the city as a moral hierarchy, depicting the wealthy in a ballroom vignette as the highest story of the urban house. Subsequent levels portray urban vignettes of increasing poverty and desperation, from a tableau of labor lines, to one of an impoverished rag picker with her children, to

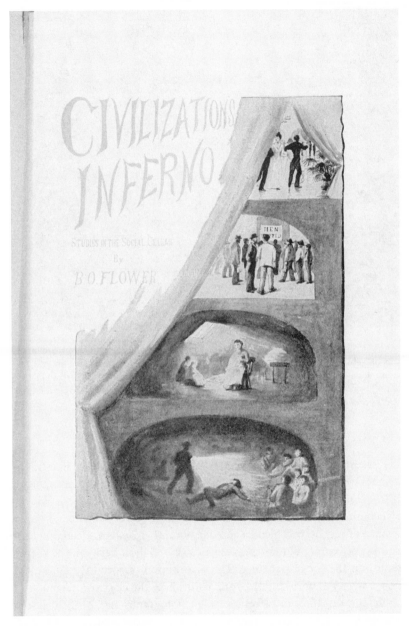

FIGURE 6. Benjamin Orange Flower, frontispiece to *Civilization's Inferno; or, Studies in the Social Cellar*, 1894. Flower uses a popular Social Gospel trope that originated as an architectural schematic that drew from medieval allegory and Reformation noetic technologies.

FIGURE 7. Jacob A. Riis, "Burnt-out Building," c. 1890. By courtesy of the Museum of the City of New York. Familiar with Social Gospel architectural tropes such as Flower's Dantean reference, Riis's Christian audiences would have understood this image as emblematic of the narrative structure of Christian allegory, applied in this case to the conditions of Riis's urban "underworld" or Flower's "social cellar."

the lowest level of the social cellar, where the dispossessed huddle together near the prostrate body of a fallen man. This, the text announces, is "the hot-bed of moral and physical contagion."[52] The image's ironic social commentary requires that all the vignettes be read together, as a sequence of scenes, in which each scene not only reveals a social and economic declension, but also reveals a causal relation between the scenes built into the social structure. The distribution of social resources, the image suggests, both stabilizes and naturalizes the class stratification.

In one of Riis's most remarkable photographs (fig. 7), "Burnt-out Building," fin de siècle audiences saw the colossal structure of a multilevel building gutted by fire, the architectural levels visually performing the structure of homiletic aesthetics, oscillating between the material and spiritual, the immanent and transcendent. For religious audiences

trained in the architectural paradigms of Calvinist homiletics and familiar with the many Dantean references of Social Gospel literature, the
building's charred skeleton—covered with hanging sheets of ice—would
have evoked the levels of Dante's inferno, actualized through the realities of tenement poverty as Riis's urban underworld.

Civilization's Inferno reflects the novelization of Beecher's sermonic
strategy: the revival of the deep epistemic structure of Puritan heuristics
in an allegory designed to make moral and spiritual knowledge immediately intelligible and experientially available. While Beecher did this
through narrative forms, Riis, like Flower, uses the new visual media of
the virtual-tour narrative in his stereopticon presentations and books to
literally transpose the audience into an allegorical frame in a historically
unprecedented intensification of homiletic realism, measured by the increased proximity between aesthetic form and the immediacy of experience. Riis invites his audience to join him on a tour of the tenement
slum. "Suppose we look into one?" he asks.

> Be a little careful, please! The hall is dark and you might stumble over the
> children pitching pennies back there. Not that it would hurt them; kicks and
> cuffs are their daily diet. . . . Here where the hall turns and dives into ut-
> ter darkness is a step, and another, another. A flight of stairs. You can feel
> your way, if you cannot see it. . . . Here is a door. Listen! that short hacking
> cough, that tiny, helpless wail—what do they mean? . . . The child is dying of
> measles.[53]

Like Beecher's sermonic aesthetics of immediacy—inflected with the
pronominal first- and second-person plural that his ministerial predecessors used to personalize damnation—Riis calls our attention to sounds
and smell, fostering the sensuous reality initiated by the stereopticon images. Cautiously exploiting the nineteenth century's fear that poor ven-
tilation spawned disease, Riis asks, "Is it close? Yes! What would you
have? All the fresh air that ever enters these stairs comes from the win-
dows of dark bedrooms that in turn receive from the stairs their sole
supply of the elements." Appeals to touch and sound sharpen the verisimilitude of Riis's own virtual tour: "That was a woman filling her pail
by the hydrant you just bumped against," he explains as his audience encounters unfamiliar obstacles and sounds along the tour (*Other Half* 38).
Later, he invokes other odors as his audience descends with him into
"the bowels" of the tenement: "The spice of hot soapsuds is added to

the air," he tells us, "already tainted with the smell of boiling cabbage, of rags and uncleanliness all about" (41). Riis's attention to how the full range of senses flesh out visual experience recalls the fulsome descriptions of Beecher's hellish house, even as it emphasizes the reality of experience as something shaped by each agent's engagement.[54] The architectural city's lowest level, like the icy bottom of Dante's inferno, is Blackwell's Island Asylum for insane women—another name strangely evocative of moral allegory. Here, the inmates' "incessant, senseless chatter betrays the darkened mind" (*Other Half* 202)—for Riis, *the* black well of human existence.[55]

For Beecher's Calvinist ancestors, the house operated as an encyclopedia—or *technologia* as the divines called it—a unifying system or frame for the seven arts comprising the circle of knowledge. What Perry Miller and Walter Ong term the Puritans' "noetic" system is still visible in Abbott's 1836 homiletic manual.[56] Using the architectural frame as a mnemonic device, Abbott instructed Sunday school teachers in the method of organizing moral knowledge:

> The true principle [is] to lead the pupil over the ground in the natural track, acquiring knowledge first in detail, and arranging and classifying it, as he proceeds. The worth and utility of what he learns, will depend upon the fulness [sic], and freshness, and vitality of his individual acquisitions, and scientific system should be gradually developed as the apartments of it can be occupied. The building is beautiful in itself . . . but it is valuable, chiefly as a means of securing and preserving from derangement and loss, the valuables it contains. (*Way* 304–5)

As with the cemetery tour, homiletic strategies relied on this organizing principle of spatial paradigms to instill moral order and to arrange knowledge in ways compatible with both memory recall and a systematic association between spatial cues and moral sentiment and specific knowledge—or, in some conditions, even prompts for a specific response or action. The spatialized paradigm found its way into broader use in pedagogies that shifted from religious to secular literature and institutions. John Dewey, for instance, advocated this homiletic feature in his spatial theory used to organize classrooms at the Laboratory School of the University of Chicago. In what he calls Dewey's "Social Gospel" phase—he had just relocated from the University of Michigan, where he organized a Sunday school—Robert B. Westbrook writes of Dewey's

spatialized pedagogy: "Dewey was calling upon teachers to artfully arrange things in the classroom so that 'the right social growth' could be
assured."[57] Even in this instance, the spatial paradigm as a supplement to
active instruction was meant to help children regulate and modify their
own behavior in the absence of constant adult supervision. Yet herein lay
the difficulty. The key in the homiletic tradition was to find a balance between engaged instruction, independent or self-motivated moral learning, and permitting the inexperienced too much spiritual autonomy, too
soon. While Jacob Abbott cautioned against too great a latitude in allowing the young unregulated freedom by "making every pupil an independent investigator and discoverer" (*Way* 305), he nonetheless advocated an immediacy in which the student followed a "natural track"—a
predesigned and guided, interactive course—in order to discover and
sort a range of information. While received wisdom disembodied information, creating abstractions that severed knowledge from activity, the
homiletic revealed knowledge to be the byproduct of action. This is precisely why, in the century before, Jonathan Edwards's epistemology formulated in "A Divine and Supernatural Light" granted supremacy to
perception over understanding, elevating experience—the "sense of the
heart"—over what Edwards, following Locke, called notional, or book,
learning. When an individual knows the taste of honey, he has a more
accurate understanding than that "by which he knows what a triangle
is."[58] Process rather than knowledge was the objective of homiletic pedagogy. If for Abbott received knowledge was the fish that fed the hungry
for a day—to use a popular Social Gospel homily—the homiletic process
taught the hungry to fish that they might eat for a lifetime.

Beecher's sermon demonstrates the house's heuristic function as an
allegory of the categories of sin, a technology for imposing order upon
chaos. Having conceptualized the moral pitfalls awaiting them, young
Christians could safely navigate what for Beecher had become a more
dangerous landscape than the allegorical bogs, fens, sloughs, and snares
that threatened the spiritual progress of Bunyan's seventeenth-century
pilgrim. Freighted with moral meaning, Beecher's "wards" form a blueprint of the evils that result in a Christian's demise. Each room's interior
becomes a microallegory of the sin contained within the allegory's larger
frame. In the ward associated with the sin of inebriation, for instance,
the walls "ooze" blood, a symptom of the stomach ulcers from which alcoholics were believed to suffer, and the "bloody expectorant" that these
ulcers occasioned. The ward associated with fornication is crowded

with people covered with festering sores, venereal disease's most visible symptom.

If Beecher's house of hell took the form of a city, Riis's underworld city was designed as a house. Like Beecher, Riis breaks New York down by its preexisting wards, repeatedly drawing attention to existing spatial divisions, including "Hell's Kitchen," "the Bowery," "Hell's Basement," and the "Homestead." Similar to Beecher's five wards depicting the phases of a child's moral decline, Riis's wards accrue social meaning identified with the particular ethnic populations inhabiting them. While using contemporary racial constructions, he frames the space not so much to codify putative ethnographic stereotypes as to push his audience to question them, a strategy that would intensify over the course of his career. As Riis himself increasingly broke down ethnic categorizations in his own mind over the twenty-five-year course of his poverty work, he also provided his audience with a firsthand account with which to reevaluate the very suppositions that had guided his early work. By stratifying the urban occupants into the separate floors of a house, from the parlor's social elite down to the "social cellar's" desperately poor, reformers like Riis used the architectural frame to help their readers not only to see the topography of urban poverty and racial and class hierarchies, but also to question and overturn these hierarchies by mapping the inverse relation between earthly success and spiritual redemption.[59] It was a relation that gave teeth to the disquieting biblical and homiletic edicts: "The first shall be last and the last shall be first," and "The poor shall inherit the kingdom of heaven."

In this context, Riis inoculated his audience against the irrational fears of tenement visitation, much as Edwards's generation created experience by linguistically prodding the senses to create physiological reactions. The continual influx of immigrants, Riis wrote in *Children of the Poor*—his 1892 sequel to *How the Other Half Lives*—"forces layer after layer of this population up to make room for the new crowds coming in at the bottom, and thus a circulation is kept up that does more than any sanitary law to render the slums harmless to the outside."[60] By dividing the city into "stories," and allowing the viewing auditor to see humanity from multiple angles, Riis sought to free his audience from its own social limitations. The allegory's architectural frame and Riis's hauntingly emblematic and holographic slides produced intimations that the sensible world—space itself—merely veiled eternal dimensions. Rather than externalizing perspective, the kind of socio-spiritual "cubism" that the virtual tour offered encouraged viewing auditors to see social evaluation, judgment, empirical data—even sense-based epistemology—as a flattening out or "materializing" of reality's double dimension.

The Interactive Text

Riis's virtual-tour narratives aimed to do more than introduce middle-class audiences to human misery from a safe vantage: it sought to motivate their active engagement with urban social problems. In doing so, it joined the Social Gospel to contend with two prevailing social ideologies of noninterference, one religious and one secular. The former, a strain of salvation through grace, for which social standing was a portent, resigned the impoverished to their own fallen nature and God's inscrutable design to justify social indolence in the presence of need—a theological hand-washing that William James shamed as the Christian's "moral holiday."[61] In the latter, liberal Spencerians attached capital's free-market mechanism to the theory of social evolution to advance an ideology of what we might think of as laissez-faire determinism, in which society, like nature, evolved through an undisturbed cycle of natural regulation and selection. In this view, success, failure, struggle, death, and renewal were the touted engines of social progress and evolution. By the 1890s, we recall from the previous chapter, a spate of Social Gospel publications emerged and mixed with secular arguments that associated urban poverty and social malaise with institutional and social causes. Hamlin Garland's *Main-Travelled Roads* (1891) and Walter Wyckoff's *Workers East* (1897) and *Workers West* (1898), for example, attributed the intellectual and emotional impoverishment that led to cycles of class crime and destitution to the drudgery of day labor, factory conditions, and class exploitation. Looking ahead to the proletariat novels of the 1930s, these works achieved their apogee in the period with Edwin Markham's controversial 1899 poem, "The Man with a Hoe," which created alarm on several fronts, particularly by its suggestion that environment irrevocably bestialized humanity, forever deadening spiritual aptitude.[62]

By the time Riis's stereopticon lectures were fully developed, both the Social Gospel and homiletic guides such as Stead's and Sheldon's works had fused with reform to advocate individuals' capacity to effect change, and to reverse the social entropy and political torpor produced by providential and scientific fatalism. The homiletic's interventionist

ethic answered a renewed emphasis among nineteenth-century Edward-
sians on individual volition and positive freedom.[63] The revived focus
on human agency gave credence to the formerly heretical salvation-
through-works doctrine, exposing predestinarianism's overweening presumption that privileged a social and spiritual elect. Volitional agency,
and thus a person's capacity for social mediation, made individual redemption inseparable from social salvation. By advocating individuals'
moral musculature, Christian socialists and Social Gospel adherents
who, like Riis, were strongly influenced by socialism, gave expression to
Progressive Era optimism in the form of new humanist theologies, not
the least among them the popular Christian evolution movement, what
Henry Martyn Simmons digested in his 1882 guide on the evolutionary
implications of humanity's "unending genesis" toward Messianic perfection, rendered in humanity's increasingly visible Christlike phenotype.[64]
In so doing, they liberalized Protestant humanism, transforming a belief that spiritual aptitude developed selectively in and among the young
to a faith that endowed all individuals with a lifelong capacity for moral
growth and spiritual maturation.

As we saw in the last chapter, the socially oriented theology of ministers in Henry Ward Beecher's generation had initiated a growing pattern
among Civil War–era evangelical reformers to stimulate individual forays into social activism. In efforts similar to Beecher's staged slave auction, in which he raised a freedom fund for fugitive slaves in the North,
ministers across the nation in the last years before the Civil War and the
initial decades after had begun to transform Protestant pedagogy from
a passive emphasis on social charity—traditional alms in which churches
regularly tithed congregants to support charity houses, orphanages, and
social programs administered at a distance—toward a new aesthetics of
immediacy designed to stimulate active engagement with social problems.[65] As with Beecher and, later, Charles Sheldon, ministers sought
not just to fix social problems through conventional charity programs
but to immerse audiences in the personal trauma of larger, specific social
ills—to connect their congregants to social suffering, their agency to social relief. In what would eventually inform the earliest tenets of Muscular Christianity, they believed that once their flocks personally encountered human pain, they would be transformed from social observers to
soldier activists marching beneath a millennialist banner into the worst
regions of urban destitution and squalor. In the idiom of his homiletic

pedagogy—in an expression Beecher never tired of repeating—he was teaching his congregation not only to fish, but to be fishers of men.

Riis joined Beecher in using the pulpit and lectern for sociopolitical reform. Although each used this method toward different ends, the highlighting and mapping of social and demographic conditions became a primary tool for both in helping their audiences engage contemporary urban challenges. Beecher emphasizes demographic shifts as he leads his audience from room to room in the hellish house. From the vestibule through which the child passes as he crosses into the First Ward, subsequent rooms become dirtier and more crowded, each possessing greater suffering, noise, and confusion. What becomes apparent is that Beecher's vision of hell is distinctly urban, poor, ethnic, and uneducated— immigrant, one might say. This is not surprising, however, when we recall that in 1847—the year he revises "The Strange Woman's House"—he relocated from Indianapolis to Brooklyn as pastor of Plymouth Church, to the very ward Riis would call home less than twenty-five years later, to the very church in which Riis would on many occasions present his own virtual-tour narratives. Beecher's fear of urban space and dense populations of the poor is present in his warnings to the young not to "make [their] heads a metropolis of base stories, the ear and tongue a highway of immodest words" ("Strange Woman" 208). Just across the East River from the village atmosphere of Brooklyn Heights, New York's verticality, with its submerged layers of corruption and uncatalogued, unregulated vices, sins, and diseases, provided the structure for Beecher's vision of hell.

A generation later, Riis's earliest tours followed the social and demographic emphases of Beecher's schematic topography. By drawing so closely on the form and content of homiletic structure, Riis immersed his virtual-tour narratives in prevailing moral constructions of race. Ethnically labeled photographs form the central narrative structure. The Italians of the fourth ward, for instance, live under the worst sanitary conditions. Photographed in prone positions, theirs is the disorder of idle resignation that "afflicts" Mediterranean cultures. The Irish of the "bloody sixth" and twenty-first wards are quick to wrath. Relaxing their inhibitions, excessive drinking renders them difficult to assimilate. Located near "the Bend," the Jews of "Jewtown" suffer from cupidity, a symptom, Riis tells the reader, of their "commercial instinct." The German, though "order-loving," lives a life reduced in meaning by the "monotony" of his surroundings. The African American embodies the moral failing captured in photographs of "Black and Tan Saloons," liminal spaces blurring racial boundaries. The Chinese—for Riis, the most vulnerable to slipping on the ontological chain of being—are "stealthful like the cat" in their social evasion. What for Beecher's generation was the tenement's refusal of moral closure—with its labyrinthine architecture—was for its Social Gospel heirs simply the social disorder that homiletic schematization sought to contain and organize in the name of civic and social reform. For Beecher, the tenement's gothic space had allegorized the sins of religious and legal equivocation, the false routes of logic, the blind alleys of reason, the microdivisions whose excess of sign defied the very order that homiletic architecture would impose. Evacuated of much of its moral freight, for Riis, it simply symbolized a disruption in the order that promoted meaningful self-regulation. While Riis uses conventional postbellum racial taxonomies—a blend of Judeo-Christian moral order and late-nineteenth-century scientized racism—in *How the Other Half Lives,* his lectures and editorials after 1892 begin, with increasing frequency, to reflect a significant reevaluation of race, from conventional stereotypes predicated on biology to transracial characteristics of the impoverished shaped solely by environment. Increasingly for Riis, tenement misery became an allegory of domestic disarray, in which Christian duty obligated intervention through the reformer's role of what he called the national "housekeeper."

How the Other Half Lives bears vestiges of the moral and secular typology of mid-nineteenth-century racial taxonomies that Riis's magic lantern projected onto the urban demography. The fear of social chaos created by masses who went unaccounted required ordering for what in Beecher's sermons was a zoology of the "vicious": imported "serpents from Africa," "lions from Asia," "lizards and scorpions and black tarantulas from the Indies" ("Strange Woman" 211). Beecher's xenophobia took the form of a transmogrified chain of being, by which the city became civilization's urban jungle. Merging with Social Darwinism and Louis Agassiz's legacy of late-century Lamarckian determinism, this zoology informs Riis's own fear, not of the immigrant socialized and integrated, but of those left to tenement environs, where, he writes, "the latent possibilities for evil that lie hidden within" transforms man into a brute.[66] As Riis writes of orphans like Tony, "Home, the greatest factor of all in training of the young, means nothing to him but a pigeon-hole in a coop along with so many other human animals" (*Other Half*

138). Tenement slums contain the "packs," "herds," "flocks," "clutches," and "swarms" that inhabit "rookeries," "colonies," "coops," and "dens," a categorical nomenclature he revises to describe, not individuals— and, finally, not demographic or ethnic groups—but the dangers of de- based environments ill suited for helping humans achieve their social and spiritual possibility. Riis turns Beecher's judgment back upon the middle class for their complacency toward, if not agency in, humanity's bestialization.

Because Riis's descriptions unfold on the sensational side of senti- mentalism and sometimes employ ethnic labels in seemingly rigid ways, recent criticism often dismisses his work as sentimentalism that, in June Howard's assessment, represents the "poor only in the most clichéd terms."[67] Riis's work certainly risks presenting the "other's" suffering not as an object for intervention, but as an object inviting self-reflexivity, the difference, as Howard puts it, "between empathy and observation, between treating an other . . . as a producer of signs and as a sign."[68] But this, I think, is key to understanding the complete trajectory of Riis's ca- reer: while his earliest work rises out of distinctive Progressive Era pro- cesses of social formation, the political project that gradually emerged from his ethnic cartography departed sharply from that of many of his contemporaries, and as years advanced, Riis became increasingly criti- cal of his own early racial judgments and a biting critic of human taxon- omies that both fostered and justified urban ghettoization. Embodying the spiritual transformation homiletic literature advocated in the Social Gospel tradition, Riis's social views underwent a gradual conversion af- ter the mid-1890s, as he came to see what he frequently referred to as the "Maker's image" beneath the rags and grime of the city, beneath the fragile shells of the mentally ill, and beneath the color of skin. Much of Riis's work after 1897—scores of essays, newspapers articles, and magic- lantern lectures delivered across the nation and regularly in New York City and at Chautauqua, New York—have never been collected, repub- lished, or reconstructed, rendering *How the Other Half Lives* as the fi- nal word and enduring legacy of a life tirelessly dedicated to the na- tion's poor. The archive does not bear out the quick and easy critical judgments predicated on presentist assumptions about Riis's best-known work or the hundreds of extant photographs that survive from his pro- grams of social reform. Riis's was the first sustained voice raised in de- fense of the insane, the mentally incompetent, and children born with severe disabilities (in what, sounding strikingly modern day, Riis called "special needs"), and, in an age still governed by a Victorian culture of silence, denial, and institutionalized isolation and abandonment, one of the first reformers to speak out for children most at risk for sexual exploitation. His is a legacy of liberal humanism scarcely matched in his own day.

In the emerging social sciences, in many progressive reform leagues, and in state and local legislative corridors, ethnic demography had become a tool of both description and analysis, as racial and class traits became explanatory factors for poverty, crime, and other components of urban despair. The gradual shift in social and political sentiments that shaped Riis's work from his first lectures to his final essays reveals the homiletic narrative's power to initiate self-reflection and transform one's own social awareness and political engagements. Whereas the labels Beecher used to categorize sin provided middle-class audiences with a clear portrait of good and evil, merit and sloth, grace and judgment, Riis intended his ethnography to expose the "realities" of tenement life so that listeners armed with an understanding of pain and suffering could act to alleviate such despair. His demographic tour drew on familiar schema that were intended more to stabilize and control the inevitable spin of moral allegory by giving structure and meaning to the horrifying depths of human suffering in already racialized ghettos than to naturalize ethnic difference. It is, I argue, this destabilization of meaning—moral allegory unmoored form its homiletic frame—that constituted the "unreality" that Amy Kaplan has identified as the perennial concern of the best-known, conventionally recognized, late-nineteenth-century American literary realists.[69] Riis's attempt to re-anchor the chaos of poverty, crime, and contagion within the structures of moral order and potentiality of social reform—depicted through homiletic realism—is the representational equivalent of what Kaplan calls the secular realists' attempt through discursive representation to comprehend and manage dramatic social transformation: "Like contemporary social reformers, they engage in an enormous act of construction to organize, re-form, and control the social world."[70] Ultimately, Riis drew on ethnic taxonomies not as static categories for social critique, but, rather, to question the divisions instilled by class difference, one of the primary disturbances to the sense of an ordered reality. Only by providing a structured portrait of poverty, insanity, sorrow, and need—most often, as with his portraits of Tony, Jacob, Mike, and Katie, redacted through children representing every ethnic group—could he spur his magic-

lantern audiences to engage social problems they would otherwise encounter only in the abstract. Only by installing that structured portrait
within a homiletic frame could Social Gospel reformers mitigate class
difference through an appeal to Christianity's alleged social leveling,
epitomized by and embodied in, as we saw in the last chapter, the person
of Christ, the divine tramp.

Using his press coverage to excoriate the city for "interring" the sick
and homeless on Blackwell's Island, Riis accused the city of a policy of
"dealing with the poor that simply looked at getting them out of the sight
of their happier fellows whom their misery offended."[71] "On these is-
lands," he tells his audience, "there are no flexible twigs, only gnarled,
blasted, blighted trunks, insensible of moral or social influence" (*Other
Half,* 203).[72] Alluding to the suicides' judgment in Dante's inferno—in
which they are imprisoned in trees—Riis uses the example of the Blackwell's inmates, "patients inflicted with suicidal mania" (*Other Half* 203),
to impress upon his audience the need for immediate intervention in poverty, before despair renders sufferers' minds inflexible, and necessity renders their vices habitual. Like Beecher's, Riis's aesthetics of immediacy
gave viewing auditors the perception of an authentic experience, making
them feel the irresistible gravity of hopelessness and habituation.

Riis's virtual-tour narratives struck a nerve within Progressive Era
audiences and, particularly, among Beecher's generation; the era's flurry
of social reform activities confirms that many Americans accepted and
engaged homiletic blueprints for civic engagement. Upon reading *How
the Other Half Lives,* for example, the elderly James Russell Lowell—
whose poetic allegory about Christ as a modern beggar who finds no
Christian aid prefaces not only Riis's book, but also books by Edward
Everett Hale, Milford Howard, Walter Wyckoff, W. T. Stead, and Jack
London—wrote to Riis, "I have read your book with deep and painful
interest. I felt as Dante must when he looked over the edge of the Abyss
at the bottom of which Gergon lay in ambush. . . . I found it hard to get
asleep the night after I had been reading it."[73] Writing for the same audience, Flower would name his virtual-tour narrative, *Civilization's Inferno,* after Dante's allegory. More than a metaphor, his title indexes the
hermeneutic tradition to which Lowell referred. Benjamin O. Flower
tells his reader that "there is no need to wander into other worlds for
hells of God's creating," for "Man has made an under-world, before
which the most daring imagination of poet or seer staggers. Over its portals," he intones, "might well be blazoned the soul-freezing inscription

which Dante beheld as he entered the under-world."[74] Sharing Beecher's
Calvinist training, Lowell, like the Congregationalist-trained Flower,
recognized in Riis's work the homiletic paradigm, which Riis fashioned
after the visual-narrative realism of Beecher's heuristic allegory. Lowell's sleepless night and "pained conscience" activated by reading Riis's
book demonstrate the "readerly" interaction to which Royall Tyler referred when he satirized John Bunyan's readers for laboring in real time
alongside Bunyan's pilgrimming protagonist. If Bunyan's Christian is a
struggling Everyman on a quest for personal redemption, so is Riis's impoverished immigrant (a word close in meaning to the etymology of pilgrim, or "stranger in the land"), with whom readers like Lowell came
to identify. By approaching *How the Other Half Lives* from within the
ascending materialist epistemology, against which turn-of-the-century
Christian idealists like Dewey and Josiah Royce vainly labored, modern critics have lost sight of this homiletic's allegorical structure, its spiritual dimension. From inside this religious hermeneutic, however, these
comments suggest how Riis's aesthetics of immediacy inculcated readers in the salvation or destruction of all. Riis's Social Gospel contemporary Henry Wood explained the putative consequences for the middle-
class's failed stewardship: "Humanity is one. I am living and loving, not
for myself, but for the race. If I rise, I help lift all about me, and if I fall,
I drag others down. . . . We live the life of humanity—others in us, and
we in them. We cannot be saved disconnected from relations."[75] The Social Gospel advocates filled the void between what William James called
the "discontinuous entities" of "knower and known" not with any of
the standard theories James identified as "Representative," "Common-
Sense," or "Transcendentalist," but with what seemed to them the most
material bridge of all, pain.[76] Lowell's testimony illustrates the virtual
tour's homiletic potential to overcome social barriers by collapsing the
reformer and poor into a single perceiving, suffering body.

Unlike Beecher and his contemporaries in secular reform, Riis struggled to separate the individual from the "masses," to view slums not as a
glimpse into a metaphysical hell, but, as he taught Flower to see them, a
hell made by man. While campaigning against Spencerian and religious
hereditary doctrines with the slogan that "no children were bad by nature; there was no such thing as total depravity," he modified Beecher's
Calvinist eugenics—in which moral degradation is not racially fixed or
gendered but bequeathed to children through the moral defects of their
parents—to account only for environmental effects.[77] In so doing, he at-

tached a temporal imperative to the rescue of tenement inhabitants. Because for Riis and a generation influenced by Horace Bushnell's Christian nurture theology, the effect of "bad environment," not morality, "becomes the hereditary of the next generation," dirt and darkness were, for him, the malevolent forces imperiling the nation.[78] "[I] naturally want to let in the light," Riis recorded; "I will have no dark corners in my own cellar; it must be whitewashed clean."[79] For Riis, the burst of magnesium that brought the "underworld" to view became a metaphor for the new century's enlightenment: a synthesis of the lights of science and spiritualism. Armed with new technologies and the shield of faith, he set out to harrow the tenement underworld, saving the as-yet-unhardened from a tragic end, from the lowest level of the urban hell, the "darkened mind." Or as Flower diagnosed the spiritual consequences, the "extinguished soul," a phrase loaded with recrimination for those failing in their Christian stewardship.

Riis's virtual tour departed from its precursor by realigning the Puritan forensic arts (*technologia*) with new "arts" of visual technology. This technology transformed and clarified the images of urban life, revealing not the pattern of good and evil seen in homiletic sermons, but a disorganized world of daily life rife with possibilities for social action. This is what William James meant, when in 1904, in "A World of Pure Experience," he muses that "Empiricism flirts with teleology,"[80] ascribing meaning to the social world in order to grant social intervention greater purpose. After touring Chicago slums, John Dewey expressed the same optimism about urban distress that captivated Riis's audiences. In the tenor of Social Gospel humanism, Dewey wrote to his wife: "Think of the city as 'hell turned loose' and yet not hell any longer, but simply material for a new creation."[81] In this instance—and true to homiletic purposes—teleology precedes empiricism; narrative directs action.

The Timeless Flash of Light:
The Spiritual Realism of Photography

Raised in the homiletic tradition, American Protestants learned to interact with religious texts in a manner that is difficult for more secular modern readers to understand. Particularly lost to posthomiletic audiences is the second sight claimed by nineteenth-century Christian audiences to bring specific kinds of religious narrative vividly to life. Elizabeth

Cady Stanton, for instance, grew up in the "flock" of the famed revivalist Charles Finney and recalled in her 1897 autobiography his religious training's lasting impact. Like his evangelical cohorts, Finney sought to produce piety on a mass scale by drawing upon the visually oriented homiletic tradition. In the context of massive revival meetings, faith became a matter of sight; awakening in piety meant seeing the reality their sermons verbalized. Garnering second sight thus fulfilled the homiletic injunction whose intent Abbott had digested in the slogan: "Present everything in such a way as to convey vivid pictures to the mind" (*Way* 279).

Stanton recalled how on one "memorable occasion" Finney seemed to summon Satan to frighten backsliding parishioners into renouncing their sin and renewing their faith. Sixty-five years later, she described the event as still "indelibly impressed on my mind":

> One evening he described hell and the devil and the long procession of sinners being swept down the rapids, about to make the awful plunge in the burning depths of liquid fire below, and the rejoicing hosts in the inferno coming up to meet them with the shouts of the devils echoing through the vaulted arches. He suddenly halted, and, pointing his index finger at the supposed procession, he exclaimed: "There, do you not see them!"
>
> I was wrought up to such a pitch that I actually jumped up and gazed in the direction to which he pointed, while the picture glowed before my eyes and remained with me for months afterward. . . . Fear of the judgment seized my soul. Visions of the lost haunted my dreams. Mental anguish prostrated my health. Dethronement of my reason was apprehended by my friends. . . . Returning home, I often at night roused my father from his slumbers to pray for me, lest I should be cast into the bottomless pit before morning.[82]

Stanton's memory, taking form in the homiletic realism of Finney's Edwardsian legacy, provides yet another instance of the imaginative capacities Social Gospel audiences possessed for turning visually oriented language into vivid realities. Her ability both to perceive and describe such images in evocative detail illuminates how the gap between what the viewer sees and what is "present"—what, we recall, Stanton's contemporary Stephen H. Bradley described as a sermonic scene of hellish suffering that "appeared to be taking place"—becomes the imaginative space in which texts become interactive.[83] As with Beecher's and Riis's narratives—and similar to the cemetery or Chautauqua as virtual tour—the aesthetics of immediacy furnished a space within a narrative framework designed to secure the viewing auditor's identification with an allegorical sequence of rooms and with a progressive story of moral decline or redemption.[84] By effecting a somatic identification between reform agents and the destitute, the repetition of suffering produced by homiletic simulation generated the most authentic social knowledge— personal experience. Through the exertion of the Spirit "in the exercise" of the individual faculties, to use Edwards's phrase, the sermon's words were made manifest in the flesh of the godly, through perceptions that register as *sensible* expressions of love, fear, and self-loathing. While, no doubt, as in the case of Finney, ministers' theatrical performances added to the impact of homiletic language, so, too, did audiences' training in spiritual sight. If Stanton did not descend into hell, she stood at its brink. Finney's visually evocative sermon of sinners falling into the hellish chasm was consummated in her "prostrate health" and "unthroned reason," and, like the village Increase Mather summoned in his homiletic depiction of Judgment, the anxiety that leads Stanton to wake her father in the night for his prayers of intercession demonstrates the homiletic legacy of narrative personalization. If, as Increase Mather insisted, fathers could testify against their children in death, then they could, as Stanton believed, surely intercede on their behalf in life. If her visceral reaction and, in turn, her father's response both highlight how far the early nineteenth century, in its muscularization of human volition, had come from Mather's and Edwards's belief in the soul's passivity, it is because Stanton's response makes visible the sermon's interactive dimension, the affective strategies by which the narrative elicits identification and motivates action.

In its emphasis on experiencing both the literal and the divine through the acquisition of second sight, homiletic pedagogy cultivated a double vision among Protestants who encountered life as a religious narrative. The homiletic had prepared Stanton's mind to translate verbal imagery into visual reality, not as metaphor, but as an allegorical realization of the literal world and its corresponding dimension, the immutable divine that could only be fleetingly glimpsed by the sensible. Only by seeing perishing souls fall into the chasm of the eternal deep, only by experiencing the terror of Satan's presence as a personal reality, could Stanton locate herself within the allegorical frame of Finney's regenerative narrative.

It is the occult nature of religious faith to see things that are not empirically present. The Platonic roots of Anglo-American Protestantism had long nurtured the belief that a veil divided the sensible world from the spiritual, tempting divines with its revelatory potential, while also reminding them of its impenetrable presence. The Puritan division between the visible and invisible church and the soul's unrequited, earthly desire for its perfect completion in Christ prepared the need and way for new epistemological attempts to ascertain knowledge of the divine.[85] John Locke's empiricism simultaneously thwarted this inquiry and opened new avenues for its pursuit. Turn-of-the-twentieth-century psychologists and philosophers like Henry Wood, William James, Josiah Royce, John Dewey, and George A. Coe sought to move past the perceived revelatory power of the veil, arriving at new ways to explain an organic connection between mysticism and the ordinary functioning of the human mind. Wood, for example, assured his audience that death, like a nap, was little more than a "transition" to the "real": "Man lays aside the curtain which, in his servitude to the senses, he has hung between God and himself, and calls the process death. . . . All *real* life is eternal life." [86] In a remarkable passage in *The Varieties of Religious Experience,* James even suggested the possibility that the subconscious or "subliminal conscious" was a receptacle for divine communication in language reminiscent of the gentle theology of Elizabeth Stewart Phelps:

> The lower manifestations of the Subliminal, indeed, fall within the resources of the personal subject: his ordinary sense-material, inattentively taken in and subconsciously remembered and combined, will account for all his usual automatisms [spiritual manifestations]. But just as our primary wide-awake consciousness throws open our sense to the touch of things material, so it is logically conceivable that *if there be* higher spiritual agencies that can directly touch us, the psychological condition of their doing so *might be* our possession of a subconscious region which alone should yield access to them. The hubbub of the waking life might close a door which in the dreamy subliminal might remain ajar or open. (*Varieties* 197; original emphasis)

Later, James more explicitly holds the subconscious up as a receptor for divine impressions: "The notion of a subconscious self," he writes, "certainly ought not . . . to be held to *exclude* all notion of a higher penetration. If there be higher power able to impress us, they may get access to us only through the subliminal door" (*Varieties* 198). From James's pragmatic point of view—and from the agnostic end of belief—a connection to a higher spiritual realm could not be discounted. At the secular end of true faith, James's religious contingency bespeaks the extent to which most Americans firmly believed in a reality beyond the senses. For this national majority, James's pragmatism was a lifeline of little value, a system in progress that, for genuine believers, would seem to produce faith value from its own faithlessness.

Whether defended by faith or science, the extraordinarily saintly, those with second sight, and those with a tentative hold on this world—children, the dying, spiritualists—were afforded glimpses behind the veil. Faith, then, was a measure of the believer's extrasensory perception. As Abbott admonished his audience,

> Make it your aim, not merely to see what is visible to the eye, but to read its hidden meaning, and take pleasure, not in novelty and strangeness, but in the clearness with which you understand and appreciate every common phenomenon. Be intimately conversant thus with a moral and spiritual world, to which the external one around you will be the medium of access. He who does this, will find his mind filled with a thousand recollections and associations that, by means of a power which is neither imagination or memory, but something between, will furnish him with illustrations of all which he wishes to teach;—illustrations true in spirit, though imaginary in form. (*Way* 319)

In the homiletic, the visual attributes of verbal illustration specified the process between "imagination and memory" by which the external world became a "medium of access" to the spiritual's hidden meaning. As such, verbal illustration was the catalyst of homiletic realism.

The chiliastic enthusiasm attached to the terminus of both century and millennium and the syncretism of what Louis Menand has called an age in which "psychic phenomenon, religious belief, and science" were inextricably entwined made the 1890s an auspicious time for spiritualism.[87] As Robert Taft demonstrated in *Photography and the American Scene* (1938), the camera had been associated with the occult since its invention. The ability to capture images, the daguerreotype's hologrammatic quality, the ghosting patterns produced by movement during exposure, and the palimpsestic depth and nuances of photographic chiaroscuro together supported claims about the camera's ability to register spiritual presences invisible to the naked eye. In *Reading American Photography,* Alan Trachtenberg traces the late-nineteenth-century perception that the camera could capture authentic essences, that it sees beneath the subject's mask, beneath the ontological constructions, cultural assumptions, and social prejudices that we impose on others.[88] Unlike the human mind, the camera was not, Riis believed, temporally and spatially conditioned; it was not susceptible to the habituated illusion of relational order.

The homiletic's use of allegorical tableaux made photography an ideal tool for Social Gospel reform. Protestant pedagogy's development of homiletic realism had anticipated the autoptic veracity and otherworldliness of early photography. Riis's audience came prepared to see the fluctuating superimposition of the material and spiritual worlds. Photography thus provided an ideal second fundamental strategy for engaging the imaginative space of faith: the visualization of spiritual reality at a time when the hegemony of a scientific epistemology and a materialist ontology diminished religious habits of imagination, threatening the analogical capacity on which typology—indeed the whole of the Calvinist hermeneutic—was predicated. As Abbott had described the appropriately trained "seer" in his homiletic manual earlier in the century, "The ordinary exhibitions of human action, though opaque . . . and spiritless to others, are bright and transparent to him. He sees a spiritual world through the external one, and the spectacle which thus exhibits itself all around him, is clothed thus with a double interest and splendor" (*Way* 317). Even at century's end, William James, deemed an influential voice in rational inquiry, held out the possibility for other realities: "the world of our present consciousness is only one out of many worlds of consciousness that exist . . . and that although in the main their experiences and those of this world keep discrete, yet the two become continuous at certain points" (*Varieties* 408). It is these points Riis's photographs sought to make evident. Hailing the camera as the "greatest of human triumphs over earthly conditions," Oliver Wendell Holmes described the photograph in precisely the language conventional to the description of things spiritual, "the divorce of form and substance."[89] With its ability to freeze movement and whitewash darkness, Riis used the new technology of flash photography to wage war with what he called the "principles of darkness," to make the misery of the urban reality "bright and transparent," as Abbott had put it, with "the double interest and splendor" of spiritual resonance.[90] The magnesium's blinding burst illuminated the degradation of tenement life, just as its light became Riis's metaphor of salvation in the urban house. By situating each image within the virtual-tour frame, Riis did not just capture; he actively reshaped a sordid social reality in the service of specific pedagogical ends.

FIGURE 8. Jacob A. Riis, "Minding the Baby—Scene in Gotham Court," c. 1890. By courtesy of the Museum of the City of New York. Riis manipulates this domestic scene of mother and children through an ethereal representation that, for Christian audiences, evokes a pattern of "ironic ghosting."

Photography offered Riis a medium suited to capturing the palimp-sestic correspondence between visible and spiritual realms. In his pho-tographs of children, for example, the mother often appears a "spec-tral presence." In "Minding the Baby" (fig. 8), she seems to be reaching out to catch her child as it slides from an older sibling's lap. The image's fuzzy resolution signals the woman's motion, a quality associated with Riis's candid shots, in which he surreptitiously entered homes, captur-ing occupants unaware. But this photograph is hardly candid. Riis de-liberately captured the mother in motion, using the technology's more primitive features to create a supernatural realism. Gifted with a camera and possessing hundreds of photographs from which to select his pub-lished prints—supplying photographs, in fact, to other urban reformers like Helen Campbell—Riis staged the scene. Requiring a fraction of a second for exposure, "taking a picture" had advanced dramatically from the daguerreotype phase, when, depending on light availability, exposure required from twenty seconds to three minutes. In this photograph, Riis set the woman in motion, opening the shutter at precisely the moment she enters the lens's frame. An "accident" referred to as "ghosting," the result creates a spectralized image and gives a transparent quality to objects in motion. Enabling his audience to see "the spiritual world through the external one," the image spectralizes the mother in the service of homiletic realism to remind us that her children are orphans, practically speaking, if not in actuality. She is missing: she died in childbirth, fell to prostitution, or succumbed to sweatshop labor. Her spectral image links material poverty to its spiritual consequence. Applying the religious hermeneutic to a virtual-tour narrative, Flower illustrates the proper way to read these images within the homiletic frame: inductively, from a seemingly implicit meaning backward in time to an explicit one, to reveal the viewers' culpability in the causal chain of suffering, despair, and death: "They seem of another world; they are of another world; driven into the darkness of hopeless existence."[91]

This is why, in his juxtaposition of Riis's "sentimentalized" photography with what he claims is the "frontal directness" and simplicity of Walker Evans's Depression-era photography (best known for his collaboration with James Agee in *Let Us Now Praise Famous Men*), Miles Orvell overlooks the religious efficacy of Riis's photography, by construing it in secular terms as a sympathetic yet stylized and voyeuristic portrait of immigrant and working classes. Indeed, images throughout Riis's stereopticon tours seem initially to trade in the visual conventions of sentimental domesticity, inviting viewers to draw quick conclusions from the cultural resonances they evoke. Affect-saturated tropes such as destitute orphans, childhood disease and starvation, and sacrificing mothers engage viewers' empathy in the politico-aesthetic tradition of sentimentality. Yet, this tradition is all the more affecting because the sentimental is meant to give way through spiritual sight to the authenticity of experiencing another's pain as an expiating sacrifice commensurate with Christ's atonement for the world. Riis's visual texts are interactive for what they require from the audience: a recognition of sentimental tropes that in turn invite a creative act of misrecognition, or second sight. Through the aesthetics of immediacy, Riis framed these familiar images, using sentimental conventions to destabilize the semiotic production of realism— making the social world newly visible to audiences through an optics of the divine. Here, the image evokes an alternative reality by tapping into his audience's religious belief, opening an aperture into the spiritual world that, in James's words, "the hubbub of the waking life might have closed, but . . . which in the dreamy Subliminal might have remained ajar" (*Varieties* 181). As with the photograph above, the childhood mortality and poverty Riis portrays suggest the temporal limits of the sensible world. So, too, for his audience, suffering resonates with a chiasmic typology, where, in the popular parable of rich man and beggar, eternal Life rewards the suffering poverty of a Lazarus and eternal Death the selfish luxury of a Dives.

For Beecher, the city as house is composed of "volumes of monster-galleries in which the inhabitants of old *Sodom* would have felt at home" ("Strange Woman" 210). His hell, strikingly cast in the mold of a tenement slum, is synonymous with New York's ghettos, with "stacked houses, burning streets, reeking gutters, everlasting din of wheels, and outcry of voices . . . of life in the city."[92] The contagion threatening middle-class culture is for Beecher the "common sewer of society, into which drain the concentrated filth of the worst passions, of the worst creatures, of the worst cities" ("Strange Woman" 210). His allegorical cityscape verifies the fallen state of those within, a Calvinist remnant of social status as a sign of election or reprobation. In Beecher's tableau of urban outcasts, God passes judgment on Sodom and Gomorrah. Riis's cityscape by contrast casts the reformer in the role of Abraham, who, upon learning of the cities' fate, bargained with God for its salvation if ten innocents might be found. "Were they all bad, those dens I hated?" Riis admonishes himself in his 1901 autobiography, *The Making of an American.* "Yes, hated," he muses, "with all the shame and the sorrow and the hopeless surrender they stood for? Was there not one glimpse of mercy that dwells in the memory with redeeming touch?" In the breath with which he raises the question, he answers it: "Yes, one. Let it stand as testimony that on the brink of hell itself human nature is not wholly lost. There is still the spark of His [God's] image, however overlaid by the slum."[93] Unlike Abraham's nephew Lot, who found none worthy of salvation, Riis finds many: "It is not an uncommon thing to find sweet and innocent girls," he writes in *How the Other Half Lives,* "singularly untouched by the evil around them, true wives and faithful mothers, literally 'like jewels in a swine's snout,' in the worst of the infamous barracks" (122). In his photograph entitled, "In the home of an Italian rag-picker, Jersey Street" (fig. 9), Riis portrays one such jewel, a mother and child.

This image of a mother cradling a swaddled infant is Riis's version of the New World nativity. With doleful gaze drifting upward, his Ma-

FIGURE 9. Jacob A. Riis, "In the Home of an Italian Ragpicker, Jersey Street," c. 1890. By courtesy of the Museum of the City of New York. For Riis, this New World Madonna emblematically depicts the stakes of Christian indifference and solicits through the stereopticon media a call for his audiences' personal intervention in tenement poverty.

donna strikes a pose of spiritual reflection, a pose at odds with the filth that surrounds her. Near at hand are the instruments that tie her to a base existence, to a close affinity with dirt, disease, and destitution. This living tableau demonstrates another side to homiletic allegory's "realism." The galvanized washing tubs, bundles of dirty rags, even the dustpan, signal the toiling life of a washerwoman—details that stand in contrast to the religious iconography and the mother's distant, heavenward gaze. High overhead, the straw hat is the only reminder of the natural world, the pastoral setting of nativity, the green world from which urban depravity seduced Beecher's rural youth. Daylight and its absence are invoked both by the straw from which the hat has been woven, and the hat's function to protect its wearer from the sun. The high walls and cropped ceiling, and the ladder standing near the mother, as though she must ascend from a great depth to reach the light, increase the illusion of depth, the feeling of entombment. Riis's city inverts Beecher's image of rural innocence swallowed up by urban abomination. Read through the appropriate hermeneutic lens, the photograph overturns its implicit sentimentalism to become a visual metaphor of spiritual reality—a deferred transcendence, a purgatory awaiting a social harrowing. The tableau of spiritual realism is the more apparent for the extremity of the suffering it exposes, and the repetition—the Gilded Age's memento mori—implied by life's generational cycle (mother/ child) and, as the broom, dustpan, and rags imply, by the futility of placing one's store in earthly things. First and last, the image appeals to spiritual rather than social justice where moth and rust do corrupt.

Riis's photography engaged viewers in the invisible world that lay beyond the apparent reality of projected images. Riis accomplished this engagement through a technical manipulation of the photographic medium, by ghosting. But he did so as well through a manipulation of the image's content and iconography that I call "ironic ghosting." Through a discordant juxtaposition of visual and spiritual realities, ironic ghosting creates hermeneutic space for the occult apprehension of truth. Riis imports sentimental tropes into his picture story, while at the same time shifting these familiar tropes to disrupt their implicit meaning. Essentially, he places a modern notion of *seeing* as an implicit act against an older hermeneutic practice of seeing as *reading,* an explicit act manipulated by carefully crafted tableaux. As in his image of mother and child, ironic ghosting disrupts the gestalt effect by which we immediately take in the whole of the photographic image. In this alien environment—a nativity set in an inverted pastoral scene—the familiar trope becomes unstable: flashing (like slide projection itself) between the familiar and the distorted, a disjuncture between the beautiful and damned, a process of proto-Brechtian audience alienation that, in modern psychological parlance, we might think of as cognitive dissonance. Unlike the irony associated with the critical hermeneutics of secular postmodernism, however, sentimental irony creates this dissonance *in the service of* a sincere recommitment to humanism, in order to elicit and secure his audiences' commitment to spiritual truths that defy the apparent facts of social difference.

If, as Riis informs us in the accompanying text, the room is windowless and without natural light, what is the source of its artificial light? There is no indication of a lantern or fire. Riis's "flash light" has seemingly caught the mother and child in total darkness, illuminating momentarily a virtue buried in this underworld, a virtue identified by the photograph's emblematic presentation. As a contemporary reviewer observed, the "rayless vault" and other images in Riis's magic-lantern lecture frame the virtual-tour narrative as a mission to harrow hell. Writing for *The Critic* on December 18, 1892, this reviewer praised Riis's tour for "strengthening faith in God," and Riis for having "gone down into the depths of humanity, and into the homes where sunlight is but little known, and [having] come back, to call out the rest of humanity, to tell them how their brothers and sisters live."[94] From this perspective, Riis's poor are suspended in a liminal world, between damnation of perpetual darkness and the salvation of light. The mother's look of forbearance belies her peril, a spiritual resignation that to all appearances must outlive her mortal form. Many twentieth-century critics have claimed that Riis's photographs were unmediated. But despite his claims of having burst unannounced into darkened rooms in the dead of night, Riis designed many of his photographs as religious emblems in larger narratives of homiletic realism.[95]

The images in Riis's virtual-tour narrative pursue yet another strategy of ironic ghosting, borrowing from the homiletic tradition even as they adapt it to photographic technology. Unlike Beecher's visual language of excess, Riis relies on photography's claim to represent reality. In fact, his occasional graphic descriptions stand in contrast to the restraint shown in his photographs. He occasionally writes of alcohol sold in saloons as so toxic to the body that he refers to it as "blood baths," and of little children so inebriated that, while unconscious, they are "killed and half-eaten by rats" (*Other Half* 169), yet his photographs never reveal such lurid scenes, much less the equivalent of Beecher's visual language. Nor do they advance the clinical "realism" prized by turn-of-the-century sociology, such as Robert W. DeForest and Lawrence Veiller's 1903 *Report of the New York State Tenement House Commission,* which, in the name of scientific objectivity, exhibits such images as the indigent stripped naked in baths or awaiting examination, or photographs of fouled tenement apartments.[96] To do so would be to ground his viewing auditors in the sensible world—in the copiousness of sensual, rather than spiritual, detail. Against Abbott's admonition, it would be to invite "pleasure in novelty and strangeness," to which photography was already susceptible. Through ironic ghosting, Riis redirects his audience's gaze inward upon an erstwhile invisible truth.

Riis's strategy of ironic ghosting was inspired by a homiletic convention that embedded irony within sentimentalism to produce a discordant jolt resulting from the friction between two familiarly paired representations, in which one representation has been slightly skewed or shifted. Beecher's sermon offers several instances of this ironic sentimentalism. In the Third Ward, for example, an adolescent girl, dressed in rags and covered in festering sores, "cries out to her sweet and virtuous mother," who, Beecher tells us, has but lately been translated into a "glorious angel" ("Strange Woman" 202). Viewed against the popular conception of the mother as "angel of the hearth" and spiritual guardian of her young, the child's moral condition is the more surprising. But the narrative holds still another twist. In contrast to the youth's eternal suffering emerges the irony of a mother whose salvation has been occasioned by her death from a grief brought about by knowledge of her child's damnation. As with the photographs above, Riis continually ironizes the sentimental tropes of motherhood, the earthly legislator of divine law. In "A Home Nurse" (fig. 10), for example, he inverts the trope of mothers nursing dying children. Here, the baby nurses a dying mother. Who, then, the photograph implies, will guide, guard, and cherish the child?

In these various ways, Riis restages or inverts romantic tropes, appealing to an incongruity of image and language to alienate his audience from the comforting stasis of a prescripted sentimentalism. "Street Arabs in Night Quarters" (fig. 11) depicts three orphans posed in sleep against an exterior tenement staircase. Their sentimentalized postures— like satyr infants of a Veronesean green world—gradually reveal a tension with the urban environment, the cold pavement and brutal city streets, a juxtaposition Riis crystallizes by his reference to "street Arabs" like Tony as urban "Huck Finns." Embedded within the implicit, autoptic epistemology of the photograph—the image's power to narrate itself—lies a subliminal pattern, which gradually reorients our vision of the photograph against sentimental convention.[97] The audience's hermeneutic training gradually renders the epistemology explicit, initiating a homiletic tradition that, as Lowell's response to Riis's book suggests, turn-of-the-century audiences could still take for granted. As with the lantern slide show from which it drew its aesthetic strategies, its technologies of homiletic realism, Riis's book engaged audiences by appealing to the affective conventions of faith.

These images also appeal to the affective conventions of typology. If we think back to the discussion of cemetery visits as homiletic tours, we can see an interpretive context that religious audiences in the American

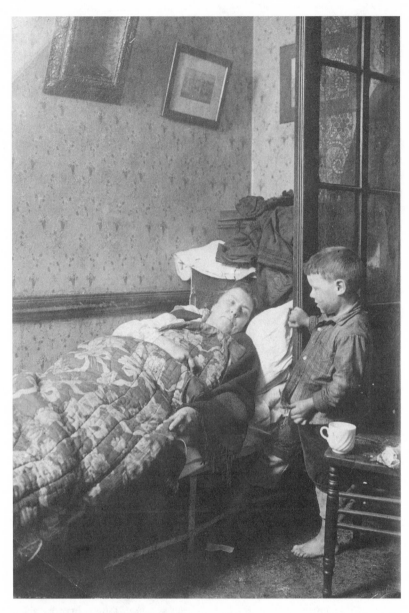

FIGURE 10. Jacob A. Riis, "A Home Nurse," c. 1890. By courtesy of the Museum of the City of New York. Riis's seemingly sentimental portrait exposes middle-class indifference to suffering through the ironic inversion of a typological domestic scene of a mother nursing a dying child.

FIGURE 11. Jacob A. Riis, "Street Arabs in Night Quarters," c. 1890. By courtesy of the Museum of the City of New York. Riis invokes the pastoral scene of sleeping satyrs to highlight, by contrast, the blighted urban conditions under which homeless children lived.

Calvinist tradition would have brought to Riis's stereopticon lectures and images. A feature of cemetery contemplation, as Sally Promey has demonstrated, was the role gravestone images played in the initiation of the viewer's spiritual introspection. These reiterative analogues worked together in, across, and outside time to strengthen the faithful's double vision, their capacity simultaneously to see the spiritual through the corporeal, and to see their likeness to venerated saints, and thus glimpse their place in God's scheme. Additionally, the slate from which they were carved could, when wet, appear blank, a penetrating reminder of the absence of loved ones, an erasure that served equally as a reminder of the vanity of life, the futility of acquiring property, reputation, or fame. Such emblematic cues as "figurative portraits of deceased saints," decorative skulls bespeaking bodily metamorphosis and spiritual translation, and scripted messages worked in tandem to catalyze the viewer's typological imagination.[98]

Audiences trained in typology would have interpreted such images carved in the stone reflexively. As mirroring devices, emblematic images of saints or portraits bracketed by sacred symbols would have instigated a process of visual objectification in the service of scrutinizing, testing, and performing the self as type, and thus, as Promey argues, imagining the self "anchored in a divine moral economy of grace."[99] Similarly, Riis's spiritualization of the poor, emblematically depicted in spiritually evocative poses—as angelic, pietistic, innocent, spiritually resolved, and above all suffering—would have suggested a universal, transcendent type. In that all Christians bore the impress of Christ's image—though, according to the Social Gospel, none more than the indigent—Riis's religious audiences were prepared to see the spiritual superimposed onto the luminous portraits of the tenement poor. Like the struggling protagonists of Sheldon's and Wright's novels, the humanity Riis brought to light through stereopticon projection offered exempla for viewers' own self-transformation. As with the images of dead saints inscribed on colonial gravestones, Riis's portraits—with the fragile ephemerality they conveyed—were vivid, pressing reminders of the viewer's own salvific need to be transfigured from particular to type.

*　*　*

By incorporating photography into the virtual-tour structure, Riis reinvigorated an older heuristic for shaping perception, innovating upon Abbott's cognitive track by which audience's imaginations were regulated and directed, their emotions modulated and focused. No act of free association could initiate the communal realism required for second sight or conversion to the cause of social reform. Riis's virtual-tour narrative had to enact a reality of experience so authentic that the audience would, through a kind of visceral exchange, experience a repetition of the poor's suffering. Only through alliances of suffering promoted by the Social Gospel's Pauline creed could reformers and the impoverished be united in the assurance of social redemption. We will "close the gap in the social body, between rich and poor," Riis counseled, "only when we have learned . . . to weep with the poor."[100]

In his photograph entitled "Prayer-time in the Nursery—Five Points House of Industry" (fig. 12), Riis stages a prayer circle of children in white nightgowns, gracefully arced for the camera, each kneeling in prayer. He draws on the Victorian cult of children, emphasizing their

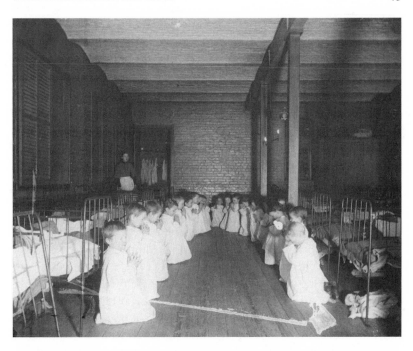

FIGURE 12. Jacob A. Riis, "Prayer-time in the Nursery—Five Points House of Industry," c. 1890. By courtesy of the Museum of the City of New York. This scene stages the prayer from the *New England Primer,* while the accompanying text reveals the contradiction between the angelic representation of Victorian children and the physical exploitation of impoverished orphans.

vulnerability in relation to the barnlike environs. But in jarring discord with the Victorian belief in heaven-protected innocence, the photograph reveals a startling contradiction. Riis describes the children kneeling in a prayer he titles (in capital letters): "Now I lay me down to sleep, I pray the Lord my soul to keep," a prayer enshrined for generations in *The New England Primer.* His abrupt midverse break compels the reader to complete the well-known prayer, printed in virtually all versions of *The New England Primer* since its origination in the seventeenth century.[101] Ventriloquized through the mouths of affluent adults, the prayer's provision for a child's sudden death adds poignancy to an already absurd irony: "If I should die before I wake, I pray the Lord my soul to take." Although disturbing, the prayer still seems at one with the photographic sentimentalism, until one sees the turn homiletic realism takes.

Should any miss the contradiction of youth and death, of helpless innocents and brutal suffering, of angelic essence and hellish existence,

Riis reveals a devastating detail. "Too often," he announces, "their white night-gowns hide tortured little bodies and limbs cruelly bruised by inhuman hands."[102] It was a message made familiar in the concurrent lectures of T. Dewitt Talmadge, whose revised homiletic realism marked the shift from Calvinism's punitive moralism (Finney's sinners swept over the brink of hell's chasm) to Riis's innocents destroyed by social complacency: "Look at the pale cheek, who bleached it? Look at the gash across the forehead, a drunken father struck it there. . . . The death-knell has already begun to toll, and the angels of God fly like birds over the plunge of a cataract. While such children are on the brink they halt, and throw out their hands, and cry: 'Help! Help!'"[103] The numerous descriptions of children's plight magnified the effect of Riis's ironic ghosting. Everett Burr, another Social Gospel minister, opined: "The children are everywhere . . . in the gutters, beneath the horses' feet on the street, children in the alley ways, on the stairs, everywhere, mowed down."[104] With Burr, Walter Swaffield warned of the "multitudinous little lives swept into the struggling, seething world of social night as driftwood borne to shore by storm-lashed ocean waves"—a premature harvest of the hope that children signified in the Progressive Era.[105] In a burst of light, the photograph, like the irony of Beecher's child in hell, is transformed from a sentimental depiction of children kneeling before a loving God—an image resonating of Victorian productions of angelic guardians drawing lost children back from the chasm's verge—to its ghost, an ironic sentimentalism rendered stunning in contrast to what it seems to be, but is not.

Because the hermeneutic process of translating pictorial language into a visual realism presupposed a trained imagination, the Calvinist homiletic was ripe for the verisimilitude of photography. Like Beecher's step-by-step frames of the youth's damnation, Riis's virtual-tour narrative chronicled the allegory of Tony's moral fall. The "Regeneration of 'Our Tony,'" printed in the *Buffalo Evening News* on November 18, 1898, reported that "talking for two hours, Riis described Tony 'in all his phases of degraded development, from the ragged infant to the old tout in the prison cell.'" Even newspaper reports of Riis's presentations relied on a prephotography vocabulary that registered language's possibility to body forth images. Still indebted to the visual tradition of the eighteenth-century Puritan sermon and to the traditions of *ars rhetorica* and *ut pictura poesis*—coming into the colonies and early nation with the emergence of a professional class (lawyers and doctors, like ministers, trained in the classical *ars rhetorica*) and an end-of-the-century vogue for painterly and plastic arts, these contemporary descriptions referred to photography's "drawing," "depicting," "painting," or "sketching" the truth. The semantic ambiguity at play in these terms underscores the interpretive shift and epistemological watershed separating recent assessments of Riis's work as exposé and the traditional homiletic understanding of it as a medium for second sight.[106] Such language of representation demonstrates a structure of meaning—a visually oriented hermeneutic—that had prepared listeners and readers for photographic realism long before its appearance.[107]

A photograph operates as a discrete unit of knowledge, even when its interpretive possibility is limitless. Yet the moral sources of subjectivity available for this interpretation do not reside outside history any more than the processes of identity formation remain constant across class, culture, and time. Although recent criticism persists in viewing Riis's photographs as part of the voyeuristic process of class identity formation, Karen Halttunen has shown that nineteenth-century humanitarians as often saw in both suffering and representations of suffering a threat to values integral to middle-class identity. Reformers worried that exposure to pain and suffering might deaden the very humanist impulses that prompted them to aid the impoverished.[108] Riis defended the intervention in poverty from both these contemporary views, arguing tirelessly for a moral duty to confront destitution, even as he boldly denounced those whose gaze was unsympathetic: "We did not gloat over the misfortunes of those we described," he writes in his autobiography of fellow "house-keepers"; "We were reporters, not ghouls."[109] For Riis, the distinction could not be clearer: the appropriate study of poverty through any medium was linked to social action. If his photographs seem to us to stabilize cultural markers of difference through a technological medium that privileges visual distinction, the homiletic frame, like that unfolding Tony's life, turned a judgment predicated on visual difference back upon the spectator, indicting him or her for failing to recognize humanity—Christ's image stamped—beneath the ephemerality of appearance. The failure to see beneath the surface announced an absence of spiritual sight. In the homiletic context, Riis's images subordinated rather than heightened visual difference—the transient markers of race, class, and culture—to suffering, the authentic index of the humanity experienced by rich and poor alike.

If his photographic tours seem to us today alien spectacles for middle-class consumption, an affirmation of what is moral, decent, and "American" in the face of all who are not, they were also, for countless of Riis's contemporaries, heuristic guides for action, ways of conceptualizing change. Through the aesthetics of immediacy, the second sight of the social acquired on virtual tours of urban slums effected one's conversion to the cause of social reform. Riis's modernization of homiletic realism through an innovative use of new visual media homiletics offered a practical means of interpersonal engagement across social barriers: it was a technology for remaking the social contract. Through their awakened faith in his spiritual reality, audiences believed "our Tony" to be an actual child, many seeking to adopt him. Their faith in Tony's spectral kinship was a function not of photography's mimetic power to represent social reality, but rather of its occult power to render visible the invisible web of religious obligation that united all Christians in the new covenant of the urban community, or what Riis would call the "new tenement neighborhood." This was a realism different from the literary aesthetics of secular "slumming" in the service of authentic social knowledge as an end in itself. Riis's virtual-tour narratives created the possibility for actual social reform: new homes were built, education promoted, relief funds initiated, parks and playgrounds established, labor laws passed, and an informed and armed citizenry actualized, all for the sake of Tony and other illusions by which Riis made urban poverty not only visible, but intolerable.

The New Media of Homiletic Realism

Over the last two decades many children and young adults from evangelical congregations began sporting brightly colored bracelets, t-shirts, and caps with the imprint "WWJD?"—"What Would Jesus Do?" The participants in this growing interdenominational movement may have imagined that they were onto something new in the form of spiritual identification the question telegraphs, but in fact, as we have seen, the movement has a long history. Grounded in heuristic practices stretching back to the Middle Ages and central to the most popular form of narrative in late-nineteenth-century American culture, it spread across the United States, assisted by evangelical ministers who fused Lockean empiricist psychology with a range of Enlightenment epistemological schemes. Condensed within the WWJD question is a radical modern version of the *imitatio Christi* that reprises earlier forms of Christian practice while adapting them to contemporary—even secular—heuristic frames.

It seems to me that the value of studying these Protestant hermeneutic traditions and the heuristics they produced is self-evident. But such a study also provides a unique understanding of our own contemporary culture, so deeply divided between the sacred and the secular, between religious and political concerns. I continue to be surprised by the number of audience members I meet during public speaking engagements on religious history who openly confess—sometimes with a hint of self-congratulation—their incredulity at religion's pervasive relevance for many Americans today. Citing an instance in which a public official invoked God or scripture as his or her moral source, proffering an anecdote about a politician's disclosure of faith or "sin," these individuals ask what happened to the split between church and state. Such bewilderment stems from an assumption that we are a secular society, that our origins in Enlightenment doctrines of natural rights and classical models of democracy and republicanism have insulated our political institutions from religious beliefs and from the moral certainty with which faith-based majorities might press their values on a political minority.

The celebrated though largely unexamined split between church and state assumes that religion is something that happens in private, far removed from the political and intellectual institutions that safeguard the notion of the self-evident neutrality of Enlightenment rationalism. Yet the idealization of a constitutionally protected and institutionally reinforced split along the religious/secular, church/state divide is hardly universal. The majority of the religious have never doubted the influence of religion in the political realm or the faith-based intentions of the founding generations. It is the nonreligious or the high-church or liberal denominations who contend that the strident public resurgence of evangelical fundamentalism over the last few decades is anachronistic. At a loss for adequate mechanisms to historicize fundamentalism—and perhaps prompted by the apostolic primitivism promoted by biblical literalism—contemporary critics read evangelicals as simple throwbacks to a distant age. This reading permits the continuation of the historical narrative that secularists most cherish, not least because it mirrors and reinforces the values of a contemporary academy that sees the nation's origins, history, and culture as a progressively secular stream, ever widening as it flows through time.

This is not to say that religion has gone unexamined. From the intellectual tradition propounded by Perry Miller to the proliferation of cultural studies of religion in recent decades to the current explosion of best-selling trade books by such critics as Garry Wills, Charles Taylor, Steven Waldman, and Daniel Dennet, religion has been the subject of considerable intellectual inquiry.[1] Yet religious culture continues to elicit a sense of surprise, befuddlement, and mystification among mainstream intellectuals. We are writing about religion more, while seeming to understand it less. Repeatedly and consistently, across disparate disciplinary, critical, and methodological frameworks, one sees the same interpretive strategies, which read religious literature, as well as the populations most implicated in its historical consumption, within the ascendancy of secularism. Consequently, religious genres and their primary audiences appear temporally displaced from the landscape of modernity. Popular religion remains elusive, even incomprehensible, because the media forms that are so central to its adaptation and success remain submerged or beyond the periphery of most secularists' critical scope. But far from the world that Enlightenment modernity left behind, religious heuristics have integrated modern epistemologies in deeply historical ways, producing genealogies of experience and textual hermeneutics that become visible only when we reorient our own critical gaze to see how divergent religious groups—across time, culture, and class—read religious texts and experience their faith. The reluctance to do so leads to critical blind spots that forestall an assessment of religious literature, perpetuating the false binary of a secular/sacred split that obfuscates mutual understanding by seeing religious experience as mysterious and atavistic.

Recent work on secularism locates the emergence of Enlightenment-based values within the "West," viewing modernity within a temporal frame that assumes its universality.[2] These accounts differentiate societies based on the extent of their contact with Enlightenment ideals. Religious fundamentalism thus gets contained within a temporal divide reinforced by contemporary geopolitics. Yet the record does not bear out this neat division. The Enlightenment has long been a significant part of American cultural identity, and as such promoted the shared values and secular ideals that make the WWJD question appear a vestigial artifact of a distant time, as if the global fundamentalism that we wish to locate elsewhere and root in a distant prerational epoch had somehow infiltrated our national borders. It troubles our intellectual sensibilities to see that the religious other is also our own.[3] One of our oft-told metanarratives recounts the nation's religious origins in the seventeenth century, annually commemorated at Thanksgiving when the Indians (a homogenous group in the popular imagination) came to the starving colonists' rescue, sharing their New World secrets about farming, fishing, and trapping. But in the next century, this story continues, America became more secular, shaking off the shackles of religious oppression and intolerance, paving the way for the emergence of a secular public sphere. The embrace of Enlightenment rationalism, Revolutionary "natural-rights" doctrines, the Industrial Revolution, scientific determinism, post–Civil War imperialism, national urbanization, and a new mode of American exceptionalism in the exuberant affirmation of two world wars further drove religion out of the public sphere. As simplistic as this popular story sounds, it has had plenty of encouragement from historians, not perhaps in so many words, but often in historical narratives that seem implicitly to suggest a progressively secular teleology.

Perry Miller's *The New England Mind* exemplifies this narrative with a remarkable subtlety that masks its own contradictions: the study of religion requires a certain distance from it, as if to shield modern, secular political and academic ideologies from religion's corruptive influence. With his David-and-Goliath homily of James Franklin's 1721 battle against Boston's Puritan oligarchy over freedom of the press, Miller created an apt, chapter-length representation of the eighteenth century as an age that saw the triumph of secularization.[4] While the dying theocracy, embodied in Boston's Increase and Cotton Mather, initially prevailed, silencing James Franklin's newspaper, *The New-England Courant,* they ultimately lost the war, symbolized when the real David in Miller's drama, James's young apprentice brother Benjamin, takes center stage. Young Ben, of course, outwits the overweening father-son duo, overcoming theocratic tyranny with his Yankee precocity, in the name of our most cherished future constitutional amendment. Miller's anecdote, however, is not free from the ideology of its own time, the technological optimism of secular humanism, given new flesh by the victories of World War II. In a synecdochic compression that conflates Franklin's mythic fame as Enlightenment proponent in an age of reason and revolution with his renown as Yankee scientist, inventor, and statesman, Miller packs both attributes into the nascent promise of the nation figured as a twelve-year-old boy destined for greatness (the part for the whole), illustrating, with devastating satire, not only the waning future of the "Puritan juggernaut," but also how the episode augured the diminution of faith-based social regulation. Similar to his tendency to aggrandize Puritan leaders (among others, John Wise, Roger Williams, Solomon Stoddard, Jonathan Mayhew) whose political, theological, and doxological iconoclasm foreshadowed the American Revolution and plebiscitary democracy—Miller's narrative tacitly celebrates as inevitable the triumphant destiny of science, political secularism, manifest destiny, and American exceptionalism.[5]

Of course this is a serious reduction of Miller's erudite and influential study, but we need to re-examine its implicit mythology of secularism triumphant. That triumphalism reappears in many accounts of

Anglo-American religious history, from elementary readers to college textbooks. Another way in which Miller's work has shaped religious historiography is in its bias for histories of formal theology—intellectual traditions coming out of seventeenth- and eighteenth-century seminaries—and against popular evangelicalism, faith, and belief on the ground, in the everyday lives of ordinary individuals. Until recently, religious and social histories have too often left popular culture out of the accounting. By focusing on the intellectual history of American religion—on the "Puritan canopy," antinomianism, the Old School/New School Protestant divisions, the Harvard-Yale schism, the Unitarian/Trinitarian split, and the like—historians have inadvertently skewed the record. These more formal religious traditions, while important for their percolation into popular culture, tended to lean liberal, rationalistic, and even secular, particularly because they emerged from institutions of higher learning and were thoroughly imbricated with classical studies.

This focus on the intellectual and orthodox histories of American Christianity is understandable, for it is not easy to talk about religious experience, much less to strike a balanced critical perspective, a measured tone, about a subject popularly invested with emotional fervor and ideologically yoked to the moral (and biblical) imperative to reject anything "lukewarm" (Revelations 3:16). Perhaps surprisingly, one encounters this tendency to personalize religious faith—to speak from a position of moral and sectarian certainty—even among religious studies scholars, whatever their discipline. Any critic seeking to negotiate the many points of view that American Protestantism engenders inevitably confronts the sensitivities inherent in the subject—both as a lived practice and as a field of inquiry. Grounded in exegesis and prizing individual interpretation, Protestantism now, as throughout its history, is rife with—indeed predicated on—the assumptions of "personal" positions, elevating the status of anecdotal evidence and individual perspective. It is a part of our culture about which people, whatever their point of view, tend to feel strongly. Thus, although much research has appeared on the various eighteenth-, nineteenth- and twentieth-century theological movements now considered "orthodox" or "formal" (and hence, perhaps, suitably academic), far less exists on the popular movements that appropriated, explained, and disseminated important theological debates. Unless we understand how those on the ground have interpreted doctrine, responded to it, and passed it along, we cannot fully comprehend how religious points of view shape popular culture, or how spiritual values inform everyday life. The cultural and political polarity of our present time speaks pressingly for just such an informed understanding.

These questions have particular relevance for literary studies. While work on popular Christianity has increased in the past two decades, little has infiltrated literary critical perspectives. The American Protestant homiletic tradition that thrives today among various denominational groups has been further obscured because many scholars tend to adopt a homogeneous reading epistemology, assuming that one reads a devotional text as one would read a newspaper, a romance, or a thriller. Despite the range of alternative secular interpretive and readerly practices described by literary and cultural critics as diverse in their disciplinary or methodological approaches as Michael Denning, David D. Hall, Janice Radway, and Jane Tompkins, a widespread assumption persists that in the last two centuries readers have approached the written word with the same critical, aesthetic, or didactic orientation regardless of their religious or secular commitments, professions, class, or cultural background.[6] It is this unexamined assumption that forestalls a serious reassessment of popular religious literature broadly conceived—an oversight, I believe, that significantly distorts our conceptions of American cultural and literary history. Why might it matter that we reexamine interdenominational Protestantism, understanding how religious literary forms were tied to pre-Reformation heuristics designed to exercise and activate auditors' and readers' volition? How do we recover the religious interpretive practices with which believers approached these texts if we rely on critical models predicated on a secular worldview that rejects a priori a spiritual teleology?

The legacy of homiletic identification has, since the end of the Social Gospel era—and since its appropriation by a generation shaped by the deeply fundamentalist Pentecostal Movement in the first few decades of the twentieth century—had a conservative, insular cast. While the interventionist ethic this legacy fostered continues to thrive among liberal Christian groups seeking social justice, its ethos of activism among fundamentalists has also fostered a strong conservative agenda promoting political change through the formation of formidable voting blocks and through legislation, local referenda, and judicial appointments. We cannot, I think, understand the controversy surrounding Mel Gibson's *The Passion of the Christ*—the simultaneous mix of gentle Jesus and vengeful Messiah—or the paradoxical "right to life"/"death with dignity" faceoffs over individuals in "persistent vegetative states," no matter how we personally feel about these cultural and political issues, without understanding this overlooked religious tradition. Neither, surprisingly enough, can we understand what many would regard to be in stark contrast to Gibson's film, Martin Scorsese's *The Last Temptation of Christ.* Far from being a product of an irreligious, vulgar secularism, Scorsese's film, like Gibson's, had its immediate origin in a religious humanism that, by the late nineteenth century, popularly depicted Christ not as a deity removed from the daily struggle of weak humanity, but as a man tempted and tortured by passions all too human. The spiritual therapeutics such representations offered are lodged in the idea that Christ had to be fully human, had to suffer all aspects of humanity's febrile existence, if his example—and the individual's identification with him— were to mean anything.

This epilogue, then, is not meant to signal finality, the completion of a project whose subject is fully realized, but rather to suggest the need to continue the study of American homiletic texts and practices into the twentieth and twenty-first centuries. As the *Left Behind: Eternal Forces* video game with which I began this book suggests, the ability to concretize spiritual abstractions into the reality of everyday life remains a central concern of homiletic pedagogy. The last few years, in fact, have increasingly witnessed the arrival on the evangelical scene of other forms of paratextual pedagogies predicated on the phenomenological, on the perceptual limits of reality. The Creation Museum in northern Kentucky, a stone's throw from Cincinnati, Ohio, and the Holy Land theme park in Orlando, Florida, are two such new Protestant technologies similar in function to the hell house and the *Eternal Forces* video game. While undoubtedly instances of a pattern R. Laurence Moore has called "selling God," these and other commercial Christian ventures are driven primarily by the perceived need to initiate novices into the actuality of biblical truths through experiences that are visible, visceral, and thus "real."[7] The Creation Museum promotes the Genesis story over scientific explanations of the origin of human life. Just inside the museum doors a kiosk explains the difference between a "creation" and an "evolutionary" paleontologist, detailing how each offers different interpretations of the same fossil.[8] The Holy Land theme park—a neighbor of Disney World—offers, as *USA Today* characterized it, the "Holy Land Experience" where "Jesus Christ is crucified and resurrected . . . six days a week."[9] Like the hell house, the park simulates a highly interactive space, in which audiences not only view enacted biblical vignettes and parables, witnessing Christ healing a blind man or converting a tax collector, or viewing the crucifixion in vivid realism, but also react as an actor portraying Jesus in first-century garb walks among them, picking up children and passing by those eager to touch his robes, as if to absorb his virtue. The centerpiece of both the pedagogy and the visitors' experience is the daily pageant of the crucifixion, in which "Snarling Roman soldiers whip and drag [Christ], and somber audience members watch. Some quietly weep at a pageant bloody and cruel."[10] Referred to by its promoters as a "living biblical museum," the Holy Land daily showcases the emphasis many evangelicals continue to place on forms of realism that, while enacted in real time, are no less narratological than the Puritan cemetery and the Chautauqua tours, or the virtual-tour narratives into which ministers like Henry Ward Beecher and reformers like Jacob Riis encouraged the young to "enter in imagination" more than a century and a half ago.

Given the cultural inundation of modern media images, it is tempting to assume—as cultural critics sometimes do—that no contemporary image requires the range of imaginative engagement that the pedagogical conventions of eighteenth- and nineteenth-century Protestantism did. Consider Margaret Miles's assertion that there is a greater "possibility of watching" the religious images produced today by media technologies "passively, with little investment of imaginative embellishment."[11] While largely true, this generalization, by shearing forms of modern media from their genealogy in older heuristic traditions and by assuming a common epistemology between the sacred and the secular, risks misgauging the heuristic function of specialized media forms. In its examination of the past, this book has attempted to shed light on how heuristic practices still employ affective modes of reading and interpretation both as the vital mechanism for the individual's spiritual self-transformation and as a catalyst for spiritual and communal identifications that continue into our own time.

Notes

Introduction

1. *The Holy Bible: Old and New Testaments in the King James Version* (New York: Nelson, 1972).

2. http://www.leftbehindgames.com/pages/the_games.htm, accessed November 12, 2006. In response to criticism about the game encouraging violence, its makers now emphasize that players "conduct warfare using the power of PRAYER and WORSHIP as more powerful weapons than guns." http://www.lbgstore.com/migagilebeet.html; accessed April 18, 2008.

3. The righteous comprise one of six unit types: Friends; Recruiters (disciple, evangelist, and missionary); Influencers (musician, praiser, worship leader, and prayer warrior); Builders (regular, advanced, and foreman); Healers (medic, nurse, doctor); and Soldiers (regular, special, elite, spy, and sniper). Enemies comprise one of two unit types: Criminals (thug, thief, and mob boss); and Pretenders (pretender, secularist, activist, and cult leader). Players search the urban terrain for converts, inducting them through inspirational messages and devotional exercises into the paramilitary resistance that advances against the "Global Community" or "GC" (loosely modeled on the United Nations). All who are left behind after the Rapture (those unsaved at the time) must either convert to Christianity or join the GC against the Tribulation Force. There is no neutrality or amnesty in the end-of-times battle for souls.

4. http://www.leftbehindgames.com/pages/the_games.htm.

5. John Ness, "Gamers' Good News," *Newsweek,* March 6, 2006, 11–12.

6. Authored by Jerry B. Jenkins and Tim LaHaye, the story begins with *Left Behind,* followed by *Tribulation Force, Nicolae, Soul Harvest, Apollyon,* and others.

7. Millennialism has a long history in American Protestantism. While Millennialists agreed that Christ would return to judge and rule the world for a thousand years, they were divided as to whether his rule would follow the Judgment or

precede it. Premillennialists believe Judgment will precede Christ's reign among the saints. Postmillennialists conversely believe Christ will return to reign on earth with the saints for a thousand years before judging humanity. American Protestants were in wide disagreement about when the millennium would begin, though many denominational leaders speculated on the subject. Jonathan Edwards, for instance, felt that the end times were no more than 250 years away; other leaders, including Barton Stone and Alexander Campbell, believed it to be imminent. Most famously, William Miller predicted the actual date of July 16, 1843, for Christ's return. See McDermott, *One Holy and Happy Society,* 50–60, 77–82.

8. To the extent that it has been designed around militaristic institutions and strategies—and envisions the Apocalypse as a theater of modern war with insurgencies and counterinsurgencies—it draws equally on Mel Odom's Left Behind spin-off novels, the Military Series, which includes *Apocalypse Dawn, Apocalypse Crucible,* and *Apocalypse Burning.* While the Left Behind novels have been controversial, their extension into electronic media has, in some quarters, produced more concern. Apart from a broad range of public criticism, the *Left Behind: Eternal Forces* video game debuted to mixed reviews even among evangelicals in the United States. Focus on the Family, the Promise Keepers, and Concerned Women for America have all hailed the game's relevance as an effective tool of Christian outreach, education, and practical training, yet other conservative Christian organizations—the Campaign to Defend the Constitution and the Christian Alliance for Progress, among other ministries—have decried the game's violence and potential for religious polarization, enjoining their members to boycott sales.

9. For a full discussion of the homiletic novel, see chapter 3, a portion of which also appeared in *PMLA* as "'What Would Jesus Do?'"

10. "Undeserving poor" became a popular expression in reform guides, sermons, and social exposés of all types in the last decades of the nineteenth century. Jacob Riis, B. O. Flower, Helen Campbell, and other Social Gospel adherents used the phrase to describe those individuals and families who suffered poverty not from a lack of industry or moral character (a common narrative) but from a lack of opportunity, education, or a scarcity of living-wage jobs.

11. Stafford, *Good Looking,* 9.

12. While it is not easy to define the term "evangelical" and "evangelicalism," I have found George Marsden's emphasis on "born-again" status to be one key component of evangelicalism, and genealogy—common Reformation heritage and scriptural-literalist tendencies—another. For a full discussion of evangelicalism, see Marsden, *Evangelicalism and Modern America,* especially the introduction. Similarly, the religious historian Randall Balmer has defined *evangelical* as "conservative Protestants—including fundamentalists, evangelicals, pentecostals, and charismatics—who insist on some sort of spiritual rebirth as

a criterion for entering the kingdom of heaven, who often impose exacting be-
havioral standards on the faithful, and whose beliefs, institutions, and folkways
comprise the evangelical subculture in America"; in Balmer, *Mine Eyes Have
Seen the Glory,* 8.

13. Such a loosely controlled regulatory system was meant to focus the pilgrimages of the faithful, even as, conversely, it increasingly instrumentalized
human volition—the individual's capacity to will or nil in all things spiritual—
by endorsing Protestants' quintessential spiritual immunity, "liberty of conscience." Debates about the nature and autonomy of the individual's conscience
as a privileged space of divine communion and direction began in England after the first stages of the Reformation, due in part to what the fugitive divines to
New England felt was the censorship of their objections to Archbishop William
Laud's provision for uniformity from the pulpit. Subsequently debates about liberty of conscience received a great deal of focus from both the clergy and laity in
the New England leadership. For a good summary of the issues, see Cotton, *The
Controversie.*

14. Wright, *That Printer of Udell's,* 59–60.

15. Historically, naturalism has been treated as a form of realism, its distinguishing generic differences often elided. June Howard suggests that naturalism
differs from literary realism with the figure of the spectator and the gaze as organizing principle, yet these generic distinctions hardly seem to belong to naturalism alone. See Howard, *Form and History,* esp. v–xi.

16. Sundquist, *American Realism,* viii.

17. Kaplan, *Social Construction,* 5.

18. Barrish, *American Literary Realism,* 129, 130, 155. Barrish's final chapter applies realism's aesthetic value to five critics—Lionel Trilling, Paul De Man,
John Guillory, Joan Copjec, and Judith Butler—suggesting "that double-edged
'realer-than-thou' moves . . . have a rich history in American literary culture"
that will "help us . . . to better grasp some ins and outs" of "recently prominent
competitions for critical prestige" (130). Each of the critics he examines thus
tries to "stake out realer-than-thou, more-material-than-thou, and even dirtier-
than-thou . . . approaches to literary studies" (130). While not among Barrish's
examples, his point about critics and authors is realized in instances such as Parrington's comment in *Main Currents of Thought* that James "was never a realist"
but "was a self-deceived romantic, a last subtle expression of the genteel, who fell
in love with culture and never realized how poor a thing he worshipped" (240),
or Michael Davitt Bell's comment on William Dean Howells: "What is Howellsian realism, after all, but a lie that claims to be truthful, a form of literature that
claims *not* to be 'literary,' a deployment of style that claims to *avoid* 'style'" (*The
Problem of American Realism,* 66; original emphasis).

19. For a good survey of these representative criticisms, see Kaplan, *Social
Construction.*

NOTES TO PAGES 8-9

20. In *The Real Thing,* for example, Miles Orvell observes that "the tension between imitation and authenticity is a primary category in American culture" (xv). Orvell outlines this tension as a historical trajectory that saw the Victorian obsession with realism, a culture of imitation, displaced by a twentieth-century mode of modernism, a culture that valued authenticity. While demonstrable and insightful in a secular context, Orvell's representative thesis loses its footing in a Protestant worldview.

21. Without the religious teleology or eschatology, Alfred Habegger, in *Gender, Fantasy and Realism in American Literature,* perceptively attributes American realism not to the standard genealogy in European influences but to American sentimentalism—descending not from "Hawthorne, Emerson, George Eliot, Turgenev, or Flaubert," but rather "from popular women's fiction by way of two sissies" (65), William Dean Howells and William James. In his precursors to realism, Habegger lists a number of novels often categorized as sentimental: Susan Warner's *The Wide, Wide World,* Augusta J. Evans's *St. Elmo,* Adeline Whitney's *The Gayworthys,* Elizabeth Stuart Phelps's *The Gates Ajar,* and Mrs. E[mma] D. E. N. Southworth's *The Hidden Hand.* These works forecast realism because realist fiction concerns particular issues at a given historical moment, for which we must turn to "the books that were in the air at the time, the sort of people who read and liked these books, the social divisions within the reading public and the configuration of genres that appealed to these groups, the stereotypes of men and women that happened to be getting a lot of attention, and most important of all, the exact state of the ongoing concern about the nature of womanhood" (viii). An unacknowledged point relevant to my purposes is that each of these works addresses religious themes.

22. For the best treatment of the mix of nineteenth-century Protestant evangelicalism and spiritualism, see Taves, *Fits, Trances, and Visions;* for the extent to which public intellectuals and philosophers such as William James, John Dewey, and Josiah Royce (all with no overt formal Christian affiliation) were caught between a commitment to an empirical ontology and a deep interest in spiritualism, see Menand, *The Metaphysical Club.* For an assessment of the political dimensions of spiritualism see Castronovo, *Necro Citizenship.* For an overview of secularism in relation to faith, see Casanova, *Public Religions,* esp. 11–39.

23. Examples of a universal truth beyond human ken are numerous in eighteenth- and nineteenth-century Protestant sermons. For example, instructing his congregation to look beyond the appearance of empirical fact in his sermon "Salvation Achieved Only in the Present Life," Samuel H. Cox catechizes his audience: "What then are the archetypes of the truth of the gospel? The things that are unseen and eternal! The infinite Realities of God!" (iii).

24. Wood, *Ideal Suggestion,* 58; original emphasis.

25. For a theological explanation of original sin—sometimes referred to as "indwelling sin"—and its Augustinian legacy, see Walter, *The Body of Death*

Anatomized. In an oft-quoted passage in its own time, Walter underscores why original sin is called "the radical sin": "*Indwelling sin* is the *root* of all *actual sins.* All the sins of our *Lives* proceed from the Sin of our *Nature.* The *Corruption of the Heart* is the rise and spring of all sinful thoughts, words and deeds. . . . 'Tis the sin of sins, the mother and nurse of all sins, seminally containing in it every sort of kind of sins; it is therefore more Evil than all *actual sins*"(10; original emphasis).

26. Sundquist, *American Realism;* Foote, *Regional Fictions,* 40. In *Determined Fictions,* Mitchell comes to a similar conclusion for the naturalists who ordered worlds where the unified self, under close scrutiny, tends to fracture and disintegrate. Naturalist texts, he suggests, are determined fictions where "the closer one attends to the self, the less it tends to cohere—as if the very process of depiction somehow dismantled subjectivity, breaking the self apart piece-by-piece and absorbing it into an indifferent world" (17).

27. Henry Wood explains the use of the material as a way to imagine the spiritual: "Theology, therapeutics, sociology, and ethics have also been greatly obscured by the thick dust of materialism. But at last science is coming to a late and forced conclusion that the so-called properties of matter are only sensuous limitations. They are simply provisional and educational, for matter plays an important part as a foil in soul-development" (*Ideal Suggestion,* 81).

28. "Red-letter authority" is a phrase that entered the evangelical idiom with the 1901 publication of Louis Klopsch's red-letter edition of the New Testament; Klopsch surveyed a range of ancient and modern Bible commentaries to ascertain which New Testament passages were likely spoken by Christ.

29. The concern that fin de siècle authors evinced for what Amy Kaplan identifies as "the growing sense of unreality at the heart of middle-class life"—thus initiating their discursive attempts to reconstitute the social world—was, for the religious, to split hairs, ontologically speaking. The real and the unreal were the same thing: they differed only in the untutored (unregenerated) perceptions that granted normative middle-class persons, objects, and values—as opposed to the quasi-allegorical unreality of technology, poverty, vice, "foreigners," and the destitute—not a greater but a more legitimate claim to realness (*Social Construction,* 9).

30. In their recent studies of the development of literary realism, William Morgan and Michael Hames-García ground the search for its moral bearings not in Protestantism's deferral of divine knowledge (figured most often as the desire for divine justice), but in the empirical domain, in a pragmatic and denaturalized framework for reclaiming the language of normative values and formulating "open-textured" ideals and freedom from "the concrete possibilities" embedded in the social (Morgan, *Questionable Charity;* Hames-García, *Fugitive Thought,* 32). While Morgan and Hames-García foreground the possibility of evaluating the empirical foundations of normative claims in an effort to achieve a more ac-

curate understanding of reality, homiletic realism denies the empirical assumptions that ground such claims.

31. A range of critics have written specifically on perspective but none more provocatively than Mark Seltzer, who claims that the realist novel depends on a fantasy of surveillance through the totalizing vision of omniscient narration, which, in the final analysis, constitutes a "criminal continuity" between authorial vision and social control. Seltzer, "*The Princess Casamassima,*" 116.

32. Trachtenberg, "Experiments in Another Country," 144.

33. I will return to a discussion of realism and idealism at greater length in chapters 3 and 4. See also Taves, *Fits, Trances, and Visions,* 12–40.

34. Pizer, "American Literary Naturalism," 353.

35. Wood, *Edward Burton,* 5; Warner, "Modern Fiction," 157; James, *Literary Criticism,* 185; Bierce, *Devil's Word Book,* 194.

36. Lathrop, "The Novel and Its Future," 321, 317, 318.

37. For an extended history of the spiritual and early modern concept of how the material is tied to a larger cosmic structure—what Charles Taylor refers to as the *"ontic logos"*—see Taylor's *Sources of the Self,* especially the chapter on Augustine.

38. James, "The Art of Fiction," 408, 406. For James's agnosticism and Calvinist lineage, see Banta, *Henry James and the Occult,* 38–42; and Matthiessen, *The James Family,* 82–84.

39. See, e.g., Bell, *Problem of American Realism.* In contradistinction to Kaplan, Bell ultimately deems the realist project a failure.

40. Kaplan, *Social Construction,* 8.

41. For an assessment of Alcott's *Little Women* as a realist novel, see Elaine Showalter's introduction to *Little Women,* vi–xii.

42. A knowledge of how religious audiences instrumentalized literature for social, moral, and spiritual ends requires us to reassess Kaplan's (*Social Construction*) otherwise astute admonition against viewing nineteenth-century literary realism as "a progressive force exposing social reality" (7) or evaluating it in terms of its capacity to reflect a "ready-made setting" (8).

43. Of the many critics of realism sampled here, June Howard most vehemently opposes the possibility that discursive modes can represent or reflect the social world as a "naïve" project. She writes, "My task is not to set literary texts against a 'history' or 'reality' whose own textuality is for that purpose repressed, but rather to trace how naturalism is shaped by and imaginatively reshapes a historical experience that, although it exists outside representation and narrative, we necessarily approach through texts" (*Form and History,* xii). Yet if historical experience exists outside of representation, how can it be recovered through any form of narrative or through any approach to a text? Her argument, while illuminating, goes too far, offering in the place of the representation of experience through the literary an obscure notion of other extratextual representa-

tional modes (see *Form and History,* esp. chap. 1). I favor Kaplan's more sympathetic caution: "Realism simultaneously becomes an imperative and a problem in American fiction. It neither compensates for the absence of a complex social fabric nor records a naïve belief in the correspondence between language and the intractable material world; rather it bridges the perceived gap between the social world and literary representation" (*Social Construction,* 9). When I invoke "imitation and authenticity" here, I have in mind Miles Orvell's *The Real Thing,* a study that has been a useful counter to my own thinking. While applicable to secular culture, his thesis that American culture "is forever wedded to a dialectic between authenticity and imitation" (299) throws into relief how overlooking the homiletic tradition skews American cultural and literary history.

44. Jakobson, "Two Aspects of Language," 111. This essay originally appeared in 1956.

45. Hughes, "The Biblical Play," 312.

46. I want to note early in this study that by *Puritan* I do not refer only to the Congregationalists who settled in New England, beginning in the Plymouth Colony, but rather to all branches of seventeenth-century Calvinism. Like Congregationalists, John Bunyan's Baptist congregants considered themselves Puritans, as did many Anabaptists (a sect of Baptists opposing infant baptism), a broad cross-section of early Arminians like John Milton, Scottish and English Presbyterians, and many Anglicans, who believed that individuals could effect their own salvation by pursuing conversion. Arminians—following the theology of the sixteenth-century Dutch Protestant Jacobus Arminius—broke with Calvinists (Presbyterians, Baptists, Congregationalists, and Anglicans) over the doctrines of predestination and election. In *True Religion Delineated,* Jonathan Edwards's student Joseph Bellamy offers a particularly useful definition of Arminianism, because his explanation emphasizes how much Arminians had (heretically) reintroduced human volition into religion: "As to the opinion of the *Arminians,* that God equally *designed* Salvation for all Men, purposing to offer Salvation to all, and use Means with all, and leave all to their own Free-Will, and save . . . those only, who of their own Accord will become good Men" (356; original emphasis).

47. For a useful study of childrearing practices and the Calvinist emphasis on pedagogy, see Greven, *The Protestant Temperament.* For a seminal study of religious texts with which the first three generations of Anglo-American Calvinists supplemented their devotional practices, see Hambrick-Stowe, *The Practice of Piety;* see also Brown, *The Pilgrim and the Bee.*

48. I discuss the hell house in more detail in chapter 1; the instance of the "Jesus Camp" is by fiat, one example among many. I mention it because Heidi Ewing and Rachel Grady's recent documentary *Jesus Camp* (Magnolia Pictures) makes this particular pedagogy widely available.

49. For Weems's influence on early nineteenth-century book markets and re-

ligious book consumerism, see Zboray, *A Fictive People.* Zboray argues that increases in reading, writing, and print culture catalyzed the antebellum shift from agrarian to industrial culture. For a fascinating series of case studies of this process, see Augst, *The Clerk's Tale.*

50. For the influence of American evangelicalism on eighteenth- and nineteenth-century republicanism, see Howe, "Realism and Politics in Antebellum America," and "The Evangelical Movement."

51. David S. Reynolds paved the way for subsequent studies on the influence of popular literature on nineteenth-century religious culture in *Faith in Fiction.* For more on the emergence of religious institutions see Nord, *Faith in Reading.* Nord's work focuses on the way in which the American Bible Society, the American Tract Society, and the American Sunday School Union helped shape modern publishing practices and, more broadly, American business practices. For a useful study of the emergence of religious civic institutions and other voluntary associations, see Boylan, *Sunday School,* which illustrates how specialized institutions such as the temperance societies (especially the Women's Christian Temperance Union), the YMCA, and like-minded organizations helped to indoctrinate the young in the moral objectives of middle-class American women who were attempting, in the language of the time, to create a national evangelical "mental universe."

52. See Reynolds, *Beneath the American Renaissance,* esp. pp.15–41. For a helpful history of emerging religious literature, see Reynolds, *Faith in Fiction.* This work addresses more literary authors who since 1981 have enjoyed increasing attention in interdisciplinary curricula, including Royall Tyler, Susanna Rowson, Henry Ward, Catherine Sedgwick, Lydia Maria Child, Sylvester Judd, and William Ware. The homiletic authors addressed in this study are less literary and, in most instances, more concerned with Protestant education, theology, and spiritual practices.

53. I have found two works indispensable in formulating ideas about the role of reading in conceptualizing and imagining the reader's reality: Brewer, *The Pleasures of the Imagination,* and "Reconstructing the Reader." For a useful summary of how "unfiltered" images and other forms of ocular evidence can produce a seductive sense of "reliability," see Burke, *Eyewitnessing,* 21–33. For two recent studies of twentieth-century Protestant women's readerships, see Mountford, *The Gendered Pulpit,* and Neal, *Romancing God.*

54. Cooper, *How and Why the Young Should Cleanse Their Way,* 5.

55. See Fliegelman, *Prodigals and Pilgrims,* 1–3, n2. I will return to this transformation of childhood in chapter 1 and to subsequent scholarship on the topic.

56. For the religious, the ascendancy of empiricism was redacted through a number of popular religious authors, including the Lockean apologist Isaac Watts in England; Anglicans Joseph Butler and Bishop George Berkeley; Berkeley's American disciple, the Yale-educated, Congregational apostate Samuel

Johnson; and, perhaps most significantly, Johnson's one-time Yale charge and
the age's most important Calvinist apologist, Jonathan Edwards, whose own ambivalent relationship to Locke's materialist reality helped fuel evangelical revivals that swept the colonies. I will return to this at greater length in chapter 1.
See Fiering, *Jonathan Edwards's Moral Thought,* and *Moral Philosophy at
Seventeenth-Century Harvard;* Laurence, "Jonathan Edwards, John Locke";
Knight, "Learning the Language of God"; and McClymond, "Spiritual Perception in Jonathan Edwards."

57. Locke, *Essay Concerning Human Understanding,* 444; hereafter cited in
text as *Essay.* This empirical legacy led to other conclusions about the need for
experience in order to develop moral understanding. Rationalized Protestantism in such denominations as the Unitarians and other more liberal evangelical groups and independent congregations tolerated, if not encouraged, a certain amount of experience with sin, not simply so the young would recognize it,
but also because they believed that volition—the individual's moral choice—had
to be predicated on knowledge. One example among many of this belief taken to
its logical conclusion is the tradition of *rumspringa* (Pennsylvania Dutch: "running around") practiced among many Amish communities, in which older adolescents are encouraged to leave their communities and enter into the world to
experience the vices and sins of outside communities. See, e.g., Lucy Walker's
documentary, *The Devil's Playground.*

58. Edwards, "Divine and Supernatural Light," 423; hereafter cited in text as
"Divine Light." Watts, *Catechisms,* vi; hereafter cited in text as *Catechisms.*

59. The paradigmatic passage popularly quoted in homiletic literature is
the parable of the "strange woman's house" (Proverbs 9:13–18). Also popularly
quoted is I Peter 3:3–4: "Whose adorning let it not be that outward adorning of
plaiting the hair, and of wearing of gold, or of putting on of apparel. But let it be
the hidden man of the heart, in that which is not corruptible."

60. For a useful survey of such pedagogical material with little theoretical ap-
paratus, see MacLeod, *A Moral Tale.* For how children's literature shaped social
values even in the secular realm, see Westeroff, *McGuffey and His Readers.* Revising Richard Mosier's study of McGuffey in *Making the Modern Mind* (1947),
Westeroff painstakingly separates the contributions McGuffey made to the
McGuffey Reader from those offered by later authors after McGuffey retired.
He makes the case for why McGuffey's brand of Congregationalism mattered
to the reader's ideology and thus to the shape American education took, since it
was the most widely used reader in the country for almost a century (1836–1920).
He demonstrates how McGuffey's theology bespeaks American social views and
values, including salvation, righteousness, piety, work ethic, thrift, and kindness.
As later editions of the reader began to drop the first three values, it unwittingly
contributed to the secularization of public education.

61. On Coleridgean influences, see generally Nicolson, "James Marsh and

the Vermont Transcendentalists"; Feuer, "James Marsh"; and Duffy, introd. to *Coleridge's American Disciples.* For what is still the best background on Puritan Platonism, see Miller, *The New England Mind: The Seventeenth Century,* chaps. 1–3; Colacurcio, "The Example of Edwards," 61–62; and the unpublished dissertation of Emily Stipes Watts, "Jonathan Edwards and the Cambridge Platonists" (University of Illinois at Urbana-Champaign, 1963). See also Ellis, "The Puritan Mind in Transition." For an excellent example of Puritan Platonism, see Winthrop's "A Modell of Christian Charity," in which he likens members of the community to the several limbs and organs of the body of Christ, demonstrating how interlocking members create a Christian domain that corresponds with the spiritual world.

62. John Dewey, for instance, was influenced in his assessment of children's aptitude by his early study of James Marsh's "Preliminary Essay" in Coleridge's *Aids to Reflections,* and by Professors Joseph and Henry Torrey's influence at the University of Vermont and in the broader intellectual circles of postbellum New England. See Benedict, *An Exposition.* On Dewey in that "system," see Commager, *The American Mind,* esp. 78–110.

63. In 1860 Bushnell extensively reworked this early version, abbreviating the title to *Christian Nature.* For a discussion of the influence on Bushnell's belief that children were born with both good and bad potential, see Macleod, *A Moral Tale,* esp. 90–93. See also Horace Bushnell, "An Argument."

64. History of the book scholars have elevated the place and importance of ephemeral print—almanacs, chapbooks, broadsides, newspapers, catechisms, and the like—as agents in the proliferation of literacy and in the development of cultural attitudes and beliefs. Besides the chapters by David Paul Nord ("A Republican Literature") and Victor Neuburg ("Chapbooks in America") in *Reading in America,* and William J. Gilmore's treatment of these genres in *Reading Becomes a Necessity of Life,* see Margaret Spufford's study of chapbooks in England, *Small Books and Pleasant Histories.*

65. Love, *Mirror of the Blessed Life of Jesus Christ,* prologue II, 14–16.

66. Chaucer, *The Canterbury Tales,* vii, 484–85.

67. Potter, *The English Morality Play,* see esp. 45–57.

68. Bazire and Colledge, *The Chastising of God's Children.*

69. In the seventeenth century, most Protestants followed the ancient Catholic practice of infant baptism; the Anabaptists were a notable exception, for which they were often brutally persecuted by Congregationalists, Presbyterians, and Baptists. The shift to an age of informed consent (generally seven and older) was undoubtedly influenced by the emergence of seventeenth-century contractualism, but it also bespoke the gradual erosion in the doctrine of election (limited atonement) and the gradual muscularization of volition, both of which emphasized the need for the convert to make a moral choice. All of these conditions

worked constitutively with emerging evangelicalism in the eighteenth century and its attendant, if initially implicit, introduction of a doctrine of works. On the importance of children's requisite capacity to form consent, see Walker, *Introduction to American Law;* also, because requisite capacity is a requirement for consent as a trigger for the marriage contract, I have found Joel Prentiss Bishop's landmark *Commentaries on the Law of Marriage and Divorce* particularly useful.

70. *Spiritual Milk* appeared in more than 100 editions (still extant) in the 150 years between 1650 and 1800, including versions translated into Algonquian and other Native American languages before 1700. It was also regionalized, as, for instance, *Spiritual Milk for Boston Babes.* It remained widely popular until the Civil War among a broad range of Protestants, represented, for example, by the great antebellum publisher Joel Munsell (whose last edition appeared in 1885), and John Boyle, Edward Draper, Ira Webster (1843 and several later printings), and Henry Overton (1846).

71. *Spiritual Milk*'s insistence on the link between spiritual failure and bodily corruption likely reminded readers with middle-class aspirations of the way in which human appetite figured prominently in tent-revival sermons of the lower classes that they eschewed. For that reason, Cotton's homiletic manual continued to shape generations of the lower- and working-class faithful up to and through the American Civil War. More than thirty editions appeared after 1800, and five after 1900. Ira Webster of Harford, Connecticut, for instance, published at least seven editions of the *New England Primer* with Cotton's "Milk for Babes" "attached" between 1843 and 1855.

72. George Morton's *Mourt's Relation,* for example, a narrative history of the Plymouth Colony pilgrims published around 1626, was optimistic in its assessment of New World resources available to the initial settlers. But it was also filled with explicit warnings about both the physical and spiritual danger of communal dispersion for New World colonies.

73. I have found Gilmore's *Reading Becomes a Necessity of Life* helpful in thinking through a broader range of reading responses. His categories of "Hardscrabble," "Self-Sufficient Farmstead," "Self-Sufficient Hamlet," "Fortunate Farmstead," and "Fortunate Village" aptly illustrate how geography and economic conditions played an important part in the delineation not only of reading material but also of interpretive practices. As Gilmore argues, "The concept of a series of rural living situations shaping distinctive reading communities has important implications for the study of cultural life and of the formation of public opinion in a nation more than five-sixths rural in 1830" (360). Religious templates and masterplots brought a level of interpretive stability to religious and exegetical practices among the cultural diversity within communities next to one another. For a useful treatment of how publications such as Thomas Prince's pe-

riodical *The Christian History* helped create and spread an intercolony sense of communal grace and inspiration during the Great Awakening, see Lambert, *Inventing the "Great Awakening,"* 113–14 and 212–40.

74. Hambrick-Stowe, "The Spirit of the Old Writers," esp. 281–84.

75. See Matthew P. Brown, *The Pilgrim and the Bee: Reading Rituals and Book Culture in Early New England* (Philadelphia: University of Pennsylvania Press, 2007), see esp. 1–20.

76. Hollinger, "Jewish Intellectuals."

77. Broadhead, *Cultures of Letters,* 5.

78. Walter Scott, the founder of the Disciples of Christ and author of influential *The Gospel Restored* (1836), for instance, worked with a number of fellow exhorters, including Alexander Campbell and Barton Stone, to initiate the New Testament "restoration" movement. This movement profoundly altered traditional hermeneutic practice among a range of evangelical groups by promoting biblical literalism and shearing the New Testament interpretation of all learned commentaries, including the widely received conventional glosses of the Patristic tradition.

79. On a distinctive African American sermon style, see Frey and Wood, *Come Shouting to Zion;* Hatch, *The Democratization of American Christianity;* Brooks, *American Lazarus;* Brekus, *Strangers and Pilgrims,* 25–26; and Taves, *Fits, Trances, and Visions.*

80. If, as Joanna Brooks argues, African American religious narrative "yields up its secrets only to faithful, suspicious, and vigilantly inductive readers" (*American Lazarus,* 117), then we must be doubly suspicious and doubly vigilant when tracing the import of Protestant typologies, returning to the historicist roots of cultural studies and multiculturalism, for nothing altered the meaning of religious master narrative more than the pressing exigencies of time and place.

81. So vehement was the Protestant imperative that each individual read the scriptures for him- or herself that historians of the book have recently begun to give greater credence to the Protestant requirement for individual interaction with scripture as an important impetus to the promotion of print in the late eighteenth century. See Brown, afterword to *Printing and Society in Early America,* 302; and Gilmore, *Reading Becomes a Necessity of Life.*

82. For post-Revolutionary religious movements that sought to unify all sects under the name "Christian" and all churches as the "Christian Church" or the "Church of Christ," see Williams, *Barton Stone,* 183–249.

83. Morgan, "Visual Religion," 51.

84. David Morgan explains both the reason for post-Reformation iconoclasm—while also acknowledging its overstated status—and the reason for a continued sense of that iconoclasm among modern evangelicals: "Such iconophobia is certainly implicit in the stark contrast that many Protestant respondents drew between biblical word and visual image" ("Would Jesus Have Sat

for a Portrait?" 82). Herbert Schneidau points out that Jewish monotheism with its unseen God was a departure from the iconographical-based faiths that Jews were combating (*Sacred Discontent*). For a useful summary of the differences between Protestant and Roman Catholic distinctions and uses of the visual, see Dillenberger, *The Visual Arts and Christianity in America*. See especially chapters 1 and 2, in which Dillenberger addresses the differences between the visual art forms and Christianity brought to the New World by English Puritanism and Spanish Catholicism.

85. Strictly speaking, Anglicans were Calvinists, but because the Anglican church preserved many features of the jettisoned Catholic church—against which Separatists and Nonconformists defined their own reform—they are also remarkably different from their Protestant counterparts in the Presbyterian, Baptist, Congregational, and, later, Methodist movements.

86. While certainly theoretically more complex, Douglas's influential account in *The Feminizing of American Culture* of how nineteenth-century sentimental fiction reflected the "base religiosity" of postbellum evangelicalism largely recapitulates this metanarrative. It was the nineteenth century that feminized the Puritan legacy. In her study, Douglas reduces both middle-class religion and female authorship to the now-critical epithet the "minister and the lady," an "elite" mid-to-late-nineteenth-century alliance formed to consolidate power in order to occupy the void left by the dissolution of traditional ministerial hegemony and to buttress flagging Victorian mores and notions of gentility. Douglas alleges that this cultural coalition popularized a "debased religiosity" by a "sentimental peddling of Christian belief for its nostalgic value," largely through popular literature. Critically filtered through Gramscian Marxist analysis, Douglas's work argues that ministers and women exerted a formidable conservative influence on American society through the vehicle of narrative, marked by "heel-dragging" when it came to political activism.

Douglas opines the demise of the "neo-orthodox" (7), religious theologians and even radically secular critics (she counts Perry Miller among this group) who valued the complex ideas behind American Calvinism. In contrast to the purveyors of "the rituals of that Victorian sentimentalism that did so much to gut Calvinist Orthodoxy" (7–8), she praises the ministerial luminaries such as Edwards and his following—Samuel Hopkins, Joseph Bellamy, and Nathaniel Emmonds—who "constituted the most persuasive example of independent yet institutionalized thought . . . [and who] exhibited with some consistency the intellectual rigor and imaginative precision difficult to achieve without collective effort, and certainly rare in recent American annals" (6–7). As much as we might admire Edwards's and the New Divinity School—their ideas are taken seriously in this study—we also have to acknowledge the real psychological brutalization that Calvinist doctrines perpetrated on millions of people through the eighteenth and nineteenth centuries. For a balanced counter to Douglas and older

social histories by Norman F. Furniss and Richard Hofstadter that viewed evangelical cultures as antimodernist, see Marsden, *Fundamentalism and American
Culture.*

87. For an analytical history of the Weber-Tawney thesis, see Bushman,
From Puritan to Yankee; for a revision of this thesis, see Morgan, "The Puritan
Ethic."

88. See Duffy, *The Stripping of the Altars.*

89. In so doing, visual culture historians have moved the critical conversation beyond what Larry J. Reynolds has called the "'sister arts' criticism" of the
1970s and 80s. Reynolds, "American Cultural Iconography."

90. Several good studies have recently emerged on religious reading. Brown's
The Word in the World provides an in-depth understanding of the history
of religious books and the cultures of reading they fostered. The attention to
nineteenth-century consumerism and commercialism builds on R. Laurence
Moore's *Selling God,* adding to the contradictions Protestants negotiated: How
could one produce and sell religious works while remaining apart from the concerns of the world? How should one value (materially and spiritually) parabiblical texts? The work's focus on regional differences in communities' values about
such religious texts is particularly illuminating.

91. Denning, *Mechanic Accents;* Hall, *Cultures of Print,* and *Lived Religion
in America;* Janice A. Radway, *Reading the Romance: Women, Patriarchy, and
Popular Literature* (Chapel Hill: University of North Carolina Press, 1984);
Tompkins, *Sensational Designs.* I discuss these various reading models in chapter 3.

92. Miles, "Image," 170.

93. For a discussion of the spiritual construction of this transhistorical vision
of the self in conceptions of American history and in the individual's agency in
manifest destiny, see Pocock, *The Machiavellian Moment,* part 1.

94. Through the narrator in his best-selling homiletic novel *In His Steps*
(1896; discussed at length in chapter 3), Charles Sheldon dramatized the desire
to build soul-sustaining alliances by making the body a living testament to another's pain: "There had sprung up in them [the Christian protagonists] a longing that amounted to a passion, to get nearer the great physical poverty and the
spiritual destitution of the mighty city. . . . How could they do this except as they
became a part of it, as nearly as one man can become a part of another's misery?
Where was the suffering to come in, unless there was an actual self-denial apparent to themselves . . . unless it took this concrete, actual, personal form of trying
to share the deepest suffering and sin of the city?" (223).

95. While in the last century the notion of being in and not of the world has
manifested a preoccupation with the literal in daily life, it is still meant to foster double vision. In an example of this literal extremism, Balmer, in *Mine Eyes
Have Seen the Glory,* states "Generations of children in fundamentalist house-

holds were instructed to eschew 'worldliness,' and to adhere to strict codes of morality that forbade card-playing, gambling, cosmetics, motion pictures, dancing, alcohol, and tobacco. Some of the proscriptions have eased somewhat in evangelical circles, but the suspicion of worldliness, of theological and cultural innovation, endures" (43–44).

96. For donor portraits in medieval books of hours, see Wiek, *Time Sanctified;* and Duffy, *Marking the Hours.*

Chapter One

1. Also called "judgment houses" and "scream houses"; see Hannah Sampson, "Broward Church's 'Scream House' Hopes to Scare the Hell out of You," *Miami Herald,* October 23, 2003.

2. John Moore, "'Hell House' to See the Stages of Sin," *Denver Post,* October 8, 2006; http://www.denverpost.com/theater/ci_4333367.

3. The Hell House Kit urges, "Do your very best to buy or purchase a meat product that will resemble as much as possible pieces of a baby that are being placed in the glass bowl for all to see." Quoted from "'Hell House' Kits Selling Nationally," *Christianity Today,* October 7, 1996.

4. In a similar scene depicting lost virginity, Denver's *Rocky Mountain News* reports that "a girl has her boyfriend spend the night in her parents' bed while they are out of town. The demon guide tells her, "'The dog you just slept with is Prince HIV, and he doesn't even know it!'" Sue Lindsay, "Gay Union Portrayed in Hell House," September 29, 1999; see also Sam Howe Verhovek, "Using Ghouls to Get to God," *New York Times,* October 27, 1996.

5. Jim Yardley, "Church's Haunted House Draws Fire," *New York Times,* October 29, 1999.

6. Beecher, "The Strange Woman's House," 206; hereafter cited in text as "Strange Woman."

7. See my "Cultivating Spiritual Sight," and Beecher, "The Strange Woman's House," 178.

8. Several influential scholars have noted the shift in sermon tone and content from the seventeenth to the eighteenth century. See Stout, *The New England Soul.* While Stout suggests that hellfire sermons were rare before 1740—a date denoting the apogee of the New England revivals that we, in retrospect, refer to as the First Great Awakening—I move the date back in time about twenty years (155).

9. Stout, *The New England Soul,* 155.

10. Shepard, *Thomas Shepard's Confessions,* 115. Several studies on colonial and early national literacy reveal how many individuals, particularly women, could read but not write; claims about illiteracy are thus often misleading. In

terms of religious instruction, for instance, both the Anglicans and Methodists determined to teach the poor to read but not to write. See Rule, *Albion's People,* and Kathryn Sutherland, "'Events . . . have made us a world of readers.'" See also Monaghan, "Literacy Instruction," in which Monaghan demonstrates that New England colonial women could often read but not write, and argues that the familiar "x" as a signature does not signify illiteracy. She argues that the literacy rates in colonial New England were much higher than originally believed. For a sampling of the literature on U.S. literacy, see Lockridge, *Literacy in Colonial New England;* Gilmore, *Elementary Literacy;* and Kaestle, "The History of Literacy." For useful study reading and literacy in practice, see Jackson, *Romantic Readers.*

11. Quoted in Stout, *The Divine Dramatist,* 153.

12. Stanton, *Eighty Years and More,* 42–43.

13. Foxcroft, *Cleansing Our Way in Youth,* 87; hereafter cited in text as *Cleansing Our Way.* Similarly, in *The Doctrine of the Passions Explained,* Isaac Watts asserts the usefulness of fear: "The anger of God is the most proper object of our fear, as we are sinful creatures; nor can sinners fear the anger of God too much, 'till they have complied with the appointed methods of his grace" (139).

14. On the theology of cruelty, see Chamberlain, "The Theology of Cruelty."

15. For a historical evaluation of revivalism and the emergence of the supplicant's salvific independence, see Hatch, *The Democratization of American Christianity,* 195–201; McLoughlin, *Modern Revivalism;* and Bernard A. Weisberger, *They Gathered at the River.*

16. The English Presbyterian Isaac Taylor testified to Edwards's international influence on ministers and congregants from a number of denominations. In his assessment of Edwards's influence on the Anglican ministry, he writes in his *Essay on the Application of Abstract Reasoning to the Christian Doctrines,* "In the reaction which of late has counterpoised the once triumphant Arminianism of English [E]piscopal divinity, the influence of Edwards has been much greater than those who have yielded to it have always professed" (21).

17. James, *Varieties of Religious Experience,* 300; original emphasis. Hereafter cited in text as *Varieties.*

18. The influence of Locke in the American colonies cannot be gainsaid. For the best treatment of Locke's pervasive influence on religious culture, historical shifts in the perception of children's aptitudes, and epistemology, see Fliegelman, *Prodigals and Pilgrims,* see esp. 4–5, 12–15, 58–59, 111.

19. In *The English Morality Play,* Robert Potter points out that the "theme of the coming of death" is "well recognized, particularly in its relation to the cult of death which swept fifteenth-century Europe in the wake of the plague" (20).

20. For a useful sketch of the "Pauline-Augustinian-Calvinist tradition" and a survey of the literature on the bondage of human will in that tradition, see Ramsey, introd. to "Edwards and John Locke," 49–51.

21. *The New-England Primer,* 22.

22. In *How and Why the Young Should Cleanse Their Way* (1716), the Reverend William Cooper, Benjamin Colman's associate at Brattle Street Church in Boston, justifies God's ways to man as a response to "that Original Corruption which we all bring into the World with us" (5). God owes humanity nothing, Cooper intones, because "the Nature of man has miserably lost its Primitive purity, and has a permanent viciousness and corruption brought upon it; is tainted with the Evil disease which cleaveth fast to it, and is hereditary, so as that none can be clean who is born of a Woman." Without Colman's restraining influence, Cooper's colleague Thomas Foxcroft was not so delicate. In graphic terms, he conveyed the extent of God's aversion to sinning humanity, who were "a loathsome stench in the nostrils of the holy God, and an odious spectacle to angels" (*Cleansing Our Way* 6). Beginning with an anatomy of humanity's corruption, Foxcroft reiterates humanity's birthright in the Fall: "The whole head is sick, the whole heart is faint, there is no soundness in them, nothing but bruises and putrifying sores. Their wounds stink and are corrupt, They are all over an unclean thing, and as for their Nativity, in the day they were born, they were cast out in the open field to the loathing of their persons, weltring in their own blood, their whole spirit, soul and body filled with loathsome disease" (*Cleansing Our Way* 6).

23. Refusing to sign Laud's "Thirty-Nine Articles of the Church of England," which mandated uniformity among the clergy by a signed profession of "divine right of the episcopacy," hundreds of dissenters like Shepard were turned out of their pulpits and hounded by government censors. Exercising their "liberty of conscience," nonconforming ministers preached in unauthorized venues, but were threatened with prison. As William Prynne—who lost his ears for defaming Charles I's consort Queen Henrietta Maria—discovered, the long arm of the church wielded a saber. Under the Carolinian crown, ecclesiastical law, which historically could not touch life, limb, or property, had become a menacing presence.

24. See Slotkin, *Regeneration through Violence.*

25. Mather, *Magnalia Christi Americana,* 634–36.

26. A favorite trope of the early modern American sermon, "arrows" creased the hearts, livers, and lungs of the damned. In his sermon *Pray for the Rising Generation,* Increase Mather asked his audience, "Do you not see the Arrow of Death come flying over your heads?" (22). Foxcroft warned of "arrows" and "firey darts" that come as sinners sleep (*Cleansing Our Way* 65). Even Edwards, nephew of the famed Indian captive John Williams and, after losing his pulpit at Northampton, missionary to the Wampanoags in western Massachusetts, pictured God's wrath in the form of fiery arrows.

27. Milton, *Paradise Lost,* 140.

28. Isaac Watts, *Philosophical Essay on Various Subjects,* viii–ix. Speaking

further to the pervasiveness of Locke's great work, Isaac Watts observes, "There are many admirable chapters in that book and many truths in them, which are worthy of letters of Gold."

29. While recent scholarship might take issue with Perry Miller's well-known assertion of the decline in Puritan piety between the first and fourth generations as a historical fact, they cannot take issue with the late-seventeenth-century perception of a declension, for the record is filled with sermons lamenting the decline in piety from generation to generation. For a recent reevaluation of the "declension thesis," see Kamensky, *Governing the Tongue*, 99–126.

30. Unlike the Presbyterians of Scotland, who set up a central governing body to govern and unify individual congregations, Congregationalists in New England held to the principle that each congregation enjoyed sovereignty. They constructed each congregation on the model of the visible church. Based on the ninth chapter of the book of Romans, the Anglo-American Puritans believed that the immutable church—the "invisible church"—was composed of the elect, those individuals preordained by God to enjoy salvation. Modeled on the Augustinian notion of earthly representation of this "invisible church," the "visible church" was composed of those in the congregation who believed themselves to be recipients of God's grace and who could convincingly justify their inclusion among the elect to the membership body. See Morgan, *Visible Saints*.

31. Mather, *Pray for the Rising Generation*, 12.

32. Cotton, *The Covenant of Gods Free Grace*, 19.

33. In his final sermon before the Northampton congregation on July 1, 1750, following the council's decision to terminate his services, Jonathan Edwards strenuously warned against the infiltration of Arminianism and its message of "conditional" rather than "irresistible" grace, and the threat it posed to the doctrine of election: "The progress they [Arminians] have made in the land, within this seven years, seems to have been vastly greater, than any time in the like space before: and they are still prevailing and creeping into almost all parts of the land.... And if these principles should greatly prevail ... it will threaten the spiritual and eternal ruin of this people, in the present and future generations." Dwight, *The Works of President Edwards*, vol. 1, 649–50.

34. For a history of the doctrine of original sin and Edwards's account of it, see Holbrook's introduction to Edwards's *Original Sin,* and Smith, *Changing Conceptions of Original Sin*, esp. 1–35; see also Conrad Wright's revised view of original sin as a dividing issue among colonial Calvinists in *Beginnings of Unitarianism in America*, 58–114.

35. Hobbes thus argued in *The Leviathan* as "Common Power, to keep them [the people] in awe, and to direct their actions to the common benefit," the sovereign instills the fear of violent death in his subjects as a means of preventing uprisings. On "collective consent," he argued that the "only way to erect a common power ... is, to conferre all their [subjects'] power and strength upon one

Man, or upon one Assembly of men, that may reduce all their Wills, by plurality of voices, unto one Will" or the "Collective Will" (120). In *On the Citizen,* Hobbes formulates his idea of "negative freedom": "But once a commonwealth is formed, every citizen retains as much liberty as he needs to live well in peace, and enough liberty is taken from others to remove the fear of them. Outside the commonwealth every man has a right to all things, but on the terms that he may enjoy nothing. In a commonwealth every man enjoys a limited right in security" (116).

36. Pearse, *The Great Concern,* 41.

37. The doctrine of universal salvation (broadly understood in the seventeenth and early eighteenth century) technically meant salvation for all, believers and unbelievers alike. See, e.g., Caldwell, "The Doctrine of Universal Salvation Unscriptural." Later in the nineteenth century, the term *universal* often signified open salvation for any believer, as opposed to the doctrine of predestination.

38. See Holifield, *The Covenant Sealed.*

39. The material success of the plantation and its broad colonization to western New England continued to foster spiritual complacency, and the partial covenant only undermined the motivation for full membership. By the first decade of the eighteenth century, many in the third and fourth generations were content with the social status and salvific hope afforded by half-way membership. As their ministers complained, they were too satisfied with spiritual limbo to undertake the emotional pilgrimage required to ascertain whether or not they had an assurance of grace. To a generation enjoying longer lives and the fruits of colonial expansion, the prospect of hell's suffering as a correlative of life, like the early New England winters of deprivation and hunger, seemed ever more remote. Although the jeremiads threatened new physical hardships—a renewal of the demonic assault that had made early Puritan life hell on earth—life in the material world seemed to be getting steadily better, not worse, for the complacent "half-way" children of the covenant.

40. Crawford, *Seasons of Grace.* The gentler image of God took hold in the colonies and nation much slower than in Britain, and these shifting views spread unevenly. The influential New Light Presbyterian Barton Stone, a principal architect of the Cane Ridge revival, came, as late as 1805, to the conclusion that because Jesus revealed the only true God ("He that hath seen me hath seen the Father," John 14:9) and because Jesus was the savior of sinners, God was love. He was thus able once and for all to discard the depiction of the "dreadful God of vengeance, wrath and fury." Stone, *A Reply,* 5.

41. Edwards, *Life of David Brainerd,* 20; hereafter cited in text as *Life.*

42. Less than four generations before, Hutchinson pronounced that her learned brethren's conversion morphology rendered "preparations" the equivalent of works—and therefore was Arminian or, she implied, even the Catholic doctrine of salvation. As opposed to Whitefield's Calvinist Methodists, the Wes-

leyan Methodists and emerging New Light Presbyterians and Congregationalists were the first Calvinists to break with the doctrine of predestination in any unified way. See Hall, "The Examination of Mrs. Anne Hutchinson."

43. While Wesleyan Methodists opposed the doctrine of predestination, Baptists and New Light Congregationalists and Presbyterians simply did not emphasize it. The architects of these revivals—among them Samuel Davies, James McGready, and Barton Stone, all followers of Jonathan Edwards—represent the various stages of this doctrine's rejection. For a description of how this doctrine and opposition to it shaped the Kentucky revivals leading up to Cane Ridge, see Williams, *Barton Stone,* 17–21.

44. Haroutanian, *Piety versus Moralism;* Meyer, *The Democratic Enlightenment;* May, *The Enlightenment in America,* chap. 3.

45. Watt, *The Rise of the Novel,* see esp. chap. 2.

46. See esp. Breen, "An Empire of Goods," and "'Baubles of Britain'"; and "Toward a History of the Standard of Living." For a study of the transformation of cultural life through institutions, see Peter Clark, *British Clubs and Societies.* See also Gilmore, *Reading Becomes a Necessity of Life,* in which Gilmore describes how even rural areas were dramatically altered: there was "a vast transformation in the forms of cultural exchange and the commercialization of material and social existence as the Upper Valley became enmeshed in a regional market economy linked to the transatlantic commercial world" (18).

47. In *Barton Stone,* Williams credits the Enlightenment's emphasis on common sense as a principal cause in the decline of predestination theology in the colonies and early nation (3).

48. In his tract justifying smallpox inoculation—which Jonathan Edwards had printed in Boston—Increase Mather excoriated as a "crying iniquity" those who labeled smallpox vaccinations as "a work of the Devil, and a going to the Devil," as a "shocking blasphemy." He accused his and Cotton's attackers for being "much more likely to bring the plague among us, than the practice, which they so ignorantly and maliciously do charge with such imaginary consequences." "Several Reasons," 2.

49. While not oversimplifying the historical record, we must recognize that colonial American religious communities—before the Enlightenment, at the threshold of the scientific revolution, and preindustrial—were, in many ways, closer to medieval culture than our own. The neat historical divide we sometimes imagine the Protestant Reformation to have been, isolating what came before from what came after, was actually a messy, protracted, grass-roots-driven cultural, political, and theological transition. See Hatch, *The Democratization of American Christianity,* esp. 49–66; Walzer, *The Revolution of the Saints;* and Goodwyn, *The Populist Moment,* xii–xxiv, 34–35, and 293–96.

50. Huizinga, *The Waning of the Middle Ages,* 138.

51. Ibid.

52. The lyric is number 239 in *Middle English Lyrics,* ed. Luria and Hoffman.

53. Perhaps the best-known representation of the tradition is the grave-digger scene in *Hamlet,* in which the unearthed skull of a court jester—"poor Yorrick!"—causes Hamlet to soliloquize about the brevity of life and the common fate of humanity.

54. Promey, "Seeing the Self," 17.

55. For a different take on photographing dead children, see Karen Sanchez-Eppler, "Then When We Clutch the Hardest."

56. Cooper, "Man Humbled by Being Compar'd to a Worm," 3. Additionally, colonial gravestone carvers did not abandon the practice of decorating cemetery markers with skeletons and skulls—the Puritan memento mori—until the nineteenth century, when the focus on eternal damnation had to compete with an emerging emphasis on heaven and salvation.

57. We can see the sources of Puritan imagery in iconic works like Michaelangelo's nightmarish "Last Judgment," with its hideous, contorted multitudes of damned souls; or in older works like Dante's *Inferno,* with its vividly detailed and ordered moral cartography of the various consequences of sin (in its prevalent Social Gospel adaptation, revisited in chapter 4, an important precursor of the hell house).

58. Sewall, *The Certainty and Suddenness of Christ's Coming to Judgment,* 19.

59. Holly, "Youth Liable to Sudden Death."

60. In recalling Marvell's "To His Coy Mistress," Foxcroft reminds us that carpe diem was the period's other great answer to life's uncertainty and brevity—the answer favored by Royalists and Cavaliers. Like those Puritan ministers with whom Marvell associated, his poem's seductive speaker warns that "worms shall try/ That long preserved virginity" (Marvell, *Complete Works,* 107).

61. I am extending to M. H. Armstrong Davison's concept and timeline of the "pre-anaesthetic era" (1754–1846), developed in *The Evolution of Anaesthesia;* see esp. 73–96.

62. There has been a good deal of contention about the role Locke's work played in the transformation of early American culture. On the side of Locke's foundational role—a broad critique of interpretations of the republicanism of the period—see foremost Fliegelman, *Prodigals and Pilgrims;* also for their partial critiques of Louis Hartz's *The Liberal Tradition in America,* see Bailyn, *The Ideological Origins of the American Revolution;* Wood, *The Creation of the American Republic.* Post-Fliegelman, several recent studies emphasize the importance of Locke: see Brown's *The Consent of the Governed.* On the reception of Locke's political theory in Boston, which necessitates his epistemology, see Ohmori, "'The Artillery of Mr. Locke,'" and Breen, "Subjecthood and Citizenship."

63. Locke studied at Oxford during the Puritan Interregnum. On Locke's Puritan background, see Greaves, *The Puritan Revolution and Educational Thought.*

64. See Watts's essay, "Remarks on Some Chapters of Mr. Locke's *Essay on the Human Understanding,*" in *Philosophical Essays on Various Subjects,* 276–321. In *Catechisms,* Isaac Watts argued that he recognized children's insufficient mental capacities: "Have not many of you often wished for some easier and shorter forms of knowledge, whereby your children might have some sense of divine things and early religion let into their minds in a way more suited to their feeble capacities?" (v).

65. For a contested critical history of Edwards's idealism, see Baritz, *City on a Hill,* 47-90; Rupp, "The 'Idealism' of Jonathan Edwards"; Anderson, "Immaterialism"; for the "idealist" school, see Fisher, "The Philosophy of Jonathan Edwards"; Smyth, "Jonathan Edwards' Idealism"; and Howard, *The Mind of Jonathan Edwards.*

66. It is the extension of this un-unified self through popular evangelicalism, in fact, that would lead William James to declare as late as the twentieth century that "the Psychological basis of the twice-born character seems to be a certain discordancy or heterogeneity in the native temperament of the subject, an incompletely unified moral and intellectual constitution" (*Varieties* 140). While today we assume every individual has a subconscious, it was not until 1886 that psychology began articulating a "subliminal consciousness" or subconscious (*Varieties* 190). In terms of the persistence of an unified self among the religious, James, like George A. Coe, author of *The Spiritual Life,* argued—in the science of their times—that evangelicals evinced a more developed and "active" subconscious than non-evangelicals. Coe's work, James says, "confirm[s] the view that sudden conversion is connected with the possession of an active subliminal self" (195).

67. In their understanding of the fall, Reformation Protestants largely followed Augustine, for whom, in Peter Brown's words, "the Fall had been, among many other things, a fall from direct knowledge into indirect knowledge through signs. The 'inner foundation' of awareness had dried up: Adam and Eve found that they could only communicate with one another by the clumsy artifice of language and gestures. Above all, Augustine was preoccupied by the coexistence of this necessary but defective means of knowledge by 'signs,' with flashes of direct awareness." Brown, *Augustine of Hippo,* 261.

68. Monk, *John Wesley,* 56.

69. Taylor, *Sources of the Self.* Taylor titles his chapter on Locke "The Punctual Self."

70. In the voice of the Canticles, "I sleep, but my heart waketh" (the Latin inscription in homiletic texts was "*Ego dormio, sed cor meum vigilat*").

71. One of the most enduring refutations of Locke's denial of the soul's vigil

was Watts, "An Enquiry Whether the Soul Thinks Always," in *Philosophical Essays on Various Subjects.*

72. For a refutation of Locke's theory of dreams as decaying sense impressions, see Watts, *Philosophical Essays on Various Subjects,* 119–21. In an apt allegory of imagination divorced from the rational faculty, essentially Locke's definition of dreams, the Lockean Francisco de Goya represented dreams as the nocturnal sprites or monsters—embodied superstitions—emanating from the mind when reason sleeps. See also Wigglesworth, *The Diary of Michael Wigglesworth,* 47, 134–56.

73. In a remarkable passage, Brown indirectly suggests why Lockean materialism proved particularly devastating to Calvinists of all stamps, through their connection to the Augustinian tradition: "Augustine . . . produced a singularly comprehensive explanation of why allegory should have been necessary in the first place. The need for such a language of 'signs' was the result of a specific dislocation of the human consciousness. In this, Augustine takes up a position analogous to that of Freud. In dreams also, a powerful and direct message is said to be deliberately diffracted by some psychic mechanism, into a multiplicity of 'signs' quite as intricate and absurd, yet just as capable of interpretation, as the 'absurd' or 'obscure' passages in the Bible. Both men, therefore, assume that the proliferation of images is due to some precise event, to the development of some geological fault across a hitherto undivided consciousness: for Freud, it is the creation of an unconscious by repression; for Augustine, it is the outcome of the Fall." Brown, *Augustine of Hippo,* 261.

74. For a grasp of how much Edwards's own views of the will and volition changed (increasingly distant to Locke's own) between the time he began "Notes on the Mind" (and "Divine and Supernatural Light") and one of his last great works, "Freedom of the Will," see Paul Ramsey's introduction to the latter work in *The Works of Jonathan Edwards,* vol. 1, 11–65.

75. See Fliegelman, *Prodigals and Pilgrims,* 12–13.

76. Locke, *The Educational Writings of John Locke,* 111; Watts, *The Improvement of the Mind,* 19.

77. Ariès's controversial study (*Centuries of Childhood*) posits an origin for modern childhood in late medieval France, while Demos (*A Little Commonwealth*) and Zuckerman (*Peaceable Kingdoms*) argue for its emergence in New England somewhat later in the eighteenth century. While arguing for the "birth" of modern childhood seems more than a little reductive, it is important to note that Western notions of childhood have changed dramatically, if not uniformly or unidirectionally, over the past two millennia. For the best discussion of the broader themes of this shift, see Fliegelman, *Prodigals and Pilgrims,* 10–13.

78. Ibid., 11.

79. On the development of childhood in the nineteenth century, see Sánchez-Eppler, *Dependent States;* for a good historical introduction to American child-

hood, see Levander and Singley, *The American Child*. Descriptions of innate depravity abound in seventeenth- and eighteenth-century sermons. In *A Guide to Heaven*, the nonconformist Anglican minister Samuel Hardy (1637–1691) of Dorchester, England, provides a representative illustration of the level of depravity and its perceived contagion. This illustration is not a confession, as so many similar passages are in Puritan journals, but intended as a communal affirmation to be recited aloud: "Lazarus in all his sores, or Job on the dung hill, with his scabs and botches, were not so filthy and abominable to the eyes of man, as I am through the running sores and plagues of my heart and life, in the sight of an holy and pure God: I am more vile than the toad, than the stinking carrion in the ditch. How doth is filth stream through every duty and mercy? I drop the filthiness of sin wherever I go" (14–15). For the more liberal Congregationalists in 1899, as for many denominations today, original sin continues to be the fundamental challenge to redemption. "The most terrible and obtrusive fact in the world," Rev. John Daniel Jones tells the ministers gathered at the Second International Congregational Council in Boston in 1899, "is the fact of sin. Wherever man is found, he carries upon his soul this burden—the burden of sin, the consciousness of demerit and guiltiness in the sight of God. Any religion that seeks to be universal, any religion that seeks to meet the deepest needs of the human heart must recognize this terrible fact and deal with it" ("Distinctive Characteristics of Christianity," 102).

80. While the seventeenth-century contractualists—principally Locke and Hobbes—had, in political terms, already posited a moral shelter for the young and insane (the legal precedent for "requite capacity"), Calvinist theocracies disregarded criminal motivation and mental capacity as an ameliorative factor in their penal system. At a time when Hobbes was exempting "children, fools, and madmen" from the social contract—and thus the pain of its breach—because they did not meet the volitional bar required to form consent, the Puritans still prosecuted and executed both adolescents and the insane, as the sad fates of the young Thomas Granger for bestiality or Mary Dyer for heresy and deranged behavior, two cases of particular renown, attested. In *The Leviathan*, Hobbes writes: "Likewise children, fools, and madmen, that have no use of reason, may be personated by guardians or curators, but can be no authors, during that time, of any action done by them longer than, when they shall recover the use of reason, they shall judge the same reasonable" (133; see also Moriarty, "The True Story of Mary Dyer," 40–42; and, for Thomas Granger, see Bradford, *Of Plymouth Plantation*, 320–22). In her study of the colonial execution sermon, Karen Halttunen demonstrates that the motive for crimes, including serious felonies like murder, were inconsequential as legal criteria in colonial Calvinist communities, for all were presumed not merely capable of but predisposed to evil. See *Murder Most Foul*, esp. 7–32. For the religious, evil was its own motive. Executions were neither punishment nor deterrent so much as attempts to circum-

scribe moral contagion, to close demonic avenues into the spiritual community by weighing the welfare of the many against the one.

81. The rub in Reformation theology lay in the individual's direct access to God. While clerical mediation was anathema to the Protestant injunction for that access, religious authority's predication on education and gender survived the iconoclasm that dismantled Roman Catholic and Anglican Episcopal hierarchies. Colonial Calvinism never achieved the balance it sought between ministerial authority in local theocracies and individuals' liberty of conscience. As Harry Stout observes, in New England, government "existed primarily for religious reasons and represented, in effect, the coercive arm of the churches" (*The New England Soul,* 20); and Catherine Brekus notes that "The Anglican churches in the South, the Puritans in New England, and the Dutch Reformed in New York all prided themselves on being the guardians of public order" (*Strangers and Pilgrims,* 28).

These questions of degrees of moral knowledge and spiritual aptitude tied to age, race, and gender simply became more visible in the wake of an empirical epistemology and the privileged place it accorded human feelings over cold rationalism.

82. They also led to ingenious feats of casuistry. In a theological fiction suggested by Michael Wigglesworth's *Day of Doom,* for example, Foxcroft suggested that damned infants—those who might never have had the opportunity to add sins to the taint with which they were born—are accorded "Hell's easiest room." Foxcroft envisioned hell as a Dantean escalation of punishment; although "the wages of every sin is eternal death; and every degree of damnation is insufferable," children would suffer less than adults: "A much sorer punishment will some have than others. The degrees of misery which the wicked shall be condemned to, shall correspond with the degrees of wickedness which they are charged with" (*Cleansing Our Way* 94). But Foxcroft's solution did little to disguise the contradiction inherent in Calvinism: increasing degrees of cognizance increased both culpability and its eternal retribution, yet if the wages of sin was death, the young still suffered damnation even if the degree of sin in relation to experience mitigated the punishment. For parents this was but cold comfort. Unlike purgatory's fixed term of suffering, Protestant hell, even in the "easiest room," was for eternity. Clearly, Foxcroft's generation had already ventured out onto the slippery slope that Congregationalists, Presbyterians, Methodists, and Baptists were still trying to terrace in the mid-nineteenth century.

83. Translating the eighteenth-century dilemma back into the apostolic context, Edwards asks in "A Divine and Supernatural Light," "For if knowledge were dependent on natural causes or means, how came it to pass that . . . a company of poor fishermen, illiterate men, and persons of low education, attained to the knowledge of truth; while the Scribes and Pharisees, men of vastly higher advantages, and greater knowledge and sagacity in other matters, remained in ig-

norance?" (409). Edwards argues, of course, that knowledge for the regenerate lies above "natural causes or means."

84. Notably, Foxcroft turns to the older faculty psychology that made the passions a legitimate faculty. Descartes had linked the passions to the volition; and Locke, revising Descartes, made the passions "variants of pleasure or pain," and thus made them states of the understanding. See Nidditch's introduction to Locke's *Essay,* xxiii.

85. At midpoint in the eighteenth century, for example, John Wesley's final rejection of election finalized the break between his "Arminian" Methodists and Whitefield's "Calvinist" Methodists (the so-called "Huntingdon Connexion," after its sponsor Selina Hastings, the Countess of Huntingdon) and instigated a contentious quarrel with the Anglican episcopacy. Andover professor Leonard Woods allowed that the doctrine of election defied moral reason, but argued that it was scriptural and so merited defense. Even as late as the 1830s and 40s, Lyman Beecher still had to argue against infant damnation as the contamination of pre-Reformation doctrines. In the first half of the nineteenth century, Connecticut Congregationalism was divided between Nathaniel William Taylor, whose professorship at Yale spread the theology of volition among the three generations of ministers, and Bennet Tyler, who defended the doctrine of election from within the walls of his seminary at East Windsor, which became the symbolic seat of conservative Congregationalism.

86. Knight, *Orthodoxies in Massachusetts: Rereading American Puritanism.*

87. Testimonials of Jonathan Edwards's remarkable influence among Protestants of every stripe are numerous. One example of that influence aptly illustrates Edwards's international fame. Recalling his uncle's training in *The Memoir of William Carey,* Eustace Carey disclosed how William Carey (1761–1834)—deemed the "father of modern missions"—"was deeply imbued with North American theology. President Edwards, its great master, was his admired author. The strong and absorbing view in which he exhibited some leading principles in the system of revealed truth, seeming so clearly to explode the errors of Arminianism on the one hand, and of pseudo-Calvinism on the other, and to throw such a flood of irresistible light on the mediatorial dispensation, as perfectly captivated, and almost entranced, the ministerial circle with which Mr. Carey was connected" (88).

88. Smith, "Edwards and the 'Way of Ideas.'"

89. For arguments about the centrality of "A Divine and Supernatural Light" in the development of Edwardsian theology, and for Edwards's relation to Locke's epistemology, see Miller, *Jonathan Edwards,* 43–68. While Miller reads "Divine and Supernatural Light" in order to trace Edwards's rationalist revisions—and what, controversially, Miller saw as his modernist turn—back to Locke, I am interested in the tradition of homiletic pedagogical theory that emerges from Edwards's Lockean revisions. See also Miller, "The Rheto-

ric of Sensation," 179–80, and "Jonathan Edwards on the Sense of the Heart,"
131, 136–37; Davidson, "From Locke to Edwards"; and Laurence, "Jonathan
Edwards, John Locke." For a critical history of the "modernist" argument, see
Marsden, *Jonathan Edwards;* Opie, *Jonathan Edwards and the Enlightenment;*
and Colacurcio, "The Example of Edwards," 61–62.

90. Edwards did not embrace the level of materialism that, through Charles
Chauncy's Boston coterie, would eventually lead a rationalist branch of Congregationalist Old Lights to reject the Trinitarian Godhead (three persons in
one) as mystical and to take up a Unitarian creed, after which it would be more
than a century before any national evangelical leader would reject rational theology in an open embrace of mysticism. Perhaps no one so clearly renounced
both Locke and the doctrine of innate depravity in the same breath than the Social Gospel prophet George Davis Herron, who claimed, "I may have been converted before I was born. . . . I have never been without the inner consciousness
of God's compelling and restraining presence." Quoted in Beardsley, "Professor
Herron," 786.

91. For a discussion of Edwards and mysticism, see Riley, *American Thought,*
29.

92. By the 1740s, the epistemological shortcomings of mechanical philosophy
were becoming clear to natural philosophers as well as theologians. From the
1680s to the 1740s, natural philosophy assumed an almost purely mechanistic
perspective, incorporating "the methods and assumptions of formal mathemati-
cal reasoning into explanations for natural phenomena. The overriding impulse
was to transform contingent knowledge into certain truth, to reduce the manifold appearances of nature to simple principles." Reill, *Vitalizing Nature in the
Enlightenment,* 5. For a critique of Descartes on this point, see Watts, *The Doctrine of the Passions Explained,* 11–12, and *Philosophical Essays on Various Subjects,* iv–vi.

93. Locke lists and uses these faculties unevenly, often even collapsing them
into what he calls the "two great and principal actions of the Mind, which are
most frequently considered, and which are so frequent, that every one that
pleases, may take notice of 'em in himself, are these two: *Perception,* or *Thinking,* and *Volition,* or *Willing.* The Power of Thinking is called the *Understanding,* and the Power of Volition is called the *Will,* and these two Powers or Abilities in Mind are denominated *Faculties" (Essay* II.6.2; original emphasis). For a
good discussion of the view of technology and automated mechanisms in the seventeenth century, see Fowler, *Renaissance Realism,* 52.

94. Pearse, *The Great Concern,* 11.

95. Edwards's student Joseph Bellamy reiterates Edwards's theory of divine
light throughout his *True Religion Delineated.* He writes, for instance, "All these
things [spiritual understanding] . . . may, for substance, instantly open to view,
and the Soul immediately acquiesce in the Gospel scheme and close with Christ,

instantly, I say, upon DIVINE LIGHT's being imparted to the Soul" (388; original emphasis). Borrowing Edwards's very language, William James in 1901 still
insists that the most "vital" part of saving faith for the religious convert is "immediate and intuitive" (*Varieties* 200).

96. Suggesting Edwards's resolution without attempting to frame the mechanism by which perception, superintended by the Spirit, exerts itself in the emergent epistemology, Foxcroft writes that the "Light of the Word illuminates many
known things, elightening [sic] the eyes, and making wise the simple (Psalms 19:
7–8)" (*Cleansing Our Way* 111).

97. James, "Does 'Consciousness' Exist?" 36.

98. Responding to Immanuel Kant's "curious doctrine about such objects of
belief as God, the design of creation, the soul, its freedom, and the life hereafter," which according to Kant were not properly objects of knowledge because
such knowledge requires sense-content, James argues that "strangely enough
they have a definite meaning *for our practice.* We can act *as if* there were a God;
feel *as if* we were free; consider Nature *as if* she were full of special designs; lay
plans *as if* we were to be immortal; and we find then that these words do make
a genuine difference in our moral life. Our faith *that* these unintelligible objects
actually exist proves thus to be a full equivalent in *praktscher Hinsicht,* as Kant
calls it, or from the point of view of our action, for knowledge of *what* they might
be, in case we were permitted positively to conceive them" (*Varieties* 52; original emphasis).

99. Beecher, "Strange Woman," 206.

100. Edwards's reference to the "sweetness of the thing" as an actual sensation is taken from Locke's illustration of the pineapple in *Essay.* Locke distinguished between experiential knowledge and an abstract concept. The precept
of how a pineapple tastes for one who has never tasted it would provide an in-
exact idea, based on its "resemblance with any tastes, whereof he has the Ideas
already in his Memory" (424). But a true sense of its taste would come only by
tasting it, producing a precise idea. Illustrating the superiority of experience to
precept, Locke had argued, "Words can produce in us no other simple Ideas";
in the case of pineapple, words can compare it to other fruit, comprise a catalogue of descriptive adjectives, but could not give an idea of its exact taste. "He
that thinks otherwise," Locke challenges, "let him try if a Word can give him the
taste of a Pine Apple, and make him have the true Idea of the Relish of that celebrated delicious fruit" (424). Edwards followed Locke closely, yet altered the
context to demonstrate Locke's point by wedding language to the personal experience of his auditors who assuredly had not tasted a pineapple.

101. This was precisely the charge leveled at the devout Isaac Newton for his
theory of gravity, because to a nascent science invested in the relation of cause
and effect in natural laws, it posited action at a distance in an age that gaped
wide-eyed at the prospect of physical impulsion across vast space. Without expe-

rience, Edwards's proposition was tantamount to suggesting that the faithful receive knowledge from an unbroken chain of revelations. It would have suggested a tie with God so intimate, an individualism so radical, that if it did not deify the faithful outright—a popular indictment of perfectionists like the "Grindletonians" or the Quakers with their indwelling Spirit—it came damnably close to overturning the effects of the Fall.

102. The warning Solomon Stoddard gave the ministers of his grandson's generation about the habituation of sin was a homiletic commonplace: "Those temptations that have prevailed upon [sinners]," he reminds the young clergy, "are more like to prevail again; and if they get an habit of backsliding, they will be the more incurable: custom in any evil way, naturalizes it to men: they run more readily into the same" (*Guide to Christ,* 48; hereafter cited in text). The processes of study and learning—particularly the time involved in scriptural reading, exegesis, and application—were at odds with the acquisition of experience. While scholars note American primers' and catechisms' turn from biblical motifs to less-religious themes in the nineteenth century as evidence of secularization, I suggest that this change has more to do with an epistemological shift that privileged children's experience.

103. Edwards, "Sinners in the Hands of an Angry God."

104. While describing the connection between language and the object world, Locke had initially assumed that words formed a "simple idea" or image of the object they represented in the mind of the perceiver. As the smallest unit of experience, simple ideas, such as horse or man, could be combined to create more complex ideas, such as their fusion into a centaur. Once an idea—simple or complex—became lodged in the understanding as an "ideal apprehension," a kind of template, it provided a mold for similar perception, and through accretion, a reservoir of ideas or a "settled standard" formed by which "to rectify and adjust" new ideas, or from which to create complex ideas and "mixed modes" (*Essay* 478), the most abstract concepts. Thus far, Locke simply agreed with Augustine in *De Magistro,* in which, through a Socratic dialogue with his son, Augustine explains the arbitrary connection between sign and signified, the object referent of the sign. (*De Magistro* has been generally translated as "The Teacher"; *Against the Academicians; The Teacher.*) With Augustine, Locke argued that words were mere sounds, "voluntarily connected" by convention to the objects they came to represent. "Words in primary or immediate signification," Locke mused, "stand for nothing, but the Ideas in the mind of him that uses them" (*Essay* 407).

105. Scholars such as Will Durant, Ralph Bauer, and Susan Parrish have variously read this Baconian image. In each case, it has been interpreted as a ship on route to the New World surpassing Aristotelian knowledge, symbolized by the Pillar of Hercules. While such scholars read this image as emblematic of a link between the new science and the New World, I read it as indicative of the widening separation between knowledge and experience—produced by both the sci-

entific revolutions and the violent religious schisms of the preceding two centuries. Durant, *A Brief History,* 318–20; Bauer, *Cultural Geography,* 1–30; Parrish, *American Curiosity,* 264.

106. In his reading of Locke's philosophy of education, Jay Fliegelman makes a similar point in a secular context of the Enlightenment's emphasis of education as a process of rational self-sufficiency. The paramount obligation to educate the minds of children "was even more urgent if, as Locke's theory of mind suggested, our ideas were 'unreal representations of unknowable objects' and we were adrift in a world of appearances. For in such a world the danger of mistaking or being manipulated into mistaking a false appearance or a projected wishfulness for a certain reality was ever present" (*Prodigals and Pilgrims* 15).

107. Like Joseph Bellamy, many of Edwards's students inherited his concern with language's inability to articulate distinct and clear ideas. In *True Religion Delineated,* for which Edwards wrote the introduction, Bellamy repeatedly warned, "Using words without determinate Ideas is one principal thing which bewilders the World about Matters of Religion" (352–53).

108. Later, Watts writes, "Then children need not have such a long train of theological phrases and hard sentences imposed on their memories, while by reason of their infancy they understand very little more of them than a parrot, and talk them over almost by mechanism" (20–21). He then asks later, "How many persons are there who have been trained up from their infancy by religious parents in the knowledge of that accurate composition the *Assembly Catechism,* and could repeat it from end to end when they were very young; but they pronounced it for the most part like so much Greek or Hebrew?" (*Catechisms* 33).

109. "In this peculiarity mystical states are more like states of feeling than like states of intellect. No one can make clear to another who has never had a certain feeling, in what the quality of worth of it consists. One must have musical ears to know the value of a symphony; one must have been in love one's self to understand a lover's state of mind" (*Varieties* 302).

110. Edwards, "Some Thoughts," 388. For examples of modes of eighteenth-century inculcations, consider the 1725 edition of *The New England Primer,* which offered the following couplets for the alphabetic letters K, R, and U, respectively: "King Charles the Good, No Man of Blood"; "Rachel doth mourn for her first-born"; "Uriah's beauteous wife made David seek his life." An 1819 edition altered these examples to the following: "'Tis youth's delight to fly their kite"; "The rose in bloom sheds sweet perfume"; and "Urns hold, we see coffee and tea." This change might as easily be explained by a shift from abstract, learned knowledge to knowledge that reflected a child's experience. For more on *The New England Primer,* see Ford, *The New England Primer.*

111. By insisting on experience over education, Edwards echoed the broader currents of the new "heart-centered" revivals spreading throughout New England and the Middle Colonies in the 1740s. In its extreme, the young were not

the only ones imperiled, but at least they only imperiled themselves. Unsaved ministers imperiled their congregations. In a controversial sermon circulated in Boston and Philadelphia, Gilbert Tennent impugned unconverted ministers as "dead dogs that can't bark." "Is a blind Man fit to be a Guide in a very dangerous Way?" he asked. "Is a dead Man fit to bring others to Life?" Quoted in Chauncy, *Seasonable Thoughts,* 48.

112. It is worth pointing out that Edwards's legacy was not necessarily one he would have approved. As a New Light, Edwards sought a return to the covenant of his forebears and repeatedly denounced lay ministry, yet his theology sometimes had the reverse effect, diminishing the ministerial hegemony enjoyed by the orthodox Old and New Lights, whether Baptist or Presbyterian, Congregational or Anglican, Wesleyan or Calvinist Methodist. In invoking "immediate experience" or "spiritual sight," Edwards did not mean that they were the only requirements for ministry, but he lost control over how the reading public would interpret his work, particularly his best-selling, widely circulated "Sinners in the Hands of an Angry God." Despite his repeated rejection of lay exhorting, his work inspired many among the socially disenfranchised to claim ministerial authority for themselves. By promoting experience over both formal education and book knowledge, he unintentionally further eroded the clear distinctions between clerics and the laity. His articulation of immediate evidence anticipated the preaching and ministries of women like the radical Quaker-sect leader Jemima Wilkinson and the Shaker founder Ann Lee, who struggled against the pervasive social and religious restrictions placed on their gender. Such logic became a spiritual source and defense for a radical revoicing in the ranks of the laity. Among New Light "Separates"—the name taken by radical New Light sects splintering from their erstwhile orthodox Baptist and Congregational folds—women and men congregants, regenerate and unregenerate alike, began as early as the 1740s openly to challenge their ministers' scriptural interpretations and theological authority. Some, like Bathsheba Kingsley, whose outspoken ministry during the revivals invited censure from a panel that included Edwards, further cleaved congregations already separated from more traditional ministries.

113. Brown, *Augustine of Hippo,* 262.

114. These concerns coming to the fore in the eighteenth century have remained at the core of Christian education and homiletic instruction because evangelicals have perceived the gulf between "notional" knowledge and experience to have widened. The modern-day hell house attempts to update and answer questions posed by eighteenth-century ministers: how to convey the meaning of "everlasting" to a generation accustomed to instant gratification, to children who have not known the excruciating pace of an hour lengthened by pangs of hunger, cold, and sickness. As hell-house promoters argue, those who have no experience with chronic pain, the despair of shame, or the anxiety of unrelieved guilt

cannot comprehend the pain, misery, and fear of a place they have never seen. What could biblical descriptors such as "the worms die not" or "a great gnashing of teeth" add to the dread of those who had not witnessed the necrosis of the dying, the decay of a corpse, or been exposed to the howls of the insane? Protestant pedagogy has thus sought to personalize the afterlife with the sensible impressions conveyed through a new kind of homiletic realism, without which, as we will see in the remaining chapters, they had little hope of reforming generations believed to be increasingly caught up in a science-based ontology and a strictly sense-based, material epistemology.

115. Edwards, "Sinners in the Hands of an Angry God," 350.

116. Lemay, "Rhetorical Strategies," 187. For a good account of Edwards's use of rhetorical catalogs, see Cady, "The Artistry of Jonathan Edwards."

117. Edwards, "Distinguishing Marks," 246–47.

118. As the theological debates of the First Great Awakening rose to a fever pitch in the late 1730s and early 1740s, Britain was inundated by ministerial pronouncements and arguments for and against piety, for and against enthusiasm. Like Edwards's *A Faithful Narrative,* many of the books, pamphlets, and letters circulating in these years in the heated debates between Old and New Lights were either first published or simultaneously published in England, many facilitated in a transatlantic partnership formed between Benjamin Colman at Brattle Street Church in Boston and Isaac Watts in London. Scores of tracts were generated in this period to explain, account for, discredit, and defend localized revivals that would become the First Great Awakening. Since the debates often focused on charges against and denials of what Chauncy called the emotional "contagion" produced by religious rhetoric and the social dangers of exhorters and preachers to foment unrest with their fiery orations, it is little wonder Burke found in contemporary sermons—filled with metaphors, colloquial phrases, and word images calculated to excite auditors' passions—the most salient example of the impact that visually oriented language had on the uneducated or colonial "rustics." For a useful study tracing the epistemological continuity of revivalism and Scottish Common Sense philosophy, particularly in relation to the rhetoric of affections and the doctrine of the passions, see Rivers, *Reason, Grace, and Sentiment.*

119. Burke, *A Philosophical Enquiry,* 56; hereafter cited in text as *Enquiry.* George Whitefield was the most famous preacher in Burke's time, the most referenced in the eighteenth century. Burke's friend Henry Fielding made Whitefield the butt of a running joke about the "madness" of evangelicalism in his 1754 novel *The History of Tom Jones.* For a full discussion of Whitefield in this novel and in relation to Burke and others, see Fredson Bowers's running commentary on Fielding's satire of Whitefield throughout the footnotes of *Tom Jones.*

120. Brown, *Augustine of Hippo,* 263.

121. This new homiletic tradition of realism was not without its risks or its

detractors. For one thing, once supercharged by fear, emotions could be difficult to control. While both Edwards and Burke acknowledged that affecting the
passions energized the imagination, helping auditors and readers to personalize homiletic scripts as templates of suffering and redemption, they also allowed
that fear could overstimulate the imagination, overwhelming individuals' capacity to process and thus personalize the sermon narrative. In his various illustrations of how vivid language could both obscure the senses and yet evoke physical sensation "more strongly" than "the things they represent," Burke suggested
that while word images could become the mark of experience registered as evidence by physical response in the body, the body's reaction could itself stimulate
responses in surrounding auditors. Unwritten sermons that had not been worked
out through the conventionally preinscribed heuristic designs were considered
particularly vulnerable to error and heresy, and blasphemous for the tacit assumption that ministers were, if not endued with the Spirit as the Apostles and
disciples had been on the day of Pentecost, guilty of encouraging the impression
that they were conduits for the divine inspiration or revelation, the possibility
that Edwards had painstakingly refuted.

Because many believed with Burke that visual language circumvented the
normative sequence of the faculty psychology, subordinating reason to passion
or bypassing the rational faculty altogether and allowing the imagination free
play, revival critics assumed that it inclined individuals to extremes of enthusiasm. This was precisely where those like Chauncy found traction to undermine
Edwards's theory of how the Spirit works within Locke's epistemological model.
According to the rational theology propounded by Chauncy's Old Light cohorts,
it made them susceptible to false spiritual impressions. Edwards acknowledged
the possibility but not the certainty.

Burke's notion that religious rhetoric is political at its roots, that renegade
preachers use language to produce social upheaval, confirms a long-standing
suspicion that Protestantism would undermine social hierarchies. Within the
ranks of the lower classes, Burke and other rationalists saw the danger of the en-
thusiastic preacher as an Old Testament prophet sowing the wind to reap a whirl-
wind of social disorder and chaos. For how words could overwhelm the faculty
senses, Burke bids his reader to imagine any picture of hell's demons and compare the sensation it evokes with that evoked by Milton's description of Satan in
book I of *Paradise Lost,* which, he insists, is more conducive of sensation, for the
"mind is hurried out of itself," marshalling a "croud of great and confused images; which affect because they are crouded and confused" (*Enquiry* 57). In a final sentence, Burke overturns Locke's conclusion that experiences drawn from
our senses are the most conducive to the kind of sensation that creates a settled
standard by which individuals can measure new knowledge. "In reality," Burke
concludes, "a great clearness helps but little towards affecting the passions"
(*Enquiry* 56). Burke's description of how the "contagion" of passion evoked by

the fanatic preachers spreads from one auditor to another is the charge that the Old Light followers of Charles Chauncy were leveling against Whitefield, Edwards, Gilbert Tennent, and a host of young firebrands igniting revivals across New England, Philadelphia, and the Mid-Atlantic colonies in the decade before Burke wrote his treatise.

122. As William James explained this same effect, "It is as if there were in the human consciousness a *sense of reality* . . . more deep and more general than any of the special and particular 'senses' by which the current psychology supposes existent realities to be originally revealed. If this were so, we might suppose the senses to waken our attitudes and conduct as they so habitually do, by first exciting this sense of reality; but anything else, any idea, for example, that might similarly excite it, would have the same prerogative of appearing real which objects of sense normally possess" (*Varieties* 55).

123. Attempting to explain how spiritual reality can be experiential while lacking a clear connection to the senses, James compares the sense impression to magnetism: "It is as if a bar of iron," he writes, "without touch or sight, with no representative faculty whatever, might nevertheless be strongly endowed with an inner capacity for magnetic feeling; and as if, through the various arousals of its magnetism by magnets coming and going in its neighborhood, it might be consciously determined to different attitudes and tendencies. Such a bar of iron could never give you an outward description of the agencies that had the power of stirring it so strongly; yet of their presence, and of their significance for its life, it would be intensely aware through every fibre of its being" (*Varieties* 53).

124. The historian David Zaret usefully explains how popular religion in the seventeenth century helped to cultivate "the critical rational habits" that comprised the emergent bourgeois public sphere. Echoing the focus seventeenth-century sermons put on communal duty and discipline, the Protestant gathering also "legitimated the reasonableness of public opinion as a forum and arbiter for criticism and debate." Zaret, "Religion, Science, and Printing," 221, 223.

125. Many New Lights and Methodists taught that the Spirit troubled the sinner for a brief period. If he or she failed to make the most of what many referred to as the "day of grace," the Spirit might depart, leaving them unredeemed forever. For illustrations of the "day of grace" in Presbyterian, Congregational, and Methodist sermons, see Williams, *Barton Stone,* 22, 23n21.

126. In *Varieties of Religious Experience,* William James, following E. D. Starbuck's *The Psychology of Religion,* calls the gradual, lifelong conversion process the "volitional" type and the evangelical sudden heart change the "self-surrender" type. James writes, "In the volitional type the regenerative change is usually gradual, and consists in the building up, piece by piece, of a new set of moral and spiritual habits" (170). Speaking to the pervasive impact of "self-surrender" on all Protestant denominations, James writes, "One may say that

the whole development of Christianity in inwardness has consisted in little more than the greater and greater emphasis attached to this crisis of self-surrender" (173). James extends this logic to the radical difference in psychology between revival (self-surrender) conversion and "volitional" conversion (186).

127. Several scholars over the last forty years have followed Perry Miller's lead in downplaying Edwards's relationship to the rhetoric of fear that Miller identifies in the works of Foxcroft, Cooper, Prince, and others. Yet many of Edwards's sermons reflect the practice of his sensational theory, including such titles as "When the Wicked Shall Gave Filled Up the Measure of Their Sin," "Wrath Will Come Upon Them to the Uttermost," "The Folly of Looking Back in Fleeing Out of Sodom," "The Future Punishment of the Wicked Unavoidable and Intolerable," and "The Eternity of Hell Torments."

128. While not a doctrinal shift of much magnitude, the First Great Awakening was certainly a watershed in terms of religious practice. The indelible mark it made on the sermon was what scholars like Harry S. Stout have identified as a new mode of persuasion, one that would ultimately appeal less to the head than to the heart. Yet in comparison with the popular religious revivals gathered under the rubric of the Second Great Awakening, the first was still a bookish affair, a theological and intramural dialogue among an elite body of seminary-trained clergy.

129. Edwards, "Sinners in the Hands of an Angry God," 351.

130. Mather, *Pray for the Rising Generation,* 22.

131. Ibid., 22.

132. Mather, *An Earnest Exhortation,* 35.

133. In contrast to the Rapture-as-reunion motif popularized by the nineteenth-century sermon (addressed in the next chapter), the depiction of Judgment as an eternal severing of families produced an anxiety that, in the spiritual emotionalism of revivals, left individuals prostrate in the pews and writhing in the aisles.

134. Edwards, *Religious Affections,* 147.

135. Bradley, *A Sketch,* 6–10.

136. Clark, *Sinners in the Hands of an Angry God,* 17.

137. Gladden, *Recollections,* 59.

138. Wood, *Ideal Suggestion,* 118.

139. Abbott, *Young Christian,* 228; hereafter cited in text as *Young Christian.*

140. For the mutually constitutive influence of religious and political autonomy in the decades after the Revolution, see Sellers, *The Market Revolution,* 25–30; for an analysis of the correspondences between revivalism and democratic politics, see Hatch, *The Democratization of American Christianity,* 5–45; Howe, "The Market Revolution"; and Noll, *America's God,* esp. 130–200.

Chapter Two

1. Deerfield, about seventeen miles up river from Northampton and the pulpit of Solomon Stoddard, suffered a number of attacks after hostilities began in 1689, when, through a standing alliance with Holland, King William took the Austrian side in the war that King Louis XIV of France declared on Hapsburg Austria (known in the American colonies as "King William's War"). This act marked the beginning of the four principle struggles between France and England for control of territories in North America. The first attack on Deerfield came on September 15, 1694, four years after Schenectady had been burned by French and Indian raids and after Deerfield erected a palisade around their city. The initial episode of war ended in a truce between William and Louis, only to be resumed at William's death when France again took the side of the dethroned James II, and the newly crowned Anne declared war against France on May 4, 1702. For a full analysis of this account, see Demos, *The Unredeemed Captive.*

2. Isaac Watts usefully quotes the Reverend Matthew Henry's description of the Protestant catechism: "The main principles of Christianity which lie scattered in the Scripture are collected and brought together, and by this means they are set in a much easier view before the minds of men. Our Catechisms and Confessions of Faith pick up from the several parts of Holy Writ those passages which . . . contain the foundations and main pillars upon which Christianity is built, which we are concerned rightly to understand, and firmly to believe in the first place, and then to go on to perfection." *Catechisms,* 13.

3. Williams, *Redeemed Captive,* 35. Learning the *Assembly's Catechism* was no easy task; they were learned by heart, and the *Shorter Catechism* was composed of between 107 and 127 scriptural and doctrinal questions and answers. For a contemporary critique of this method, see Isaac Watts, *Catechisms.* For an alternative construction of the Deerfield "massacre" and captivity, see Williams, "Narrative of the Captivity of Stephen Williams."

4. Williams, *Redeemed Captive,* 36.

5. When the Bishops' Exclusion Act passed the House of Lords on February 5, 1642, Parliament became free to develop a program of religious pedagogy. On July 1, 1643, 120 of the most learned divines from Great Britain met to devise and draft a catechism. While John Cotton, Thomas Hooker, and John Davenport were all invited from the colonies, they did not attend. Not until November 25, 1647, did the committee manage to draft and Parliament approve the text of the *Shorter Catechism,* which appeared September 22, 1648, under the title *The Grounds and Principles of Religion, Contained in a Shorter Catechism (According to the Advice of the Assembly of Divines Sitting at Westminster).* For the history of *The New England Primer* and its relation to *The Westminster Confession* and the *Shorter* and *Larger Catechism,* see Ford, *The New England Primer.*

6. Williams, *Redeemed Captive,* 36.

7. Tellingly, Williams records hearing a Jesuit priest complain that during mass neither the Indian captors nor the French Jesuits could make the adult Christians "fall down on their knees to pray there, but no sooner are they returned to their wigwams, but they fall down on their knees to prayer" (*Redeemed Captive*, 39). Williams dramatically summarized the disproportionate spiritual danger suffered by children and their elders in the language of the priest's conclusion: "They could do nothing with the grown persons there; and they hinder the children's complying. Whereupon, the Jesuits counseled the Macquas to sell all the grown persons . . . a stratagem to seduce the poor children" (*Redeemed Captive*, 39). In contrast to the steadfastness of experienced Christians, the children (including, for a time, Williams's young son Samuel) converted to Catholicism.

8. Williams, *Redeemed Captive*, 30. For a study on the changing perception of children's moral capacity and the necessary means for either correcting or augmenting moral development among different Protestant groups, see Greven, *The Protestant Temperament*.

9. Mather, *Magnalia Christi Americana,* 179. Mather specifically mentions "a lesser and a larger by Mr. Norton, a lesser and a larger by Mr. Richard Mather, several by Mr. Cotton, one by Mr. Davenport and sundry others."

10. John Craig's abridged "A Form of Examination before the Communion" (1591) also enjoyed popularity in the New World colonies.

11. John Calvin had himself provided a catechism template in his "The Manner to Examine Children," affixed to his own catechism. Undoubtedly, Craig, Perkins, and others were influenced by this heuristic (see Law's introduction to Craig's *A Shorte Summe of the Whole Catechisme*). In his introduction, Craig specifically states that he has designed the catechism for children *and* the poorly educated: "I have studied to my power, to be plaine, simple, shorte, and profitabill, not luking to . . . the desire and satisffaction of the learned, as to the Instruction and helpe for the Ignorant. . . . I have broght the question and the answere to as fewe words, as goodly I could, and that for the ease of children and commoune people, who can not understande, nor gather the substance of a long question, or answer confirmed with reasons" [text does not denote page numbers].

12. Livermore, *Origin, History and Character,* 20. According to Samuel Hopkins, Jonathan Edwards "catechized the children in publick every Sabbath in summer" (*Life and Character,* 49).

13. Daniel Clark included this promise in his 1826 revision of Edwards's "Sinners in the Hands of an Angry God"—his satisfaction, no doubt, increased by his appropriation of Edwards's authority. Clark, *Sinners in the Hands of an Angry God,* 17–18; original emphasis. John Trumbull's response to reading Dent's *The Plaine Man's Path-way* speaks to spiritual text's perceived living-word authority—theologically accorded only to holy writ. A member of Thomas Shep-

ard's congregation, Trumbull was certain that Dent's text served as a "witness against" him. See Shepard, *Thomas Shepard's Confessions,* 108–9.

14. Less than twenty years after Eunice Williams's kidnapping, ministers had begun to question the efficacy of the *Westminster Confession* and the *Assembly's Catechism.* In his *Catechisms,* Isaac Watts, for instance, remonstrates against the use of this catechism for children Eunice Williams's age, illustrating in the process how much the perception of children's moral and mental capacity had changed between the catechism's mid-seventeenth-century composition and 1730. Further demonstrating how perceptions of children had changed in the post-Lockean world, Watts argues for building the understanding of children with widely ranging mental capacities: "With what care I have endeavor'd to select the most easy and necessary parts of our religion in order to propose them to the memory of children according to their ages" (viii).

In his study of Mary Rowlandson, Mitchell Breitwieser identifies an analogous gap between Puritan narrative conventions and New World experience of trauma and loss (*American Puritanism,* esp. 131–94). The Puritan captivity narrative and the particularly American frontier experience that it sought to generically encapsulate highlights the very split between matter and spirit, the personal and the universal, that the narrative traditions traced in this chapter would seek to address.

15. A perusal of the earliest catechisms and prayers of the English Reformation reveals how slow, if ever fully realized in practice, this process of stripping was. The primer issued under Henry VIII's watchful eye included a number of Catholic texts in its prayer lineup: "The Salutation of the angel to the blessed virgin Mary," "The Apostles' Creed," "Grace before and after dinner," "Matins," "The Collects," and the like. Several prayers are addressed to Jesus (while Protestants historically pray to God, in the name of Jesus), and several prayers include ascriptions and addresses to various saints and the Virgin Mary. The *Protestant Primer* of 1539—directly preceding (and legally supplanted by) the one issued by Henry VIII—includes the following prayer, "Address to the Virgin Mary": "O glorious mother of God, O perpetual Virgin Mary, which did bear the Lord of all lords, and alone of all other didst give suck unto the King of angels, we beseech thee of they pity to have us in remembrance, and to make intercession for us unto Christ, that we being supported by his help may come unto the kingdom of Heaven" (quoted in Livermore, *Origin, History and Character,* 70–71). In 1548, two years after Henry VIII's primer, the *Cranmer Catechism* largely jettisons any reference to saints or Mary, or to any ritual, ordination, or sacrament not currently practice in the Anglican Church.

16. In his *Memoir of William Carey,* "the father of the modern mission, Eustace Carey, William Carey's nephew, recalls how many, like the Anglican reverend Ryland often claimed that 'Brainerd's life ranked with him next to his Bible.' In his esteem of this eminent saint and prince of missionaries [Brainerd],

Mr. Carey was not behind him" (89). Missionary journals are filled with testimonials of having read *The Life of David Brainerd* numerous times. According to Joseph Conforti, many referred to it as the "second Bible," inferring they studied the text exegetically, as Protestants did their Bible; see Conforti, "Jonathan Edwards's Most Popular Work," and "David Brainerd."

17. In part, the Protestant emphasis on literacy and education added to ministers' difficulty in monitoring what congregants read or regulating scriptural interpretation. Yet as early as 1647, the General Court of the Massachusetts Bay Colony insisted on general literacy:

> It being one cheife [point] of y^t ould deluder, Satan, to keepe men from the knowledge of ye Scriptures, as in former times by keeping [them] in an unknown tongue. . . . It is therefore ordred, [that] every township in this jurisdiction . . . shall then forwth appoing one wth in their towne to teach all . . . children as shall resort to him to write & reade. (Shurtleff, *Records,* 203)

For the best discussion of religious atomism after the First Great Awakening, see Hatch, *The Democratization of Christianity,* 3–46, and "Millennialism and Popular Religion"; Block, *Visionary Republic;* and Moore, *Religious Outsiders,* 3–24.

18. Foxcroft, *Lessons of Caution,* i.

19. See Stout, *The New England Soul,* esp. 6–40.

20. For an interesting account of how religious promoters shaped and marketed the First Great Awakening as a public event through the texts they compiled, see Lambert, *Inventing the "Great Awakening."*

21. In his emphasis on itinerancy and suffering, Whitefield exemplifies that language: "Every thing I meet with," Whitefield writes, "seems to carry this voice with it,—'Go thou and preach the gospel; be a pilgrim on earth; have no party or certain dwelling-place.' My heart echoes back, Lord Jesus, help me to do or suffer thy will. When thou seest me in danger of nestling,—in pity—in tender pity,—put a *thorn* in my nest, to prevent me from it." In Philip, *Life and Times,* 366.

22. Engelsing, *Analphabetentum und Lekture;* Hall, "Uses of Literacy," 20ff. For a counter to Engelsing's argument that *extensive* reading leads to greater passivity, see Davidson, *Revolution and the Word,* 69–79.

23. For the "evolution of . . . Western reading practices from antiquity to the Renaissance," see in particular Stock, *After Augustine* (quote is from cover).

24. On the Protestant conception of the Bible as the "living word," see Knott, *The Sword of the Spirit,* esp. 13–41.

25. See Altick, *The English Common Reader,* 99–102; and Nord, "Evangelical Origins."

26. Calvin, *Institutes of the Christian Religion,* 61–62.

27. Wesley, *The Christian's Pattern,* ix; hereafter cited in text as *Christian's*

Pattern. Summarizing this tradition, William James noted that the mark of "born-again" conversions for American Christians was the capacity of holy writ to convey personalized, "overpowering impressions of the meaning of suddenly presented scripture texts" (*Varieties* 194).

28. Even today, popular evangelical leaders and educators such as Bill Gothard teach their followers to invoke the word against the danger of evil. Through his popular Basic Youth in Conflict program, for instance, Gothard, a moderate evangelical minister, encourages his hundreds of thousands of working- and middle-class followers to memorize the entire sixth chapter of the book of Romans. When confronted with temptation, demonic or material, he instructs them to recite the chapter aloud until the temptation abates, beginning with "What shall I say? Shall I continue in sin? God forbid," in the belief that evil—within or without—cannot dwell in the presence of such a prayer-charm.

29. We can trace such use of the scripture as *remedia* directly back to performative medieval texts. From the perception among both clerics and laymen and women in the Middle Ages that the Lord's Prayer (the *Paternoster*) operated as a *remedia, remedia* allegories within religious cycle plays emerged. In their sanction and patronage of such performances, clergy in the late Middle Ages reinforced the basic principles of homiletic reading practices, steeping them in the understanding of a hermeneutic that both reaffirmed the sanctity of the scriptures and armed ordinary individuals with a powerful weapon—a incantation charm—in their own moral defense. As Robert Potter suggests in his seminal study of medieval morality plays, the Paternoster had by the late Middle Ages become a complex homiletic engagement with the theology of the living word. Reciting the Lord's Prayer did not merely ward off temptation or evil, but incorporated a series of charms against the worst of all spiritual threats, the seven deadly sins. The supplicant was encouraged to link the prayer's seven petitions to each of the deadly sins: for example, the first, "hallowed by thy name," with pride; the second, "thy Kingdom come," with envy; the third, "thy will be done," the fourth, "give us our daily bread," with sloth; the fifth, "forgive us as we forgive others," with avarice; the sixth, "lead us not into temptation," with gluttony; and the seventh, "deliver us from evil," with lechery (Potter, *The English Morality Play*).

30. Smith, *The Life, Conversion, Preaching,* 90.

31. Methodists and Baptists drew from the laboring classes as well as the educated and professional classes. These denominations used revival-style, extempore preaching in the squares and fields to draw people into modest churches and Sunday schools. Presbyterians and Congregationalists drew more from educated, property-owning classes. The exclusivity of Calvinist theology, seminarian trained clergy, and pew rentals largely shaped the demography of Presbyterian and Congregational churches. The free-church movement propounded by religious philanthropists such as the Presbyterians Lewis and Arthur Tappan in-

augurated a trend to provide a more democratized space for worship in these denominations.

32. I will briefly return to the remarkable African American exhorters, Elaw and Lee. Abbott, *Experience and Gospel Labours*, 17.

33. Richard Whytford translated the work for Protestants as early as 1556, though its early association with Catholicism rendered it less popular in the first century after the English Reformation. For representative examples, see Luke Milbourne, *The Christian Pattern Paraphras'ed*. An English Presbyterian clergyman, Milbourne translated his edition into verse. After 1803, it was often translated with more fidelity to the Latin; see Payne, *Of the Imitation of Christ;* Challoner, *The Imitation of Christ*. It also circulated under descriptive titles: see Stanhope, *Soliloquy of the Soul,* reprinted as *The Follower of Christ* (Cincinnati: Vahreite-Freun, 1860).

34. Van Engen, introd. to *Devotio Moderna*, 25.

35. One of the most significant cultural developments in Christian practice in the seventeenth century was the broad inward turn in both Catholicism and Protestantism toward a kind of "sacred heart," the idea that each soul is a fortress for the indwelling Savior. It was this development that helped bridge the intensely devotional cultures of Protestants and Catholics, through the impact of the *Devotio Moderna*. For a good discussion of the "sacred heart," see Hambrick-Stowe, *The Practice of Piety*.

36. For an analysis of contemporary modes of reading, see Jameson, "Reification and Utopia."

37. The *Oxford English Dictionary* (2nd ed. [Oxford: Clarendon, 1989]) quotes the Lockean John Norris's homiletic manual, *A Treatise Concerning Christian Prudence; or, the Principles of Practical Wisdom, Fitted to the Use of Human Life, and Design'd for the Better Regulation of It* (1710): "To Build up men in Faith and Holiness of Life, that which we properly mean by Edification."

38. One of the best examples of how the living word was understood is in the act of bibliomancy, when readers seeks divine inspiration by opening the Bible to a seemingly random passage in the belief that what they lay their finger on is meant to guide them. In *Robinson Crusoe,* Daniel Defoe—born and raised in the Puritan tradition—depicts Crusoe in the act of bibliomancy: "I daily read the Word of God, and apply'd all the Comforts of it to my present State: One Morning begin very sad, I open'd the Bible upon these Words, *I will never, never leave thee, nor forsake thee;* immediately it occurr'd, That these Words were to me, Why else should they be directed in such a Manner, just at the Moment when I was mourning over my Condition, as one forsaken of God and Man?" (105).

39. See Frei, *The Eclipse of Biblical Narrative;* and Schneidau, *Sacred Discontent*.

40. In Thomas Graves Law's edition, in Craig's introduction, which does not denote page numbers; emphasis added.

41. See Knott, *The Sword of the Spirit,* 13–41. For an excellent study of the relation between this concept and Christian allegory, see Goldman, "Living Words."

42. Abbott, *The Corner Stone,* 14.

43. *OED.*

44. Mather, *Pray for the Rising Generation,* 22; Edwards, *Life,* 163; Pearse, *The Great Concern,* 31; Edwards, "Sinners in the Hands of an Angry God," 409.

45. In much the same way, Spenser's Red Cross Knight must fight Error, visit the House of Holiness, brave the cavern of Despair, and so forth, before finally coming to the House of Holiness. But Spenser's poetic allegory, with its archaic language and suspicious ambiguity and polysemy, could hardly serve as an effective homiletic template, let alone a teaching text for the young.

46. Miedema, "Following in the Footsteps of Christ."

47. On generic and homiletic connections between *Piers Plowman* and *The Pilgrim's Progress,* see Barbara A. Johnson's comparative study, *Reading* Piers Plowman *and* The Pilgrim's Progress.

48. See especially Bryan, *Looking Inward.*

49. *The Book of Margery Kempe,* 109. Significantly, Kempe did not write her autobiography, but narrated it to a scribe or scribes.

50. Much as they might undertake three-step programs of spiritual reform, climb the rungs on the ladder of perfection, or imagine themselves on the pilgrimages of human life, they did not generally turn those journeys into written narratives for others to read (unless, of course, they had a vision from God and could find a clerical sponsor).

51. Webster, "Writing to Redundancy."

52. It was also the place, as Max Weber taught us, where the sacred and the secular meanings of "interest" and "value" began to collapse together.

53. For useful studies on the confession narrative, see Caldwell, *The Puritan Conversion Narrative;* Cohen, *God's Caress;* and Morgan, *Visible Saints.* For a good history and analysis of colonial American deathbed testimonies, see Rivett, "Tokenography."

54. Nineteenth-century foreign mission societies, for instance, found Bunyan's protagonist even in Japanese culture. They discerned in the martial, wayfaring Samurai warrior, a type which, like the Christian knight whom he resembled, journeyed forth on a quest for self-enlightenment, assisting the afflicted whither his faith directed him. Missionaries translated Bunyan's popular allegory into Japanese, believing that homiletic identification must first particularize the universal—in this case, the Samurai as the pilgrim Christian—before it

can transcend the specificity of culture, time, and place. See Brown, *The Word in the World*, 213-42.

55. Bercovitch, *Puritan Origins*, 13.

56. David Brainerd edited and wrote a preface for an edition of Shepard's journals, titled *Mediations and Spiritual Experiences of Mr. Thomas Shepard*.

57. McGiffert, *God's Plot*, 57.

58. While Shepard's autobiography was not printed until the Nehemiah Adams edition (*The Autobiography of Thomas Shepard, the Celebrated Minister of Cambridge, New England*), it did not share the fate of Anne Bradstreet's meagerly circulated works or Edward Taylor's poetry, neither printed nor much circulated until 1937. Shepard, a revered architect of the "New England Way" in his own day and well after, was one of the most frequently cited Bay Colony theologians in the seventeenth and eighteenth centuries.

59. Edwards, "True Christian's Life," 433; emphasis added.

60. Bercovitch, *Puritan Origins*.

61. Edwards, *Images of Divine Things*, 16.

62. Such tales are epitomized by the "God's Revenge" or "Looking Glass" tales of Mason L. ("Parson") Weems and the "morality fiction" of George Lippard.

63. Similarly, the African American John Marrant—who was struck senseless by the Spirit while trying to play a boyish prank on George Whitefield, described as a "crazy man . . . hallooing" before a revival crowd—saw belatedly that the "Lord spoke" to him as he had to Lot in the form of "removes" from city to city. When he failed to make the connection between physical journey and spiritual pilgrimage, God cast him out into the "desert," the wilderness of Indian territory, without food or shelter, with nothing but "a small pocket Bible and one of Dr. Watts's hymnals," to which he repeatedly turned for devotion and inspiration. Though "the Lord tried [his] faith sharply," he preserved him like Daniel from "wild beasts" until he was finally taken captive and, after being nearly "put to death" by the Cherokee, delivered home by his captors. Marrant, *Narrative*, 15.

64. Edwards, "True Christian's Life," 439.

65. Franklin, *The Autobiography and Other Writings*, 9-11.

66. At the same time, middle-class Americans would come to think of the pilgrimage in increasingly metaphorical—and even increasingly secular—terms, imagining life as a journey fraught with significant moral struggles that lead to a spiritual fulfillment achieved through vigilant self-scrutiny and the ability to frame that life within preinscribed templates of the Christian's pattern.

67. Carey, *Carey's Library*, 19.

68. Jarena Lee, Elaw's elder contemporary and sometime preaching companion, recalled in her autobiography how Bishop Richard Allen, the black Meth-

odist minister who founded the African Methodist Episcopal Church in Philadelphia in 1819, had looked askance at her when she informed him that she had
been called to preach. But Lee reasoned, "If a man may preach, because the Saviour died for him, why not the woman? seeing he died for her also. Is he not a
whole Saviour, instead of a half one? as those who hold it wrong for a woman to
preach would seem to make it appear"; "Life and Religious Experience of Jarena Lee," 36.

69. Elaw, *Memoirs of the Life,* 87; hereafter cited in text as *Memoirs.*

70. Wesley noted just a few years before his death the pervasiveness with
which the sudden heart-change had come to mark conversions: "In London
alone, I found 652 members of our society who were exceeding clear in their experience, and of whose testimony I could see no reason to doubt. . . . And every
one of these (without a single exception) has declared, that his deliverance from
sin was *instantaneous;* that the change was wrought in a moment" (Tyerman,
Life and Times, 462; original emphasis).

71. See especially Andrews, *To Tell a Free Story,* and Moses, *Black Messiahs
and Uncle Toms,* 30–48.

72. In an epitaph worthy of one who modeled the union of the Pauline soldier and the traveling itinerant, the Reverend John Newland Maffitt eulogized
Philip Embury—one of the founders of American Methodism—at the rededica-
tion of his gravesite in 1832 (fifty-seven years after his death): "Here fell a harnessed warrior of the cross." The funeral oration and recommitment ceremony is
quoted in Wakeley, *Lost Chapters Recovered,* 137.

73. Andrews, *Sisters of the Spirit,* 134.

74. Benjamin Keach's most widely read works were *Sion in Distress; or, the
Groans of the Protestant Church; The Progress of Sin;* and the best-selling *War
with the Devil; or, the Young Man's Conflict with the Powers of Darkness*—a Socratic dialogue that anticipates C. S. Lewis's *Screwtape Letters.*

75. O'Neall, *Biographical Sketches,* vol. 1, 302.

76. Livermore, *Origin, History and Character,* 10.

77. Ibid., 11.

78. Jackson, *Works of John Wesley,* vol. 3, 294; vol. 8, 328.

79. Wesley, "An Extract," 294.

80. Bond, *Memoir of the Rev. Pliny Fisk,* 259. Fisk writes to a friend, "Brainerd desired to be 'a flame of fire' in the service of God? How should such a wish
from such a Saint shame us, who fall so far behind him!" (93). In *The Memoir of
William Carey,* Carey's nephew Eustace recalled how Brainerd—"this eminent
saint and prince of missionaries"—provided a model of conduct; his life story's
"intrinsic worth, as offering a sublime and experimental display of religious affections, through a scene of arduous labor and patient suffering, rendered it the
devotional guide of multitudes" (89). In *A Memoir of the Rev. Henry Martyn*—
a book in which John Sargent gathered excerpts from Henry Martyn's journals—

Martyn records that "Soon after . . . perusing the life of David Brainerd, who preached with apostolical zeal and success to the North American Indians, and who furnished a course of self-denying labours for his Redeemer, with unspeakable joy, at the early age of thirty-two, his soul was filled with a holy emulation of that extraordinary man: and, after deep consideration and fervent prayer, he was at length fixed in a resolution to imitate his example" (30). On May 30, 1805, he records in his diary: "Read Brainerd. I feel my heart knit to this dear man, and really rejoice to think of meeting him in heaven" (104). On February 24, 1827, Martyn writes, "The rest of the morning, till dinner time, I spent not unprofitably in reading Scripture and David Brainerd, and in prayer. That dear saint of God, David Brainerd, is truly a man after my own heart. Although I cannot go half-way with him in spirituality and devotion, I cordially unite with him in such of his holy breathings as I have attained unto" (242). At Martyn's death, his editor, John Sargent, writes, "He followed the steps of Zeigenbalg in the old world, and of Brainerd in the new; and whilst he walks with them in white, for he is worthy,—he speaks by his example, to us who are still on our warfare and pilgrimages upon earth" (502).

81. The Methodist movement, begun by Whitefield and the Wesleys, had taken root in the years just before the Revolution, led by British-born bishop Francis Asbury (1745–1816), the great itinerant book peddler Robert William (1745–1775), the "weeping prophet" Philip Embury, the Irish-born Robert Strawbridge (1739?–1781), the first American-born exhorter Richard Owen, Joseph Toy, Jesse Lee, Freeborn Garrettson (1752–1827), the firebrand Billy Hibbard, and Richard Boardman.

While Methodism began as a small Calvinist community of Oxford seminarians within the Anglican Communion, it quickly became a movement seeking to administer to the poor, particularly tenant farmers and laborers attached to England's landed estates. With its transatlantic spread, its organization of followers into communities along fixed paths became an important mode of proselytizing. By 1815, the itinerant preacher and circuit horse so integral to the Wesley brothers' revolutionary ministry were all but a thing of the past in England, except in remote areas of Wales (Hatch, *The Democratization of American Christianity*). Not so in America, where the circuit connections proliferated yearly until at least 1840, serving new settlements ever receding into the West. In the wake of the success of the Methodist blueprint, other enterprising, upstart revivalist leaders such as Alexander Campbell in Pennsylvania, James O'Kelly in Virginia, Barton Stone in Kentucky, and Elias Smith in New England (all associated with the emerging reform movement focused on "primitive" Christianity) wasted little time organizing circuits and recruiting their own armies of exhorters who— largely under the banner of the "Christian Connection" after 1830—took to the pilgrim path along the young nation's expanding margins.

82. Lee, "The Life and Religious Experience of Jarena Lee," 32.

83. Barton Stone records that at the completion of his theological training and examinations in 1796, Henry Patillo, head of the Orange Presbytery, presented him and the other candidates with Bibles and gave each the solemn charge, "Go ye into all the world, and preach the gospel to every creature" (Williams, *Barton Stone,* 16). Bishop Francis Asbury, whose self-nomination as bishop shocked the aged John Wesley, was the key figure in the transatlantic migration of Methodism. Asbury—like his defecting lieutenant from Virginia, James O'Kelly— trained an army of itinerant exhorters to ride circuits from the Eastern seaboard to frontier settlements along the nation's margins. A typical admonition to one of his itinerants in 1788 underscores the impact of universalist evangelicalism on sermon form: "If possible visit from house to house . . . to speak to each in the family about their souls. . . . Sermons ought to be short and pointed in town, briefly explanatory and then to press the people to conviction, repentance, faith and holiness. . . . So shall we speak . . . by life and application in the heart, little illustration and great fervency . . . [is] the spark of life." Asbury in a letter to Ezekiel Cooper, December 24, 1788, in *Journal and Letters of Francis Asbury,* vol. 3, 66.

84. Pilgrimage masterplots absorbed even the most literal forms of journey, especially where those journeys were already associated with salvation's vanguard, such as migrating communities like the Mormons, moving westward, or Methodists, whose army of itinerant preachers sustained the initial energies of the Second Great Awakening.

85. As the historian Charles Sellers observes, "Direct access to divine grace and revelation, subordinating clerical learning to every person's reborn heart, vindicated the lowly reborn soul against hierarchy and authority, magistrates and clergy." Sellers, *The Market Revolution,* 30; see also Hatch, *The Democratization of American Christianity,* 9–16; Noll, *America's God,* 30–87.

86. Nineteenth-century spiritual autobiographies were most often written by white men and women with little formal education, or by African American exhorters, many through amanuenses—including many slave narratives whose function within the homiletic tradition of spiritual autobiography has been subordinated within larger ethnographic, literary rubrics (see Andrews, *To Tell a Free Story,* 3–30).

87. Localized versions of *The New England Primer* often celebrated the spiritual triumph of particularly pious leaders or community members by enumerating their family losses and suffering. For example, the *New England Primer* published in 1841 in Concord, New Hampshire, includes a brief encomium on Ezekiel Rogers, who, "though he had a number of children, they all died in infancy or youth" (*The Improved New-England Primer,* 12). In the first application of his sermon "The True Christian's Life a Journey" (1733; preached again in 1753), Edwards exemplified how Christians were to draw strength in the face of loss from this narrative tradition: "This doctrine may teach us moderation in

our mourning for the death of such dear friends that, while they lived, improved their lives to right purposes. If they lived a holy life, then their lives were a journey towards heaven. And why should we be immoderate in mourning, when they are got to their journey's end?" (438).

88. Andrews, *To Tell a Free Story*, 11.

89. Andrews suggests that black slave narrators and spiritual autobiographers were aware of the constitutive nature (and rhetorical value for white audiences) of the "slavery of sin" and the "sin of slavery" (*To Tell a Free Story*, 44).

90. Gronniosaw, "A Narrative," 15–16.

91. Ann Taves, *Fits, Trances, and Visions*, 22–57.

92. In "The Biblical Play," Thomas P. Hughes notes that "the Biblical drama of 'The Lord's Passion' . . . attracted the thoughtful attention of the Church on both sides of the Atlantic, and created a considerable amount of literature on the religious drama. The history of this Passion Play is well known. It was established in the year 1633, condemned and suspended by the Church in 1779, revived in 1811, and has been reverently performed every ten years since. . . . A probable result of all this has been the infusion of religious sentiment into many modern dramatic productions, the gradual revival of the religious and Biblical play" (308).

93. Hatch, *The Democratization of American Christianity*, 134.

94. Hatch's representative assessment is, of course, substantiated, if not initiated, by contemporary outside observers—usually orthodox clergymen—alarmed by the "fanaticism" of nineteenth-century camp revival meetings. Yet such axiomatic assessments perpetuate the partisan and orthodox view of religious communities whose literacy and theology preserved the cultural hegemony from which African Americans and impoverished whites had long been excluded, thus necessitating the powerful homiletic impulse of the black body-narrative tradition.

95. In a comparison between the Alcott sisters and the fictional March sisters, Frances Armstrong (in "'Here Little, and Hereafter Bliss'") argues that "Alcott's characters contradict her rewriting [of Bunyan's allegory] and ironically come closer to Bunyan" (466–67). Even so, in the next line, Armstrong misunderstands the function of homiletic identification and the Everyman tradition in her brisk dismissal of Bunyan's plot: "Certainly no one's saintly feet are followed in the story that ensues; each girl finds her own way, her own answers to problems that really beset her" (467). For a representative treatment of *Pilgrim's Progress* in *Little Women*—both in brevity and in critics' dismissal or subversive rendering—see 467–68. For instance, Armstrong reads Jo's concern for Amy, after Amy's near fatality on the frozen river, to the total exclusion of the consideration of her lost book, as "the most dangerous silent subversion of the allegory" (468). Armstrong's insistence that "Jo has to talk about what is perceived to be her real problem, anger"—rather than "the loss of her 'little book' [which] is ap-

parently not worth discussing"—seems counterintuitive to moral order (life over object value), to the novel's broader narrative of maturation and sacrifice for others, and to late-nineteenth-century Christian values in general.

96. Vincent, *The Chautauqua Movement,* 4–5, 31; hereafter cited in text as *Chautauqua.*

97. On the Sunday School Union's objection to *Little Women,* see Zehr, "The Response of Nineteenth-Century Audiences," 333.

98. Johnson, *Reading* Piers Plowman, 2–8. Michael McKeon locates the origins of the novel in romance in *The Origins of the English Novel;* see chap. 8, "Romance Transformations (11): Bunyan and the Literalization of Allegory," 295–314. Leopold Damrosch, Jr., focuses on Puritan individualism and its relationship to the origins of the novel in *God's Plot and Man's Stories;* see esp. chap. 4, "Experience and Allegory in Bunyan," 121–86. For an example of homiletic secularization, consider the initial novels of the defrocked Unitarian minister Horatio Alger, whose first novel, *Ragged Dick* (1868), encouraged Christian virtues like honesty, charity, and chastity, and encouraged Sunday school attendance. Yet the novel also pushes "luck and pluck" as a means of social advancement, as the young protagonist's story continues in the aptly titled sequel, *Fame and Fortune; or, The Progress of Richard Hunter.*

99. Alcott, *Little Women,* 109; hereafter cited in text as *Little Women.*

100. For a detailed analysis of critics' and readers' demands and expectations, see Zehr, "The Response of Nineteenth-Century Audiences," 323–28.

101. Alcott, *Journals,* 22. The similarities between the characters and stories of *Little Women* and the biography of the Alcott family are legendary in Alcott studies, and are built into the plot of the sequel, in which Jo finally finds her voice when she writes about her own family. In the earliest years of the novel, critics and readers saw Jo as Alcott's alter ego, and encouraged by advertisements that conflated Jo and Louisa May, readers visited Concord in droves to meet her and her family. Elizabeth Sewall (1835–58), the model for Beth, dies of complications after contracting scarlet fever from the neighbor child her mother nurses. Alcott based Amy on her youngest sister, Abigail May Alcott, who had artistic aspirations and whose relationship with Alcott was marked by rivalry.

102. For a sketch of Bronson Alcott's faith beliefs, see my "Alcott, Amos Bronson," entry in *The Louisa May Alcott Encyclopedia,* 11–15. The best biography of Bronson Alcott is Dahlstrand's *Amos Bronson Alcott.*

103. For the role of religion, idealism, and Lockean education principles in Bronson Alcott's pedagogical theory, see McCuskey, *Bronson Alcott, Teacher,* chaps. 4 and 5.

104. For discussions of Bronson and Louisa May Alcott's use of allegory and their relationship with *Pilgrim's Progress,* see Shepard, *Pedlar's Progress,* 36–37; Ronda, *The Transcendental Child,* chap. 2; Strickland, "A Transcendentalist Father," esp. 56–61; Bedell, *The Alcotts,* 81.

105. In a letter to Alcott about *Little Women,* a child identifies Alcott as Jo, a representative response: "We have all been reading 'Little Women,' and we liked it so much I could not help wanting to write to you. We think you are perfectly splendid; I like you better every time I read it. We were all so disappointed over your not marrying Laurie." Quoted in Zehr, "The Response of Nineteenth-Century Audiences," 324.

106. Brainerd's journals are filled with impatient thoughts for death and salvation, as when he writes, "O the burden of such a life! O death, death, my friend, hasten and deliver me from dull mortality" (*Life* 114).

107. William James assessed nineteenth-century evangelicalism broadly "as a process of struggling away from sin, rather than of striving toward righteousness" (*Varieties* 172). Yet in their appeal to middle-class readers, postbellum homiletic texts like *Little Women* increasingly reversed this trajectory, emphasizing instead how struggling away from sin is integral to striving toward righteousness.

108. For a argument assessing Alcott's *Little Women* as a realist novel, see Elaine Showalter's introduction to *Little Women,* vi–xii.

109. Mission diaries are filled with instances of missionaries *intensively* reading homiletic texts. Henry Martyn, for example, recalls numerous occasions on which he read Bunyan's *Pilgrim's Progress,* including three times in 1805, first to himself and then to others. See Sargent, *A Memoir of Rev. Henry Martyn,* 109–110, 112, 114, 216.

110. Bunyan, *The Life and Death of Mr. Badman,* 1.

111. Edwards, "True Christian's Life," 440. Edwards's and Bunyan's allusion to the paths that lead to heaven comes from Matthew 7:13–14: "Broad is the way that leads to destruction, but strait is the way and narrow is the path that leads to Life."

112. Weems, *God's Revenge against Adultery, God's Revenge against Duelling, God's Revenge against Gambling, God's Revenge against Murder,* and *The Drunkard's Looking Glass.* See also George Lippard, *The Quaker City; or, Monks of Monk-hall: A Romance of Philadelphia Life, Mystery, and Crime.* Similar to Mr. Badman's moral decline from swearing and cursing as a child, to drunkenness, cheating, spousal abuse, and the like, *The Drunkard's Looking Glass* depicted alcoholism in successive stages, including the "FOOLISH" stage, the "DEMONIAC" stage, and the "TORPID" stage. This was not Falstaffian humor, as Weems's graphic anecdote demonstrates. In the story's opening scene, Satan promises a young minister a position of authority if he would only commit one of three sins: "Violate your sister"; "Murder your father"; or "Only get drunk." Scandalized by the first two choices, the youth quickly replies, "I'll get drunk"—"seeing nothing very terrible in that." The narrative informs the reader that "this was the very bait the devil wished him to snap at," "for reeling home the next night, from the tavern . . . fired with lust and wine, he brutally attempted

his sister!" Her father, hearing her cries, comes to her aid, "when the mad youth struck him a fatal blow on the head" (3).

113. While Bunyan's allegory told the story of Christian's journey, it did so in the abstract categories of doubt, despair, worldliness, greed, and the like. Yet homiletic identification required an ability to personalize the narrative, as the fictional Underhill illustrates in his reading of *Pilgrim's Progress,* or as Protestants were taught to do in Abbott's *The Young Christian,* or as thousands of African American Methodists and Baptists did in their performative embodiment of biblical typology. Historically, readers had had the capacity to personalize even general maxims. When reading the lines "Xerxes the Great did die / And so must you and I" in his primer as a child in the second decade of the nineteenth century, for example, the homiletic antiquarian and abolitionist George Livermore recalled the intensity of his textual identification: "I always made it a personal matter. It meant *me,* and my associations with death *then* were not of so pleasant a character as to make the thought agreeable" (*Origin, History and Character,* 12; original emphasis).

114. We might recall, too, that in the nineteenth century, industrialization had increased the number of time-related activities, including the departure of trains, the standardization of national time zones on November 18, 1883, and the standardization of opening and closing times for factories and shops.

115. Boylan, *Sunday School,* 126; see also 10–60, 160–68. In much the same way as homiletic literature sought to instill moral principles for life, Sunday schools, Boylan writes, imparted to children "the values of self-control, obedience, good habits, and fixed principles" necessary for survival and fulfillment in a rapidly urbanizing and industrializing nation (164–65).

116. For an interesting treatment of time in spiritual autobiography as the interplay between *chronos,* time measured in a progression of equal units, and *kairos,* time as an ebb and flow of freighted moments intersecting and punctuating the historical, see Bozeman, *"To Live Ancient Lives."*

117. Perhaps an overly general assessment, Luella M. Wright refers to Bunyan's Calvinism as "traditional Anglo-Catholic Arminianism" in "John Bunyan and Stephen Crisp," 96. For Bunyan's ambivalence toward Arminianism, see Greaves, *Glimpses of Glory,* 106, 598. Greaves refers to Bunyan's Calvinism at its most liberal as "Pastoral Arminianism" (110).

118. Even recent novels that privilege born-again converions, like those in the Left Behind series, must take the sinners left behind for their protagonists, rather than the righteous who are spirited away in the Rapture. The sinners' terrible awakening to their spiritual plight answers the conventional novel's insistence on character development in homogeneous time.

119. Bercovitch, *Puritan Origins,* 11–15.

120. Adams, *The Education of Henry Adams,* 9; and Holmes, *Elsie Venner,* 445, 356.

121. Tyler, *The Algerine Captive,* 26. Such literary progresses, of course, drew on visual forms of the "progress," such as Hogarth's eighteenth-century pictures of the whore's or the rake's declines. Both these visual and literary traditions had their antecedents in medieval moral allegory and liturgical drama.

122. Ibid., vi.

123. For a useful study of the Civil War's influence on Alcott's political and authorial values, see Young, "A Wound of One's Own."

124. The Everyman locution calls attention to the gendering of the typological model. For analysis of gendered language in *Little Women* and cultural— though not religious—literary forms, see Zwinger, *Daughters, Fathers, and the Novel.*

125. Stafford, *Visual Analogy,* 8–10.

126. Jehlen, "Why Did the Europeans Cross the Ocean?" 55.

127. Stowe, *Uncle Tom's Cabin,* 628. For a counterunderstanding of Stowe and Alcott and a provocative intervention that helped me think through these differences, see Hendler, "The Limits of Sympathy."

128. See the chapter "Sentimental Power," 122–46, in Tompkins, *Sensational Designs.*

129. Stowe, *Uncle Tom's Cabin,* 628.

130. Beecher, "The Sources and Uses of Suffering," 160–61.

131. Ibid., 160.

132. Abigail May ("Abba") Alcott embodies the gradual change from an ethic of Christian charity to an ethic of social activism. Between 1848 and 1850, Abigail worked in the position of "city missionary" in Boston, emphasizing education and organizing food and clothing drives. In the 1830s, she belonged to the Female Anti-Slavery Societies in Philadelphia, Boston, and Concord, which originated in the May family, associates of William Lloyd Garrison whose home was a point on the underground railroad. The Alcotts later, with Henry David Thoreau and the May clan, supported John Brown's cause and sheltered his widow at his death. Later, Louisa May Alcott would serve as a nurse at a Civil War hospital in Georgetown. See Barton, *Transcendental Wife.*

133. Warner's *House in Town: A Sequel to "Opportunities"* is third in a series that includes *What She Could* (1871), *Opportunities: A Sequel to "What She Could"* (1871), and *Trading: Finishing the Story of the House in Town* (1873). "In general," the preface to *The Dairyman's Daughter* intones, "if we want to see religion in its purest character, we must look for it among the poor of this world, who are rich in faith. How often is the poor man's cottage the palace of God? Many of us can truly declare, that we have there learned our most valuable lessons of faith and hope, and there witnessed the most striking demonstrations of the wisdom, power, and goodness of God." Legh Richmond, *The Dairyman's Daughter,* 1. Richmond's tract first appeared in the Christian Guardian under the pseudonym Simplex.

134. The turn away from innate depravity was, as Karen Halttunen points out, largely a result of the influence of Coleridgean Platonism. Louisa May Alcott's famous father Bronson, for example, had been converted by Coleridge's *Aids to Reflection* from, Halttunen argues, "a Lockean view of the child as tabula rasa to a romantic vision of the child's innate divinity" ("Domestic Drama," 235). A closer analysis of Bronson Alcott's journals suggests that Alcott had not, in fact, turned away entirely from a Lockean conception of the child as tabula rasa; rather he seems to have merged the two philosophies.

135. Phelps's literary vision of heaven as a place where, without pain or infirmity, life takes up again where it had abruptly ended was nowhere more movingly or imaginatively described then in a scene in heaven from *The Gates Ajar,* in which deceased Confederate and Union soldiers throng the compassionate, forgiving Abraham Lincoln, as the Christlike martyr stands before them bathed in the radiance of glory. By including soldiers from both sides, Phelps renders Lincoln's death a willing sacrifice that casts the Confederate soldiers in the role of the Romans, whom Christ pardons ("for they know not what they do"; 170). The daughter of Austin Phelps, the eminent antebellum Andover professor of theology, Elizabeth Phelps was no less heretical in her fiction to the Congregationalism of her father than Harriet Beecher Stowe had been to that of hers.

Chapter Three

1. In a speech before the Second International Congregational Council in Boston (1899), Albert Spicer, a member of the British Parliament, attested to fiction's function in providing just such an imaginative arena: "I would venture to say . . . that members of our churches are ready to consider these difficult questions [of social reform]. Look, for instance, at the intense interest displayed in the works of Rev. Charles E. [*sic*] Sheldon. We are told, by competent authorities, that their sale in Great Britain alone amounted to something like three millions of copies. That of itself is an indication that in the minds of multitudes there is a feeling of unrest and of willingness to be led in the direction of higher social ideas, with a view of ascertaining how they can carry out more truly Christ's command to 'do unto others as we would they should do to us'" ("Annual Address," 138).

2. For its use by missionaries in black congregations, see Luker, *The Social Gospel in Black and White.* Luker writes, "Missionary zeal was evident in Wilmington, North Carolina's, black churches where the pastors took Charles M. Sheldon's social gospel novel, *In His Steps,* as the text for their evening sermons. Their congregations were exhorted to make choices based on "What would Jesus do?" See also Beam, *He Called Them by the Lightening,* 108; and Miss Hatch, "Some Features," 441.

3. Sheldon, *Robert Hardy's Seven Days, The Twentieth Door, The Crucifixion of Phillip Strong, John King's Question Class,* and *His Brother's Keeper.* For a critical survey of *In His Steps* see Miller, *Following in His Steps,* and Boyer, "In His Steps."

4. Chamberlin, "If Jesus Were an Editor"; Sheldon, "If Jesus Were Here Today," "If I Were a Teacher," "If I Were President," and "What I Would Do If I Were a Farmer."

5. James, *Pragmatism,* 40.

6. For representative articles on diminishing membership in Congregational churches, see Evans, "Woman's Work," see esp. 287. In *If Christ Came to Chicago!* W. T. Stead quotes a representative view, when he records a man on the street as evidence of the growing crisis among the faithful about the relevance of Christ in the modern age: "He was all very well nineteen hundred years ago in Judea, but what have we to do with him in civic life in Chicago?" (12).

7. The best general study of the Social Gospel is still Hopkins, *The Rise of the Social Gospel.* Hopkins's tendency to treat the Social Gospel movement strictly as a reform ideology rather than as a theology has, I think, led to misconceptions about its transitional role in the history of American Protestantism.

8. See Brodhead's essay "Sparing the Rod" in his *Cultures of Letters;* Gates, "Susan Warner"; Lindley, "Gender and the Social Gospel Novel"; Ellen Shaffer, "Children's Books"; and Wright, *The Social Christian Novel.* See also Boylan, *Sunday School;* Bratton, *The Impact of Victorian Children's Fiction;* Reynolds, *Faith in Fiction,* in which he discusses the works of Royall Tyler, Susanna Rowson, Henry Ward, Catherine Sedgwick, Lydia Maria Child, Sylvester Judd, and William Ware.

9. Denning, *Mechanic Accents;* Hall, *Cultures of Print,* and *Lived Religion in America;* Radway, *Reading the Romance;* and Tompkins, *Sensational Designs.*

10. Miller, *Following in His Steps,* 69; Boyer, "In His Steps," 61.

11. Denning, *Mechanic Accents,* 72–73. In its function as an imaginative arena for individual and communal action, the homiletic novel tacitly serves—in the way Radway has shown of romance novels—the function of a social contract between authors and specific religious audiences. Using traditional homiletic strategies newly incorporated into the novel form, religious authors directed their readers in the proper use of this homiletic heuristic (Radway, "The Book-of-the-Month Club"; Jameson, *The Political Unconscious*). As Denning points out, however, not all texts can be reduced simply to symbolic acts; he emphasizes the extent of social "scrimmaging," intra- and intercommunally contested meanings that take place in and around texts. While Denning emphasizes the social construction of meaning—plurality of audiences, multiaccentual signs, and Gramscian demographic blocs rather than simple stratified class structures—I

want to suggest the homiletic novel's role in an act of communal collective bargaining, its purpose as an imaginative arena in which individuals and communities could test and contest the limits of moral agency and action, not theoretically, but in their application in the social world.

12. Denning, *Mechanic Accents,* 71-72.

13. On the Social Gospel, see Hopkins, *Rise of the Social Gospel;* see also Curtis, *A Consuming Faith;* and Graham, *Half Finished Heaven.* For urban reformers after about 1830, poverty and respectability were not mutually exclusive. Increasingly after 1860, religious and secular reform literature drew even sharper distinctions between the "undeserving poor" and those, presumably, more culpable. For a discussion of class identification in the nineteenth century, see Blumin, *The Emergence of the Middle Class.*

14. Quoted in Kengor, *God and Ronald Reagan,* 18-19; original emphasis. See also Morris, *Dutch,* 40-41; and Cannon, *Governor Reagan,* 72.

15. One cannot draw a clear line between homiletic works and contemporary works of naturalism because the two drew from each other. Works such as Upton Sinclair's *The Jungle* and John Steinbeck's *Grapes of Wrath,* as the latter's title suggests, use homiletic strategies to foster social reform.

16. *In His Steps* emphasizes the dialogic aspect of these communal roundtables: "Into these meetings have come all those who made the pledge to do as Jesus would do, and the time is spent in mutual fellowship, confession, questions as to what Jesus would do in special cases, and prayer that the one great guide of every disciple's conduct may be the Holy Spirit." Sheldon, *In His Steps,* 239; hereafter cited in text as *In His Steps.*

17. Denning, *Mechanic Accents,* 82.

18. Denning's notion of "multiaccentual signs" is based on Bakhtininian theory (Denning, *Mechanic Accents,* 66). In his essay "What Is the History of Books?" Darnton argues that a history of reading cannot center on the book as a material object, but must deploy a methodology focused on a "communication circuit," marked by the positions of author, publisher, printer, shipper, bookseller, and reader. (We need only think of Mason Locke Weems, who wrote and oversaw the publication and distribution of his books, often meeting personally with prospective buyers and readers.) As Darnton points out, then as now, most Americans do not read books so much as newspapers, pamphlets, broadsides, journals, magazines, typescripts, signs, and the like.

19. Boylan, *Sunday School,* 90. Christian unity was fostered on other fronts as well. In *When Church Became Theatre,* Jeanne Halgren Kilde, for instance, argues that Gothic revival architecture in the mid-nineteenth century made Christian unity "a visual feature of the American landscape itself" (72).

20. Sheldon, *Heart of the World,* 38.

21. Wood, *Ideal Suggestion,* 89; original emphasis.

22. Cave, "The Living Christ," 471; emphasis added.

23. Stead, *If Christ Came to Chicago!* 262–63. On transhistorical vision in American history, see Pocock, *The Machiavellian Moment,* 28–132.

24. Schocket, "Undercover Explorations," 110; Leonardo, foreword to London, *The People of the Abyss,* viii.

25. For an in-depth discussion of the "virtual-tour narrative" and its transition from the sermon to the literature of social reform, see my "Cultivating Spiritual Sight." For the best discussion of this discursive tradition in secular literature, see Schocket, "Undercover Explorations."

26. Recent studies of Crane, London, and Dreiser focus on depictions of poverty and vice. Many focus on social realism's role in the formation of social identity. While Riis figures in this reading, I resituate him in the Social Gospel tradition. See also Flower, *Civilization's Inferno;* Campbell, *Darkness and Daylight;* Wyckoff, *The Workers: An Experiment in Reality; The East,* and *The Workers: An Experiment in Reality; The West;* Flynt, *Tramping with Tramps.*

27. William James's "radical empiricism"—a concept developed in *Essays in Radical Empiricism*—in many ways marks the culmination of this dilemma in empiricism of how to access knowledge that could not be fully apprehended through sensory data.

28. Howard, *Form and History,* 142–82; Kaplan, *Social Construction,* 140–60; Pizer, *Theory and Practice,* 85–101; Trachtenberg, "Experiments in Another Country: Stephen Crane's City Sketches," 138–54.

29. McKeon, *The Origins of the English Novel.*

30. The phrase *veracious narrative* took on life as a descriptor for all kinds of new forms of discursive realism emerging in the 1890s after Stephen Crane used it in his journalistic sketch "An Experiment in Misery."

31. London, *The People of the Abyss,* 15.

32. Ibid., 31.

33. Nothing better illustrates this popular form of clinical "realism" prized by turn-of-the-century sociology than Robert W. DeForest and Lawrence Veiller's report for the New York State Tenement House Commission, which in the name of scientific objectivity exhibits images of the indigent stripped naked in baths or awaiting examination, or photographs of fouled tenement living spaces (*The Tenement House Problem*).

34. London, *The People of the Abyss;* Flynt, *Tramping with Tramps.*

35. Josiah Royce quoted in Clendenning, *The Life and Thought of Josiah Royce,* 252; original emphasis.

36. Crane's sociological interests and intent have been controversial. Howard Horowitz ("Maggie and the Sociological Paradigm"), for instance, argues that *Maggie* (1896) actually resists the sociological paradigms popularized throughout the 1890s that promoted individual autonomy over alleged deterministic forces such as environment. He sees *Maggie* as denial that an unconditioned consciousness might overcome an environmental shaping of the self.

37. Tourgée, *Murvale Eastman*. See also Nicholl, "The Image of the Protestant Minister."

38. Sheldon, "Practical Christian Sociological Studies," and *His Life Story*, 88–92.

39. Hughes, "The Biblical Play," 312.

40. In his survey of attitudes toward religious life, William James astutely captures the contemporary attitude many had toward the Social Gospel's embrace of poverty, while suggesting the Social Gospel's imbrication with Muscular Christianity: "Among us English-speaking peoples especially do the praises of poverty need once more to be boldly sung. We have grown literally afraid to be poor. We despise anyone who elects to be poor in order to simplify and save his inner life. . . . We have lost the power even of imagining what the ancient idealization of poverty could have meant: the liberation from material attachments, the unbribed soul, the manlier indifference, the paying our way by what we are or do and not by what we have, the right to fling away our life at any moment irresponsibly—the more athletic trim, in short, the moral fighting shape" (*Varieties* 293)

41. Boyesen, *Social Strugglers*.

42. In a biting critique of the use of science in the "re-discovery" and explanation of Jesus Christ's life, Alfred Cave, in his address before the Second Congregational Council, lamented that "This age has certainly brought to our knowledge, as never before, the Christ of history. But in the search after the Christ of history you may divert attention from the Living Christ. Our Christian faith does not depend upon a life of Christ of a strictly scientific kind, with every date exactly determined, and every spot minutely described. Settle the precise date of our Lord's birth, you have done interesting archaeological work, but your argument has brought no man nearer the kingdom of heaven. Accurately assign to years and months and days every event in our Lord's human lie, and your chronological efforts are interesting to chronologists and others, but you have conveyed to no man that Jesus is the Light of the World, the Living Bread for every hungry soul, and the Water that welleth up eternally to quench spiritual thirst. Decide the interminable dispute as to whether Jesus died on the 14th or 15th of Nisan, and again you have laid the historically inclined under obligation but you have helped no poor soul to learn that there is spiritual cleansing in the blood of Jesus. In our modern biographies of Jesus, stress is apt to be laid upon the wrong things" ("The Living Christ," 464).

43. Hughes, "The Biblical Play," 307, 312.

44. Looking back on the century from 1899, Alfred Cave observed: "We have been told on high authority that this nineteenth century, the century of so many great discoveries, has excelled its other exploits by rediscovering the Christ. The scholars and critics of the last fifty years have recovered, it is said, the lost Christ. . . . Lives of Jesus, we have been told, have been the successes of our book

markets, from the rationalistic Lives of Jesus by Paulus and Strauss and Renan to the more evangelical Lives of Farrar and Stalker and Didon" ("The Living Christ," 463–64). German scholars, notably Schaff and Strauss, initiated the new biblical historicism in the 1830s, influencing Boston Unitarians' and transcendentalists' views of biblical history and New Testament miracles: see Packer, *The Transcendentalists*.

45. In what was referred to as "the Young Christian series," this volume, the first in the series, is followed by *The Cornerstone; or, a Familiar Illustration of the Principles of Christian Faith; The Way to Do Good; or, the Christian Character Mature;* and *Hoaryhead and M'Donner; or, the Radical Nature of the Change in Spiritual Regeneration.*

46. "Over the lecture-room swept that unseen yet distinctly felt wave of Divine Presence. No one spoke for a while. Mr. Maxwell standing there, where the faces lifted their intense gaze into his, felt what he had already felt—a strange setting back out of the nineteenth century into the first, when the disciples had all things in common, and a spirit of fellowship must have flowed freely between them such as the First Church of Raymond had never before known" (*In His Steps* 208).

47. George Doran recalls that criticism of the novel as "too literal" led Revell Publishing initially to reject it (*Chronicles of Barabbas*, 26–27).

48. See May, *Protestant Churches and Industrial America*, 207; Davies, "Religious Issues."

49. Exposés on and depictions of urban poverty, the urban homeless problem, and immigration, particularly from Eastern Europe, rose dramatically after the winter of 1893–94, a critical point in the "great depression" of the 1890s. See Moeller, "Cultural Construction," 10.

50. Adams, "The Dynamo and the Virgin," 379.

51. Sheldon, *Jesus Is Here!* i.

52. Such moments of fictive representation appear tritely sentimental only when removed from the interventionist context in which homiletic literature operated. As Cathy Davidson (*Revolution and the Word*) has illustrated in tracing the various editions and reader reception of Susanna Rowson's *Charlotte Temple,* context can dramatically alter how readers interact with texts. Davidson shows how this interaction shifts depending on varying physical characteristics of the text, on marketing and other forms of institutional or ideological promotion, on the agency of authors and critics, and on programmed readerly expectations. If, as Davidson has demonstrated, different bindings, illustrations, and introductory material could transform Rowson's secular novel from an early example of realism into sentimental fiction, from a quasi-pornographic text to an object of scholarly interest—how much greater might such transformations be if directed at a mode of reading intricately connected to readers who perceived their own lives, like the typological characters about whom they read, within the

representational frame of a false—might we say *fictional*—world. It is the ability of religious readers to access the appropriate hermeneutical context that makes the homiletic novel an instrument of moral self-examination.

53. May, *Enlightenment in America,* see esp. the introduction.

54. Burder, "Sermon XXXIII," 8. Burder's two-volume *Village Sermons* was likely the most widely read sermon collection among the lower classes in most American Protestant denominations between 1815 and 1840. The Trinitarian controversy and national debate, including Burder's involvement, received much of its impetus in the Kentucky-Tennessee revivals at the beginning of the nineteenth century. The then Presbyterian Barton Stone, founder of the "Christian Church" movement, took issue with the standard statement of doctrine on the Trinity articulated by Augustine in *The Trinity* and reaffirmed in the seventeenth-century Westminster Confession and by revered divines such as Herman Witsius, a seventeenth-century Dutch Reformed theologian prized by Presbyterians and Congregationalists, who, rather than illuminating the enigma of "eternal in the Father," celebrated its "incomprehensible mystery, which surpasses all sense and reason" (*Sacred Dissertations,* vol. 1, 143). For Witsius's enduring popularity among American Calvinists, see Trinterud, *The Forming of an American Tradition,* 52–56. For a full explication of the Trinity crisis surrounding Barton Stone's "Christian Movement" and for its break with Calvinism, see Williams, *Barton Stone,* 29–45.

55. Burder, "Sermon XLIV," 6. Writing early in this debate, Burder, for instance, asserts that "In what manner the human nature was united to the divine, we cannot tell. It is enough for us, that it was so united" ("Sermon XLIV," 114). In this, Burder signals how difficult the rational process of explaining the Godhead had become, even after renowned ministers such as the Enlightenment-influenced Isaac Watts had weighed in. In "The Christian Doctrine of the Trinity," Watts defended Trinity theology against the assertions that the scripture did not teach three persons are one person, for "neither reason nor religion can require us to believe plain inconsistency" (26). Watts reduced the problem to the person of Christ, since the idea of a Holy Spirit troubled Christians less. The problem, he noted, was the identification of Christ as the "Son of God," which led individuals to assert that he was separate from God. Rather than Son of God, Watts identified Christ as the human soul "formed" by God, insisting that scriptures did not identify the Son of God as the second person in the Godhead, but as a soul formed by God and united to him well before he was conceived of Mary (468).

56. The Stone Christian movement seemed, generally at least, to embrace Arianism, which suggested that the Savior was an exalted being, a separate and lesser entity than God. The Nicene Council of 325 had opposed Arius's view that the Son was *created* (rather than "eternally begotten") out of nothing.

Nineteenth-century Socinians—influenced by the New Criticism—viewed Christ as a mere man, disagreeing, however, about his post-Resurrection status.

57. See Mullin, *The Puritan as Yankee*, 134–40. These theological debates, translated into popular movements, often appeared in homiletic novels. In *Metzerott, Shoemaker*, for example, Katharine Pearson Woods has a priest critique the belief that Christ was human: "Perhaps there are some here who think that Jesus Christ was simply a good man, not even a perfect man, far less the God-man" (265). For the shift toward modern humanism, see Noll, *America's God*, 139–40.

58. James, *Pragmatism*, 268.

59. Stead, "If Christ Came to Chicago!" 38.

60. Taves, *Fits, Trances, and Visions*.

61. The various Protestant journals published between 1875 and 1900 repeatedly feature articles on science, many going to great lengths to dismiss the very topic they inaugurate. Many ministers saved their sharpest critiques for the ministry itself. For instance, in "The Living Christ," Alfred Cave insists: "How is it that renewed and prolonged attacks on the Christian faith,—assaults from our own preachers and sustained with great intellectual vigor and with all the resources both of the older learning and of the new sciences,—have produced so little effect! How is it that the discoveries of geology, and the theory of Darwin, and the attacks on the Gospels of Strauss and the Tübingen school, and the modern criticism of the Jewish Scriptures, have had so little effect upon the rank and file of the Christian church, agitating the pulpit a great deal more than they agitate the pew?" (470).

62. Draper, *History of the Conflict*, xi.

63. See "The Problem of Job" in Royce, *The Philosophy of Josiah Royce*, 93.

64. Ibid., 97.

65. James, "Philosophical Conceptions and Practical Results," 267. James delivered this address, in which he first used C. S. Peirce's term "pragmatism," before the Philosophical Union at the University of California, Berkeley, August 26, 1898. Later, in *Varieties of Religious Experience*, James further excoriates those who turn a blind eye to social need: "Let a man who, by fortunate health and circumstances, escapes the suffering of any great amount of evil in his own person, also close his eyes to it as it exists in the wider universe outside his private experience, and he will be quit of it altogether, and can sail through life happily on a healthy-minded basis" (289).

66. While Sheldon and Royce certainly followed divergent paths in making sense of the modern world, it would be a mistake to view Sheldon as incapable of theory, or to assume that Royce did not emphasize philosophy as a living creed. Sheldon's theory is visible in the structure of his homiletics taken as

a whole, and Royce's philosophical system promoted a system of ethical practice influenced not least by his mother's fervent evangelicalism. By exploring the
duality of theory and praxis in the writings of Sheldon and Royce, we glimpse
a popular tributary of pragmatism that had its origin in millennialist evangelicalism. This genealogy, which ties pragmatism to the works of such prominent
theologians as Jonathan Edwards, Lyman Beecher, and Horace Bushnell, is evident in the subtitle William James gave his seminal book on pragmatism: *A New
Name for Some Old Ways of Thinking.* Thus, while Sheldon was a minister, his
life and work were far removed from what Stewart Cole, Norman Furniss, and
public luminaries such as H. L. Mencken and H. Richard Niebuhr—by focusing on the Pentecostal revivals of the 1920s—spurned as the anti-intellectual
tendencies of feeling-focused evangelicalism, and closer to the era's most innovative currents of philosophy: the theory and practice of pragmatism as it circulated among Christian socialists and reformers. Whereas Sheldon's practical Christianity—much like that taught in Dewey's Ann Arbor Sunday school
classes—rose out of the exigencies of shaping his congregants' daily lives, Royce's
pragmatism came from an intellectual framework in the Christian tradition of
theodicy—justifying the ways of God to man. See Cole, *History of Fundamentalism* (1931); and Furniss, *The Fundamentalist Controversy,* (1954). Both of these
earlier works influenced Richard Hofstadter's *Anti-intellectualism in American
Life.* For Hofstadter's discussion of the roots of this evangelical-oriented anti-
intellectualism, see esp. 55–117. For the best historical assessment of fundamentalism, see Marsden, *Fundamentalism and American Culture.*

67. The determinism found in American naturalism is exemplified in a passage in Frank Norris's *McTeague* (1899), in which the romance between Mc-
Teague and Trina is depicted as an irrevocable force, part external and natural,
part internal, an uncontrollable inner determinism: "McTeague had awakened
the Woman, and, whether she would or no, she was his now irrevocably; struggle
against it as she would, she belonged to him, body and soul, for life or for death.
She had not sought it, she had not desired it. The spell was laid upon her. . . . And
he? The very act of submission that bound the woman to him forever had made
her seem less desirable in his eyes. Their undoing had already begun. Yet neither
of them was to blame. From the first they had not sought each other. Chance had
brought them face to face, and mysterious instincts as ungovernable as the winds
of heaven were at work knitting their lives together. Neither of them had asked
that this thing should be—that their destinies, their very souls, should be the
sport of chance. If they could have known, they would have shunned the fearful
risk. But they were allowed no voice in the matter" (326).

68. Wood, *Ideal Suggestion,* 128.

69. For postbellum Protestantism's emphasis on volition, see Haroutunian,
Piety versus Moralism; Meyer, *Democratic Enlightenment,* chap. 3; May, *Prot-*

estant Churches and Industrial America, chap. 3; and Noll, *America's God,* 230–31, 278–83, 299–307.

70. Doran, *Chronicles of Barabbas,* 26–27.

71. Stead, *If Christ Came to Chicago!* 13.

72. Phelps, *The Gates Ajar,* 77.

73. Flower's response is representative: "This vivid allegory Jesus made the supreme test of worthiness, man's concern for the . . . the suffering. . . . As I read this passage I saw thousands in our cities starving, naked, and shelterless, and . . . thought of the hundreds of thousands of honest, hard-working Americans . . . who are to all practical purposes in prison through unjust conditions. . . . And I said: 'Surely Jesus is in Prison. But His church is not visiting'" ("Jesus or Caesar," 531).

74. Riis, *How the Other Half Lives,* hereafter cited in text as *Other Half;* Howard, *If Christ Came to Congress;* and Hale, *If Jesus Came to Boston.*

75. The edited passage is worth reproducing here for how it sets in relief the disparate beliefs about Jesus's ontological nature, whether a hero who overcame his cowardice and fear in Davis's original, or the deified man whose "God-power" acted through him, in the edited version:

> Eighteen centuries ago, the Master of this man tried reform in the streets of a city as crowded and vile as this, and did not fail. His disciple, showing Him to-night to cultured hearers, showing the clearness of the God-power acting through Him, shrank back from one coarse fact; that in birth and habit the man Christ was thrown up from the lowest of the people: his flesh, their flesh, the want of their hourly life, and the wine-press he trod along.
>
> Yet, is there no meaning in this perpetually covered truth? If the son of the carpenter had stood in the church that night, as he stood with the fishermen and harlots by the sea of Galilee, before His Father and their Father, despised and rejected of men, without a place to lay His head, wounded for their iniquities, bruised for their transgressions, would not that hungry mill-boy at least, in the back seat, have 'known the man'? That Jesus did not stand there.

Both passages are quoted from Lasseter, "From the Archives," 176. Lasseter reads the censored version as holding a key to the meaning of the story's "veiled metaphors" (176).

76. Sheldon had used the trope in his 1894 novel, *The Crucifixion of Phillip Strong.* As the young minister Phillip Strong lies dying—his health wrecked from struggling to alleviate suffering in the tenements—his wife grieves over his well-heeled congregation's rejection of his Social Gospel theology: "I have learned to believe since you came to Milton that if Jesus Christ were to live on the earth in this century and become the pastor of almost any large and wealthy church and

preach as He would have to, the church would treat Him just as Calvary Church has treated you. The world would crucify Jesus Christ again even after two thousand years of historical Christianity" (201).

77. Seltzer, "The Princess Casamassima," 116.

78. Denning, *Mechanic Accents,* 73. See Habegger, *Gender, Fantasy, and Realism in American Literature.*

79. Denning, *Mechanic Accents,* 172.

80. Later, James reiterates the point: "Discomfort and annoyance, hunger and wet, pain and cold, squalor and filth, cease to have any deterrent operation whatever. Death turns into a commonplace matter, and its usual power to check our action vanishes. With the annulling of these customary inhibitions, ranges of new energy are set free, and life seems cast upon a higher plane of power" (*Varieties* 291).

81. Flower, "Jesus or Caesar," 522–33.

82. The motivational changes deployed in poverty reform in urban centers between 1830 and 1880 is remarked on in scores of articles advocating and justifying such reform in this period. For instance, an anonymous editorial published in the "free-church" advocate Joshua Leavitt's *New York Evangelist,* July 31, 1830, titled "To Wealthy Presbyterians in the City of New York," reasons, "Our Savior preached to the poor, and thus fulfilled the predictions of the prophets. In scriptural meaning the poor are the great body of working men. The reason of his directing his efforts to this class is obvious to an intelligent observer. They are the foundation of society; all classes rest upon them. It is so in every age, and every nation; especially in this. The moral tendency is upwards. Enlightening the common people is making the whole mass wise. The poor rise and spread, and pervade, and direct, and govern all. Incidents act upon this state of things. And Christians would act philosophically as well as scripturally, if they imitated their example" (70). This writer advocates identification with Christ but not with the poor. Rather, of a piece with Leavitt's free-church support—churches free (without pew rentals) for all classes—this writer argues that helping the rich begins by helping the poor.

83. Elaw, *Memoirs,* 118; Sheldon, *The Narrow Gate,* 141.

84. Du Bois, "The Church and the Negro," 291.

85. Phelps, *The Gates Ajar,* 109.

86. Flower, "Jesus or Caesar," 533.

87. Jeanne Halbren Kilde describes how the Chatham Street Chapel, a theater converted in 1832 into an evangelical meeting hall by Lewis Tappan and William Green for the then renowned Charles Finney, both urbanized the largely erstwhile rural tent revival tradition and altered conventional church architecture into a performative space that heightened interaction between parishioners and ministers. For the influence of the Chatham Street Chapel on later church architecture, see Kilde, *When Church Became Theatre,* 22–55.

NOTES TO PAGES 190–197

88. Beecher also "ransomed" a slave in 1856; see "Ransom of a Slave-girl at Plymouth Church," 11; Saltar, *A Church in History,* 48.

89. Similarly, William T. Elsing writes, "If . . . wealthier ladies . . . would seek . . . to come into direct personal contact with the recipients of their charity, they would experience a deeper happiness and . . . a new day would dawn for many a poor, heartbroken mother who is now hopeless and longs for death to end her misery" ("Life in New York Tenement-houses," 714).

90. This relationship between sermonic form and a hermeneutics of reading has been examined in the seventeenth-century context by Lisa Gordis in *Opening Scripture.*

91. For a discussion of spatialized memory systems from the Puritan tradition, see my "Cultivating Spiritual Sight," esp. 136–37.

92. Works focused on incremental growth were part of medieval Catholic pedagogy. See Hilton's *The Ladder of Perfection* (sometimes printed as *The Scales of Perfection*) and the anonymous tracts *A Ladder of Four Rungs by Which Men May Well Climb to Heaven, The Tree of Twelve Fruits,* and *The Seven Points of True Love and Everlasting Wisdom.* For a connection between the incrementalism discussed here and twentieth-century self-help literature, see James, *Varieties of Religious Experience,* in which, in chapters titled "The Religion of Healthy-Mindedness," he writes: "The mind-cure principles are beginning so to pervade the air that one catches their spirit at secondhand. One hears of the 'Gospel of Relaxation,' of the 'Don't Worry Movement,' of people who repeat to themselves, 'Youth, health, vigor!' when dressing in the morning, as their motto for the day" (84). James's assessment anticipates such later "mind-cure" works, as Norman Vincent Peale's *The Power of Positive Thinking.*

93. See volume editors' introduction to Edwards, "The Danger of Corrupt Communication," 156–57.

94. Miller, *Jonathan Edwards,* 157–58.

95. Edwards, "Sinners in the Hands of an Angry God," 404–17.

96. Miller, *Jonathan Edwards,* 156.

97. Condemning theory without practice, Dewey writes in "The Relation of Theory to Practice in Education": "The 'best interests of the children' are so safeguarded and supervised that the situation approaches learning to swim without going too near the water" (252).

98. Other new measures included public confession of faith and the altar call. For the New Measures, see Carwardine, "The Second Great Awakening." Kilde argues that even the influence of the theater on church architecture—wide aisles that facilitated movement from the pews to the anxious bench, clear sight lines between preachers and congregants, pulpits on thrust stages—"itself may have functioned as an unacknowledged new measure" (*When Church Became Theatre,* 36).

99. In "The Biblical Play," Hughes writes, "The Biblical play has been re-

vived. The romantic religious drama has again found a place on the English and American stage, and such gorgeous scenic productions as 'Parsifal,' 'Ben Hur,' and 'The Shepherd King' have attracted attention. . . . Ministers of religion now show no reluctance to witness plays which are known to be exceptional in their moral character. Preachers do not hesitate to endorse the higher developments of the stage. Christian congregations no longer criticise [sic.] their pastors for attending the theatre" (307–8). In *When Church Became Theatre,* Kilde demonstrates the increased dramatization of preaching fostered in the Chatham Street Chapel and later advocated in urban churches throughout the country. In particular, she argues that the free-church movement meant to democratize churches by dropping pew rents empowered congregants much as the theater had traditionally done. The stage lighting, the amphitheatre effect created by the sloped floor, the unobstructed view and eye contact with the preacher afforded by the circular seating and stage, and a class newly empowered by Jacksonian ideology that entitled individuals on a first-come basis greater proximity to the minister— all heightened the sermons theatricality and gave greater emphasis on the relationship between minister and congregant (see 29–41).

100. James, "Philosophical Conceptions and Practical Results," 259.

101. Sheldon, "Practical Christian Sociological Studies," 371; *His Life Story,* esp. 88–92.

102. Sheldon, "A Local Negro Problem," 828; and *His Life Story,* 92–95; Cox, *Blacks in Topeka,* see esp. 46–82; Miller, "Charles M. Sheldon," and *Following in His Steps,* 46–65. While perhaps naïve, Sheldon's understanding of race was radical in its day. He saw the solution to American racism as particularly "colorless." "In the largest and truest sense there is no 'negro problem,'" he wrote in 1896 in an article titled "The Kingdom," "any more than there is an 'Anglo-Saxon problem.' The only problem is the 'human problem.' And it is all capable of being resolved in simple terms which apply equally to every race and condition" ("The Kingdom," 470–71).

103. Like the magic lantern lectures and "virtual-tour narratives" presented in urban centers across the nation in the 1890s by such reformers as Helen Campbell, Everett Burr, and William Elsing, Sheldon's novels and protagonists furnished communities with innovative plans that, through the machinery of the church or Social Gospel, took pragmatic form. Converging with the pragmatism of William James and Josiah Royce, Practical Christianity implored Christians and the larger public to act. For Sheldon, no theological creed superseded this single imperative: choose a Christlike course of reform and act upon it.

104. "A Negro Mission in Kentucky," *Outlook,* vol. 80, April 19, 1905, 949–50; Little, "The Presbyterian Colored Mission."

105. Williams, *America's Religions,* 170–75. See also Johnson, *Redeeming America,* 86–154.

106. Luker, *The Social Gospel,* 19.

107. Denning, *Mechanic Accents,* 136.

108. Sheldon quoted in "The Kingdom," 70.

109. "Editorial Notes," *Unitarian* 5 (1890), 594.

110. In a letter dated May 24, 1816, Weems writes, "I have certificates of the most complete Cures wrought by a single peep at the *Drunkards Looking Glass.*" Skeel, *Mason Locke Weems,* 161.

111. Denning, *Mechanic Accents,* 72.

112. Flower, "Jesus or Caesar," 528.

113. Miller, *Following in His Steps,* 130.

114. On the Protestant idea of the Bible as the "living word," see Knott, *The Sword of the Spirit,* 13–41. For an excellent study of the relation between this concept and Christian allegory, see Goldman, "Living Words."

115. While in his garden struggling with his addiction to the flesh, Augustine hears a voice say, "Sume, lege" ("take and read"), and opening the Bible at random, sees the text "not in chambering and wantonness" (*Confessions,* book VIII, chap. 5). Protestant conversion narratives are replete with such instances of bibliomancy.

116. Sheldon, *The Reformer,* 137.

117. Wood, *Ideal Suggestion,* 44.

118. Radway, "The Book-of-the-Month Club"; Jameson, *The Political Unconscious.*

119. Jameson, "Reification and Utopia," 132–33.

120. Bell, *The Problem of American Realism,* 105; original emphasis. Bell argues that James pits realism against farce in *The Princess Casamassima* in an effort to disrupt the realism the very novel initially invokes.

121. Wood, *Ideal Suggestion,* 68–69.

122. Taves, *Fits, Trances, and Visions,* see 76–117.

123. As literacy scholars like Barbara Sicherman have shown, reading in the nineteenth century continued to be a social, active experience for many Americans. In her study of the Hamilton family of Indiana, Sicherman reveals how Hamilton women drew on the enthusiasm and reform strategies garnered in their reading to shape and energize their practical engagement with social settlement work and other Progressive Era reform projects. See Sicherman, "Sense and Sensibility."

124. Frye, *The Secular Scripture,* see 21–48.

125. Royce, *Philosophy of Josiah Royce,* 169–70.

126. Roosevelt is quoted in Moore, *Selling God,* 210. Bush quotes are from the following sources, respectively: James Caroll, "The Bush Crusade," *The Nation,* September 2, 2004; Peter Ford, "Europe Cringes at Bush 'Crusade' against Terrorists," *Christian Science Monitor,* September 19, 2001.

127. Throughout the 1960s, 70s, and 80s, the annual sales was around 100,000, in more than ten separate editions, including a comic book version. However,

as Timothy Miller points out, the number of readers is much higher, as "clearly many of those millions of copies were each read by several persons" (*Following in His Steps,* 85; for more details on sales figures, see 85–88).

128. John Leland, "At Festivals, Faith, Rock and T-Shirts Take Center Stage," *New York Times,* July 5, 2004.

Chapter Four

1. Walter J. Swaffield quotes Riis's assessment of tenement dangers: "The investigations reveal a state of affairs for which nothing more horrible can be imagined, and which, although perhaps equalled [*sic*] cannot be surpassed in any European city. To get into these pestilential human rookeries you have to penetrate courts and alleys reeking with poisonous and malodorous gases arising from accumulations of sewage and refuse scattered in all directions and often flowing beneath your feet. You have to ascend rotten staircases which threaten to give way beneath every step, which in some cases have already broken down, leaving gaps that imperil the limbs and lives of the unwary. Walls and ceilings are black with the accretions of filth which have gathered upon them through long years of neglect. It exudes through cracks in the boards overhead and runs down the walls; it is everywhere" ("Round Table," 677).

2. Dewey, "Introduction to Essays," 129.

3. Blending the moral imperatives of Christian socialism with the reform-through-education premise of secular socialism, Riis's virtual tours created in the name of ethical reform an emotional and cognitive dissonance similar to the alienation effect Bertolt Brecht sought to induce in playgoers less than three decades later. But while Brecht inundated his audience with sensory stimulus to produce a gradual reorientation to social change, Riis used it to bring about immediate action, to create a pragmatic pedagogy whereby knowledge was the product of doing.

4. *Wesley Magazine,* May 1893, 22.

5. The principle ethos linking secular, progressive reform with Christian Socialism was the perceived need to intervene in childhood poverty. As Robert Wiebe observes, if "humanitarian progressivism has a central theme it was the child" (*The Search for Order,* 169).

6. Among Riis's pantheon of children whose biographies emblematized the need for intervention are "Little Nisby," "Mike of Poverty Gap," "Jacob Beresheim," and "Katie."

7. "A Golden Opportunity," *Brooklyn Eagle,* April 30, 1895.

8. The theological tradition of harrowing hell is largely a Catholic paradigm, but picks up increasing currency as a Protestant metaphor of urban reform with the East Coast decline of the virulently anti-Catholic secret society, the Amer-

ican Protective Association (APA) in the 1890s. The APA remained a powerful force until after the turn of the century—boasting a three million member following—in the Midwest and South.

9. As late as 1912, Walter Rauschenbusch could still count on his audience's familiarity with both John Bunyan's and Dante's epic allegories, which he incorporated into his homiletic allegory of social reform, *Christianizing the Social Order.* After placing readers in the role of Bunyan's pilgrim, Rauschenbusch invokes Dante's verse to encourage them to view self-sacrifice as the highest calling of Christian love: "I call on the old to make a great act of expatiation and love before they go hence. / Why will they descend to join 'the melancholy souls of those / Who lived withouten infamy or praise? / Commingled are they with the caififf [Caiaphas] choir / Of Angels, who have not rebellious been / Nor faithful were to God, but were to self'" (474).

10. See esp. Howard, *Form and History;* Kaplan, *Social Construction;* Pizer, *The Theory and Practice;* and Sundquist, *American Realism.* For an insightful discussion of the role of photography in realism and naturalism, see Trachtenberg, "Experiments in Another Country."

11. Trachtenberg, "Experiments in Another Country," 144. Stange, *Symbols of Ideal Life,* 20–25; and Castronovo, *Beautiful Democracy,* 224. While Russ and I continue to disagree over the nature of the substantive shift in middle-class perception around the erosion of religious epistemology—the passage cited from his book references material in this chapter—his arguments have been helpful to me in thinking through the epistemic differences between homiletic and secular "seeing."

12. Wood, *Ideal Suggestion,* 48–49; emphasis added.

13. See Trachtenberg, *The Incorporation of America,* 87–91. Trachtenberg suggests that by 1890, approximately "45 percent of the industrial laborers barely held on above the $500-per-year poverty line; about 40 percent lived below the line of tolerable existence, surviving in shabby tenements and run-down neighborhoods by dint of income eked out by working wives and children. About a fourth of those below the poverty line lived in absolute destitution" (89–90).

14. Berlant, "Poor Eliza," 638. See also my "A Dowry of Suffering."

15. Riis, "Reform by Humane Touch," 752.

16. James, "A World of Pure Experience," 61; emphasis added.

17. Ibid. James argues that knowledge of an object or a concept is reached through a kind of typology. "It consists in intermediary experiences (possible, if not actual) of continuously developing progress, and, finally, of fulfillment, when the sensible percept, which is the object, is reached. The percept here not only *verifies* the concept, proves its function of knowing that percept to be true, but the percept's existence as the terminus of the chain of intermediaries *creates* the function. Whatever terminates that chain was, because it now proves itself to be, what the concept 'had in mind'" (60–61).

18. Sheldon, *The Crucifixion of Phillip Strong,* 216.

19. James, "World of Pure Experience," 65.

20. For a discussion of the spiritual construction of this transhistorical vision of the self in conceptions of American history and in the individual's agency in manifest destiny, see Pocock, *The Machiavellian Moment,* part 1.

21. Wood, *Ideal Suggestion,* 55–56.

22. Ibid., 118.

23. For the best treatment of the pictorial tradition in American Protestantism, see Morgan, *Protestants and Pictures,* esp. chaps. 2–3.

24. Riis's reform, like Christian socialism generally, was deeply connected with nationalism and what he called "Christian citizenship" ("Reform by Humane Touch," 745). Riis writes that the problem New York must solve "is the problem . . . of a people's fitness for self-government that is on trial among us. We shall solve it by the world-old formula of human sympathy, of humane touch" (753). In his stereopticon lecture "Children of the Poor," Riis equated homes with citizenship. For an account of this Carnegie Library lecture, see *Pittsburgh Dispatch,* February 16, 1900. As part of his tenement reform, Riis promoted clubs, where occupants would be encouraged "to discuss there the current topics of the day," so that "when election-time came around politics would naturally come up on top. Young men so trained would, when their time to vote came, be sure to give good account of themselves" ("Special Needs," 497). Finally, Riis repeatedly connects the "decent and orderly citizen" to salvation of poor children. For instance, see "Genesis of the Gang."

25. Following the work of Michel Foucault and Guy Debord, scholars in the last two decades have demonstrated, as Eric Schocket recently argues, "how the lower classes have been both distanced and contained within the discursive structure of 'the spectacle'" ("Undercover Explorations," 111). Recent studies of Riis, Stephen Crane, Jack London, and Theodore Dreiser, among others, for example, focus on depictions of poverty and vice. In various ways, they show how the advent of social realism enabled the middle class to affirm and codify its own sense of economic and social identity through the consumption of poverty, vice, and depravity. Unhappily, even part of Riis's title, "the Other Half," lifted from Arthur Pember's *The Mysteries and Miseries of the Great Metropolis* (1874), lends itself to a simple dialectical reading, serving, in Riis's language of photography, as a "negative" from which the middle class is rendered fully visible in the form of a "positive."

26. In *The Real Thing,* Miles Orvell uses the juxtaposition between Riis and Evans to demonstrate the cultural shift between the nineteenth-century optimistic hope for the democratization of luxury through production and imitation and the twentieth-century interest in authenticity that sought to "elevate the vernacular into the realm of high culture . . . inspired by the machine's capacities to re-

cord and analyze reality and to build new artifacts" (xvi). For an informative reading of Riis, see esp. chap. 5.

27. Largely in reference to Riis, Benjamin Flower expressed the new epistemological orientation and commitment to personal agency at the heart of emerging Social Gospel reform: "There is no way in which people can be so thoroughly aroused to the urgent necessity of radical economic changes as by bringing them into such intimate relations with the submerged millions that they hear the throbbing of misery's heart. The lethargy of the moral instincts of the people is unquestionably due to lack of knowledge. . . . The people do not begin to realize the true condition of life in the ever-widening field of abject want. *When they know and are sufficiently interested to personally investigate the problem and aid the suffering,* they will appreciate . . . the absolute necessity for radical economic changes" ("Society's Exiles," 49; emphasis added). A year later, William T. Elsing promoted Social Gospel's interventionist creed: "In our cities there is too much isolation between the rich and the poor. . . . If the mother of every well-to-do home in our large cities would regularly visit, once a month, a needy family, a vast amount of good would be accomplished among the worthy poor. . . . If . . . wealthier ladies . . . would seek . . . to come into direct personal contact with the recipients of their charity, they would experience a deeper happiness and . . . a new day would dawn for many a poor, heartbroken mother who is now hopeless and longing for death to end her misery. . . . The first visit to a tenement-house might be made in the company of a city missionary, after which the most timid could go alone" ("Life in New York Tenement-Houses," 714).

28. Riis developed this metaphor in *The Battle with the Slum.*

29. Not only did Riis liberally quote Henry Ward Beecher and attend Plymouth Church, but he also wrote, early in his career, articles that took up Beecher's reform agenda; see, e.g., Riis, "Reform by Humane Touch," 745–47.

30. Riis, "Special Needs," 495.

31. *Oxford English Dictionary.*

32. The immediacy of personal experience that Riis's virtual tours produced and the fear the slums held for the middle class merges in Social Gospel advocate Hjalmar Hjorth Boyesen's 1893 homiletic novel based on Riis's virtual-tour narrative. (Boyesen and Riis often shared the lectern on the Chautauqua circuit.) After taking a virtual tour, one character declared: "I had no idea the slums were as bad as this. I feel as if I were inhaling typhus and smallpox and diphtheria in every breath I draw" (*Social Strugglers,* 267).

33. Describing the importance Jonathan Edwards assigned to the will in the act of learning, Perry Miller observed that Edwards forced "the Lockean sensationalism as far as possible away from a blank naturalistic passivity toward a creative destiny. He was making the nature of man—a creature of experience—a participant in the cosmic design, which is not static, which is not merely an object

of contemplation, but a design in time, requiring for its consummation struggle and anxiety, triumph and repeated failure" (*Jonathan Edwards,* 329).

34. For a brief discussion of the epistemological principles and pedagogies of New Divinity followers, see Noll, *America's God,* chap. 7, esp. 134–35.

35. Abbott, *The Way to Do Good,* 298–99; hereafter cited in text as *Way.* For an examination of "rumspringa," the practice in some Amish cultures of allowing adolescents to encounter vice in the world outside the religious community, see Lucy Walker's documentary, *The Devil's Playground.*

36. In a tradition we have seen, Henry Ward Beecher reminded parents and children that "the purity of imagination, of thought, and of feeling, if soiled, can be cleansed by no fuller's soap; if lost, cannot be found, though sought carefully with tears" ("Strange Woman" 212).

37. Helen Campbell's virtual tours resonate with Beecher's homiletic sermon. Speaking of the seduction of despair in the tenements, she writes, "Darkness means the devil's deeds, and [children] never get a breath except from the rooms into which they open. You sleep in one once, and there is a band around your head when you wake, and a sinking and craving at your stomach. You don't want to eat, there is nothing answers it but whiskey, and in the basement of the building you may find a smiling fiend in immaculate white apron ready to pour the bubbling glass full and usher you into the anteroom of hell" (quoted in Burr, "Social Salvation," 261–62).

38. Bunyan, *The Life and Death of Mr. Badman,* 1.

39. Pearse, *The Great Concern,* 64–65; original emphasis.

40. Ibid., 17.

41. My thanks to Tobias Gregory for taking me on a tour of this regional, historic Puritan cemetery on the Vermont-Massachusetts border, outside Colrain.

42. Pearse, *The Great Concern,* 32.

43. See French, "The Cemetery as Cultural Institution," 47; and Grant, "Patriot Graves," 79.

44. Promey, "Seeing the Self," 19–20.

45. Ibid.

46. Rivett, "Tokenography."

47. See Carruthers, *The Book of Memory;* and Yates, *The Art of Memory.*

48. The house figure was repeatedly used in Harvard senior disputations to organize and analyze arguments through dialectical reasoning. Peter Ramus joined the utility of architecture as a mnemonic system (based on Solon's building codes) with its use for organizing and compartmentalizing knowledge categories. On the relation between space, architecture, and memory in Ramism, see Ong's discussion of "Solon's Law" (*Ramus,* 280–82). Ong's study of memory in the classical rhetorical tradition is particularly salient for understanding the role of the architectural system of mnemonics in Protestant homiletics: "But the real reason why Ramus can dispense with memory is that his whole scheme

of arts, based on the topically conceived logic, is a system of local memory. Memory is everywhere, its 'places' or 'rooms' being the mental space which Ramus' arts all fill" (280). In his explanation of the transmission of Ramism at Harvard, Perry Miller defers to the very architectural trope at the core of Ramus's system of logic: A standard diagram or "blueprint" accompanied "Ramistic teaching; it show[ed] at a glance how this logic was built up as an architectural unit, all its parts fitting together, represented on this chart exactly as a house may be represented in the architect's plan. No such design could be discerned until the categories were broken up" (*The New England Mind: The Seventeenth Century*, 125). For the preponderance of the house figure in Harvard theses, see 111–206, and Morison, *Harvard College*, part 1, esp. 139–222. For examples of the division of hell into compartments, see Alexis, "Wigglesworth's 'Easiest Room.'"

49. In part, Riis's virtual tour worked against the spectacularized demography of the "city as mystery" genre, initiated by Eugene Sue's *Le Mystères de Paris* (1842–43), and taken up by American urban writers, such as George Foster, Solon Robinson, and John B. Gough, the last of whom was a temperance evangelical whose own sermons drew upon the homiletic traditions of his Plymouth Church ministers, Beecher and Lyman Abbott. Gough's interaction with homiletic pedagogy, like Robinson's, no doubt shaped the construction of his own urban narratives.

Focused largely on New York City, this American genre promoted the city's urban doppelganger, a dark twin hidden in subterranean layers beneath the streets. Karen Halttunen observes that the city-as-mystery genre borrowed the "spatial sensibility" of the eighteenth-century gothic novel, in which heroines navigated underground vaults and labyrinthine corridors while preserving their virtue and lives to escape licentious clerics, monstrous stepfathers, and assassins. I argue that the seventeenth-century Calvinist sermon tradition presupposed this use of spatial sensibility, initially drawing on the architectural metaphors in the Book of Proverbs. Halttunen points out that both the perspective and purpose of the city as mystery merge in the genre's celebration of its "Asmodean privilege." A puckish demon, Asmodeus's particular pleasure was to lift the roofs off buildings in order to peer down upon the exposed wickedness of the occupants within. In both its authorial function and readerly perspective, the city-as-mystery genre's sensationalist and didactic nature paralleled the virtual-tour narrative's design, but sharply contrasted in its purpose. City-as-mystery narratives presented not the structured allegory of religious homiletics, but rather, an aimless secular allegorical form that gave free play to readers' imaginative and associative capabilities. Like its late-nineteenth-century descendent, the "transvestite narratives" of Crane, London, and Josiah Flynt, in which narrators dress down to pass as poor or working class in order to report ventures among the "lowest strata" of humanity, the city-as-mystery genre exploited the prurient appetites of readers who sought voyeuristic titillation. Its literary structure, allowing readers to gaze down upon the wickedness secreted from urban slums, belonged to a prophylactic pedagogy that, like the homiletic, emerged from the early Calvinist sermons, but that, unlike the homiletic, distanced readers from the objects of their gaze. For an excellent treatment of class transvestism, see Schocket, "Undercover Explorations." For a useful discussion of the city-as-mystery genre, see Halttunen, *Murder Most Foul,* 124. For examples, see Gough, *Sunlight and Shadow* (1881), and *Platform Echoes* (1886); Robinson, *Hot Corn* (1854); and Foster, *Celio* (1850).

50. Beecher and Stowe, *The American Woman's Home.* For a useful study of domestic architecture and architectural metaphors in Beecher and Stowe's theory of domestic economy, see Askeland, "Remodeling the Model Home"; see also Brown, "Getting in the Kitchen with Dinah." For a broader history of the perceived role American domestic architecture played in moral development, see Wright, *Moralism and the Model Home.*

51. Like the structure of allegory, the tenement fabric conceals stories within. Flower, for instance, writes of Boston, "If the passer-by could see what the brick walls which front Hanover and other streets of the North End hide from view," if one passes into "scores of alley-ways, through the narrow corridors, or down through the cellar-like passages which line the streets," he or she enters the "courtyards of the democracy of night" ("Society's Exiles," 208). Evoking the same chapter of Proverbs as Beecher, Walter Swaffield, Flower's friend, ascribes a sinister intent: "This is a large brick block, which from the outside presents a fair appearance, but as you enter you find that the place is like the tombs of the prophets, whitewashed without, but within full of rottenness and death. The sanitary provisions are the cheapest and poorest kind; poisonous gases enough to stifle one are met on every floor. . . . Here sickness, weakness and destitution abound" ("Round Table," 670).

52. Flower, *Civilization's Inferno,* vi.

53. *Other Half* 38. While this edition adds photographs from the Riis collection not originally published in Riis's book and replaces the original ink etchings with the photographs from which they were drawn, it best captures the magic-lantern format.

54. In the same tradition, Flower similarly describes a tenement's interior in his own virtual-tour narrative: The "halls [were] dark as midnight in a dungeon; air heavy with foul odors, and seemingly devoid of oxygen; the banisters greasy and the stairs much worn, as we could feel rather than see" ("Two Hours in the Social Cellar").

55. Reminiscent of the ironic punishments of Classical Hades—that of Tantalus or Sisyphus—Riis describes the task of a group of inmates: "Beyond, on the side lawn, moves another still stranger procession, a file of women in the asylum dress of dull gray, hitched to a queer little wagon that, with its gaudy adorn-

ments, suggests a cross between a baby-carriage and a circus-chariot. One crazy woman is strapped in the seat; forty tug at the rope to which they are securely bound. . . . These are the patients afflicted with suicidal mania, who cannot be trusted at large for a moment with the river in sight" (*Other Half* 203).

56. For a useful discussion of the Calvinist noetic or cognitive systems, including Ramistic and Aristotelian logic, mnemonics, cosmology, Puritan *technologia* or seven arts, and the interlocking "encyclopedia" of knowledge, see Miller, *The New England Mind: The Seventeenth Century,* 111–238; for the best explanation of the Calvinist noetic system and tradition of Ramistic logic, see Ong, *Ramus,* esp. 270–318; for a general history of Calvinist noetic systems in the New England Calvinist tradition, see Morison, *The Puritan Pronaos.* Finally, for an illustration of how nineteenth-century American Protestant culture transformed Calvinist knowledge systems, see note 48 in this chapter.

57. Westbrook, *John Dewey and American Democracy,* 109.

58. In tracing and revising the implications of a sensory epistemology in his study of religious affections in 1746, Edwards defines knowledge in precisely the terms he had set out thirteen years earlier in "Divine and Supernatural Light," in which he divided knowledge into two categories: notional knowledge and a "sense of the heart." The passages from these two important works are worth comparing. In "Divine and Supernatural Light," Edwards writes, "There is a twofold understanding or knowledge of good, that God has made the mind of man capable of. The first, that which is merely speculative or notional. . . . And the other is that which consists in the sense of the heart: as when there is sense of beauty, amiableness, or sweetness of a thing" (413–14). In *A Treatise Concerning Religious Affections,* Edwards expands the explanation, evoking and elaborating on the same illustrations by which he first explained godly knowledge to his Northampton congregation: "There is a distinction to be made between a mere notional understanding, wherein the mind only beholds things in the exercise of a speculative faculty; and the sense of the heart, wherein the mind don't only speculate and behold, but relishes and feels. That sort of knowledge, by which a man has a sensible perception of amiableness and loathsomeness, or of sweetness and nauseousness, is not just the same sort of knowledge with that, by which he knows what a triangle is, and what a square is. The one is mere speculative knowledge; the other sensible knowledge, in which more than the mere intellect is concerned; the heart is the proper subject of it. . . . As he that has perceived the sweet taste of honey, knows much more about it, than he who has only looked upon and felt of it" (272).

59. In *Civilization's Inferno,* for instance, Benjamin Flower prefaces his study of poverty—designed after Riis's *How the Other Half Lives*—with an illustration of the class tiers contained within the frame of a house. On the highest level of the house, the picture depicts a social ball, below it, a middle-class depiction of working opportunity, and still lower, the "social cellar," in which a widow

sits with her hungry children. On the final level beneath the social cellar, "where uninvited poverty holds sway, is a darker zone: a subterranean, rayless vault—the commonwealth of the double night": the darkness of poverty that "extinguished the human soul" (99–100).

60. Riis, *Children of the Poor,* 126.

61. James, "Philosophical Conceptions and Practical Results," 267. James delivered this address, in which he first used C. S. Peirce's term "pragmatism," before the Philosophical Union at the University of California, Berkeley, August 26, 1898.

62. For controversy over Markham's poem and the range of responses, especially among the clergy, see Bremner, *From the Depths,* 106–7.

63. Haroutunian, *Piety versus Moralism;* Meyer, *Democratic Enlightenment,* chap. 3; May, *Enlightenment in America,* chap. 3; and Noll, *America's God,* 230–31, 278–83, 299–307.

64. For the slightly divergent adaptations of Darwinian evolution to Christianity, first promoted among Unitarians, see Savage's *Religion of Evolution* (1876) and *The Morals of Evolution* (1880); Simmons, *The Unending Genesis* (1882) and *New Tables of Stone* (1904); and Lyman Abbott's enormously influential *The Evolution of Christianity* (1892). For a discussion of Calvinism's shift toward modern humanism, see Noll, *America's God,* 139–40.

65. Beecher had "ransomed" a fugitive slave in 1856. For details, see "Ransom of a Slave-girl at Plymouth Church." See also Saltar, *A Church in History.*

66. For a useful explanation of the enduring prevalence of Lamarckian evolution—"the theory that species progress by the cultivation of good habits transmitted genetically from one generation to the next"—see Menand, *The Metaphysical Club,* 382.

67. Howard, *Form and History,* 132.

68. Ibid., 105.

69. Kaplan, *Social Construction,* 9–11.

70. Ibid., 10.

71. Riis, "Special Needs," 495.

72. Riis continues: By the time women arrive at Blackwell's Island, or men arrive at Ward Island, they cannot be redeemed. "No man or woman . . . who is 'sent up' to these colonies ever returns to the city scotfree. There is a lien, visible or hidden, upon his or her present or future, which too often proves stronger than the best purposes and fairest opportunities of social rehabilitation. The under world holds in rigorous bondage every unfortunate or miscreant who has once 'served time'" (*Other Half* 203).

73. Riis reproduces Lowell's letter in his autobiography, *Making of an American,* 308.

74. Flower, *Civilization's Inferno,* 101.

75. Wood, *Ideal Suggestion,* 120.

76. In "A World of Pure Experience," James summarizes the tradition: "Throughout the history of philosophy the subject and its object have been treated as absolutely discontinuous entities; and thereupon the presence of the latter to the former, or the 'apprehension' by the former of the latter, has assumed a paradoxical character which all sorts of theories had to be invented to overcome. Representative theories put a mental 'representation,' 'image,' or 'content' into the gap, as a sort of intermediary. Common-sense theories left the gap untouched, declaring our mind able to clear it by a self-transcending leap. Transcendentalists theories left it impossible to traverse by finite knowers, and brought an Absolute in to perform the salutatory act" (52–53).

77. This slogan is in Riis, "Children of the Poor," 20.

78. Riis, "The Battle with the Slum," 626. Helen Campbell, for whose book *Darkness and Daylight* Riis supplied the photographs, exhibits this Larmarkian belief: of a drunkard's children, Campbell writes, "Eleven of these came into the world, each a little more aburdened than the last with the inheritance of evil tendency. Five died before they were three weeks old, from . . . vitiated blood. Two were born idiots, and are in an asylum" (675).

79. Riis, *The Making of an American,* 423.

80. James, "A World of Pure Experience," 40.

81. Dewey quoted in Westbrook, *John Dewey and American Democracy,* 89.

82. Stanton, *Eighty Years and More,* 42–43.

83. In the sermon tradition of Finney, Henry Ward Beecher also brought fiction to life in vivid dramas. His biographer Paxton Hibben, for example, described Beecher's performance in the slave "auction" for the captured Edmonson sisters as though Beecher stood in the midst of the southern slave market he depicted, "as if he were an actor in it, himself. It [seemed] more real to him than the crowded church filled with sobbing . . . women, with shining-eyed, trembling-handed men, vicarious participants in a tremendous drama of heroism" (Hibben, *Henry Ward Beecher,* 134).

84. Sermons in the homiletic tradition often relied on a step system—usually linked to a spatial paradigm—a system that marks their roots in older memory systems: for example, see Arthur, *Ten Nights in a Bar-room* (1854); Sheldon, *Robert Hardy's Seven Days* (1898), or even the double meaning conveyed by *In His Steps;* and Beecher, *Six Sermons* (1827).

85. Edwardsian Platonism, the Scottish Common Sense School's "sixth sense," Coleridgean Platonism, Swedenborgianism, Mesmerism, transcendentalism, Universalism, and the homiletic tradition, to name but a few, were, broadly speaking, ideas and movements anchored in a belief in an *ontic* and corresponding universe and marshaled against the advancing skepticism of the rational Enlightenment. American Protestant ministers assured their followers of the gossamer-thin veil that separated the earthly realm from the divine, through

which the energies of heavenly guardians or their demonic counterparts might intercede in worldly cause and effect.

86. Wood, *Ideal Suggestion,* 134.

87. Menand, *The Metaphysical Club,* 90.

88. Trachtenberg, *Reading American Photography,* esp. 21–46.

89. Holmes, "The Stereoscope and the Stereograph," 748.

90. Riis, "Reform by Humane Touch," 738; Abbott, *Way,* 317.

91. Flower, "Society's Exiles," 37.

92. Beecher's works are peppered with contrasts between the "deep and strange joy" of the rural and the perilous moral "contradictions and burdens" of the city; see, e.g., Beecher, *Star Papers,* 112.

93. Riis, *Making of an American,* 169–70.

94. Quoted from an anonymous review of Riis's lecture, "The Children of the Poor," *The Critic,* vol. 18, December 17, 1892, 340–41.

95. While acknowledging recent theories in the relational—and thus narrative—nature of photography, many scholars remain uncritical of Riis's claims to candid photography. Ansel Adams and Alexander Alland epitomize this credulousness by their insistence that "Riis used the camera to record, not to create" (Alland, *Jacob A. Riis,* xiii).

96. DeForest and Veiller, *The Tenement House Problem.*

97. For a helpful discussion of the seductive sense of "reliability" that seemingly "unfiltered" images can provide, see Burke, *Eyewitnessing,* 41–42.

98. Promey, "Seeing the Self," 26.

99. Ibid., 13.

100. Riis, "Reform by Humane Touch," 753.

101. In his study of *The New England Primer,* George Livermore writes that this prayer was the first prayer he ever learned, and tells the anecdote that John Quincy Adams never "laid his head down" that he did not repeat the prayer (*Origin, History and Character,* 4).

102. Cross, *The Suffering Millions,* 3.

103. In Rosetta Otwell Cross, *The Suffering Millions,* 3.

104. Burr, "Social Salvation," 263.

105. Swaffield, "Round Table," 674. Often cited in relation to children in New York institutions was Amos G. Warner's famous study, *American Charities,* which put the mortality rate for institutionalized children under three at "97 per cent per annum." "Of course," Warner writes, "this high death-rate comes in part from the bad condition of the children when received. They are often marasmic, rachitic, syphilitic, half dead from drugging or neglect, or from ante-natal and post-natal abuse. Yet this does not explain entirely the high death-rate common to institutions, as is shown by the fact that strong, thriving babies droop and die in them. . . . The death-rate where children are cared for in institutions often results from positive neglect" (266–67).

106. As the reviewer of Riis's magic-lantern lecture titled "Children of the Slums" described Riis's talk "Tony's Hardships," "Riis *painted* the 'little incidents of child life,' showing how they were cared for and how, through wicked surroundings, evil associates and the neglect of Christians in better circumstances, they grew up in evil ways" ("Children of the Slums," *Indianapolis Journal,* February 19, 1900; emphasis added). On occasion, reviewers characterized the realism of Riis's virtual tour over mere language, as when a reviewer of a magic-lantern slide lecture, "How the Other Half Lives," wrote for *Coup d'Etat* (April 1892): "Riis's stereopticon views were certainly more realistic than any words could be." While this reviewer's statement signals a distinct break from an older allegorical epistemology that viewed images and language as similar in their representative capacities, other reviewers continued to use the older vocabulary to describe Riis's photographic tours, making it difficult to separate the affect produced by photography from that produced by language. The contemporary criticism again reveals the way in which the visually oriented homiletic tradition seamlessly absorbs the photograph. For one viewer of Riis's talk at the Vendome, "Squalid Abodes," printed in the *Boston Traveler* on April 19, 1891, it "was a realistic picture of life in the New York slums," a characterization that denies the photograph's discrete meaning or visual authority apart from the lecture's larger production of "a realistic picture." In an article titled "Millions of Babies," printed in the *New York Tribune* on December 18, 1896, the writer claimed that Riis "urged the need of caring for the poor, and gave graphic pictures, both pathetic and amusing, of his experience with the waifs and wanderers of all ages and sizes in this great city." While Riis used the stereopticon projection in his talk, "graphic pictures" blends the photographic referent with the verbal, suggested by the term "experience."

107. When, for instance, Henry Cabot Lodge used Riis's magic-lantern lectures to defend his immigration restrictions based on their "vivid picture" of "the degrading effect" of the "importation of the lowest forms of labor," he drew equally upon the authority of the lectures' visually oriented heuristic and its photographic realism ("The Restriction of Immigration," 34).

108. Halttunen, "Humanitarianism and the Pornography of Pain," 325–26.

109. Riis, *Making of an American,* 134.

Epilogue

1. Wills, *Head and Heart,* and *What Jesus Meant;* Taylor, *A Secular Age;* Waldman, *Founding Faith;* Dennet, *Breaking the Spell.*

2. See esp. Lilla, *The Stillborn God.*

3. Garry Wills, "The Day the Enlightenment Went Out," *New York Times,* November 4, 2004.

4. For Perry Miller's history of James Franklin's struggle with the Mathers, see *The New England Mind: From Colony to Province,* chap. 20, esp. 324–44.

5. For an extended reading of Miller's formative role in shaping and institutionalizing ideologies of imperialism in the American higher-education curriculum (the invention of American Studies predicated on an idea of exceptionalism), see Kaplan, "Left Alone in America."

6. Denning, *Mechanic Accents;* Hall, *Cultures of Print,* and *Lived Religion in America;* Radway, *Reading the Romance;* and Tompkins, *Sensational Designs.*

7. Moore, *Selling God.*

8. Barbara Bradley Hagerty, "Creation Museum Promotes the Bible over Evolution," National Public Radio, http://www.npr.org/templates/story/story .php?storyId=10498875.

9. John Raoux and Travid Reed, "Christian Theme Park a Holy Land Experience," *USA Today,* http://www.usatoday.com/news/religion/2007–07–29-holy-land-experence_N.htm.

10. Ibid.

11. Miles, "Image," 169.

Bibliography

Abbott, Benjamin. *The Experience and Gospel Labours of the Rev. Benjamin Abbott.* New York: John C. Totten, 1813.

Abbott, Jacob. *The Corner Stone; or, A Familiar Illustration of the Principles of Christian Truth.* New York: Harper, 1851.

——. *The Way to Do Good; or, The Christian Character Mature.* Boston: W. Peirce, 1836.

——. *The Young Christian; or, A Familiar Illustration of the Principles of Christian Duty.* New York: American Tract Society, 1832.

Abbott, Lyman. *The Evolution of Christianity.* New York: Johnson Reprint Corporation, 1969.

Adams, Henry. "The Dynamo and the Virgin." In *The Education of Henry Adams,* 379–90. Cambridge, Mass.: Riverside, 1916.

——. *The Education of Henry Adams: An Autobiography.* Boston: Houghton Mifflin, 1918.

Alcott, Louisa May. *The Journals of Louisa May Alcott.* Edited by Joel Myerson and Daniel Shealy. Athens: University of Georgia Press, 1997.

——. *Little Women.* Edited by Elaine Showalter. New York: Penguin, 1989.

Alexis, Gerhard T. "Wigglesworth's 'Easiest Room.'" *New England Quarterly* 42, no. 4 (December 1969): 573–82.

Alland, Alexander. *Jacob A. Riis: Photographer and Citizen.* Millerton, N.Y.: Aperture, 1974.

Altick, Richard D. *The English Common Reader: A Social History of the Mass Reading Public, 1800–1900.* Chicago: University of Chicago Press, 1957.

Anderson, Wallace E. "Immaterialism in Jonathan Edwards' Early Philosophical Notes." *Journal of the History of Ideas* 25 (1964): 181–200.

Andrews, William L., ed. *Sisters of the Spirit: Three Black Women's Autobiographies of the Nineteenth Century.* Bloomington: Indiana University Press, 1986.

——. *To Tell a Free Story: The First Century of Afro-American Autobiography, 1760–1865.* Chicago: University of Illinois Press, 1986.

Ariès, Philippe. *Centuries of Childhood: The Social History of Family Life.* New York: Vintage, 1962.

Armstrong, Frances. "'Here Little, and Hereafter Bliss': *Little Women* and the Deferral of Greatness." *American Literature* 64 (September 1992): 453–74.

Arthur, T. S. *Ten Nights in a Bar-room, and What I Saw There.* Philadelphia: Bradley, 1854.

Asbury, Francis. *The Journal and Letters of Francis Asbury,* vol. 3. Edited by Elmer T. Clark et al. London: Epworth, 1958.

Askeland, Lori. "Remodeling the Model Home in *Uncle Tom's Cabin* and *Beloved.*" *American Literature* 64, no. 4 (1992): 785–806.

Augst, Thomas. *The Clerk's Tale: Young Men and Moral Life in Nineteenth-Century America.* Chicago: University of Chicago Press, 2003.

Augustine, St. *Against the Academicians; The Teacher.* Edited by Peter King. Indianapolis: Hackett, 1995.

——. *Confessions.* Vol. 5. Translated by Vernon J. Burke. New York: Fathers of the Church, 1953.

Axtell, James, ed. *The Educational Writings of John Locke.* Cambridge: Cambridge University Press, 1968.

Bailyn, Bernard. *The Ideological Origins of the American Revolution.* Cambridge, Mass.: Belknap, 1967.

Balmer, Randall. *Mine Eyes Have Seen the Glory: A Journey into the Evangelical Subculture in America.* Oxford: Oxford University Press, 1989.

Banta, Martha. *Henry James and the Occult.* Bloomington: Indiana University Press, 1972.

Baritz, Loren. *City on a Hill.* New York: Wiley, 1964.

Barrish, Phillip. *American Literary Realism, Critical Theory, and Intellectual Prestige, 1880–1995.* Cambridge: Cambridge University Press, 2001.

Barton, Cynthia. *Transcendental Wife: The Life of Abigail May Alcott.* Lanham, Md.: University Press of America, 1996.

Bauer, Ralph. *The Cultural Geography of Colonial American Literatures: Empire, Travel, Modernity.* Cambridge: Cambridge University Press, 2003.

Bazire, Joyce, and Eric Colledge, eds. *The Chastising of God's Children.* Oxford: Basil Blackwell, 1957.

Beam, Lura. *He Called Them by the Lightening: A Teacher's Odyssey in the Negro South, 1908–1919.* Indianapolis: Bobbs-Merrill, 1967.

Beardsley, Charles. "Professor Herron." *Arena* 15 (1896): 784–96.

Bedell, Madelon. *The Alcotts: Biography of a Family.* New York: Clarkson N. Potter, 1980.

Beecher, Catharine E., and Harriet Beecher Stowe. *The American Woman's Home; or, Principles of Domestic Science; being a Guide to the Foundation of Economical, Healthful, Beautiful, and Christian Homes.* New York: J. B. Ford, 1869.

Beecher, Henry Ward. *The Life of Jesus, the Christ.* New York: Ford, 1871.

——. "The Sources and Uses of Suffering." In *The Plymouth Pulpit: Sermons Preached in Plymouth Church, Brooklyn,* 155–78. New York: J. B. Ford, 1875.

——. *Star Papers; or, Experiences of Art and Nature.* New York: J. C. Derby, 1855.

——. "The Strange Woman's House." In *Lectures to Young Men, on Various Important Subjects.* New York: M. H. Newman, 1851.

Beecher, Lyman. *Six Sermons on the Nature, Occasions, Signs, Evils, and Remedy of Intemperance.* New York: American Tract Society, 1827.

Bell, Michael Davitt. *The Problem of American Realism: Studies in the Cultural History of a Literary Idea.* Chicago: University of Chicago Press, 1993.

Bellamy, Joseph. *True Religion Delineated; or, Experimental Religion as Distinguished from Formality on the One Hand, and Enthusiasm on the Other, Felt in a Scriptural and Rational Light.* Boston: S. Kneeland, 1750.

Benedict, G. W. *An Exposition of the System of Instruction and Discipline Pursued in the University of Vermont,* 2nd ed. Burlington: Chauncey Goodrich, 1831.

Bercovitch, Sacvan. *The Puritan Origins of the American Self.* New Haven, Conn.: Yale University Press, 1975.

Berlant, Lauren. "Poor Eliza." *American Literature* 70 (September 1998): 635–68.

Bierce, Ambrose. *The Unabridged Devil's Dictionary,* ed. David E. Schultz and S. T. Joshi. Athens, Ga.: University of Georgia Press, 2000.

Bishop, Joel Prentiss. *Commentaries on the Law of Marriage and Divorce.* Boston: Little, Brown, 1852.

Block, Ruth H. *Visionary Republic: Millennial Themes in American Thought, 1756–1800.* Cambridge: Cambridge University Press, 1985.

Blumin, Stuart M. *The Emergence of the Middle Class: Social Experience in the American City, 1760–1900.* Cambridge: Cambridge University Press, 1989.

Bond, Alvin, ed. *Memoir of the Rev. Pliny Fisk, A. M.: Late Missionary to Palestine.* Boston: Crocker and Brewster, 1828.

Boyer, Paul S. "In His Steps: A Reappraisal." *American Quarterly* 23 (1971): 60–78.

Boyesen, Hjalmar Hjorth. *Social Strugglers: A Novel.* New York: Scribner's, 1893.

Boylan, Anne M. *Sunday School: The Formation of an American Institution, 1790–1880.* New Haven, Conn.: Yale University Press, 1988.

Bozeman, Theodore Dwight. *"To Live Ancient Lives": The Primitivist Dimension in Puritanism.* Chapel Hill: University of North Carolina Press, 1988.

Bradford, William. *Of Plymouth Plantation, 1620–1647.* Edited by Samuel Eliot Morison. New York: Knopf, 1952.

Bradley, Stephen H. *A Sketch of the Life of Stephen H. Bradley, from the Age of Five to Twenty-four Years; Including His Remarkable Experience of the Power of the Holy Spirit on the Second Evening of November, 1829.* Madison, Conn.: 1830.

Brainerd, David, ed. *Mediations and Spiritual Experiences of Mr. Thomas Shepard.* Boston: Rogers and Fowle, 1747.

Bratton, J. S. *The Impact of Victorian Children's Fiction.* London: Croom Helm, 1981.

Breen, T. H. " 'Baubles of Britain': The American and Consumer Revolutions of the Eighteenth Century." *Past and Present* 119 (May 1988): 73–104.

——. "An Empire of Goods: The Anglicization of Colonial America, 1690–1776." *Journal of British Studies* 25 (October 1986): 467–99.

——. "Subjecthood and Citizenship: The Context of James Otis's Radical Critique of John Locke." *New England Quarterly* 71 (September 1998): 378–403.

Breitwieser, Mitchell. *American Puritanism and the Defense of Mourning: Religion, Grief, and Ethnology in Mary White Rowlandson's Captivity Narrative.* Madison: University of Wisconsin Press, 1990.

Brekus, Catherine A. *Strangers and Pilgrims: Female Preaching in America, 1740–1845.* Chapel Hill: University of North Carolina Press, 1998.

Bremner, Robert H. *From the Depths: The Discovery of Poverty in the United States.* New York: New York University Press, 1956.

Brewer, John. *The Pleasures of the Imagination: English Culture in the Eighteenth Century.* London: Harper Collins, 1997.

——. "Reconstructing the Reader: Prescriptions, Texts, and Strategies in Ann Larpent's Reading." In *The Practice and Representation of Reading in England,* ed. James Raven, Helen Small, and Naomi Tadmor, 226–45. Cambridge: Cambridge University Press, 1996.

Brodhead, Richard H. *Cultures of Letters: Scenes of Reading and Writing in Nineteenth-Century America.* Chicago: University of Chicago Press, 1993.

Brooks, Joanna. *American Lazarus: Religion and the Rise of African American and Native American Literatures.* Oxford: Oxford University Press, 2003.

Brown, Candy Gunther. *The Word in the World: Evangelical Writing, Publishing, and Reading in America, 1789–1880.* Chapel Hill: University of North Carolina Press, 2004.

Brown, Gillian. *The Consent of the Governed: The Lockean Legacy in Early American Culture.* Cambridge, Mass.: Harvard University Press, 2001.

——. "Getting in the Kitchen with Dinah: Domestic Politics in *Uncle Tom's Cabin.*" *American Quarterly* 36 (1984): 503–23.

Brown, Matthew P. *The Pilgrim and the Bee: Reading Rituals and Book Culture in Early New England.* Philadelphia: University of Pennsylvania Press, 2007.

Brown, Peter. *Augustine of Hippo: A Biography.* Berkeley and Los Angeles: University of California Press, 1967.

Brown, Richard D. Afterword to *Printing and Society in Early America.* Edited by William L. Joyce. Worcester: University of Massachusetts Press, 1983.

Bryan, Jennifer. *Looking Inward: Devotional Reading and the Private Self in Late Medieval England.* Philadelphia: University of Pennsylvania Press, 2007.

Bunyan, John. *The Life and Death of Mr. Badman: Presented to the World in a Familiar Dialogue between Mr. Wiseman and Mr. Attentive.* Edited by Roger Sharrock and James E. Forrest. Oxford: Clarendon, 1988.

——. *The Pilgrim's Progress.* Edited by Roger Sharrock. London: Penguin, 1987.

Burder, George. "Sermon XXXIII: The Doctrine of the Trinity." In *Village Sermons; or, Sixty-five Plain and Short Discourses on the Principal Doctrines of the Gospel, Intended for the Use of Families, Sunday Schools, or Companies*

Assembled for Religious Instruction in Country Villages, vol. 2, 5–14. Brookfield, Mass.: Merriam, 1818.

———. "Sermon XLIV: The Birth of Christ." In *Village Sermons; or, Sixty-five
Plain and Short Discourses on the Principal Doctrines of the Gospel, In-
tended for the Use of Families, Sunday Schools, or Companies Assembled for
Relgious Instruction in Country Villages*, vol. 2, 111–20. Brookfield, Mass.:
Merriam & Co., 1818.

Burke, Edmund. *A Philosophical Enquiry into the Origin of Our Ideas of the
Sublime and Beautiful.* Edited by Adam Phillips. New York: Oxford University Press, 1990.

Burke, Peter. *Eyewitnessing: The Uses of Images as Historical Evidence.* Ithaca,
N.Y.: Cornell University Press, 2001.

Burr, Everett D. "Social Salvation: What the Church Can Do to Abolish the
Slums." *The Coming Age* 2, no. 3 (September 1899): 254–61.

Bushman, Richard L. *From Puritan to Yankee: Character and the Social Order in
Connecticut, 1690–1765.* Cambridge, Mass.: Harvard University Press, 1967.

Bushnell, Horace. *An Argument for "Discourse of Christian Nurture," Addressed to the Publishing Committee of the Massachusetts Sabbath School
Society.* Hartford: E. Hunt, 1847.

Cady, Edwin H. "The Artistry of Jonathan Edwards." *New England Quarterly*
22 (March 1949): 61–72.

Caine, Hall. *The Christian: A Story.* London: Heinemann, 1897.

Caldwell, David. "The Doctrine of Universal Salvation Unscriptural." In *A
Sketch of the Life and Character of the Rev. David Caldwell, D. D.*, 285–302.
Greensborough, N.C.: Swaim and Sherwood, 1842.

Caldwell, Patricia. *The Puritan Conversion Narrative: The Beginnings of American Expression.* Cambridge: Cambridge University Press, 1983.

Calvin, John. *Institutes of the Christian Religion.* Edited by Lewis Battles. Philadelphia: Westminster, 1960.

Campbell, Helen. *Darkness and Daylight; or, Lights and Shadows of New York
Life.* Hartford: Hartford Press, 1895.

Cannon, Lou. *Governor Reagan: His Rise to Power.* New York: Public Affairs,
2003.

Carey, Eustace. *The Memoir of William Carey.* Boston: Gould, Kendall, and
Lincoln, 1836.

Carey, James. *Carey's Library of Choice Literature.* Philadelphia: E. L. Carey &
A. Hart, 1836.

Carruthers, Mary. *The Book of Memory: A Study of Memory in Medieval Culture.* Cambridge, Mass.: Harvard University Press, 1990.

Carwardine, Richard. "The Second Great Awakening in the Urban Centers: An
Examination of Methodism and the 'New Measures.'" *Journal of American
History* 59 (1972): 327–40.

Casanova, José. *Public Religions in the Modern World.* Chicago: University of
Chicago Press, 1994.

Castronovo, Russ. *Beautiful Democracy: Aesthetics and Anarchy in a Global
Era.* Chicago: University of Chicago Press, 2007.

——. *Necro Citizenship: Death, Eroticism, and the Public Sphere in the Nineteenth-Century United States.* Durham, N.C.: Duke University Press, 2001.

Cave, Alfred. "The Living Christ." In *Volume of Proceedings of the Second International Congregational Council Held in Tremont Temple, Boston, Mass., September 20–29, 1899,* 463–72. Boston: Press of Samuel Usher, 1900.

Challoner, Richard, ed. *The Imitation of Christ.* New York: Benziger, 1874.

Chamberlain, Ava. "The Theology of Cruelty: A New Look at the Rise of Arminianism in Eighteenth-Century New England." *Harvard Theological Review* 85 (1992): 335–56.

Chamberlin, James A. "If Jesus Were an Editor." *Kingdom,* April 2, 1897, 820–21.

Chaucer, Geoffrey. *The Canterbury Tales.* 3rd ed. Edited by Larry Benson. Boston: Houghton Mifflin, 1987.

Chauncy, Charles. *Seasonable Thoughts on the State of Religion in New-England.* Boston: Rogers and Fowle, 1743.

Clark, Daniel A. *Sinners in the Hands of an Angry God: A Sermon by the Venerated President Edwards, Re-written, so as to Retain His Thoughts in a Modern Style.* Amherst, Mass.: Carter & Adams, 1826.

Clark, Peter. *British Clubs and Societies, 1580–1800: The Origins of an Associated World.* Oxford: Clarendon, 2000.

Clendenning, John. *The Life and Thought of Josiah Royce.* Madison: University of Wisconsin Press, 1985.

Coe, George A. *The Spiritual Life: Studies in the Science of Religion.* New York: Eaton and Mains, 1900.

Cohen, Charles. *God's Caress: The Psychology of Puritan Religious Experience.* New York: Oxford University Press, 1986.

Colacurcio, Michael. "The Example of Edwards: Idealist Imagination and the Metaphysics of Sovereignty." In *Puritan Influences in American Literature,* ed. Emory Elliott, 55–106. Urbana: University of Illinois Press, 1979.

Cole, Stewart. *The History of Fundamentalism.* New York: Richard R. Smith, 1931.

Commager, Henry Steele. *The American Mind: An Interpretation of American Thought and Character since the 1880s.* New Haven, Conn.: Yale University Press, 1950.

Conforti, Joseph. "David Brainerd and the Nineteenth Century Missionary Movement." *Journal of the Early Republic* 5 (Fall 1985): 309–29.

——. "Jonathan Edwards's Most Popular Work: 'The Life of David Brainerd' and Nineteenth-Century Evangelical Culture." *Church History* 54 (June 1985): 188–201.

Converse, Florence. *Garments of Praise: A Miracle Cycle.* New York: Dutton, 1921.

Cooper, William. *How and Why the Young Should Cleanse Their Way.* Boston: B. Green, 1716.

——. "Man Humbled by Being Compar'd to a Worm." Boston: B. Green, 1732.

Cotton, John. *The Controversie Concerning the Liberty of Conscience in Mat-*

ters of Religion, Truly Stated, and Distinctly and Plainly Handled, by Mr. John Cotton of Boston in New-England. London: Thomas Banks, 1646.

———. *The Covenant of Gods Free Grace, Most Sweetly Unfolded and Comfortably Applied to a Disquieted Soul*. London: Matthew Simmons, 1645.

Cox, Samuel H. "Salvation Achieved Only in the Present Life: Requiring a Resolute Effort." New York: Jonathan Leavitt, 1831.

Cox, Thomas C. *Blacks in Topeka, Kansas, 1865–1915: A Social History*. Baton Rouge: Louisiana State University Press, 1982.

Craig, John. *A Short Summe of the Whole Catechisme*. Introduction by Thomas Graves Law. Edinburgh: David Douglass, 1883.

Crane, Stephen. "An Experiment in Misery." *New York Press*, April 22, 1894, 2.

Crawford, Michael. *Seasons of Grace: Colonial New England's Revival Tradition in Its British Context*. New York: Oxford University Press, 1991.

Cross, Rosetta Otwell. *The Suffering Millions*. Ann Arbor: Courier Office, 1890.

Curtis, Susan. *A Consuming Faith: The Social Gospel and Modern American Culture*. Baltimore: Johns Hopkins University Press, 1991.

Dahlstrand, Frederick C. *Amos Bronson Alcott: An Intellectual Biography*. Rutherford, N.J.: Fairleigh Dickinson University Press, 1982.

Damrosch, Leopold, Jr. *God's Plot and Man's Stories: Studies in the Fictional Imagination from Milton to Fielding*. Chicago: University of Chicago Press, 1985.

Darnton, Robert. "What Is the History of Books?" In *Reading in America: Literature and Social History,* ed. Cathy N. Davidson, 27–52. Baltimore: Johns Hopkins University Press, 198.

Davidson, Cathy N. *Revolution and the Word: The Rise of the Novel in America*. New York: Oxford University Press, 1986.

Davidson, E. H. "From Locke to Edwards." *Journal of the History of Ideas* 24 (1963): 355–72.

Davies, Wallace Evan. "Religious Issues in Late Nineteenth-Century American Novels." *Bulletin of the John Rylands Library* 41 (1959): 358–59.

Davison, M. H. Armstrong. *The Evolution of Anaesthesia*. Baltimore: Johns Hopkins University Press, 1965.

Defoe, Daniel. *Robinson Crusoe*. Edited by Virgini Woolfe. New York: Random House, 2001.

DeForest, Robert W., and Lawrence Veiller. *The Tenement House Problem: Including the Report of the New York State Tenement House Commission of 1900*. 2 vols. New York: Macmillan, 1903.

Demos, John. *A Little Commonwealth: Family Life in Plymouth Colony*. New York: Oxford, 1970.

———. *The Unredeemed Captive: A Family Story from Early America*. New York: Knopf, 1994.

Dennet, Daniel C. *Breaking the Spell: Religion as a Natural Phenomenon*. New York: Penguin, 2007.

Denning, Michael. *Mechanic Accents: Dime Novels and Working-Class Culture in America*. New York: Verso, 1987.

Devil's Playground. DVD. Directed by Lucy Walker. New York: Stick Figure Productions, 2002.

Dewey, John. "Introduction to Essays in Experimental Logic." In *John Dewey: The Middle Works, 1899–1924,* vol. 4, ed. Jo Ann Boydston, 129–42. Carbondale: Southern Illinois University Press, 1977.

———. "The Relation of Theory to Practice in Education." In *John Dewey: The Middle Works, 1899–1924,* vol. 3, ed. J. A. Boydston, 252–56. Carbondale: Southern Illinois University Press, 1977.

Dillenberger, John. *The Visual Arts and Christianity in America: From the Colonial Period to the Present.* New York: Crossroad, 1989.

Doran, George H. *Chronicles of Barabbas.* New York: Harcourt, 1935.

Douglas, Ann. *The Feminizing of American Culture.* New York: Knopf, 1977.

Draper, John William. *History of the Conflict between Religion and Science.* New York: D. Appleton, 1875.

Du Bois, W. E. B. "The Church and the Negro." *Crisis* 6 (October 1913): 219.

———. "Jesus Christ in Georgia." *Crisis* 3 (December 1911): 70–74.

——— "Jesus Christ in Texas." In *Darkwater: Voices from within the Veil,* 123–33. New York: Harcourt, Brace, and Howe, 1920.

Duffy, Eamon. *Marking the Hours: English People and Their Prayers, 1240–1570.* New Haven, Conn.: Yale University Press, 2006.

———. *The Stripping of the Altars: Traditional Religion in England, c. 1400–c. 1580.* New Haven, Conn.: Yale University Press, 1992.

Duffy, John J. Introd. to *Coleridge's American Disciples: The Selected Correspondence of James Marsh.* Amherst: University of Massachusetts Press, 1973.

Durant, Will. *A Brief History of Civilization from Ancient Times to the Dawn of the Modern Age.* New York: Simon & Schuster, 2001.

Dwight, Sereno E. *The Works of President Edwards,* 10 vols. New York: Carvell, 1829–30.

Edwards, Jonathan. "The Danger of Corrupt Communication among Young People." In *The Works of Jonathan Edwards: Sermons and Discourses, 1739–1742,* vol. 22, ed. Harry S. Stout and Nathan O. Hatch. New Haven, Conn.: Yale University Press, 2003.

———. "The Distinguishing Marks of a Work of the Spirit of God." In *The Works of Jonathan Edwards,* vol. 4, ed. C. C. Goen, 213–88. New Haven, Conn.: Yale University Press, 1972.

———. "A Divine and Supernatural Light." In *The Works of Jonathan Edwards,* vol. 17, ed. Mark Valeri and Harry S. Stout, 405–26. New Haven, Conn.: Yale University Press, 1999.

———. *Essay on the Application of Abstract Reasoning to the Christian Doctrines.* Boston: Crocker and Brewster, 1832.

———. *A Faithful Narrative.* London: John Oswald, 1737.

———. *Images of Divine Things.* Vol. 11 of *The Works of Jonathan Edwards,* ed. Wallace E. Anderson. New Haven, Conn.: Yale University Press, 1993.

———. *The Life of David Brainerd, Chiefly Extracted from His Diary by President Edwards.* New York: American Tract Society, 1833.

——. *Religious Affections.* Vol. 2 of *The Works of Jonathan Edwards,* ed. John E. Smith. New Haven, Conn.: Yale University Press, 1959.

——. "Sinners in the Hands of an Angry God." In *The Works of Jonathan Edwards,* vol. 22, ed. Harry S. Stout and Nathan O. Hatch, with Kyle P. Farley, 404–17. New Haven, Conn.: Yale University Press, 2003.

——. "Some Thoughts Concerning the Present Revival." In *The Great Awakening,* ed. C. C. Goen, 388. New Haven, Conn.: Yale University Press, 1972.

——. "Subjects of the First Work of Grace May Need a New Conversion." In *The Works of Jonathan Edwards,* ed. Perry Miller, John E. Smith, and Harry S. Stout, vol. 22, 181–202. New Haven: Yale University Press, 1957.

——. *A Treatise Concerning Religious Affections.* Edited by John E. Smith. New Haven, Conn.: Yale University Press, 1959.

——. "The True Christian's Life a Journey towards Heaven." In *The Works of Jonathan Edwards,* vol. 17, ed. Perry Miller, John E. Smith, and Harry S. Stout, 427–46. New Haven, Conn.: Yale University Press, 1957.

Elaw, Zilpha. *Memoirs of the Life, Religious Experience, Ministerial Travels, and Labours of Mrs. Elaw.* In *Sisters of the Spirit,* ed. William L. Andrews, 53–160. Bloomington: Indiana University Press, 1986.

Ellis, Joseph J. "The Puritan Mind in Transition: The Philosophy of Samuel Johnson." *William and Mary Quarterly* 28 (1971): 26–45.

Elsing, William T. "Life in New York Tenement-Houses, as Seen by a City Missionary." *Scribner's Magazine* 40, no. 73 (June 1892): 697–721.

Emerson, Ralph Waldo. *Lectures and Biographical Sketches.* Boston: Houghton Mifflin, 1883.

Engelsing, Rolf. *Analphabetentum und Lekture: Zur Sozialgeschichte des Lesens in Deutchland zwischen feudaler und industrieller Gesellschaft.* Stuttgart: Metzler, 1973.

Evans, Margaret J. "Woman's Work: A Change of Emphasis Needed." In *Volume of Proceedings of the Second International Congregational Council Held in Tremont Temple, Boston, Mass., September 20–29, 1899,* 281–90. Boston: Press of Samuel Usher, 1900.

Feuer, Lewis. "James Marsh and the Conservative Transcendentalist Philosophy: A Political Interpretation." *New England Quarterly* 31 (1958): 3–31.

Fielding, Henry. *Tom Jones.* Edited by Fredson Bowers. New York: Modern Library, 1985.

Fiering, Norman. *Jonathan Edwards's Moral Thought and Its British Context.* Chapel Hill: University of North Carolina Press, 1981.

——. *Moral Philosophy at Seventeenth-Century Harvard: A Discipline in Transition.* Chapel Hill: University of North Carolina Press, 1981.

Fisher, G. P. "The Philosophy of Jonathan Edwards." In *Discussions in History and Theology,* 227–52. New York: Scribner's, 1880.

Fliegelman, Jay. *Prodigals and Pilgrims: The American Revolution against Patriarchal Authority, 1750–1800.* Cambridge: Cambridge University Press, 1982.

Flower, Benjamin Orange. *Civilization's Inferno; or, Studies in the Social Cellar.* Boston: Arena, 1893.

——. "Jesus or Caesar." *Arena* 9 (March 1894): 522–33.

——. "Society's Exiles." *Arena* 4 (June 1891): 37–54.

——. "Two Hours in the Social Cellar." *Arena* 5 (April 1892): 646–53.

Flynt, Josiah. *Tramping with Tramps: Studies and Sketches of Vagabond Life.* New York: Century, 1899.

Foote, Stephanie. *Regional Fictions: Culture and Identity in Nineteenth-Century American Literature.* Madison: University of Wisconsin Press, 2001.

Ford, Paul Leicester. *The New England Primer: A History of Its Origin and Development.* New York: Columbia University Press, 1962.

"Forum: Toward a History of the Standard of Living in British North America." *William and Mary Quarterly* 45 (1988): 116–70.

Foster, George. *Celio; or, New York Above Ground and Under-ground.* New York: DeWitt and Davenport, 1850.

Fowler, Alastair. *Renaissance Realism: Narrative Images in Literature and Art.* Oxford: Oxford University Press, 2003.

Fox, John, Jr. *The Heart of the Hills.* New York: Scribner's, 1913.

——. *The Little Shepard of Kingdom Come.* New York: Scribner's, 1903.

Foxcroft, Thomas. *Cleansing Our Way in Youth, Press'd as the Highest Importance; and Observing the Word of God Recommended, as the Only Sufficient Means.* Boston: S. Kneeland, 1719.

——. *Lessons of Caution to Young Sinners.* Boston: S. Kneeland and T. Green, 1733.

Franklin, Benjamin. *The Autobiography and Other Writings on Politics, Economics, and Virtue.* Cambridge: Cambridge University Press, 2004.

Frei, Hans W. *The Eclipse of Biblical Narrative: A Study in Eighteenth and Nineteenth Century Hermeneutics.* New Haven, Conn.: Yale University Press, 1974.

French, Stanley. "The Cemetery as Cultural Institution." *American Quarterly* 26 (1974): 37–59.

Frey, Sylvia R., and Betty Wood. *Come Shouting to Zion: African American Protestantism in the American South and British Caribbean to 1830.* Chapel Hill: University of North Carolina Press, 1998.

Frye, Northrop. *The Secular Scripture.* Cambridge, Mass.: Harvard University Press, 1976.

Furniss, Norman F. *The Fundamentalist Controversy.* New Haven, Conn.: Yale University Press, 1954.

Gates, Sondra Smith. "Susan Warner and the World of Sunday School Fiction." *Arizona Quarterly* 60, no. 4 (2004): 1–31.

Gilman, Bradley. *Ronald Carnaquay: A Commercial Clergyman.* New York: Macmillan, 1903.

——. *A Son of the Desert.* New York: Century, 1909.

Gilmore, William J. *Elementary Literacy on the Eve of the Industrial Revolution: Trends in Rural New England, 1760–1830.* Worcester, Mass.: American Antiquarian Society, 1982.

——. *Reading Becomes a Necessity of Life: Material and Cultural Life in Rural New England, 1780–1835.* Knoxville: University of Tennessee Press, 1989.

Gladden, Washington. *Recollections.* Boston: Houghton Mifflin, 1909.

Goldman, Peter. "Living Words: Iconoclasm and Beyond in John Bunyan's *Grace Abounding.*" *New Literary History* 33 (Summer 2002): 461–89.

Goodwyn, Lawrence. *The Populist Moment: A Short History of the Agrarian Revolt in America.* New York: Oxford University Press, 1978.

Gordis, Lisa. *Opening Scripture: Bible Reading and Interpretive Authority in Puritan New England.* Chicago: University of Chicago Press, 2003.

Gough, John B. *Platform Echoes; or, Living Truths for Head and Heart.* Hartford, Conn.: A. D. Worthington, 1886.

———. *Sunlight and Shadow; or, Gleanings from My Life Work.* Hartford: A. D. Worthington, 1881.

Graham, William C. *Half Finished Heaven: The Social Gospel in American Literature.* Lanham, Md.: University Press of America, 1995.

Grant, Susan-Mary. "Patriot Graves: American National Identity and the Civil War Dead." *American Nineteenth Century History* 5, no. 3 (Fall 2004): 74–100.

Greaves, Richard L. *Glimpses of Glory: John Bunyan and English Dissent.* Stanford, Calif.: Stanford University Press, 2002.

———. *The Puritan Revolution and Educational Thought: Background to Reform.* New Brunswick, N.J.: Rutgers University Press, 1969.

Greven, Philip J., Jr. *The Protestant Temperament: Patterns of Child-Rearing, Religious Experience, and the Self in Early America.* New York: Knopf, 1977.

Gronniosaw, James Albert Ukawsaw. *A Narrative of the Most Remarkable Particulars in the Life of James Albert Ukawsaw Gronniosaw, an African Prince, as Related by Himself.* In *Slave Narratives,* edited by William L. Andrews and Henry Louis Gates, 1–34. New York: Library of America, 2000.

Habegger, Alfred. *Gender, Fantasy and Realism in American Literature.* New York: Columbia University Press, 1982.

Hale, Edward Everett. *How They Lived in Hampton: A Study of Practical Christianity Applied in the Manufacture of Woodens.* Boston: Smith, 1888.

———. *If Jesus Came to Boston.* Boston: Smith, 1894.

Hall, David D. *The Antinomian Controversy, 1636–1638.* Durham, N.C.: Duke University Press, 1990.

———. *Cultures of Print.* Amherst: University of Massachusetts Press, 1996.

———. "The Examination of Mrs. Anne Hutchinson at the Court of Newtown." In *The Antinomian Controversy, 1636–1638,* 311–48. Durham, N.C.: Duke University Press, 1990.

———. *Lived Religion in America.* Princeton, N.J.: Princeton University Press, 1997.

———. "The Uses of Literacy in New England, 1600–1850." In *Printing and Society in Early America,* ed. William L. Joyce et al., 1–47. Worcester, Mass.: Oak Knoll, 1983.

Halttunen, Karen. "The Domestic Drama of Louisa May Alcott." *Feminist Studies* 10, no. 2 (Summer 1984): 233–54.

———. "Humanitarianism and the Pornography of Pain in Anglo-American Culture." *American Historical Review* 100, no. 2 (April 1995): 303–34.

——. *Murder Most Foul: The Killer and the American Gothic Imagination.* Cambridge, Mass.: Harvard University Press, 1998.

Hambrick-Stowe, Charles E. *The Practice of Piety: Puritan Devotional Disciplines in Seventeenth-Century New England.* Chapel Hill: University of North Carolina Press, 1982.

——. "The Spirit of the Old Writers: The Great Awakening and the Persistence of Puritan Piety." In *Puritanism: Transatlantic Perspectives on a Seventeenth-Century Anglo-American Faith,* ed. Francis J. Bremer, 277–91. Boston: Massachusetts Historical Society, 1993.

Hames-García, Michael. *Fugitive Thought: Prison Movements, Race, and the Meaning of Justice.* Minneapolis: University of Minnesota Press, 2004.

Hardy, Samuel. *A Guide to Heaven.* Hartford, Conn.: O. D. Cooke, 1815.

Haroutunian, Joseph. *Piety versus Moralism: The Passing of the New England Theology.* New York: Harper & Row, 1970.

Hatch, Miss. "Some Features of the Work among the Freedman." *Missionary Review of the World* 17 (June 1894): 441.

Hatch, Nathan O. *The Democratization of American Christianity.* New Haven, Conn.: Yale University Press, 1989.

——. "Millennnialism and Popular Religion in the Early Republic." In *The Evangelical Tradition in America,* ed. Leonard I. Sweet, 113–30. Macon, Ga.: Mercer University Press, 1984.

Hendler, Glenn. "The Limits of Sympathy: Louisa May Alcott and the Sentimental Novel." *American Literary History* 3 (Winter 1991): 685–706.

Hibben, Paxton. *Henry Ward Beecher: An American Portrait.* New York: George H. Doran, 1927.

Hilton, Walter. *The Scale (or Ladder) of Perfection.* Westminster: Art and Book Company, 1908.

Hobbes, Thomas. *Leviathan.* Edited by Richard Tuck. Cambridge: Cambridge University Press, 1991.

——. *On the Citizen.* Edited by Richard Tuck. Cambridge: Cambridge University Press, 1991.

Hofstadter, Richard. *Anti-intellectualism in American Life.* New York: Knopf, 1963.

Holbrook, Clyde A. Editor's introd. to *Original Sin,* vol. 3 of *The Works of Jonathan Edwards,* ed. John E. Smith, 1–101. New Haven, Conn.: Yale University Press, 1970.

Holifield, Brooks E. *The Covenant Sealed: The Development of Puritan Sacramental Theology in Old and New England, 1570–1720.* New Haven, Conn.: Yale University Press, 1974.

Hollinger, David A. "Jewish Intellectuals and the De-Christianization of American Public Culture in the Twentieth Century." In *New Directions in American Religious History,* ed. Harry S. Stout and D. G. Hart, 262–86. New York: Oxford University Press, 1997.

Holly, Israel. "Youth Liable to Sudden Death; Excited Seriously to Consider Thereof and Speedily to Prepare Thereto." Hartford, Conn.: Thomas Green, 1766.

Holmes, Oliver Wendell. *Elsie Venner: A Romance of Destiny.* Boston: Houghton Mifflin, 1892.

———. "The Stereoscope and the Stereograph." *Atlantic Monthly,* June (1859):
738–49.

The Holy Bible: Old and New Testaments in the King James Version. New York:
Nelson, 1972.

Hopkins, Charles Howard. *The Rise of the Social Gospel in American Protestantism.* New Haven, Conn.: Yale University Press, 1940.

Hopkins, Samuel. *The Life and Character of the Late Reverend Mr. Jonathan
Edwards.* Boston: S. Kneeland, 1765.

Horowitz, Howard. "Maggie and the Sociological Paradigm." *American Literary History* 10 (Winter 1998): 606–38.

Horton, J. B. *In His Steps; or, The Rescue of Loreen.* London: n.d.

Howard, June. *Form and History in American Literary Naturalism.* Chapel Hill:
University of North Carolina Press, 1985.

Howard, Leon, ed. *The Mind of Jonathan Edwards.* Berkeley and Los Angeles:
University of California Press, 1963.

Howard, Milford W. *If Christ Came to Congress.* New York: Howard, 1894.

Howe, Daniel Walker. "The Evangelical Movement and the Political Culture
of the Second Party System." *Journal of American History* 77 (March 1991):
216–39.

———. "The Market Revolution and the Shaping of Identity in Whig-Jacksonian
America." In *The Market Revolution in America: Social, Political and Religious Expressions, 1800–1880,* ed. Melvyn Stokes and Stephen Conway,
259–81. Charlottesville: University of Virginia Press, 1996.

———. "Religion and Politics in Antebellum America." In *Religion and American Politics: From the Colonial Period to the 1980s,* ed. Mark A. Noll, 121–45.
New York: Oxford University Press, 1990.

Hughes, Thomas P. "The Biblical Play: A New Development of the Drama." *The
Critic* 45 (1904): 307–12.

Huizinga, Johan. *The Waning of the Middle Ages: A Study of the Forms of Life,
Thought, and Art in France and the Netherlands in the Dawn of the Renaissance.* New York: St. Martin's, 1949.

*The Improved New-England Primer; or, An Easy and Pleasant Guide for the In-
struction of Children, Containing Many Explanatory Notes, and References
to the Scriptures.* Concord, N.H.: Roby, Kimball & Merrill, 1841.

Ingraham, Joseph Holt. *The Prince of the House of David; or, Three Years in
the Holy City: Being a Series of Letters of Adina, a Jewess of Alexandria,
Sojourning in Jerusalem in the Days of Herod, Addressed to Her Father, a
Wealthy Jew in Egypt. And Relating, as by an Eye-Witness, All the Scenes
and Wonderful Incidents in the Life of Jesus of Nazareth, from His Baptism
in Jordan to His Crucifixion on Calvary.* New York: Pudney & Russell, 1855.

Jackson, Gregory S. "Cultivating Spiritual Sight: Jacob Riis's Virtual-Tour Narrative and the Visual Modernization of Protestant Homiletics." *Representations* 83 (Summer 2003): 126–66.

———. "'A Dowry of Suffering': Consent, Contract, and Political Coverture in

John W. De Forest's Reconstruction Romance." *American Literary History* 15, no. 2 (Summer 2003): 277–310.

———. " 'What Would Jesus Do?': Practical Christianity, Social Gospel Realism, and the Homiletic Novel." *PMLA* 121 (2006): 641–61.

Jackson, H. J. *Romantic Readers: The Evidence of Marginalia.* New Haven, Conn.: Yale University Press, 2005.

Jackson, Thomas, ed. *The Works of Rev. John Wesley, A.M.: Sometime Fellow of Lincoln College, Oxford.* 14 vols. 3rd ed. London: Wesleyan Conference Office, 1872.

Jakobson, Roman. "Two Aspects of Language and Two Types of Aphasic Disturbances." In *Language and Literature,* 95–114. Cambridge, Mass.: Belknap Press of Harvard University Press, 1987.

James, Henry. "The Art of Fiction." In *Partial Portraits,* 375–408. London: Macmillan, 1888.

———. *Literary Criticism: French Writers; Other European Writers; The Prefaces to the New York Edition.* New York: Viking, 1984.

James, William. "Does 'Consciousness' Exist?" In *Essays in Radical Empiricism,* 1–36. Lincoln: University of Nebraska Press, 1996.

———. *Essays in Radical Empiricism.* Lincoln: University of Nebraska Press, 1996.

———. "Philosophical Conceptions and Practical Results." In *Pragmatism,* 255–70. Cambridge, Mass.: Harvard University Press, 1975.

———. *Pragmatism.* Cambridge, Mass.: Harvard University Press, 1975.

———. *The Varieties of Religious Experience: A Study in Human Nature; Being the Gifford Lectures on Natural Religion Delivered at Edinburgh in 1901–1902.* New York: Longmans, Green, 1902.

———. "A World of Pure Experience." In *Essays in Radical Empiricism,* 39–91. Lincoln: University of Nebraska Press, 1996.

Jameson, Fredric. *The Political Unconscious: Narrative as a Socially Symbolic Act.* Ithaca, N.Y.: Cornell University Press, 1980.

———. "Reification and Utopia in Mass Culture." *Social Text* 1 (1979): 130–48.

Jehlen, Myra. "Why Did the Europeans Cross the Ocean? A Seventeenth Century Riddle." In *Cultures of United States Imperialism,* edited by Amy Kaplan and Donald Pease, 41–58. Durham, N.C.: Duke University Press, 1993.

Jesus Camp. DVD. Directed by Heidi Ewing and Rachel Grady. Magnolia Pictures, 2007.

Johnson, Barbara A. *Reading* Piers Plowman *and* The Pilgrim's Progress: *Reception and the Protestant Reader.* Carbondale: Southern Illinois University Press, 1992.

Johnson, Curtis. *Redeeming America: Evangelicals and the Road to the Civil War.* Chicago: Dee, 1993.

Jones, Jesse. *The Christian Commonwealth.* Commonwealth, Ga.: Christian Commonwealth, 1900.

Jones, John Daniel. "Distinctive Characteristics of Christianity." In *Volume of Proceedings of the Second International Congregational Council Held in*

Tremont Temple, Boston, Mass., September 20–29, 1899. Boston: Press of Samuel Usher, 1900.

Kaestle, Carl F. "The History of Literacy and the History of Readers." *Review of Research in Education* 12 (1985): 11–53.

Kamensky, Jane. *Governing the Tongue: The Politics of Speech in Early New England.* Oxford: Oxford University Press, 1997.

Kaplan, Amy. "'Left Alone in America': The Absence of Empire in the Study of American Culture." In *Cultures of United States Imperialism,* ed. Amy Kaplan and Donald Pease, 3–21. Durham, N.C.: Duke University Press, 1993.

——. *The Social Construction of American Realism.* Chicago: University of Chicago Press, 1988.

Keach, Benjamin. *Sion in Distress; or, The Groans of the Protestant Church.* 3rd ed. Boston: Samuel Green, 1683.

Kempe, Margery. *The Book of Margery Kempe.* Edited and translated by Lynn Staley. New York: Norton, 2001.

Kengor, Paul. *God and Ronald Reagan: A Spiritual Life.* New York: Harper, 2004.

Ker, Patrick. *The Map of Man's Misery; Or, The Poor Man's Pocket-Book.* Boston: Samuel Phillips, 1692.

Kilde, Jeanne Halgren. *When Church Became Theatre: The Transformation of Evangelical Architecture and Worship in Nineteenth-Century America.* New York: Oxford University Press, 2002.

Knight, Janice. "Learning the Language of God: Jonathan Edwards and the Typology of Nature." *William and Mary Quarterly* 48, no. 4 (October 1991): 531–51.

——. *Orthodoxies in Massachusetts: Rereading American Puritanism.* Cambridge, Mass.: Harvard University Press, 1994.

Knott, John R. *The Sword of the Spirit: Puritan Responses to the Bible.* Chicago: University of Chicago Press, 1980.

LaHaye, Tim, and Jerry B. Jenkins. *Apollyon.* Wheaton, Ill.: Tyndale House, 1999.

——. *Left Behind.* Wheaton, Ill.: Tyndale House, 1995.

——. *Nicolae.* Wheaton, Ill.: Tyndale House, 1997.

——. *Soul Harvest.* Wheaton, Ill.: Tyndale House, 1999.

——. *Tribulation Force.* Wheaton, Ill.: Tyndale House, 1996.

Lambert, Frank. *Inventing the "Great Awakening."* Princeton, N.J.: Princeton University Press, 1999.

Lathrop, George Parsons. "The Novel and Its Future." *Atlantic Monthly,* September 1874, 313–24.

Lasseter, Janice Milner. "From the Archives: The Uncensored Literary Lives of *Life in the Iron Mills.*" *Legacy* 20 (2000): 175–90.

Laurence, David. "Jonathan Edwards, John Locke, and the Canon of Experience." *Early American Literature* 15 (1980): 107–23.

Lee, Jarena. *The Life and Religious Experience of Jarena Lee.* In *Sisters of the Spirit: Three Black Women's Autobiographies of the Nineteenth Century,* ed. William L. Andrews, 25–48. Bloomington: Indiana University Press, 1986.

Lemay, J. A. Leo. "Rhetorical Strategies in *Sinners in the Hands of an Angry God* and *Narrative of the Late Massacres in Lancaster County.*" In *Benjamin Franklin, Jonathan Edwards, and the Representation of American Culture,* ed. Barbara B. Oberg and Harry S. Stout, 186–203. New York: Oxford University Press, 1993.

Levander, Caroline F., and Carol J. Singley, eds. *The American Child: A Cultural Studies Reader.* New Brunswick, N.J.: Rutgers University Press, 2003.

Lilla, Mark. *The Stillborn God: Religion, Politics, and the Modern West.* New York: Knopf, 2007.

Lindley, Susan Hill. "Gender and the Social Gospel Novel." In *Gender and the Social Gospel,* ed. Wendy J. Deichmann Edwards and Carolyn De Swarte Gifford, 185–201. Urbana: University of Illinois Press, 2003.

Lippard, George. *The Quaker City; or, Monks of Monk-hall: A Romance of Philadelphia Life, Mystery, and Crime.* Philadelphia: G. B. Ziebler, 1844.

Little, John. "The Presbyterian Colored Mission." In *An Era of Progress and Promise, 1863–1910: The Religious, Moral, and Educational Development of the American Negro since His Emancipation,* ed. William Newton Hartshorn, 233–47. Boston: Priscilla, 1910.

Livermore, George. *The Origin, History and Character of the New England Primer.* New York: C. F. Heartman, 1915.

Locke, John. *The Educational Writings of John Locke.* Edited by James Axtell. Cambridge: Cambridge University Press, 1968.

——. *An Essay Concerning Human Understanding.* Edited by Peter H. Nidditch. Oxford: Clarendon, 1975.

Lockridge, Kenneth A. *Literacy in Colonial New England: An Enquiry into the Social Context of Literacy in the Early Modern West.* New York: Norton, 1974.

Lodge, Henry Cabot. "The Restriction of Immigration." *North American Review* 152, no. 410 (1891): 27–37.

London, Jack. *The People of the Abyss.* Foreword by Micaela di Leonardo. New York: Macmillan, 1903.

Lorimer, Wright, and Arthur Reeves. *The Shepherd King: A Romantic Drama in Four Acts and Five Scenes.* Mount Vernon, NY: [N. p.], 1903.

The Louisa May Alcott Encyclopedia. Edited by Gregory Eiselein and Anne K. Phillips. Westport, Conn.: Greenwood, 2001.

Love, Nicholas. *Mirror of the Blessed Life of Jesus Christ.* New York: Garland, 1992.

Luker, Ralph E. *The Social Gospel in Black and White: American Racial Reform, 1885–1912.* Chapel Hill: University of North Carolina Press, 1991.

Luria, Maxwell S., and Richard L. Hoffman, eds. *Middle English Lyrics.* New York: Norton, 1974.

MacLeod, Anne Scott. *A Moral Tale: Children's Fiction and American Culture, 1820–1860.* Hamden: Archon, 1975.

Markham, Edwin. *The Man With the Hoe.* New York: Doubleday and McClure, 1900.

Marrant, John. *Narrative of the Life of John Marrant . . . Giving an Account of His Conversion.* Halifax: J. Nicholson, 1808.

Marsden, George M., ed. *Evangelicalism and Modern America.* Grand Rapids: Wm. B. Eerdmans, 1984.

———. *Fundamentalism and American Culture: The Shaping of Twentieth-Century Evangelicalism, 1870–1925.* Oxford: Oxford University Press, 1980.

———. *Jonathan Edwards: A Life.* New Haven, Conn.: Yale University Press, 2003.

Marvell, Andrew. *The Complete Works of Andrew Marvell,* vol. 1, ed. Alexander B. Grosart. London: Robson and Sons, 1872.

Mather, Cotton. *Magnalia Christi Americana; or, The Ecclesiastical History of New-England, in Seven Volumes.* Edited by Thomas Robbins. Hartford: Silas Andrus, 1853.

Mather, Increase. *An Earnest Exhortation to the Children of New England to Exalt the God of Their Fathers.* Boston: Timothy Green, 1711.

———. *Pray for the Rising Generation; or, A Sermon Wherein Godly Parents Are Encouraged, to Pray and Believe for Their Children.* Cambridge, Mass.: Samuel Green, 1678.

———. "Several Reasons Proving That Inoculating or Transplanting the Small Pox, Is a Lawful Practice and That It Has Been Blessed by God for the Saving of Many a Life." Boston: S. Kneeland for J. Edwards, 1721.

Matthiessen, F. O. *The James Family.* New York: Knopf, 1947.

May, Henry F. *Enlightenment in America.* Oxford: Oxford University Press, 1976.

———. *Protestant Churches and Industrial America.* New York: Harper, 1949; reprint, New York: Octagon, 1963.

McCuskey, Dorothy. *Bronson Alcott, Teacher.* New York: Macmillan, 1940.

McClymond, Michael J. "Spiritual Perception in Jonathan Edwards." *Journal of Religion* 77, no. 2 (April 1997): 195–216.

McDermott, Gerald R. *One Holy and Happy Society: The Public Theology of Jonathan Edwards.* University Park: Pennsylvania State University Press, 1992.

McGiffert, Michael, ed. *God's Plot: The Paradoxes of Puritan Piety, Being the Autobiography and Journal of Thomas Shepard.* Amherst: University of Massachusetts Press, 1972.

McKeon, Michael. *The Origins of the English Novel, 1600–1740.* Baltimore: Johns Hopkins University Press, 1987.

McLoughlin, William G., Jr. *Modern Revivalism: Charles Grandison Finney to Billy Graham.* New York: Ronal Press, 1959.

Menand, Louis. *The Metaphysical Club.* New York: Farrar, Straus, and Giroux, 2001.

Meyer, Donald H. *The Democratic Enlightenment.* New York: Putnam, 1976.

Miedema, Nine. "Following in the Footsteps of Christ: Pilgrimage and Passion Devotion." In *The Body Broken: Passion Devotion in Late-Medieval Culture,* ed. Alasdair MacDonald, Bernhard Ridderboff, and Rita Schlusemann, 73–92. Grongingen: Egbert Forsten, 1998.

Milbourne, Luke. *The Christian Pattern Praphras'ed; or, The Imitation of Christ.* London: Roger Clavel, 1696.

Miles, Margaret R. "Image." In *Critical Terms for Religious Studies,* ed. Mark C. Taylor, 160–72. Chicago: University of Chicago Press, 1998.

Miller, Perry. *Jonathan Edwards.* New York: Sloane, 1949.

——. "Jonathan Edwards on the Sense of the Heart." *Harvard Theological Review* 41 (1948): 123–45.

——. *The New England Mind: From Colony to Province.* Cambridge, Mass.: Harvard University Press, 1953.

——. *The New England Mind: The Seventeenth Century.* New York: Macmillan, 1939.

——. "The Rhetoric of Sensation." In *Errand into the Wilderness,* 167–83. Cambridge, Mass.: Harvard University Press, 1956.

Miller, Timothy. "Charles M. Sheldon and the Uplift of Tennesseetown." *Kansas History* 9 (1986): 125–37.

——. *Following in His Steps: A Biography of Charles M. Sheldon.* Knoxville: University of Tennessee Press, 1987.

Milman, Henry Hart. *The Martyr of Antioch: A Dramatic Poem.* London: John Murray, 1822.

Milton, John. *John Milton: Paradise Lost.* 2nd ed. Edited by Alastair Fowler. London: Longman, 1998.

Mitchell, Lee Clark. *Determined Fictions: American Literary Naturalism.* New York: Columbia University Press, 1989.

Moeller, Susan D. "The Cultural Construction of Urban Poverty: Images of Poverty in New York City, 1890–1917." *Journal of American Culture* 18, no. 4 (1995): 1–16.

Monaghan, E. Jennifer. "Literacy Instruction and Gender in Colonial New England." In *Reading in America: Literature and Social History,* ed. Cathy N. Davidson, 53–80. Baltimore: Johns Hopkins University Press, 1989.

Monk, Robert C. *John Wesley: His Puritan Heritage.* 2nd ed. Lanham, Md.: Scarecrow Press, 1999.

Moore, R. Laurence. *Religious Outsiders and the Making of Americans.* New York: Oxford University Press, 1986.

——. *Selling God: American Religion in the Marketplace of Culture.* New York: Oxford University Press, 1994.

Morgan, David. *Protestants and Pictures: Religion, Visual Culture, and the Age of American Mass Production.* Oxford: Oxford University Press, 1999.

——. "Visual Religion," *Religion* 30 (2000): 41–53.

——. "Would Jesus Have Sat for a Portrait?" In *Religion, Art, and Visual Culture,* ed. S. Brent Plate, 81–88. New York: Palgrave Macmillan, 2002.

Morgan, Edmund S., ed. *The Diary of Michael Wigglesworth, 1653–1657: The Conscience of a Puritan.* New York: Harper & Row, 1965.

——. "The Puritan Ethic and the Coming of the Revolution." *William and Mary Quarterly* 24 (1967): 3–18.

——. *Visible Saints: The History of a Puritan Idea.* New York: New York University Press, 1963.

Morgan, William M. *Questionable Charity: Gender, Humanitarianism, and Complicity in U.S. Literary Realism.* Lebanon: University of New Hampshire Press, 2004.

Moriarty, G. Andrews. "The True Story of Mary Dyer." *New England Historical and Genealogical Register* 104 (January 1950): 40–42.

Morison, Samuel Eliot. *Harvard College in the Seventeenth Century.* Cambridge, Mass.: Harvard University Press, 1936.

———. *The Puritan Pronaos: Studies in the Intellectual Life of New England in the Seventeenth Century.* New York: New York University Press, 1936.

Morris, Edmund. *Dutch: A Memoir of Ronald Reagan.* New York: Modern Library, 1999.

Morton, George. *Mourt's Relation: A Journal of the Pilgrims in Plymouth.* Boston: J. K. Wiggin, 1865.

Moses, William J. *Black Messiahs and Uncle Toms: Social and Literary Manipulations of a Religious Myth.* University Park: Pennsylvania State University Press, 1982.

Mosier, Richard David. *Making the American Mind: Social and Moral Ideas in the McGuffey Readers.* New York: King's Crown, 1947.

Mountford, Roxanne. *The Gendered Pulpit: Preaching in American Protestant Spaces.* Carbondale: Southern Illinois University Press, 2003.

Mullin, Robert Bruce. *The Puritan as Yankee: A Life of Horace Bushnell.* Grand Rapids, Mich.: Eerdmans, 2002.

Neal, Lynn S. *Romancing God: Evangelical Women and Inspirational Fiction.* Chapel Hill: University of North Carolina Press, 2006.

Neander, August. *The Life of Jesus Christ in Its Historical Connexion and Historical Development.* London: Bell, 1880.

Neuburg, Victor. "Chapbooks in America." In *Reading in America: Literature and Social History,* ed. Cathy N. Davidson, 81–113. Baltimore: Johns Hopkins University Press, 1989.

The New-England Primer. Boston: S. Kneeland and T. Green, 1735.

Nicholl, Grier. "The Image of the Prostestant Minister in the Christian Social Novel." *Church History* 37, no. 3 (1968): 319–34.

Nicolson, Marjorie H. "James March and the Vermont Transcendentalists." *Philosophical Review* 34 (1925): 28–50.

Nidditch, Peter H., ed. *An Essay concerning Human Understanding,* by John Locke. Oxford: Clarendon, 1975.

Noll, Mark A. *America's God: From Jonathan Edwards to Abraham Lincoln.* Oxford: Oxford University Press, 2002.

Nord, David Paul. "The Evangelical Origins of Mass Media in America, 1815–1835." *Journalism Monographs* 88 (1984): 1–30.

———. *Faith in Reading: Religious Publishing and the Birth of Mass Media in America.* New York: Oxford University Press, 2004.

———. "A Republican Literature." In *Reading in America: Literature and Social History,* ed. Cathy N. Davidson. Baltimore: Johns Hopkins University Press, 1989.

Norris, Frank. *McTeague: A Story of San Francisco.* In *Frank Norris, Novels and Essays,* ed. Donald Pizer, 261–572. New York: Library of America, 1986.

Norris, John. *A Treatise concerning Christian Prudence; or, the Principles of*

Practical Wisdom, Fitted to the Use of Human Life, and Design'd for Better Regulation. London: Samuel Manship, 1710.

Odom, Mel. *Apocalypse Burning.* Wheaton, Ill.: Tyndale House, 2004.

——. *Apocalypse Crucible.* Wheaton, Ill.: Tyndale House, 2004.

——. *Apocalypse Dawn.* Wheaton, Ill.: Tyndale House, 2003.

Ohmori, Yuhtaro. "'The Artillery of Mr. Locke': The Use of Locke's 'Second Treatise' in Pre-Revolutionary America, 1764–1776." PhD diss., Johns Hopkins University, 1988.

O'Neall, John Belton. *Biographical Sketches of the Bench and Bar of South Carolina.* Charleston, S.C.: S. G. Courtenay, 1859.

Ong, Walter. *Ramus: Method and the Decay of Dialogue; From the Art of Discourse to the Art of Reason.* Cambridge, Mass.: Harvard University Press, 1958.

Opie, John, ed. *Jonathan Edwards and the Enlightenment.* Lexington, Mass.: Heath, 1969.

Orvell, Miles. *The Real Thing: Imitation and Authenticity in American Culture, 1880–1940.* Chapel Hill: University of North Carolina Press, 1989.

Oxford English Dictionary. 2nd ed. Oxford: Clarendon Press, 1989.

Packer, Barbara. *The Transcendentalists.* Athens: University of Georgia Press, 2007.

Parrington, V. L. *Main Currents of Thought.* Volume 3 of *The Beginning of Critical Realism in America: 1860–1920.* New York: Harcourt, Brace, 1930.

Parrish, Susan Scott. *American Curiosity: Cultures of Natural History in the Colonial British Atlantic World.* Chapel Hill: University of North Carolina Press, 2006.

Payne, John. *Of the Imitation of Christ.* Stanford, N.Y.: Daniel Lawrence, 1803.

Pearse, Edward. *The Great Concern; or, A Serious Warning to a Timely and Thorough Preparation for Death.* 18th ed. London: J. Robinson, 1694.

Pember, Arthur. *The Mysteries and Miseries of the Great Metropolis . . . Being the Disguises and Surprises of a New-York Journalist.* New York: D. Appleton, 1874.

Phelps, Elizabeth Stuart. *The Gates Ajar.* Boston: Fields and Osgood, 1869.

——. *The Story of Jesus Christ.* Boston: Houghton, 1897.

Philip, Robert. *The Life and Times of Reverend George Whitefield.* New York: D. Appleton, 1838.

Pizer, Donald. "American Literary Naturalism: The Example of Dreiser." In *Documents of American Realism and Naturalism,* ed. Donald Pizer, 344–54. Carbondale: Southern Illinois University Press, 1998.

——. *The Theory and Practice of American Literary Naturalism: Selected Essays and Reviews.* Carbondale: Southern Illinois University Press, 1988.

Pocock, J. G. A. *The Machiavellian Moment: Florentine Political Thought and the Atlantic Republican Tradition.* Princeton, N.J.: Princeton University Press, 1975.

Potter, Robert. *The English Morality Play: Origins, History, and Influence of a Dramatic Tradition.* Boston: Routledge & Kegan Paul, 1975.

Promey, Sally M. "Seeing the Self 'in Frame': Early New England Material Practice and Puritan Piety." *Material Religion* 1, no. 1 (March 2005): 10–46.

Radway, Janice A. "The Book-of-the-Month Club and the General Reader: The Uses of Serious Fiction." In *Reading in America,* ed. Cathy N. Davidson, 259–84. Oxford: Oxford University Press, 1989.

———. *Reading the Romance: Women, Patriarchy, and Popular Literature.* Chapel Hill: University of North Carolina Press, 1984.

Ramsey, Paul. Introd. to "Edwards and John Locke." In *The Works of Jonathan Edwards,* vol. 1, ed. Perry Miller, Harry S. Stout, et al., 49–51. New Haven, Conn.: Yale University Press, 1958.

Ransom, R.C. *The Pilgrimage of Harriet Ransom's Son.* Nashville: Sunday School Union, 1949.

"Ransom of a Slave-Girl at Plymouth Church." *Independent,* February 9, 1860, 9–11.

Rauschenbusch, Walter. *Christianizing the Social Order.* New York: Macmillan, 1912.

Reill, Peter Hanns. *Vitalizing Nature in the Enlightenment.* Berkeley and Los Angeles: University of California Press, 2005.

Renan, Ernest. *The Apostles.* New York: Carleton, 1966.

———. *The Life of Jesus.* London: Lévy, 1864.

Reynolds, David S. *Beneath the American Renaissance: The Subversive Imagination in the Age of Emerson and Melville.* Cambridge, Mass.: Harvard University Press, 1988.

———. *Faith in Fiction: The Emergence of Religious Literature in America.* Cambridge, Mass.: Harvard University Press, 1981.

Reynolds, Larry J. "American Cultural Iconography: Vision, History, and the Real." *American Literary History* 9 (1999): 381–95.

Richmond, Legh. *The Dairyman's Daughter: An Authentic and Interesting Narrative in Five Parts.* London: J. Evans, 1809.

Riis, Jacob A. "The Battle with the Slum." *Atlantic Monthly,* May 1899, 626–34.

———. *The Battle with the Slum.* New York: Macmillan, 1902.

———. *Children of the Poor.* New York: Scribner's, 1892.

———. "Children of the Poor." *Charities,* December 1900, 20–21.

———. "Children of the Slums." *Indianapolis Journal,* February 19, 1900.

———. "Genesis of the Gang." *Atlantic Monthly,* September 1899, 301–5.

———. *How the Other Half Lives: Studies among the Tenements of New York.* New York: Dover, 1971.

———. *The Making of an American.* New York: Macmillan, 1919.

———. "Reform by Humane Touch." *Atlantic Monthly,* December 1899, 745–52.

———. "Special Needs of the Poor in New York." *Forum,* December 1892, 492–502.

Riley, I. Woodbridge. *American Thought: From Puritanism to Pragmatism.* New York: Holt, 1915.

Rivers, Isabel. *Reason, Grace, and Sentiment: A Study of the Language of Religion and Ethics in England, 1660–1780.* Cambridge: Cambridge University Press, 1991.

Rivett, Sarah. "Tokenography: Narration and the Science if Dying in Puritan Deathbed Testimonies." *Early American Literature* 42, no. 3 (Fall 2007): 471–94.

Robinson, Solon. *Hot Corn: Life Scenes in New York Illustrated.* New York: De-Witt and Davenport, 1854.

Ronda, Bruce Allen. "The Transcendental Child: Images and Concepts of the Child in American Transcendentalism." PhD diss., Yale University, 1975.

Royce, Josiah. *The Philosophy of Josiah Royce.* Edited by John K. Roth. Indianapolis: Hackett, 1982.

Rule, John. *Albion's People: English Society, 1714–1815.* London: Longman, 1992.

Rupp, George. "The 'Idealism' of Jonathan Edwards." *Harvard Theological Review* 62 (1969): 209–26.

Saltar, Stefan. *A Church in History: The Story of Plymouth's First Hundred Years under Beecher, Abbott, Hillis, Durkee, and Fifield.* Brooklyn, 1949.

Sánchez-Eppler, Karen. *Dependent States: The Child's Part in Nineteenth-Century American Culture.* Chicago: University of Chicago Press, 2005.

———. "'Then When We Clutch the Hardest': On the Death of a Child and the Replication of an Image." In *Sentimental Men: Masculinity and the Politics of Affect in American Culture,* ed. Mary Chapman and Glenn Hendler, 64–85. Berkeley and Los Angeles: University of California Press, 1999.

Sargent, John, ed. *A Memoir of the Rev. Henry Martyn, B. D.* London: R. B. Steely and W. Burnside, 1830.

Savage, Minot J. *The Morals of Evolution.* Boston: S. E Cassino, 1880.

———. *The Religion of Evolution.* Boston: Lockwood, Brooks, 1876.

Schaff, Philip. *The Person of Christ: The Miracle of History.* Boston: American Tract Society, 1865.

Schenck, Ferdinand Schureman. *The Sociology of the Bible.* New York: Board of Publication of the Reformed Church of America, 1909.

Schneidau, Herbert N. *Sacred Discontent: The Bible and Western Tradition.* Berkeley and Los Angeles: University of California Press, 1977.

Schocket, Eric. "Undercover Explorations of the 'Other Half'; or, The Writer as Class Transvestite." *Representations* 64 (1998): 109–27.

Scott, Walter. *The Gospel Restored.* Cincinnati: O. H. Donogh, 1836.

Selement, George, and Bruce C. Woolley, eds. *Thomas Shepard's Confessions.* Boston: The Society, 1981.

Sellers, Charles. *The Market Revolution: Jacksonian America, 1815–1846.* New York: Oxford University Press, 1991.

Seltzer, Mark. "*The Princess Casamassima:* Realism and the Fantasy of Surveillance." In *American Realism: New Essays,* ed. Eric J. Sundquist, 95–118. Baltimore and London: The Johns Hopkins University Press, 1985.

Sewall, Joseph. *The Certainty and Suddenness of Christ's Coming to Judgment: Improved as a Motive to Diligence in Preparing for It.* Boston: B. Green, 1716.

Shaffer, Ellen. "The Children's Books of the American Sunday-School Union." *American Book Collector* 17, no. 2 (1966): 20–28.

Sheldon, Charles M. *The Crucifixion of Phillip Strong.* Chicago: McClurg, 1894.
——. *The Heart of the World.* New York: Revell, 1905.
——. *His Brother's Keeper; or, Christian Stewardship.* Chicago: Congregational Sunday-School and Publishing Society, 1896.
——. *His Life Story.* New York: George H. Doran, 1925.
——. "If I Were a Teacher." *Household,* April 1936, 36.
——. "If I Were President." *Christian Herald,* May 1936.
——. "If Jesus Were Here Today." *Christian Herald,* December 1945.
——. *In His Steps: "What Would Jesus Do?"* Chicago: Advance, 1897.
——. *Jesus Is Here!* New York: Hodder, 1914.
——. *John King's Question Class.* Chicago: Advance, 1899.
——. "The Kingdom." *Missionary Review of the World,* June 1896, 470–71.
——. "A Local Negro Problem." *Kingdom,* April 1896, 828.
——. *The Narrow Gate.* Chicago: Advance, 1903.
——. "Practical Christian Sociological Studies." *Andover Review,* October 1890, 371.
——. *The Redemption of Freetown.* Chicago: Advance, 1899.
——. *The Reformer.* Chicago: Advance Publishing, 1902.
——. *Robert Hardy's Seven Days: A Dream and Its Consequences.* Chicago: Advance, 1898.
——. *The Twentieth Door.* Chicago: Advance, 1893.
——. "What I Would Do If I Were a Farmer." In *Report of the Kansas State Board of Agriculture,* vol. 24, 210–15. Topeka: State Board of Agriculture, 1905.
Shepard, Odell. *Pedlar's Progress: The Life of Bronson Alcott.* Boston: Little, Brown, 1937.
Shepard, Thomas. *The Autobiography of Thomas Shepard, the Celebrated Minister of Cambridge, New England.* With additional notes by Nehemiah Adams. Boston: Pierce and Parker, 1832.
——. *Thomas Shepard's Confessions.* Vol. 58 of *Publications of the Colonial Society of Massachusetts Collections,* ed. George Selement and Bruce C. Woolley. Boston: The Society, 1981.
Showalter, Elaine. Introd. to *Little Women,* by Louisa May Alcott. New York: Penguin, 1989.
Shurtleff, Nathaniel B. *Records of the Governor and Company of the Massachusetts Bay in New England.* Boston: William White, 1853.
Sicherman, Barbara. "Sense and Sensibility: A Case Study of Women's Reading in the Late-Victorian America." In *Reading in America: Literature and Social History,* ed. Cathy N. Davidson, 201–25. Baltimore: Johns Hopkins University Press, 1989.
Sienkiewicz, Henryk. *"Quo Vadis": A Narrative of the Time of Nero.* Trans. Jeremiah Curtin. Boston: Little, Brown, 1897.
Simmons, Henry Martyn. *New Tables of Stone and Other Essays.* Boston: James H. West, 1904.
——. *The Unending Genesis; or, Creation Ever Present.* Minneapolis: Echo Simmons, 1937.

Skeel, Emily Ellsworth Ford, ed. *Mason Locke Weems: His Works and Ways.* Vol. 3 New York, 1929.

Slotkin, Richard. *Regeneration through Violence: The Mythology of the American Frontier, 1600–1860.* Middletown, Conn.: University Press, 1973.

Smith, Bernard. *Forces in American Criticism: A Study in the History of American Literary Thought.* New York: Harcourt, Brace, 1939.

Smith, Claude A. "Edwards and the 'Way of Ideas.'" *Harvard Theological Review* 59 (1966): 153–73.

Smith, Elias. *The Life, Conversion, Preaching, Travels, and Sufferings of Elias Smith.* Portsmouth, N.H.: Beck & Foster, 1816.

Smith, H. Shelton. *Changing Conceptions of Original Sin.* New York: Scribner's, 1955.

Smyth, E. C. "Jonathan Edwards' Idealism." *American Journal of Theology* 1 (1897): 950–64.

Spicer, Albert. "Annual Address." In *Volume of Proceedings of the Second International Congregational Council Held in Tremont Temple, Boston, Mass., September 10–29, 1899,* 137–38. Boston: Press of Samuel Usher, 1900.

Spufford, Margaret. *Small Books and Pleasant Histories: Popular Fiction and Its Readership in Seventeenth-Century England.* London: Methuen, 1981.

Stafford, Barbara. *Good Looking: Essays on the Virtue of Images.* Cambridge, Mass.: MIT Press, 1999.

———. *Visual Analogy: Consciousness as the Art of Connecting.* Cambridge, Mass.: MIT Press, 1999.

Stange, Maren. *Symbols of Ideal Life: Social Documentary Photography in America, 1890-1950.* Cambridge: Cambridge University Press, 1989.

Stanhope, George. *Soliloquy of the Soul.* Bennington, Vt.: Darius Clark, 1816.

Stanton, Elizabeth Cady. *Eighty Years and More, 1815–1897.* New York: European Publishing, 1898.

Stead, William T. *If Christ Came to Chicago! A Plea for the Union of All Who Love in the Service of All Who Suffer.* Chicago: Laird, 1894.

Stock, Brian. *After Augustine: The Meditative Reader and the Text.* Philadelphia: University of Pennsylvania Press, 2001.

Stoddard, Solomon. *A Guide to Christ; or, The Way of Directing Souls That Are under the Work of Conversion. Compiled for the Help of Young Ministers.* Boston: J. Allen, 1714.

Stone, Barton. *A Reply to John P. Campbell's Strictures on Atonement.* Lexington: Joseph Charles, 1805.

Stout, Harry S. *The Divine Dramatist: George Whitefield and the Rise of Modern Evangelicalism.* Grand Rapids, Mich.: Eerdmans, 1991.

———. *The New England Soul: Preaching and Religious Culture in Colonial New England.* New York: Oxford University Press, 1987.

Stowe, Harriet Beecher. *Uncle Tom's Cabin; or, Life among the Lowly.* Philadelphia: H. Altemus, 1990.

Strauss, David. *The Life of Jesus, Critically Examined.* London: Chapman, 1846.

Strickland, Charles. "A Transcendentalist Father: The Child-Rearing Practices of Bronson Alcott." *Perspectives in American History* 3 (1969): 5–73.

Sue, Eugène. *The Mysteries of Paris.* London: Chapman and Hall, 1845–46.

Sundquist, Eric J., ed. *American Realism: New Essays.* Baltimore: Johns Hopkins University Press, 1982.

Sutherland, Kathryn. "'Events . . . Have Made Us a World of Readers': Reader Relations, 1780–1830." In *The Romantic Period,* ed. David Pirie, 1–48. London: Penguin, 1994.

Swaffield, Walter J. "Round Table: 'The Tenement House Curse.'" *Arena,* April 1894, 659–83.

Taft, Robert. *Photography and the American Scene: A Social History, 1839–1889.* New York: Macmillan, 1938.

Taves, Ann. *Fits, Trances, and Visions: Experiencing Religion and Explaining Experience from Wesley to James.* Princeton, N.J.: Princeton University Press, 1999.

Taylor, Charles. *A Secular Age.* Cambridge, Mass.: Belknap, 2007.

———. *Sources of the Self: The Making of the Modern Identity.* Cambridge, Mass.: Harvard University Press, 1989.

Taylor, Isaac. *Essay on the Application of Abstract Reasoning to the Christian Doctrines.* Boston: Crocker and Brewster, 1832.

Tompkins, Jane. *Sensational Designs: The Cultural Work of American Fiction, 1790–1860.* New York: Oxford University Press, 1985.

Tourgée, Albion. *Murvale Eastman: Christian Socialist.* New York: Fords, 1890.

"Toward a History of the Standard of Living in British North America." *William and Mary Quarterly* 45, no. 1 (January 1988): 116–70.

Trachtenberg, Alan. "Experiments in Another Country: Stephen Crane's City Sketches." In *American Realism: New Essays,* ed. Eric J. Sundquist, 138–54. Baltimore: Johns Hopkins University Press, 1982.

———. *The Incorporation of America: Culture and Society in the Gilded Age.* New York: Hill and Wang, 1982.

———. *Reading American Photography: Images as History, Matthew Brady to Walker Evans.* New York: Noonday Press, 1990.

Trinterud, Leonard J. *The Forming of an American Tradition: A Re-Examination of Colonial Presbyterianism.* Philadelphia: Westminster, 1949.

Tyerman, Luke. *The Life and Times of the Rev. John Wesley, M.A.* Vol. 1. New York: Harper, 1972.

Tyler, Royall. *The Algerine Captive.* Hartford: Peter B. Gleason, 1816.

Van Engen, John, trans. *Devotio Moderna: Basic Writings.* New York: Paulist Press, 1988.

Vincent, John H. *The Chautauqua Movement.* Boston: Chautauqua Press, 1886.

Wakeley, J. B. *Lost Chapters Recovered from the Early History of American Methodism.* New York: Carlton and Porter, 1858.

Waldman, Steven. *Founding Faith: Providence, Politics, and the Birth of Religious Freedom in America.* New York: Penguin, 2007.

Walker, Timothy. *Introduction to American Law.* Philadelphia: P. H. Nicklin & T. Johnson, 1837.

Wallace, Lew. *Ben-Hur: A Tale of the Christ.* New York: Harper, 1880.

———. *The Boyhood of Christ.* New York: Harper, 1888.

Walter, Nehemiah. *The Body of Death Anatomized: A Brief Essay Concerning the Sorrows and the Desires of the Regenerate, upon the Sense of Indwelling Sin, Delivered at the Lecture in Boston, 1706.* Boston: John Draper, 1736.

Walzer, Michael. *The Revolution of the Saints: A Study in the Origins of Radical Politics.* Cambridge, Mass.: Harvard University Press, 1965.

Warner, Amos G. *American Charities.* New York: T. Y. Crowell, 1894.

Warner, Charles Dudley. "Modern Fiction." In *The Relation of Literature to Life,* 135–67. New York: Harper, 1897.

Watt, Ian. *The Rise of the Novel: Studies in Defoe, Richardson, and Fielding.* London: Chatto & Windus, 1957.

Watts, Isaac. *Catechisms; or, Instructions in the Principles of the Christian Religion, and the History of Scripture, Composed for Children and Youth.* London: E. Matthews, 1730.

———. "The Christian Doctrine of the Trinity; or, Father, Son, and Spirit, Three Persons and One God, Asserted and Proved, with Their Divine Rights and Honors Vindicated." In *The Works of the Late Reverend and Learned Isaac Watts,* 6 vols. London: J. and T. Longman, 1757.

———. *The Doctrine of the Passions Explained and Improved.* Elizabeth-Town: Shepard Kollock, 1795.

———. *The Improvement of the Mind; or, A Supplement to the Art of Logic; to Which is Added a Discourse on the Education of Children and Youth.* London: James Blackstone, 1741.

———. *Philosophical Essay on Various Subjects.* London: Richard Ford, 1734.

Webster, Tom. "Writing to Redundancy: Approaches to Spiritual Journals and Early Modern Spirituality." *Historical Journal* 39, no. 1 (1996): 33–56.

Weems, Mason Locke. *The Drunkard's Looking Glass, Reflecting a Faithful Likeness of the Drunkard.* Philadelphia, 1818.

———. *God's Revenge against Adultery, Awfully Exemplified in the Following Cases.* Philadelphia, 1818.

———. *God's Revenge against Duelling; or, the Duellist's Looking Glass.* Philadelphia: J. Bioren, 1821.

———. *God's Revenge against Gambling, Exemplified in the Miserable Lives and Untimely Deaths of a Number of Persons.* Philadelphia, 1821.

———. *God's Revenge against Murder.* Baltimore: Bell & Cook, 1814.

Weisberger, Bernard A. *They Gathered at the River: The Story of the Great Revivalists and Their Impact upon Religion in America.* Boston: Little, Brown, 1958.

Wesley, John. *The Christian's Pattern; or, a Treatise of the Imitation of Christ. Written Originally in Latin, by Thomas à Kempis. With a Preface, Containing an Account of the Usefulness of This Treatise.* London: C. Rivington, 1735.

———. "An Extract of the Reverend Mr. John Wesley's Journal, from May 6, 1760 to October 28, 1762." In *The Works of the Reverend John Wesley,* vol. 3, ed. Thomas Jackson, 294. London: Wesleyan Conference Office, 1872.

Westbrook, Robert B. *John Dewey and American Democracy.* Ithaca, N.Y.: Cornell University Press, 1991.

Westeroff, John H., III. *McGuffey and His Readers: Piety, Morality, and Education in Nineteenth-Century America*. Nashville: Abingdon, 1978.

Whitney, Adeline. *The Gayworthys: A Story of Threads and Thrums*. Boston: Loring, 1865.

Wiebe, Robert. *The Search for Order, 1877–1920*. New York: Hill and Wang, 1968.

Wiek, Roger S. *Time Sanctified: The Book of Hours in Medieval Art and Life*. New York: G. Brailler, 1988.

Wigglesworth, Michael. *Day of Doom; or, A Poetical Description of the Great and Last Judgment*. Boston: John Allen, 1715.

———. *The Diary of Michael Wigglesworth, 1653–1657: The Conscience of a Puritan*, ed. Edmund S. Morgan. New York: Harper & Row, 1965.

Williams, D. Newell. *Barton Stone: A Spiritual Biography*. St. Louis: Chalice Press, 2000.

Williams, John. *The Redeemed Captive Returning to Zion: A Faithful History of Remarkable Occurrences in the Captivity and Deliverance of Mr. John Williams*. Boston: Samuel Hall, 1795.

Williams, Peter. *America's Religions: Traditions and Cultures*. New York: Macmillan, 1990.

Williams, Stephen. *Narrative of the Captivity of Stephen Williams, Who Was Taken by the French and Indians at Deerfield*, ed. George Sheldon. Deerfield, Mass.: Pocumtuck Valley Memorial Association, 1889.

Wills, Garry. "The Day the Enlightenment Went Out." *New York Times*, Nov. 4, 2004.

———. *Head and Heart: American Christianities*. New York: Penguin, 2007.

———. *What Jesus Meant*. New York: Penguin, 2006.

Winthrop, John. "A Modell of Christian Charity." Collections of the Massachusetts Historical Society. http://history.hanover.edu/texts/winthmod.

Witsius, Herman. *Sacred Dissertations on What Is Commonly Called the Apostle's Creed*. 2 vols. Translated by Donald Fraser. Edinburgh: A. Fullarton, 1823.

Wood, Gordon S. *The Creation of the American Republic, 1776–1787*. Chapel Hill: University of North Carolina Press, 1969.

Wood, Henry. *Edward Burton*. Boston: Lee & Shepard, 1890.

———. *Ideal Suggestion through Mental Photography: A Restorative System for Home and Private Use*. Boston: Lee & Shepard, 1893.

Woods, Katharine Pearson. *Metzerott, Shoemaker*. New York: Cromwell, 1889.

Wright, Conrad. *The Beginnings of Unitarianism in America*. Boston: Starr King, 1955.

Wright, Gwendolyn. *Moralism and the Model Home: Domestic Architecture and Cultural Conflict in Chicago, 1873–1913*. Chicago: University of Chicago Press, 1980.

Wright, Harold Bell. *The Shepherd of the Hills*. Chicago: Book Supply, 1907.

———. *That Printer of Udell's: A Story of the Middle West*. Gretna, La.: Pelican, 1996.

Wright, Luella M. "John Bunyan and Stephen Crisp." *Journal of Religion* 19 (April 1939): 95–109.

Wright, Robert Glenn. *The Social Christian Novel.* New York: Greenwood, 1989.

Wyckoff, Walter. *The Workers: An Experiment in Reality: The East.* New York: Scribner's, 1897.

———. *The Workers: An Experiment in Reality: The West.* New York: Scribner's, 1898.

Yates, Frances. *The Art of Memory.* Chicago: Chicago University Press, 1966.

Young, Elizabeth. "A Wound of One's Own: Louisa May Alcott's Civil War Fiction." *American Quarterly* 48 (September 1996): 439–75.

Zaret, David. "Religion, Science, and Printing in Public Spheres in Seventeenth-Century England." In *Habermas and the Public Sphere,* ed. Craig Calhoun, 212–35. Cambridge, Mass.: MIT Press, 1993.

Zboray, Ronald J. *A Fictive People: Antebellum Economic Development and the American Reading Public.* New York: Oxford University Press, 1993.

Zehr, Janet S. "The Response of Nineteenth-Century Audiences to Louisa May Alcott's Fiction." *American Transcendental Quarterly* 1 (December 1987): 323–42.

Zuckerman, Michael. *Peaceable Kingdoms: New England Towns in the Eighteenth Century.* New York: Knopf, 1970.

Zwinger, Lynda. *Daughters, Fathers, and the Novel: The Sentimental Romance of Heterosexuality.* Madison: University of Wisconsin Press, 1991.

Index